Library of
Davidson College

LABOUR'S DOORSTEP POLITICS IN LONDON

By the same author
The Methodology of Comparative Research (contributor and co-editor with Robert T. Holt)
Political Parties in Action: The Battle of Barons Court (with Robert T. Holt)
The Political Basis of Economic Development: An Exploration in Comparative Political Analysis (with Robert T. Holt)
The Soviet Union: Paradox and Change (co-editor with Robert T. Holt)
The Soviet Dictatorship (with Herbert McClosky)
The New Japan (with Harold S. Quigley)

Published with assistance from the Roger E. Joseph Memorial Fund for greater understanding of history and public affairs, a cause in which Roger Joseph believed.

LABOUR'S DOORSTEP POLITICS IN LONDON

John E. Turner
Regents' Professor of Political Science
University of Minnesota

University of Minnesota Press
Minneapolis

© John E. Turner 1978

All rights reserved. No part of this publication may be reproduced or transmitted, in any form or by any means, without permission

First published 1978 by
THE MACMILLAN PRESS LTD

Published in the United States by the University of Minnesota Press

Library of Congress Catalog Card Number 77–99160

ISBN 0 8166–0843–1

Printed in Great Britain

TO ELSIE

who has done so much, so well, for so long

Contents

Preface	ix
1. Labour Party Organization: a Look at the Bottom	1
2. Labour Party Organization: a View from the Lower Tier	41
3. Socio-economic Settings in Three Constituencies	83
4. The Constituency Parties: Goals, Organizational Structures, and Key Party Roles	120
5. Constituency Parties in Action	157
6. Outlooks of the Activists	226
7. Involvement, Motivations, and Inducements	282
8. Summary and Conclusions	312
Notes	330
Bibliography	367
Index	387

Preface

Although scholars who reflect upon British politics have long felt the need for 'grass roots' studies of local parties, some of them have grown more vocal in the last few years about this gap in our knowledge. Consider, for example, the comment of Professor Hindess: 'Quite simply, there is remarkably little evidence concerning grass-roots politics (below the level of the council chamber) or of changes therein.'[1] According to Professor Birch: '. . . very little is known about the agents and active party workers who keep the party organizations alive in the constituencies. . . .'[2] And Reg Race, in his article in a Fabian Society pamphlet, makes the point even more bluntly: '. . . it ought to be made clear that we know next to nothing about the actual operation of local and constituency Labour parties, and even less about the role or attitudes of crucial individuals in the party structure, such as full time agents.'[3] The purpose of this study is to tilt the spotlight toward three local Labour parties during a nine-month period in order to see how they really operated and to learn more about the people who engaged in party work 'on the doorstep'.

The author first became interested in Labour Party politics at the constituency level in 1951 when he visited the headquarters of several organizations to examine their structures and to get a 'feel' for the way in which they functioned. On numerous trips within Britain since that time he has made it a point to stop at the central Labour committee room in a number of towns and cities he has visited, interviewing the agents and other key political leaders. While he often asked the same questions, none of these contacts involved systematic research with a definite project in mind; he was largely concerned with developing a background for classroom teaching. Over this lengthy time-span, the author has conducted interviews in forty-six constituency Labour parties and three borough parties, and he has had numerous discussions with officials in Transport House, as well as three regional offices. In addition, he has observed the following types of activities: six general elections and one contest for the borough council; one Labour Party Annual Conference and one national gathering of the Trades Union Congress; three parliamentary selection conferences; one annual meeting of the Young Socialists; and one conference of the London Labour Party.

The opportunity for systematic research effort came in 1961–62 when the author spent a sabbatical year in London. The project that supplied the material for this volume, however, was not initially included in the author's program. He was engaged in another research endeavor which kept him moving from the London School of Economics to the British Museum and then to the House of Commons. This, he felt, was a somewhat restricted sort of existence, and he sensed the need for 'real-life' contact with ordinary political activists. To fit this purpose, he hit upon the idea of selecting three Labour parties – one in a safe constituency, one in a marginal district with a sitting Labour M.P., and one in hopeless territory – and to see if it were possible for him to become attached to these organizations as a 'participant observer' for a period of months. The aim, quite candidly, was to enrich the author's teaching background as he carried out the project for which leave had been granted. When he discussed the idea with his academic colleagues, they were rather dubious about the prospects of getting the local parties to cooperate.

The author nevertheless decided to try to secure the necessary authorization, and lodged his request with Mr Peter Robshaw, secretary of the London Labour Party, indicating his interest in the constituency parties in Bermondsey, Fulham, and South Kensington. Mr Robshaw was most helpful, and he passed the request on to the local party agents. A favorable response from the organization in South Kensington came quite quickly, and after a lengthy interview with the voluntary secretary/agent, the author attended the November meeting of the General Management Committee. This experience was valuable in providing knowledge about party procedures and enabled him to plan his work in more detail. Shortly thereafter, arrangements were made with the other two organizations. As he widened his contacts, held more interviews, and attended more meetings, he began to realize that the project could be more than just a teaching-enrichment program – that indeed it could be developed into a manageable research endeavor.

The objective of the exercise was to study, during the same time-period, three Labour parties which had the same general structure but which operated in vastly different environmental contexts. The author attended all of the General Management Committee meetings, several Executive Committee meetings, and certain ward meetings, taking notes on the proceedings. He observed virtually all of the constituency party activities (including a long march from Bermondsey to Hyde Park on May Day!), but conflicting ward engagements made it impossible for him to keep up with more than a modest number of them. He had numerous interviews with the three agents, as well as lengthy consultations with other party and ward officers and with a good number of activists who held no official posts. He also had access to the annual reports of the three parties, their financial statements and membership records, and other relevant documents and newspaper accounts.

Participant observation, of course, presents some difficulties. No one in the three organizations – not even the agents – knew exactly what the author was after, and in the initial stages of the project he occasionally heard activists whisper, 'He is studying us!' But one advantage of observation over a period of months is that the investigator becomes a familiar part of the organizational landscape and is able to carry on his work without attracting much notice. The author remembers a very heated controversy which erupted at the regular meeting of the one of the parties; the next morning one of the participants remarked to a colleague: 'That was a great show we put on for our American professor last night! He was in the corner where he always sits, and we forgot that he was there.'

Before very long the author had established sufficient rapport that he was invited to attend the parties' social functions, which helped to deepen his understanding of the organizations and provided opportunity for some 'informal' interviewing. Understandably, it took a bit longer for an American professor to sink roots in the Bermondsey party, where the activists were working-class folk, than in the other two organizations. But he knew that he had gained some acceptance when they invited him to attend the party 'bingo session', and he was told that he had 'made it' when a week later they requested him to take a turn at calling the numbers.

Toward the end of his stay, the author received official permission from each General Management Committee to send a mail questionnaire to every member. This instrument was designed to elicit conventional information about social background and political career patterns and to probe such matters as their reasons for wanting to become involved in local party affairs, their political aspirations, their perceptions of the problems confronting their organizations, and their opinions on the controversial issues which had arisen during the party meetings. The questionnaire included forced-choice items with spaces for open-ended comments. After two follow-up letters, the response rate was as follows: South Kensington, 97 per cent; Fulham, 82 per cent; and Bermondsey, 59 per cent. The total rate of return was 76 per cent (142 respondents). The poorer response rate in Bermondsey was a source of some worry. The author discovered, however, that some of the older people could not face up to the task of filling out the long forms, and that some of the others hesitated to return their questionnaires because they were employees of the borough council. He interviewed a small sample of the non-respondents and concluded that a larger rate of return would not have changed the Bermondsey data significantly.

The 1961–62 period was a good 'political season' for a study of these Labour parties as organizations. The unilateralist controversy was still raging, the question of Britain's entry into Europe was raised for the first time, the struggle over the issue of Commonwealth immigration came to a head, and the Macmillan Cabinet introduced its plan for reorganizing local government in London. In addition, the party agents were beginning to gear up for the next general election (which was eventually held in 1964), and, of course, they were called upon to fight a borough council election in May 1962.

The author – through such research techniques as participant observation, the examination of documents, and the analysis of census data and socio-economic data drawn from the questionnaires – has attempted to address such questions as: What was the impact of environment upon the goals, structures, and operation of the three parties? In what ways did these organizations seek to respond to their environmental challenges? What functions do constituency parties perform, and how did each of these units set about performing them? What were the roles of the agents and the Members of Parliament? What were the attitudes of particular categories of activists toward the important issues of the day? Who were the 'ideological enthusiasts' and how numerous were they? What sorts of people were the most involved in local political work? What seemed to motivate them to be active? Were the local parties able to take advantage of an 'inducement' system in order to encourage their members to work hard in behalf of the organizations?

A study of only three party cases, especially when they are drawn from one urban center, obviously has limitations. The author has tried, whenever possible, to minimize this weakness by comparing each of the parties with roughly comparable organizations in the Greater London area. The constituency parties were selected on the basis of their contrasting political environments, i.e., so that there would be a variety of party types. This means that when we analyze the attitudes of the activists, we are dealing with a relatively small number of people – a situation over which the author had no control. Despite the small size of the population, however, we are able to deepen our knowledge about activists' outlooks, especially when the statistical associations are strong and the findings are congruent with those in the literature. But in some areas the number of cases is so small that the refined points in the analysis can be nothing more than suggestive. The study is also constrained by the fact that it is largely confined to one time-period; hence, the results are only cross-sectional comparisons. As already indicated in several places, this project was carried out in the early 1960s and is being published more than a decade later. The author makes no apologies for this delay. At the time of the study, the people in the three parties were very much involved in their internal disputes, and in some instances the personal stakes were high. The passage of time has healed most of the wounds; the leadership has changed; and most people regard the controversial encounters as history. Delayed publication permits a much more candid analysis than would have been possible six or seven years earlier. Moreover, in the intervening period the investigator was able to look at the parties in subsequent general elections, especially in

1964 and 1966. Besides, if a study of this type has merits, it should be just as valuable in 1978 as it would have been in 1968. (One disadvantage is that the prose occasionally had to be cast in the present tense in the interest of a smoother literary style. Technically, such topics as the socio-economic settings of the constituencies should be written in the past tense, but the sentence structure becomes too cumbersome.)

The first two chapters of the volume are intended to acquaint American readers with the organization and operation of the Labour Party. Chapter 1 describes the various elements of a constituency party and the problems it encounters, and Chapter 2 discusses the Party structures that exist *above* the constituency level, but this is done from the vantage point of the lower tier. We begin the analysis of the constituency parties in Chapter 3 by looking at their socio-economic settings. Chapter 4 introduces the reader to the goals, organizational patterns, and key roles of each party, while Chapter 5 examines the operation of the parties in terms of the functions they are expected to perform. In Chapter 6 we turn to an examination of the political outlooks of the activists, and in Chapter 7 we look at their degrees of party involvement, their motivations and political aspirations, and the system of 'rewards' and 'satisfactions' employed by each organization.

Instructors of the English language would undoubtedly shudder if the author were to describe this research undertaking by the hackneyed expression, a 'labor of love'. They might feel more comfortable with the statement that it was an 'enterprise of endearment', but only slightly so. Anyway, this was a 'fun project' which brought the investigator into contact with warm, dedicated, and hospitable people. The author's feelings bring to mind the words of St. Matthew (though they were applicable to a much different situation): 'I was a stranger and [they] took me in!' This book owes a great deal to the General Management Committee delegates in the three parties who were willing to subject themselves to scholarly scrutiny. They were always courteous in answering sticky questions, and they were most helpful in supplying the information that was crucial to the study.

The author owes a major debt to the three agents – John R. Thomas of Bermondsey; Leslie H. Hilliard, C.B.E., of Fulham; and Maurice Barber of South Kensington. Without their full cooperation, the project could not have been carried out. In the many hours they spent with him they never hesitated to answer the questions frankly and completely, and they never refused to make requested documents available. The author came to have enormous respect for their expertise, and he is particularly appreciative of their trust.

Debts were also incurred outside the boundaries of the three constituencies. The London School of Economics supplied the investigator with an office which facilitated the research. At various times, important help and advice were given by Pat Cavenaugh of Transport

House; Tom Cox, M.P.; the late Alan Clarke; Richard L. Leonard; Ivor S. Richard; and Clifford Tucker.

The author gratefully acknowledges the logistical and financial support provided by the University of Minnesota – the Graduate School, the Office of International Programs, the College of Liberal Arts, and the Computer Center. Despite crippling retrenchment, the chair-person of the Political Science Department, Samuel Krislov, made clerical and research assistance available when it was most needed. Expressions of appreciation are also due to the patrons of the Winton Fund, and to Mr Frank M. Rarig and Mr Walter S. Rosenberry III who were instrumental in providing funds from the Charles A. Weyerhauser Memorial Foundation.

Also deserving of thanks are the people who assisted in the computer work – James Minar, Dr Steve Chan, and especially Stanley Feldman, who also read the manuscript; the young ladies who helped with the library research – Elaine Kuczek, Nancy Guthrie, and Debra Turner; and the willing secretaries who did most of the typing – Sue Brown, Barbara Freeman, and Debbie Trefz. The author is also indebted to the highly competent staffs of the University of Minnesota Press and the Macmillan Press for transforming sheets of typed paper into book form.

This book has been influenced in many respects by the years of intellectual contact the author has had with his colleague, Professor Robert T. Holt. The collaborative endeavors have been both stimulating and enjoyable; the joint effort in the Barons Court constituency in 1964 and 1966 has had its impact upon this study. Professor Holt read the manuscript and made helpful comments.

A number of other colleagues kindly consented to rearrange their hectic schedules to consult with the author from time to time and to read and criticize the typed draft. He wishes to record his appreciation for the valuable suggestions offered by Professors Roger W. Benjamin; Raymond D. Duvall; William Morris; W. Phillips Shively; Charles Walcott; and by his advisee, Bruce Williams. In accord with the recognized customs of academia, however, the writer absolves his friends from all responsibility and accepts it as his own.

JOHN E. TURNER

July 1977

I will not cease from mental fight,
Nor shall my sword sleep in my hand,
Till we have built Jerusalem
In England's green and pleasant land.

> William Blake
> '*Milton*' (1804)

1 Labour Party Organization: a Look at the Bottom

As one of the leaders of a local Labour party answered questions put to him by an American visitor, he began to relate some of his experiences in politics, and the highlights of an active political life flashed across his mind. In his whimsical style he showed signs of enjoying these moments of recollection, as though perhaps his civic responsibilities gave him little time to muse about the past.

His political career was typical of many Labour stalwarts who grew active in politics during the inter-war years. He had joined the 'movement' when only a lad in his teens when the party in his district suffered from electoral famine. During these lean years and later in more rewarding times he had done his share of work 'on the doorstep', delivering literature and canvassing voters, arranging for bazaars and raffles, and collecting dues from party members. After serving out his apprenticeship in minor posts, he had been elected ward secretary, then treasurer of the constituency party, and eventually he had worked his way up to the chairmanship of the organization.

At an early point in his career, a growing involvement in party affairs prompted him to stand for a seat on the borough council. The first two election battles had been hopeless endeavors, but the third fight gave him a razor-thin majority. After this victory and a few successful encounters on the chamber floor, he was selected as a candidate in the borough's 'safer' wards, and now he was completing his twentieth year of service on the council. His veteran status in local government had naturally elevated him to positions of leadership and responsibility.

In discussing his political role, the Labour leader pointed out that his work cut across several spheres of activity. He had started out in the ward organization where he resided, and he was still an officer in that unit. But, since he represented a different ward as a member of the borough council, he had a responsibility to that ward as well. This meant that he had to listen to citizens' complaints in the ward, and he was expected to attend at least some of the party's monthly meetings there. Moreover, since the boundaries of the borough were coterminous with those of the parliamentary constituency, his duties as an officer in the local constituency party drew him into national politics. Whenever a general election was scheduled, he was a key figure in the campaign to get the Labour candidate elected to the House of Commons.

The local Labour partisan was careful to observe that if he had lived in a different constituency, his political career might have taken a markedly different turn. He was fortunate now to be in a safe Labour area where the outcome of an election was never in doubt and where his political position was unlikely to be challenged successfully. Here he could afford to pour his energy into the work of the council, for the party demands upon him were not as pressing as they would be in a constituency with less Labour support. The big problem that he and his colleagues had to face was that of apathy – keeping people interested in politics when the local opposition was weak and political contests were not even close. His political career might have followed a different course if he had lived in a marginal constituency where every election is hard-fought and the specter of defeat is always present. Even more different would have been that career if he had lived in a hopelessly Conservative constituency, where the Labour party tries to maintain an organization and to keep up the morale of a small band of workers without the slightest hope of victory at the polls.

He knew what it was to tramp the pavement in a despairing search for Labour votes, for that was the story of his early political experience. He had joined the movement during a discouraging era when it was difficult for the Labour Party to get a hearing and to recruit enough people to handle its organizational tasks. But, with the development of new industry in his borough and the movement of workers into the district's cheaper flats, the social composition of the area began to change. Manual workers and some middle-class groups – disturbed by poor housing and chronic unemployment – became awakened to the need for social reform. As these people grew disillusioned by the other parties, they began to turn to Labour, and the party gradually increased its strength, gaining respectability because of the performance of Labour members on the council. The political complexion of the district underwent further change during the war when working-class people were moved into the area as a result of the 'blitz'; and in the immediate post-war years more voters developed an interest in the party as the Labour government unfolded its program. Thus, in a sense, he asserted, his own political career had been tied to the 'social revolution' which gradually swept him into a position of electoral security.

The local notable had few regrets about his political work, past and present. To be sure, his duties on the council were extremely demanding and consumed much of his leisure time; indeed, he had had only eight evenings to himself during the previous month. Moreover, the hours he spent on council activities were without remuneration, since the British do not provide salaries for their elected representatives in local government. Far from being compensated, his service to the borough actually cost him money, for very often his council work prevented him from earning overtime wages on his regular job and sometimes he had to take time off from work in order to carry out his civic assignments. He carefully pointed out, however, that his long record of volunteer service was appreciated; his council colleagues had once elected him mayor of the borough – an honor which made him proud and had been well worth the financial sacrifice.

'Why do I get so involved in party work and the activities of the council?', the Labour leader asked, almost rhetorically. 'Because I believe in the Labour Party and the principles it stands for. We have built up our party in this constituency by dint of hard work, and we take pride in servicing the needs of the people who live here. If you will pardon me for saying so, we do a jolly good job running this borough! But, quite apart from the political side, I enjoy the fellowship with people in the party who are ordinary citizens, just like I am. The party is more than just politics and political discussion; it is the center of our social activities as well. Without my work in the party, my life would not be complete.'

It did not take the American interrogator long to realize that he was talking to a dedicated party activist who believed in the 'cause' and for whom the party served as the central focus of his intellectual and social life. Individuals of this type, of course, are to be found in all political parties. The corps of activists in each organization are the volunteer workers who can always be counted upon to meet voters on the doorstep and to handle routine clerical tasks – work that has to be done if the party is to make an impact on the electorate. Moreover, it is from the group of motivated partisans that individuals are singled out to occupy leadership roles in the organization. Without a solid core of activists in a political organization, the party machine would soon break down.

The British party system places heavy demands upon its activists in that it seeks to involve them on a continuing basis. Unlike most American parties, the British parties do not disband their organizations after a parliamentary election, but continue to hold their regular meetings, to sponsor conferences and training programs, to recruit new members, and to canvass voters in preparation for the next encounter. If they want to be successful at the polls, political organizers have to keep their party machines from getting rusty because the electoral system requires that most of the local parties get ready for an election every year and, periodically, for two or even more in a single year. For example, they have to be prepared to fight regularly scheduled elections for the borough and county councils. Although the pattern is not uniform, a local party in a borough has to tune its machine for an election every year to fill one-third of the seats on the council, and it usually has to fight a separate election for the county council every third year. A government at the national level may run its five-year term, but party organizers can never be certain when a parliamentary election will be called; many of them had been anticipating the 1964 general election for almost two years before the Prime Minister eventually set the date. Moreover, a local party may be summoned without much notice to compete in one or more by-elections, since vacant seats on the local councils and in parliament are filled through special elections. This schedule of some staggered and some uncertain voting contests encourages party leaders to cultivate healthy organizations at the grass roots, even though the success may be patchy.

In this study we shall be examining the organization, leadership, and activities of three local Labour parties in the London area. But before we turn our attention to these three units, it will be useful to describe in a general way the organizational structure of local Labour parties in the urban centers of Britain. Then, in the next chapter, we shall briefly look at the regional and national structures of the Labour Party, especially as they affect the local parties. Such an exposition will hopefully provide us with a general field of vision within which we can focus more sharply upon the three objects of this study.

LABOUR PARTY ORGANIZATION: AN OVERVIEW

The structure of the Labour Party, like that of most organizations, has been shaped by the circumstances of history. Prior to 1918, its leaders were intent upon mobilizing support outside parliament in an effort to build up working-class representation at Westminster, and they welded together a number of separate groups (mostly trade unions and socialist societies) into a loose federation. Following the organizational pattern of the Trades Union Congress, these groups affiliated with the Labour Party. Under this arrangement of affiliated collectivities, no provision was made for the enrollment of *individual* members; an individual could participate in the political movement only by joining one of the affiliated organizations.

At the end of World War I, the Party's constitution was modified, under the guidance of Arthur Henderson and Sydney Webb, to permit the recruitment of individuals who had no connections with the unions or socialist societies. This meant that a set of local constituency parties enrolling individual members was grafted on to the federation, which eventually took the form of a four-dimensional alliance: individual members who join at the ward or branch level; and affiliated members who are linked with the Party through their trade unions, co-operative organizations, or socialist/professional societies (like the Fabian Society Socialist Medical Association, etc). Each of these components is entitled to representation at the constituency level and in the higher tiers of organization.

The 1918 reforms also committed the Labour Party (including the affiliated trade unions) to a socialist platform. The long-term objective, which still excites the idealism of many Labour stalwarts, is inscribed in the Party's constitution: 'to secure for the workers by hand or by brain the full fruits of their industry and the most equitable distribution thereof that may be possible upon the basis of the common ownership of the means of production, distribution, and exchange, and the best obtainable system of popular administration and control of each industry or service.'[1]

Since the Labour Party is pledged to achieve its socialist purpose by democratic means, it must compete for support in the electoral marketplace. Like most parties, it seeks power in order to put its policies into effect. But the policies of the Labour Party are of a special type; they presumably flow from a philosophical perspective which makes a critique of existing society and enunciates as a major objective the reconstruction of the social order. That the Labour Party is branded with a special stamp has more than once been indicated by Harold Wilson: '[It] is more than a political organization; it is a crusade, or it would be better that it did not exist.'[2]

While the imprecision of the stated goals, as well as questions of timing and strategy, make it possible for a wide variety of outlooks to claim cover under Labour's umbrella, the 'class interpretation of politics' and the 'radical critique' of the social order probably require that the organization be catalogued as an 'ideological' party in James Q. Wilson's typology.[3] Some members, to be sure, may join the ranks for ambiguous or even personal reasons, but the fact remains that a good number sign up because of the Party's 'reconstructive' program or its socialist goals. Indeed, some of the 'committed' would even be willing to forego power rather than have the goals compromised. As we shall see later on, the twin objectives of electoral victory and the building of a socialist society have always generated conflict within the organization; the Party's leaders and activists are by no means in complete agreement on what the immediate or even the ultimate goals should be.

For the vast majority of Labour activists, however, the winning of elections is the immediate goal to be pursued, and the organizational pattern of the federation is designed for this purpose. At the lowest tier is the *ward* or *branch*, which enrolls the individual members of the Party and which may have a women's unit or a youth section attached to it. At the next highest level is the *constituency Labour Party*, which is the basic unit of Labour Party organization. The wards or branches send delegates to the governing body of this unit, as do the trade unions and other groups that are affiliated with the local party. In the case of a large metropolitan area, there may be two or more constituency parties whose activities, especially in the field of local government, are coordinated by a *district Labour party* (formerly called a *borough Labour party*), to which each constituency party and affiliated components send representatives, subject to the approval of the National Executive Committee (NEC). In the case of a large metropolitan area which is a county embracing a number of boroughs, the *county Labour party* takes the form of a coordinating committee on which the various constituency parties within the territory are represented for the purposes of developing policy and managing county elections. Above the constituency, district, and county levels is the *regional organization*, which is designed to assist the local parties and to link them with the national headquarters. At the top of the organizational pyramid are several structures with which the constituency parties have important connections: the *Party Conference*, which is the main representative organ of the national Party outside of parliament; the *National Executive Committee*, which is the administrative arm of the Conference; and the *Parliamentary Labour Party*, which comprises all of the Labour M.P.s in the House of Commons, as well as the Labour members of the House of Lords.

Our main purpose in this chapter is to examine the patterns of organization in the local constituency parties and the problems that these units face. In the next chapter we shall look at the upper layers of Labour Party organization in order to see how a constituency party fits into the federated structure and to describe the relationships it has with the agencies that rank above it in the hierarchy. We must remember, however, that the several hundred local parties in Britain's urban areas occupy a spectrum which allows for considerable variation. Moreover, the recent reorganization of local government has necessitated a restructuring of the lower Party units, the outcome of which is unclear at the moment.[4] How the constituency parties operate depends upon such factors as the nature of the locale and the size of the Labour vote, the capabilities of the agent (if there is one), the organization's financial resources, the degree of consensus among the party activists, etc. Hence, in drawing the picture we shall have to be content with broad-pencilled contours, since available information on the actual operation of local parties is inadequate for firm generalizations.

FUNCTIONS OF THE CONSTITUENCY PARTY

The local constituency party is the crucial unit of Labour Party organization, for it is the agency through which propagandists and candidates approach the voters. Most activists want their local party organizations to be as influential as possible in electoral contests and in exerting an impact upon the community. This primary goal requires certain secondary or *operational objectives* if the unit is to be organizationally effective (or, indeed, if it is to survive). These operational objectives may be listed as follows:

1. *Recruitment of new members.* Both the tradition of the Labour Party

and its chronic lack of funds dictate that most of the work in the constituencies has to be done by volunteer workers. An adequate supply of such help is especially important at election time because of the statutory limitations on campaign disbursements. The local party needs to develop a reservoir of manpower from which it can draw its leading activists who will occupy official posts in the ward organizations and at the constituency level, and from which it can recruit a larger group of ordinary workers who will be asked to handle routine clerical and doorstep assignments. Even though a local party is too small to become very bureaucratic, it nevertheless has a distinct ordering of agencies and offices with clear-cut duties and patterns of authority, particularly during election campaigns. This means that the constituency organization needs people who possess certain skills or who have the interest and the time to learn them. A well-run party is also concerned about the recruitment and retention of young people as replacements for veterans who are no longer able to serve; an aging organization obviously faces a problem of survival. A party that is successful in its membership drives presents the image of vitality to the local community and is able at the same time to broaden its financial base through the collection of dues. It also increases its chances of drawing interested, qualified people into the corps of regular activists who will become party officers and council candidates, and into the ranks of the volunteers who are needed in propaganda and election campaigns. It hardly needs to be mentioned that a good constituency organization sponsors attractive social activities designed to retain the interest and deepen the loyalty of the activists upon whom it is so dependent.

2. *Education and training of party workers.* The local party facilitates the political education of its activists through the distribution of pamphlets and the sponsorship of discussion forums. This enables them to receive training in oral expression and to become better informed about public issues so that they can help to generate political awareness among ordinary citizens. The activists also need to be trained for the political roles they are called upon to play; they have to be knowledgeable about parliamentary procedure, the processes of local government, and election laws and campaign organization.

3. *Coordination of workers' activities.* A constituency party has to make sure that its human resources are deployed effectively and that the activities of the volunteers are woven together in a united effort. Inherently, this involves an effective system of communication. While the coordination problem has to be resolved in any political association, it assumes added importance in the Labour party because of its federated structure and because so many of its volunteers work only on a part-time basis when their schedules permit. Coordination becomes especially important during an election campaign when as many as 200 to 400 workers may be involved intermittently.[5]

If the party is sufficiently affluent, it maintains a central headquarters in the district which has facilities for group meetings and serves as a nerve-center for the organization. The party premises are run by a small staff (finances permitting), which carries on its work under the direction of an agent — a professional political organizer who is employed by the constituency unit, ideally on a full-time basis, although in many instances he may be a part-time volunteer without pay.[6] In directing and coordinating the party effort, the central headquarters becomes involved in a two-way communications flow: (1) it receives information, directives, and requests from agencies outside the constituency — the national headquarters in Transport House, the regional office, political units at the borough level, affiliated organizations, and other constituency parties — and it transmits the information to designated party activists who carry it back to their wards or local affiliated groups; and (2) the agent and his staff generate an information flow from the ward parties and other lower-tier organizations to the central headquarters where the data are processed, problems are identified, and information is made available on a constituency-wide basis to the officers who need it and also to functionaries in the national headquarters who request it.

4. *Policy-making.* Like any organization, a local Labour party has to make decisions with respect to the management of its internal affairs. But, as one would expect in an association that emphasizes internal democracy, the policymaking function extends much farther than mere housekeeping. At the local level, the party is confronted on a day-to-day basis with borough problems which are often of greater interest to voters than broader national questions. As these problems arise, policies have to be shaped and implementing strategies adopted. If the constituency coincides with the borough, the local party, working though the Labour representatives on the borough or county councils (called the Labour Group), has a wide range of autonomy in local matters and is usually able to work out its own program without the restraints of national Party decisions which apply to wider issues. By the same token, the local party is relatively free to develop its own issue foci and other strategies during election campaigns. On a wider front, the activists participate in policymaking to a limited extent through the institutionalized procedure of submitting resolutions (and sometimes questionnaire responses) to the National Executive Committee and the Party Conference. The policymaking process in a constituency organization poses special difficulties by virtue of the fact that it is a coalition of interests which are prone to keep a sharp lookout for their rights. While the delegates to the General Management Committee (GMC) are influenced by the plenary discussions, they sometimes fall under conflicting pressures as a result of their status as the representatives of their respective groups.

5. *Conduct of election campaigns.* Since the emphasized objective is to

win elections, the local party assumes responsibility for the selection of a parliamentary candidate and for the recruitment and selection of candidates for the local councils. Unlike the American system, these candidates are all chosen from within the organization. As the campaign begins to get under way, the party calls up its army of volunteer workers who engage in two lines of activity: (1) the contacting of voters through the distribution of leaflets and window bills; and (2) the identification – and later the mobilization – of probable supporters through canvassing and door-knocking efforts.

6. *Management of local affairs.* When Labour wins control of the local council, its active workers – by themselves if the parliamentary constituency is coterminous with the borough and in collaboration with other local parties if the borough covers more than one constituency – are called upon to operate the system of local government. In some respects, the borough council functioning in its locale resembles the House of Commons functioning in a national setting, with the councillors bearing responsibility for their wards just as a Member of Parliament is expected to look after his constituents. When a Labour party does a good job of 'running the borough', it strengthens its political base, which sometimes makes the election of an M.P. easier.

7. *Liaison between public officials and ordinary citizens.* A good constituency party is alert to the needs and attitudes of the electorate it represents. This means that it must facilitate contact between the public officials it sponsors – the Member of Parliament (or the prospective candidate) and the local councillors – and the inhabitants of the area.

8. *Finance of the organization.* Obviously, no local organization can carry out its activities effectively without adequate funding, and each constituency organization is responsible for pulling together the financial resources that are needed to pay the salaries of the staff, to maintain the premises, to secure propaganda materials, etc. Some parties try to use fund-raising ventures as means for enticing Labour supporters to become dues-paying members. The challenge is to develop stable sources of revenue without detracting hazardously from other organizational tasks.

An approaching election usually serves as a stimulus for political effort, but electoral contests occur only periodically, and in the interlude between campaigns other cementing influences have to be developed if the party is to continue to be effective and kept in trim for the next encounter. An organization that for all practical purposes dismantles its machinery after an election fosters apathy among its members and loses the opportunity to be effective in its non-electioneering functions. Thus, the building of a strong constituency party is a continuing process; people have to be drawn into the network well in advance of an election, and their life in the party has to be made sufficiently attractive for them to remain involved. We shall now examine the ways in which a constituency party organizes itself to perform the functions expected of it, and the problems that it encounters in handling its responsibilities.

ORGANIZATION AT THE WARD/BRANCH LEVEL

The main subdivision of a constituency Labour party is the ward or 'branch'. The latter is a recent structural change stemming from the reorganization of local government in Britain. The new patterns of local government cut through many of the wards and other units upon which Labour Party organization was based, and in 1974 the Party was forced to adjust its machinery to fit the new arrangement and thus be more efficient in fighting local government elections.[7] The Party Conference decided that the nuclear organization would be called the 'branch' and that the constituency parties would be given flexibility in forming their subordinate units on basis of electoral convenience or 'community of interest', subject to the approval of the National Executive Committee. In many areas the ward units remain the same but operate under a different name. Though technically wrong, we shall refer to them as 'wards' because they still function as electoral divisions for local councils in a good many urban centers, and because they were the party units when this study was made.

Ward Activities

The primary objective of the ward organization is to keep its machine tuned up in the interim between elections so that it can be moved into top gear the moment an election is scheduled.[8] It serves as the focal point for a variety of activities, most of which are carried out under the direction of the governing bodies and administrative officers of the local party.

One of the important assignments of a ward organization is the recruitment of individual members, and it is through the ward machinery that they participate in local party affairs. To qualify for membership in this category, individuals must be at least fifteen years of age, British subjects or citizens of Eire, or residents of Great Britain for more than one year. Besides having to live in the constituency or be registered to vote there, they must be members of a *bona fide* trade union if they are eligible, and are required to contribute to the political funds of their unions. All individual members sign statements indicating that they endorse the constitution, principles, and policies of the Labour Party, and that they do not belong to any political organization which has been proscribed by the Party Conference. This latter requirement is designed to protect the Party against infiltration by extremist groups, especially Communists and Trotskyists. An individual whose application for admission is rejected by the ward organization may appeal the decision to the GMC at the constituency level. A person must be registered as an individual member if he or she wishes to become a Labour candidate in a local or parliamentary election, a delegate to the Party Conference, or a member of the GMC.

The Labour Party also has a category of affiliated members – those who have joined a trade union or some other group that is affiliated with the Labour Party or is recognized by the NEC as being eligible for affiliation. Needless to say, the overwhelming majority of affiliated members secure attachment to the Party through their trade unions, and a portion of their union dues is turned over to the Party. This means that many of them are members of the national Party without being members of the local constituency party. They may be affiliated members of the local party, however, if their unions have chosen to affiliate with it. Members with affiliated status are not very conspicuous in the ward organizations and are rarely to be found among the activists in the local party.

An individual member of the Labour Party is obliged to pay a minimum fee of £1.20 per year, except for retired people who pay at a reduced rate determined by the local party. It falls upon the ward organization to see that the subscriptions are collected. This is done by personal visitation monthly or quarterly, and these visits are considered to be a mechanism through which the ward can keep in touch with its members and learn about their problems.

The individual members of the local party are invited to attend the ward club's monthly meetings, which are held in a nearby school, the local library, the party premises, or a private home. Although much of the meeting time is devoted to organizational and 'housekeeping' matters, the officers usually try to arrange for a speaker or to generate a discussion of public affairs. At these ward gatherings, ordinary party members have opportunities to voice their feelings on policy issues and to draw up resolutions. If a member's resolution is approved by the ward party, it is transmitted to the General Management Committee for consideration there. Influential members of the ward organization often serve on the borough council, and they are expected to attend the meetings of the ward they represent. This enables them to answer questions about local government policy, to hear complaints about high rents or poor street-lighting, and to listen to rank-and-file views on local issues.

An active ward organization tries to hold its members together by sponsoring various social and welfare activities. These include dances, fellowship 'socials', hikes, day outings to resort areas, theater parties, bingo evenings, and similar engagements. Activities of this sort often attract newcomers to the district who are eager to strike up friendships, as well as older residents who feel a need to enrich their social lives. In addition to improving morale through widened social contact, some of these ward-sponsored activities bring revenue into the treasury. The more active members of some ward groups undertake welfare projects—the scheduling of children's parties and sports events, bus trips for old-age pensioners, visits to the sick, and the like. Such projects not only serve to focus the members' attention on concrete objectives, but also help to touch up the party's image at the grass roots.

As suggested earlier, however, the main reason for building an organization at the ward level is to assist the constituency party in fighting elections. When a campaign is in the offing, the officers and other members of the ward party share responsibility for selecting the candidates. At an election for the borough council, for example, they act in collaboration with the Executive Committee of the constituency party or other units in choosing candidates to stand in their ward. In the case of a parliamentary election, each ward is entitled to nominate an eligible candidate who, along with competing candidates, will be considered by the governing bodies of the constituency party.

Once the parliamentary standard-bearer or the candidates for the local council have been chosen, the constituency party officials usually delegate responsibilities to the ward officers who in turn assign tasks to reliable members in their organization. People have to be recruited to deliver literature, to distribute window stickers, to address envelopes, and to staff the committee rooms (precinct headquarters). But the most crucial task that is usually assigned to the wards is that of identifying voters who are likely to cast their ballots for Labour.

Voter identification is a detailed information-gathering activity which is based upon the election register. Issued periodically by the local government authorities, the register carries the name of every eligible voter, his address, and his registration number. The aim is to secure an accurate 'marked register', i.e., an indication of the likely political allegiance of every elector in the ward—and, of course, in all of the wards in the constituency. Labour supporters who have moved to a different residence within the area have to be recontacted, and sympathetic electors who have moved away but who are still entitled to vote in the constituency have to be traced and a postal vote (absentee ballot) and some party literature sent to them. Ward activists also process the claim forms for the postal votes of incapacitated people, taking the initiative in getting the doctor's signature. But the most important task is to compile the list of resident voters who are inclined toward Labour, including young people who have just reached voting age and people who have recently moved into the ward. The objective of this exercise is to compile, store, and retrieve information so that on polling day transportation can be supplied for people who need it and, more important, door-knocking campaigns can be organized to remind Labour's supporters to vote. An accurately marked register is built up over the years and is kept current—a resource-devouring endeavor.

Alert leaders are on the lookout for voter information in news stories in the local press, letters to the editor, and informal conversation. The bulk of the information about voters' inclinations, however, comes from the door-to-door canvass, which an efficient ward organization conducts at frequent intervals, intensifying the effort at election time.

When the ward leaders decide that their records should be updated (usually during a campaign), they dispatch teams of canvassers to designated areas to engage each voter listed on the canvass card in a brief doorstep conversation. The objective is not to convert; it is merely to appraise the elector's voting intentions. On the basis of this doorstep encounter, the canvasser marks the card 'Labour', 'Conservative', or 'Liberal' (some cards provide only for a designation of 'For' or 'Against'), or 'Doubtful' if it appears that the voter has not yet made up his mind. Canvassing estimates of a voter's political leanings may be corroborated over a period of time by noting the consistency of his responses to the Labour people who call upon him, his willingness to put up a window bill, and his attitude toward the party workers who ask him for his registration number when he comes out of the polling station. (It is by relaying these numbers back to the committee rooms that the party's election workers determine which of their supporters have already voted and which have yet to be routed out.)

Thus, a good ward organization is a vital component of a constituency party. Without it, the tasks of recruiting new members, collecting subscriptions, and canvassing for electoral support would have to be done entirely through the party's central headquarters. Given the size of the territory to be organized on a day-to-day basis and the need to coordinate the activities of scores of volunteers during election campaigns, a set of efficient ward organizations affords a pattern of decentralized administration which can be put into operation when the centralized model is considered to be impractical or undesirable.

Organization of Ward Activities

The legal subdivisions of a ward are polling districts (precincts), and a local Labour party carries its organization down to this level for propaganda and election purposes. This enables the ward officers to hand routine assignments over to lower-tier administrators who are more easily recruited when the territory they have to cover is small. The person responsible for the work in this subdivision is the polling-district secretary, a person who has detailed knowledge about the political complexion of the area. He knows where the Labour support lies – who will be certain to vote on election day, who will need some prodding, and who is incapacitated and needs help in getting to the polls. When the party schedules a bazaar, he knows where to go for donations and for help in running it. In a well-run polling district with plenty of volunteers, the distribution of literature and the other door-to-door work may be assigned on a street basis; or where there are huge blocks of flats, the work may be apportioned block by block. When the polling district organization is weak, of course, the work falls upon the ward secretary.

At their annual meeting, the ward members elect the principal officers: the chairman, the secretary, and the treasurer. If the ward is active, an adequate distribution of responsibility may require a secondary level of officials – a social secretary who arranges the ward's social gatherings, a political education officer who tries to keep the members informed about public issues by scheduling speakers and making literature available, and a minute secretary who records the party's official proceedings. The elected officers constitute the ward party's executive committee – a body that meets to discuss the affairs of the organization and to present recommendations at the ward meetings. Although the officers are elected for one-year terms, they may be re-elected, and it is not unusual for some of the leaders to serve for long periods of time, especially in wards that have a stable membership. Many wards have won a reputation for effectiveness because a handful of devoted activists have invested their spare time in party activities for many years.

While the chairman and other officials play important roles, major responsibility for organization falls upon the ward secretary, one of the key figures in a constituency party. He keeps the membership records, remains in touch with the members, and sets the agenda for meetings, sometimes arranging for the speakers. It is the secretary's responsibility to maintain a record of all party activities in his area, including the marked register, and to make periodic reports to officials in the constituency headquarters. In many wards, the secretary is so knowledgeable about the district that constituency officials are content to put him in charge of the canvass and the recruitment and supervision of the volunteer workers during election campaigns. To a lot of residents, the secretary symbolizes the party, and they seek him out when they have complaints or want to express themselves on a local issue. The secretary then relays the messages to the appropriate authorities, often requesting a report on the action taken. This ward official is in a position to command respect if he exhibits organizing ability and demonstrates his loyalty to the organization. But responsibility of this sort is time-consuming, and in some areas the job goes begging. As Ron Hayward, the Labour Party's General Secretary, once pointed out, 'When we talk about Ministers and ward secretaries, . . . I suppose that the latter may be more important than the former. The Prime Minister has a long list of people dying to become Ministers; we have a very short list of people wanting to be ward secretaries.'[9]

Patterns and Problems of Ward Politics

The description we have offered is that of well-organized wards, and we have observed some that measured up. But in many places the scenario records ward party structures in decay. According to an official report, '... there are not a few parties who succeed in keeping ward committees in active operation in every ward; there are more which have a committee functioning in most of the wards but not in all of them; and there are some where the numbership is so small that no proper ward organization can exist at all.'[10] Often the deterioration has occurred in the strongly Labour areas.

The general problem of declining individual membership in the constituency party as a whole will be treated later. It will suffice at this juncture to report that unexciting ward meetings in the urban areas can hardly compete with television programs, the attractions of city life, and obligations of competing loyalties. As a result, the overwhelming majority of individual members do little more than pay their dues (provided that someone comes along to collect them), and the few activists who show up regularly for the meetings carry the organizational load. This means that a small group of people may be consigned to positions of ward leadership for a long time. Such a situation creates problems when, in the absence of adequate replacements, the leaders grow old in harness, lacking the energy, the time, or the innovative ideas required for organizational effectiveness. Obviously, too, a party unit dependent upon the devoted few is likely to wither when the leaders move away or for some other reason have to terminate their responsibilities. This sometimes happens when a ward officer is elected to the borough council to represent a different ward and finds himself with competing demands for his time.

An equally difficult problem is that of keeping existing membership rolls intact owing to the instability of the population in Britain's metropolitan areas since the war. Slum clearance programs, for example, have caused the relocation of working-class voters to other areas, and some middle-class people, forced out of the high-rent districts, have purchased homes or signed leases in areas that have traditionally been Labour's preserve. Population shifts, which may affect from 10 to 15 per cent of the constituency's electorate in any given year, often change the political complexion of the wards — a situation that makes an updated voting register more imperative but also more difficult. Very often the movements of population have resulted in an amalgamation of wards or a redrawing of the boundary lines. As a consequence of this reorganization, the leaders of a given ward sometimes find themselves in a different unit, and the old ward is left without experienced activists to give it direction. It hardly needs to be mentioned that changes in ward boundaries entail a remodeling of the party structure, the recruitment of new officers, and fresh canvassing efforts so that the ward can mobilize its resources within the new framework.

In light of these developments, it is small wonder that the machinery for collecting members' subscriptions has broken down. In the old days the collection of dues was done by volunteers who sensed the importance of the revenue for the local party and the need to maintain contact with individual members. In recent years, however, the party has turned over the job to hired collectors – usually old-age pensioners or other Labour people in need of supplementary income – who retain a proportion of the yield (usually 25 per cent). But the use of paid helpers has not solved the problem of gathering in the subscriptions. The task is a bit arduous for old people, and the remuneration is unattractive to the able-bodied. For these reasons there is usually a shortage of collectors, and when the call goes out for volunteers to assist the hired personnel, the people most likely to respond are those whose limited time could be better spent on other assignments. In many local parties, the average level of dues paid is less than the amount required under Party rules.

ORGANIZATION AT THE CONSTITUENCY LEVEL

The ward units, which are composed of individual members, do not have affiliated organizations. Moreover, in contrast with the Conservative Party, the individual members from all of the ward clubs never meet together in a large assembly. It is at the constituency level that the representatives of the various components of the federation in the locality join together in common cause – delegates who speak for the individual members in the wards and spokesmen from trade unions, socialist societies, and other groups. In this integrative function, the local party is patterned after the national organization. Its official responsibility is to direct the political effort in the constituency and to further the goals of the Labour Party within its jurisdiction.

Constituency Party Activities

We have already listed the major functions of a constituency party, and have examined some of the activities it supervises at the ward level. This treatment will undoubtedly elicit a response from critics who have recently taken a censorious view of these units.[11] The skepticism stems largely from the experience they have had with declining activity in the local parties, and from the studies they have read concerning the negligible impact that 'good organization' seems to have had upon electoral results.[12] At the moment, the slight evidence we have is conflicting, and we shall not have a more definitive answer until more rigorous studies are made – with appropriate control groups – in a series of general and local elections.

The most telling criticism is levelled at the vote-gathering function of the local parties. According to the argument, many constituencies are non-competitive, and energetic campaigns in such areas become a 'meaningless ritual'; in these districts, electioneering activities should be held to a minimum and the activists transferred to marginal areas where they stand a chance of affecting the result.[13] It is true that some political effort in 'safe' electoral units is wasted, and no one can argue against an efficient deployment of resources. But rather than 'scaling down' their election activities, some local parties should be challenged by such developments as Labour's loss of council seats in Labour areas to their opponents in recent years, the apparent disenchantment of working-class voters with the Labour Party, and the increasing volatility of the electorate.

In any event, no one seems to advocate the dismantling of the constituency parties; the critics would merely amplify certain functions and play down others. As we already observed, the local parties at the present time are responsible for the recruitment and retention of individual members, the development of political education programs and propaganda campaigns, the training of party workers, and the coordination of their activities. They also serve as vehicles for policy-making, especially in internal matters and in local affairs and to a lesser extent in the national organization.[14] One of its primary obligations is to conduct election campaigns, including the important task of selecting candidates. If the party is successful in local elections, it becomes involved in managing the borough, and in any event it usually serves as a link between elected public officials and ordinary citizens. Finally, the constituency organization concerns itself with the financing of its activities.

Organization for the Performance of Party Functions

The governing body of a constituency party is the General Management Committee, to which individual members from each ward,[15] the affiliated organizations, and certain ancillary units are entitled to send delegates. The individual members of a ward club are usually represented by the secretary, who sits *ex officio* with the right to vote, and by other delegates elected annually, the number depending upon the size of the membership. Similarly, the trade unions, socialist societies, and cooperative units that have affiliated with the local party have a right to appoint delegates to the GMC. A union branch, for example, may be entitled to send one representative for every fifty members or part thereof up to a maximum of five. The Women's Section is ordinarily allocated two delegate positions, as are the Young Socialists, though provision is sometimes made for awarding more GMC seats to the youth sections as their membership grows. The basis of representation for all groups is set by the General Management Committee and endorsed by the National Executive Committee.

In urban centers, the largest block of GMC delegates comes from the wards, since some trade unions do not bother to select representatives, and even when they do, many of their delegates are unable to attend regularly. A good number of people who are active in their unions, however, come on to the GMC as delegates from their wards. In the active ward parties, the members often compete for GMC seats, making their representation less stable than that of the trade union branches. But when a ward member is defeated in the race for a delegateship, he sometimes manages to get on the GMC anyway by becoming a representative of an affiliated organization which may be experiencing difficulty in filling its quota of seats. All GMC members are elected for one-year terms, but they may be re-elected. The composition of the GMC in safe Labour territory usually remains stable, the delegates being returned for long periods of time.

The members of the General Management Committee usually meet at a fixed time each month in a central place to deliberate on the party's affairs, to present the views of the groups they represent, and to pick up information to take back to their wards or the affiliated organizations. A GMC meeting typically handles an agenda of business like the following:

1 Call to order by the Chairman.
2 Minutes of the Previous Meeting.
3 Matters arising from the Minutes.
4 Apologies sent by members who are unable to attend owing to sickness or conflicting engagements.
5 Correspondence. (This includes notification of any action taken by the national headquarters [Transport House], as well as announcements of public meetings, special conferences, and other activities organized by Labour Party groups outside the constituency.)
6 Executive Committee Report. (This body, which is elected annually by the GMC from among its own members, considers the party's affairs in a preliminary way and brings in recommendations for discussion.)
7 Reports from Officers.
   (a) Secretary.
   (b) Treasurer.
   (c) Political Education Officer.
   (d) Meetings Officer.
   (e) Social Secretary.

8 Reports from Ward Organizations. (These include a statement of each ward's activities during the previous month, as well as an announcement of its total membership.)
9 Reports from Other Organizations.
 (a) Young Socialists
 (b) Women's Section.
10 Parliamentary Report. (This is an account given by the Member of Parliament on the major issues being dealt with in the House of Commons and on the situation in the Parliamentary Labour Party.)
11 Reports on Special Conferences attended by the party's representatives.
12 Report on the Labour Group in the Borough Council and a Discussion of Local Questions.
13 Resolutions sent forward by Ward Organizations or Affiliated Groups.
14 Other Urgent Business of which advance notice has been given.

The GMC meetings operate under standing orders which set the time of adjournment, unless the members vote to suspend them.

These gatherings are often criticized for their 'dull reports' and the 'humdrum' discussions about organization. As with many meetings of every political faith, the agenda is not always inspiring. But it is worthwhile to observe that the assembly helps to meet two important needs in an organization composed of diverse interests and outlooks. First, the GMC meeting serves as a forum for competitive discussion on whatever subject, and from the interchange of opinions an acceptable decision can be hammered out. Second, the meeting facilitates an exchange of information so that the representatives of each group know what the others are doing. Thus, not only do the delegates bring information and views from their respective clienteles, but they also carry back other types of information about policy and overall party activities to the wards and affiliated bodies.

Despite the 'meeting weariness' that sets in during the exchange of information, most parties manage to devote some time to the discussion of policy. Most of the activists who are faithful to the GMC are concerned about issues, and the intensity of their feeling sometimes livens up the proceedings. A policy debate might erupt from the contents of a report or an ordinary item for action; the M.P.'s report often opens up current questions of local and national importance, providing scope for the expression of individual and group views; and a resolution sent forward by one of the wards might generate argument over an issue. Whether or not a controversial question has been 'settled' at the GMC meeting, the keenest of the partisans will probably continue the exchange of ideas at the nearby public house, where libation stimulates comradely communion.

Attendance at GMC meetings obviously varies with the type of constituency and the vitality of the organization. While no comprehensive study has been made of urban parties, an educated estimate would place the normal attendance figure at between 50 per cent and 60 per cent of the delegates. The press of other loyalties, work on the nightshift, and competition with the excitement of urban social life tend to push up the absentee rate. But on certain occasions – when a parliamentary candidate is to be selected, when a controversial item appears on the agenda, or even when the annual meeting is called – the attendance book usually records a more complete roster.

The party elects its officers at the annual meeting of the General Management Committee, which is usually held early in the year. The major officials – called the 'executive officers' – typically include the chairman, two vice-chairmen, the treasurer, and the secretary (who is in most cases the agent). The most coveted post is the chairmanship, for in an area of Labour strength its occupant is counted among the top political figures. The vice-chairmen also emerge from contested elections. Very few people struggle to become treasurer, because the work is arduous, the responsibility is great, and the money is scarce. In addition to the major officials, the GMC elects a set of 'non-executive' functionaries who perform specialized tasks: a political education officer, a youth officer, a meetings officer, a social affairs officer (or committee), etc. Most of these positions are uncontested, the people involved having been recruited beforehand.

At the annual meeting, the GMC also elects from its membership a smaller steering group known as the Executive Committee. Responsible to the parent body, the Executive Committee handles ordinary business matters and discusses in a preliminary way the important concerns of the party, ways to foster its development, and its official stand on current issues. This Committee has significant powers in the selection of a parliamentary candidate, being authorized to make a nomination of its own and to draw up a 'short list' of nominees from which the GMC may make a choice.[16] The Executive Committee prepares reports and makes recommendations which are presented to the governing body for consideration.

The party's executive officers are automatically members of the Executive Committee by virtue of their position, while the non-executive officers usually hold seats without voting rights, although they may be elected to full status in another capacity. As in the case of the GMC, each component of the federation claims representation on 'the Executive', and the election is carried out in sections. In other words, the ward delegates representing the party's individual members nominate and vote for their own representatives, as do the trade unions and other affiliated organizations – all on the basis of a prescribed allocation of seats. Except for the trade union places, which may be filled by volunteers, the seats on the Executive Committee are often hotly contested. Since party matters are usually brought to this body first and its members are bound individually to support the group decision, the Executive Committee can be a powerful force within a constituency organization, and people who are interested in influencing policy or who are motivated toward power are often eager to serve on it.

One of the key roles in the better organized constituency parties is that played by the secretary/agent who, initially selected by the General Management Committee, continues to hold his post so long as he and his colleagues on the GMC are happy in harness. A professional organizer, he is responsible for all that is entailed in building an efficient machine and keeping it in good running condition. To develop and hold together an organization of volunteer workers who can entertain no hope of *material* rewards and can easily withdraw when they become discontented is a challenging assignment, and the successful agent is a rare combination of diplomat, strategist, financial manager, and expert organizer.

An important but often unnoticed part of an agent's work is in the area of recruitment. To be sure, he initiates and supervises membership drives, but the recruitment effort he undertakes on his own is more specifically targeted. He must be continually on the lookout for individuals who exhibit a capacity for leadership. He seeks to draw them into the organization, to gradually increase their responsibilities, and to encourage them to use talents they may not have been aware of.

More than any other local officer, the agent knows what is going on in the organization, for he constitutes the nucleus of the communications network. As the manager of the central headquarters, he handles the correspondence and maintains the party's records, collecting the necessary information from the wards and other units, and he is the sole point of contact between the constituency and the organizers in the regional and national offices. It is through the agent that information is transmitted to the various officers and units within the constituency and to the external agencies and organizations.

The agent's expertise and his command of important information enable him to be helpful in the party's decision-making function. As the chief administrative officer, he is a member of its governing bodies, and he works closely with the other officers in identifying problems and in offering suggestions for their resolution. But, even though he is expected to 'give a lead', he cannot afford to become too involved in controversial matters, for if he appears to be 'taking sides', he runs the risk of alienating some of the members and thus jeopardizing his effectiveness as a leader. Indeed, part of his responsibility is to thwart the development of factional rivalries and personal feuds, which often requires him to mediate conflicts and to smooth ruffled feathers. Transport House attempts to screen the candidtes for agency work so as to weed out those who lack the necessary skills, and it admonishes the agents to follow the principle of toleration and neutrality.[17]

It is during an election campaign that the position of the agent becomes most conspicuous.[18] When the campaign officially gets under way, the local party as a *formal organization* temporarily goes out of commission. This is done for several reasons. First, except for recent legislation authorizing the candidate's political affiliation to be listed on the ballot, British law does not recognize the status of a party as such; statutory recognition is given only to the candidate and the person who is responsible for running his campaign (the agent). Second, the dissolution of the party organization makes it possible for the candidate to divorce himself from any improprieties of which a few party volunteers may be accused. Third, British election law severely limits campaign expenditures, and the party officers naturally want to avoid having to include the costs of normal party operation as part of their campaign disbursements. Fourth, by dispensing with its regular meetings during the campaign, the party is able to avoid formal discussion of issues that might have divided the members, and attention can be focused on the winning of the election.

When the party dissolves, the agent assumes full responsibility for campaign activities. The various Representation of the People Acts define in intricate detail his legal duties and obligations, and the penalties for violations are severe for both the agent and the candidate. The funds that are collected go through the agent's hands and only he can authorize their expenditure. Although he usually consults with the candidate and his task-oriented campaign staff, he has to assume the risk of the final decisions. In a political sense, of course, he cannot behave as an autocrat. To be successful in putting together an efficient campaign organization, he has to delegate authority and he has to maintain cordial relations with his colleagues so that he can command their full support. He is answerable to the whole party when it comes back into operation.

To many Labour veterans who have never grown accustomed to the requirements of a 'modern' political organization, the agent sometimes appears as the local symbol of a needless bureaucracy, and he becomes an easy target when things do not work out according to plan. He bears the responsibility of a manager, but his dependence upon volunteer labor make it impossible for him to apply the sanctions that are available to executives in other types of organizations. His success lies in his ability to gain the confidence of his people and to inspire them to work together. This means that he often has to listen sympathetically as they recount their personal problems, and to utter kind words of recognition at the appropriate time. Without an effective agent, the local party machine soon begins to sputter.

Patterns and Problems of Constituency Party Politics

1. *The financial problem.* While the local parties usually get some financial help from the trade unions or Transport House and develop money-raising schemes of their own, most of them lack a stable fiscal base, which stops them from performing at high-level capacity. Some parties, for example, have to carry on their work without adequate premises, operating out of a single room or even a private home. Still more serious is the inability of most of them to employ a full-time agent, and they are forced to rely upon a part-time organizer or an unpaid volunteer. From a peak of slightly less than 300 full-time agents in the early 1950s, the number had dwindled to 95 by 1976.[19]

The financial problem is complicated by the fact that some of the parties that are relatively well off, often as a result of subsidies from union branches, operate in safe Labour districts where the need for funds is not so critical. Some agents naturally gravitate toward these financially sound and electorally safe organizations where the responsibilities are less demanding and where they are not required to spend so much time raising money for their own salaries. The paucity of funds has contributed to the deficient organization in some marginal constituencies which are strategic to the outcome of a parliamentary election. During the general election of 1964, for example, only about half of the marginal seats held by Labour and the winnable seats held by the Conservatives could claim the services of a full-time, professional agent. At the same time, agents were employed in 22 per cent of the safe Labour districts and in 10 per cent of the constituencies where Conservatives were almost sure to win.[20]

While the leaders in Transport House have customarily felt constrained by their own limited resources, they have given grants to some marginal constituencies to enable them to retain the services of a full-time agent. In 1969, the Party introduced a more systematic program of agent employment in the form of a partial National Agency Service. Under this scheme, Transport House financed about 40 agency positions (in some cases with contributions from the local parties), and in 1974 most of these agents were employed in marginal constituencies.[21] The high drop-out rate among agents stems largely from the low salary scale. Transport House negotiates minimum pay levels with the agents' trade union, and the agents are left to bargain with their local parties for higher wages provided that resources are available. But in many cases the party's revenue is so uncertain that the agent has to promote fund-raising ventures in order to collect his pay, often at the expense of his regular political work. Under these circumstances, it is remarkable that the Labour Party has been able to retain as many good agents as it has. Many of them stay on, despite the poor remuneration, because they enjoy the 'sport' of politics and the challenge of organizational work, and because they are devoted to the 'cause'.[22]

2. *Recruitment of members.* For more than two decades, local Labour parties have been wrestling with the problem of declining membership. According to the quotas suggested by the national organizers in the late 1950s, a constituency organization should aim to recruit a membership base equal to 12.5 per cent of the supporting electorate.[23] Most local units, however, are unable to come close to hitting this target. Individual membership in the Labour Party reached its peak in 1952, and the latest report indicated a decline of about one-third from the 1952 figure.[24]

Existing information permits no more than speculation about the reasons for the lack of political involvement at the local level. As Britain has grown more affluent since the war, some people who might have been drawn into politics during a depression era have not felt the need to become active in Labour's cause, and the new attractions of urban life compete for their leisure time. According to an official analysis in the 1950s, the availability of consumer goods and the prospect of a higher standard of living encouraged more married women to take jobs and more men to work overtime — a development that affected 'not only political attitudes but also the numbers of voluntary workers willing and able to carry on election activities'.[25] Young married women in the 30-40 age-bracket, who might be searching for ways to relieve the monotony of their home chores, may not be enthusiastic about joining a political study group where older women discuss the affairs of the local coop and recall the hardships of the General Strike. Some people who were once active have grown disenchanted with politics, possibly on ideological or policy grounds.

In most constituencies, it is a job to get younger people interested in the party. They have never experienced the poverty that turned their parents to political action, and the weekly dance or the cinema are more appealing than ward meetings or an opportunity to deliver leaflets in council flats. Many of the youngsters who have developed an interest in Labour politics have been inclined to adopt rigid or extreme views on particular issues, creating problems for the party organizers who seek to restrain them. It is not unusual for conflicts of outlooks to erupt between the young people and the older members, who are sometimes reluctant to hand over responsibility to the young. When the 'generation gap' becomes serious in the party, the young people are tempted either to persist in their 'irresponsible' behavior, or, seeing little opportunity for advancement, to withdraw from the organization.

A few of the organizational difficulties that local parties sometimes encounter are related to the type of clientele that Labour recruits from the working-class areas. Many of the administrative assignments which have to be carried out, especially under the pressures of a campaign, require *continuity of performance* for maximum efficiency. The processing of postal votes, for example, is a fairly complex operation, and unless one person is able to supervise the entire project, the work may become fragmented and many of the cases may not be carried through to completion. The Conservative Party enjoys the services of more paid help than do either of the competing parties, and both the Conservatives and the Liberals — rooted solidly in the middle class — draw in volunteer workers who not only have had the advantage of more *formal* education and hence possess more clerical skills, but are also more flexible in their jobs and home schedules. The Labour volunteers, on the other hand, have often had to terminate their formal education prematurely at an earlier age and their level of administrative and clerical skills is somewhat lower, although they quickly develop such skills through political experience. Moreover, very few of the Labour workers can afford to take time off from their regular work (although some are willing to sacrifice their holiday leaves) to devote themselves to administrative supervision for long periods. For the most part, they have to engage in party activities during the evening, after completing their shift in the factory, or on weekends. The women who fold literature, address envelopes, and prepare canvassing cards cannot afford to employ someone to cook the meals and take care of the children, and so they must adjust their political schedules to the imperatives of home life. With so few helpers available on a full-time basis, the agent often falls heir to the task of seeing that the important jobs get done, but competing demands upon his time make it impossible for him to supervise every major task down to the last detail.

3. *Doctrinal disunity*. Like most left-wing movements, the Labour Party has to navigate periodically through storms of ideological controversy. Given its recruitment policy, its traditionally 'non-theoretical' approach to doctrine, and the existence of democratic machinery for the expression of dissenting views, a 'smooth passage' would be unreal.[26] More than the other parties, Labour tends to attract people who are politically conscious and concerned about issues, and the different shades of opinion cover a wide spectrum. Applying tests of 'orthodoxy' only to the revolutionary Marxists, it welcomes into its ranks individuals with uncomforming outlooks, as well those with more conventional views. The notion has long persisted that a 'ginger group' on the left is healthy for the organization, since it serves as a check upon the leadership, helping to keep the flame of principled socialism aglow. Elements of Labour's rank and file harbor a respect for the sincere rebel or the 'stormy petrel', and they do not hesitate to protect the dissenters (or even to elect them to Party offices), even though they may fervently disagree with their politics.[27] A tolerant party is a potentially fissiparous organization, and the Labour Party has periodically gone into convulsions over such moral crusades as 'pacificism', 'Maxtonism', 'Crippsism', and, more recently, 'Bevanism' and 'unilateralism'.

As an offshoot from a tolerant, pragmatic culture, the Labour Party never constructed a coherent and rigid theoretical framework, and its members tend to define socialism in terms of the particular policies or doctrinal tenets to which they have an emotional or intellectual attachment. Instead of hammering out a systematic philosophy, the Labour people sought agreement on a set of policies designed to attack the citadels of social injustice and to improve the condition of the disadvantaged — public ownership of the 'commanding heights of the economy' (largely through the nationalization of particular industries), full employment, and welfare services.

In the immediate post-war years, the Attlee Government managed to institute nearly all of the domestic reforms that Labour had espoused since 1918. And by 1955, with the major planks in its traditional platform already nailed down (and even accepted by the new Tory regime), many people began to ask serious questions: What is the *purpose* of the Labour Party? How can it retain its distinctive character as a protest movement? Some leaders — later called 'revisionists' — tried to develop a new philosophical structure capable of dealing with contemporary problems which Labour's traditional doctrine did not envisage and for which it supplied no obvious answers. These attempts at platform-building kindled disagreement among Party stalwarts over the meaning of socialism and the 'proper order of priorities'. Harold Wilson used an analogy to describe the turmoil:

> ... the Labour Party has something in common with an old stagecoach. I don't mean that it's out of date, but in this sense that if it's rattling along at a rare old speed most of the passengers are so exhilarated, perhaps one or two are so sea-sick, that they don't start arguing or quarrelling; but as soon as it stops they all get out and start arguing about which way we ought to go. The important thing is to keep it at an exhilarating speed.[28]

The issue came to a head in 1959, after Labour had lost its third general election in a row. In their diagnosis of the Party's ailments, some leaders argued that technological advance, full employment, and the welfare state had drastically changed the nature of British society, shrinking the size of the working class and producing an ethos of affluence which stimulated the desires of ordinary people for modern household appliances, television sets, and holidays on the continent.[29] They detected an erosion of Labour's traditional support, and they saw the need to recapture the loyalty of mobile groups and to appeal to the expanding middle class. To become attractive to voters who do not live on the poverty line and never experienced the dole, the Labour Party would have to change its depression mentality and rid itself of its 'cloth-cap' image. This, according to the revisionists, requires a critical examination of the Party's traditional assumptions and the development of an imaginative set of options to replace nationalization, which is not popular with the voters. 'Revisionism' in the British Labour Party has its analogue in other socialist parties on the continent.

To many Labour people on the left, the revisionist approach represents a betrayal of true socialist principles. According to Richard Crossman, '... politicians whose sole object, or even whose main object, is to regain office tend to be opportunists, to hedge and to equivocate in order to appease the voter ... But a Left-wing party which adopts such tactics destroys itself.'[30] In the eyes of those attached to traditional views, the Labour Party ought to be glaringly different from its competitors both in outlook and program. A distinctive organization cannot afford to mark time merely to consolidate its gains; it has to have well-defined goals; — it has to 'go somewhere'. Without a clear objective, the organization would lose much of its dynamism. The anti-revisionists echo the words of Aneurin Bevan: '... we should not forget that the main road to Socialist advance is open to us if we have the courage to tread it. But there is a great danger of being seduced down side roads or stopping to pick flowers on the way.'[31] In their outlook, delaying the journey to the New Jerusalem by watering down the program and pausing to consolidate gains is like stopping along the sidepaths to gather daisies. If the Party's chief purpose is merely to govern and to pick up the mistakes of the other side, the entire job should be turned over to the Conservatives who can do it better because they enjoy the confidence of the business community.

Rather than having the Labour Party transformed into a 'do-nothing' organization, many left-wing crusaders prefer a sojourn in the political wilderness until a majority of the electorate becomes wise enough to support a radical overhaul of the social order. The proponents of root-and-branch socialism would pay no attention to floating voters, the new mobiles into the middle class, or wavering Tories. Instead they would spend their time trying to convert the trade unionists and other working-class people who presently stay away from the polls or vote Conservative. They confidently predict that, with these proletarian groups on Labour's side, the Party could win every election without having to dilute its doctrine in an effort to convert people who are instinctively hostile to socialism.

Not unexpectedly, these ideological cross-currents in the national Party spill over into the constituency parties, which become lively forums when certain policy questions are injected. Such conflicts are difficult to analyze on a left-right continuum, for the composition of the contending factions varies according to the issue being considered. As was true at the national level, the group that opposed German rearmament was not identical with the faction that was labelled 'Bevanite', and the unilateral disarmers were not uniformly the same people who opposed entry into the Common Market. A local party usually has a sizeable 'in-between' group whose members are largely preoccupied with organizational matters but who are vulnerable to mobilization on particular issues (for example, public ownership). While the left-versus-the-right framework tends to oversimplify the situation, it is nevertheless the case that a constituency party has some non-militants or 'pragmatists' who tend to be more concerned with organizational effectiveness rather than the fine points of doctrine and are inclined to support the moderate policies of the national leadership. It is also true that nearly every party has a nucleus of militant members who look upon themselves as the guardians of the sacred tablets and try to keep the party in hot pursuit of 'true socialist objectives'. The ideological stance of this group is usually predictable; its members can move easily and quickly from 'Bevanism' to 'Victory for Socialism' to 'Unilateralism', pausing at each transitional stage only long enough to draw up emergency resolutions on foreign policy.

The ability of the ideological enthusiasts to exert influence in local Labour parties depends, of course, upon the local situation and the personalities and performance records of the militants. They are usually unable to capture control in a safe Labour constituency, where the tradition of loyalty to the Party's leadership tends to be strong. They are more successful in the parties that operate in marginal districts and especially in areas dominated by the Conservatives. It is also important to note that the members who are primarily concerned with organizational affairs take a dim view of 'ideological disrupters' unless they are willing to do their share of doorstep work; the militants who are willing to undertake the routine tasks are likely to wield more influence in a party than their associates who may be just as articulate but who are less industrious. But despite the work records of the ideological enthusiasts, frosty relationships tend to develop between them and the pragmatists.[32] The pragmatists naturally seek to solidify their strength by bringing into the party individuals who share their views. By the same token, the militants continually search for additional support, especially if their success is contingent upon dislodging their opponents from party offices. As the struggle begins to grow in intensity, the crusaders are inclined to move farther to the left. A move slightly to the right would obviously bring them closer to the people they are challenging, and a jump shift that puts them to the right of their opponents does not produce encouraging rewards in a movement whose ideological boundary stops, in reality, at the political center. Thus, the distribution of power within a constituency party often reinforces the doctrinal rigidity of the crusaders; and struggles for political influence become interlaced with ideological differences. Fortunately for the local organization, the factions that are involved in a doctrinal dispute are usually committed to the 'rules of the game', and an episode of verbal combat in a GMC meeting invariably ends before the pub closes. Moreover, the need for team solidarity at election time softens the ideological rivalries and helps to keep the party integrated. But when an issue is particularly divisive and the emotional temperature runs high, the job of holding the unit together is likely to tax the endowments of an organizing genius.

PROFILES OF CONSTITUENCY PARTY TYPES

In evaluating three very different local Labour parties, we may derive benefit from the construction of three 'profiles' – abstract pictures of what a party in a safe Labour area, a party in a marginal constituency, and a party in a solid Conservative district look like.[33] Such abstractions, of course, are not 'real'; they do not refer to any particular organization in any particular locality. They are merely 'image' devices to facilitate comparisons with real parties in live settings. As indicated earlier, we are concerned only with parties operating in urban environments.

In painting these pictures, we shall be looking at three elements: (1) the size of the Labour majorities in the three types of constituencies; (2) the socio-economic milieu of the districts; and (3) the nature of the party – in terms of organization, leadership, and special problems – in each of the settings. Given the nature of this study, the latter point is of greatest concern to us.

Size of the Labour Majority

The experts – both party organizers and academicians – classify constituencies along one basic dimension: the size of the majority of a given party. In Labour's catalogue, a 'safe' district is where the level of Conservative opposition is so low that the Labour Party is assured of such a wide margin of victory that the outcome is never in doubt. As one veteran described the situation, 'In these areas, we wouldn't need to bother counting the ballots; we could just weigh them!' A 'marginal' district, on the other hand, is marked by vigorous inter-party competition, and both sides have a chance to win. The Party's managers in Transport House often use a 5000-vote majority as a rule of thumb, since the incumbent party could be dislodged by a shift of about 2500 votes. As the opposite end of the continuum, a 'hopeless' constituency is one in which the Tories are able to smother their Labour opposition by huge majorities.

Obviously, the Party's strength in a particular locality may undergo change over a span of time. As we have already suggested, movements of population as a result of slum clearance, the building of freeways, and the development of public (or 'council') housing can modify the complexion of the electorate. Moreover, the boundaries of a constituency can be shifted through 'redistribution' (reapportionment), which is carried out more regularly and more systematically in Britain than in the United States. Then, too, traditional party voting patterns may be affected by sudden shifts in the attitudes of voters over issues or programs that arouse strong feelings. In the case of Labour voters, however, disaffection is more likely to be translated into abstentions rather than votes for the opposition. These demographic, geographic, and attitudinal changes can transform a safe Labour district into a marginal one or even into a hopeless one. By the same token, a marginal seat can be rendered safe or a hopeless seat modified so that Labour has a sporting chance.

Socio-Economic Milieu

The size of a Labour majority in a constituency is merely a reflection of the socio-economic character of the area. What, then, is the nature of a safe, a marginal, and a hopeless constituency in terms of its economic features and its social base?

A safe Labour district in an urban center is usually marked by the following characteristics:

1. Industrial sites dot the landscape, providing many of the natives with employment near their homes. Conspicuous in the area are large or medium-size factories, workshops, and warehouses in which trade union organization is strong. This means that the local party stands a good chance of linking itself with local union branches, and it will probably have a good number of affiliated members.

2. The population is made up largely of manual workers and other people who are not far removed from the working class on the occupational scale (clerical workers, shopkeepers, and the like). A relatively small proportion of the inhabitants will have had the advantage of formal education beyond the elementary level. The low incidence of social mobility is matched by the low degree of geographic mobility; a large segment of the residents will have either been born in the district or lived there most of their adult lives. The population, in other words, is relatively homogeneous in terms of social class, and the socializing influences — working-class origin, elementary education, and length of residence in the area — often tend toward a uniformity of outlook on certain social and political issues and a suspicion of 'outsiders'.

3. The relatively undiversified nature of the population is accompanied by a similarity of living standards. No sharp differences in wealth mark or divide the community. 'Posh' residential districts rarely exist. The people live either in private rental property of ancient vintage, or, if they are fortunate, in new council housing.

A marginal constituency features a different socio-economic profile which, as one would expect, combines elements of the safe and the hopeless.

1. Although some local industry exists, large factories and workshops are few in number, and the party's link with trade union branches is weaker than it is in the safe districts. Some of the inhabitants are employed locally, but the constituency tends to be a dormitory area, with people leaving home each day to work in other sections of the metropolis.

2. The population is a mixture of social classes. To be sure, the component of manual workers is still strong, and the number of clerical workers in the 'lower middle class' is larger than in the safe district. But the party also draws in from the more opulent neighborhoods a scattering of people in intermediate supervisory and managerial jobs and a few from the professions. This means that a conspicuous segment of the population will have had post-elementary education, particularly at the secondary or training-school levels. Compared with the safe constituency, the incidence of geographic mobility is higher, and a larger proportion of the inhabitants will be newcomers to the area, having moved in from the higher-rent districts. The people residing in a marginal constituency lack the homogeneity of social class that is typical of a safe Labour area, and the differing levels of education and social and geographic mobility promote a wide variety of experience which often contributes to differing outlooks on certain social and political issues.

3. An area that supports a heterogeneous population embraces a variety of living standards, with differences in incomes and life styles being readily noticeable. Most of the poorer people live in privately rented accommodations – often Victorian mansions converted into small flats or 'bed-sitter' units – but some have council housing. A few sections of the constituency, however, are exclusive residential areas with owner-occupied dwellings and expensive apartments.

A hopeless Labour constituency stands in marked contrast with the other two types.

1. No significant local industry exists, and trade union membership is nominal at best. The area is almost entirely residential, and the bulk of the inhabitants travel to other districts for daily employment.

2. While the population is mixed, the tilt is heavily in the direction of the non-manuals – the regular clericals and shopkeepers, but, even more, those who are employed in professional, managerial, and intermediate supervisory jobs. This means that the incidence of post-elementary education is high – a vehicle in part for significant social mobility. The population, however, tends to be unstable, with some people moving in and others moving out to the suburbs where they can own their own homes or to other districts where rents are lower. While such an area has a heavy concentration of middle-class people, it cannot usually be classified as 'homogeneous'. The instability of the population,

the lack of communication between social statuses, and the fact that people spend their daytime hours away from their residential neighborhoods are not conducive to the development of a 'local community spirit' or strong local institutions.

3. Although the middle class predominates, a diversity of living standards is clearly evident. Many people command very high salaries, but a significant number of the lower-grade clericals experience difficulty in balancing their budgets. Council housing is minimal, if it exists at all. Most of the people live in expensive rented apartments or in costly homes of their own. The impecunious segments of the population live in cheaper, converted flats or in bed-sitters.

The Nature of the Party

The fact that each of these types of constituencies contains a different social base and exhibits different patterns of voting behavior obviously influences the character of the Labour party that is called upon to operate in the particular setting.

1. *The Party in an Urban Safe District.* (*a*) Even though the party has a near monopoly on the electoral market, its leaders are still concerned about the primary goal, the winning of elections. They are usually interested in securing as heavy a turnout of voters as possible in order to pile up a 'healthy' majority, if for no other reason than to make the 'mandate' look respectable in their territory. Sometimes the size of his margin of victory is a prestige symbol for the incumbent Member of Parliament. This fixation on gathering a large surplus of votes is fairly widespread in Labour strongholds, and Schattschneider's admonition that 'knockout victories' are unnecessary and wasteful would be especially applicable to the British system.[34] Excessive preoccupation with the local scene sometimes leads to tensions between the constituency party and the regional organizer over the question of how many campaign workers should be transferred to marginal districts in order to improve the chances of the Labour Party nationally.[35]

(*b*) The party in a safe Labour district frequently selects a local person as its candidate for the parliamentary seat — often someone from the candidate list of the trade unions. This may stem from a desire to have an M.P. who is 'one of them' — who understands their problems and will be readily accessible. It may also stem from a desire to reward a local stalwart for conspicuous service to the party and the borough council. Local M.P.s of this type are often 'good constituency men', but not many of them rise to national prominence in the House of Commons.

(*c*) Another primary objective of the local party is to manage the affairs of the borough, since it commands a majority of seats on the council. Particularly in areas where the Conservative opposition has lost its vigor, it is not unusual for friction to develop between the party organization and the Labour Group on the council. The party activists feel that the Labour Group owes its existence to them, and they insist upon being kept informed about and being able to discuss policy questions which affect the borough. The members of the Labour Group, on the other hand, resist what they regard as an infringement upon their legislative prerogatives. This tension may be exacerbated when some borough councillors become so absorbed in their council work that they cannot find the time for ordinary party tasks. The alleviation of these difficulties requires an adequate communication mechanism between the party's GMC and the council's Labour Group. For a local party to remain immune from attack by a revitalized opposition, it has to devote itself to the task of detecting and attacking local problems. In recent years local parties in Labour strongholds have temporarily lost control of their councils because they had grown insensitive to the concerns of their electorates.

(d) The activists in a non-competitive Labour constituency usually focus their attention upon local rather than national issues. The party does not regularly submit resolutions to the Party Conference, but when it does, the statements will probably deal with 'bread-and-butter' issues or an aspect of local government. A branch of the Young Socialists usually does not thrive in such a 'non-ideological' environment, and hence it does not become a strong vehicle for party work. Though the local activists discuss problems of foreign policy, they tend to respond to the cues of the national leadership on such questions. They are likely to become most aroused when a national figure from the 'intellectual' wing of the movement attacks one of Labour's 'sacred cows', such as public ownership. The social homogeneity of the area is conducive to a wide measure of agreement on issues involving traditional socialist doctrine.

(e) Given the emphasis on local issues, the factions that emerge within the party are less likely to be rooted in ideological differences than in personality conflicts and divisions among cliques. In working-class constituencies of this sort, strong leaders have ample opportunity to cultivate bases of personal support, which may be grounded in family ties or in an aggregation of factional alliances. In the absence of viable competition from the Tories, the party can enjoy the luxury of these surrogate oppositions within its structure.

(f) In nearly all of the safe Labour districts, apathy is the real enemy. This apathy is to be found not only among the voters but also among the party members. It is a challenge for people to remain active in the GMC or in the wards on a sustained basis when they already know the outcome of the next race. Without the threat of Tory opposition, only the most dedicated to the cause or those who desire to advance in politics manage to keep their enthusiasm alive. More often than not, party meetings are poorly attended, candidacies for party posts and council seats are difficult to fill, membership drives become infrequent, and ward organizations wither on the vine. Some parties that enjoy majorities of over 20,000 enroll fewer than 1000 individual members in their organizations, a tiny fragment of the support they win at the polls.[36] A deficient intake of new members is a sure indication that the local party has begun to age.

(g) Even the attempts of leaders to focus upon operational objectives, such as the sponsorship of social activities designed to keep present members interested and to bring new members in, run into difficulty in heavy Labour districts. For example, the homogeneity of the population and the lack of geographic mobility help to foster a local 'community' with highly developed social institutions. This means that the people are able to interact in other settings without having to become involved in the party's network. A person does not have to meet his friends at party headquarters and spend a dreary evening stuffing envelopes; he can see them at bingo games or in the working men's club and have more fun. Another difficulty stems from the fact that the trade union branches in the area drain off important talent and compete with the party for the member's leisure time. A potential party worker may be more interested in the bread-and-butter struggles of his union at the industrial level, where unpredictable results still generate excitement.

(h) The nagging problems of apathy, sluggish recruitment, factionalism based upon personal allegiances, and an aging membership take their toll when it comes to filling the many posts that are needed in the party, on the council, and in the borough. Complaints are frequently heard about the poor quality of some borough council candidates, and sometimes the recruitment of ward officers and minor officials at the constituency level is difficult. As older people become ensconsed in certain posts for long periods of time and jobs are passed around among a few stalwarts, the organization begins to take on an undesirable appearance. The image of an aging structure is unattractive to most young people, and there is little infusion of young blood. Faltering recruitment of younger members may also be a function of the low turnover of officer personnel which dims the prospect of easy mobility within the organization. The charge is sometimes made that the party's veterans who have grown comfortable in their positions are not cordial to newcomers who might rock the boat or become political competitors. The oldtimers who have settled into their roles develop operating procedures that achieve sanctity through time, and they may resist changes that are needed if the party is to survive.

(i) The party activists in a safe Labour district aspire predominantly to local positions – in the party, on the borough council, or as mayor of the borough. Very few are interested in becoming Members of Parliament. This is another way of saying that political aspirations are greatly influenced by social class. Manual workers and people in the lower clerical grades tend not to set their sights beyond the boundaries of the local community. The few who aspire to parliamentary careers tend to be trade union activists who hope to realize their objective through sponsorship by their unions.

2. *The Party in an Urban Marginal District.* (*a*) In an area where the political barometer is unsteady, the local party has an opposition to subdue, and the winning of elections is clearly the primary objective. Labour activists work hard for a majority, not so much for the prestige it brings, but because it is a matter of victory or defeat. The question of transferring local workers to adjacent districts at election time does not arise; instead, the problem is one of absorbing and of utilizing effectively the workers who are sent in from other constituencies where the Tory challenge is not threatening.
(*b*) The local party in a marginal constituency is more likely to select a person from the outside as its parliamentary candidate.
(*c*) The party in a marginal area is faced with the problem of governing the borough at least part of the time. This means that it, too, can be vulnerable to controversy with the Labour Group on the council and is in need of a liaison mechanism to ease the strain. Both the party activists and the members of the Labour Group, however, are likely to be aware of the fact that the costs of allowing dissension to come into public view are higher than they are in a safe district. In the first place, a strong Conservative opposition will be watching – eager to take advantage of disarray in the Labour camp. In the second place, how the party handles itself in dealing with council matters is perceived by some to have an influence on how the voters will behave in borough council and parliamentary elections.
(*d*) Although the activists must necessarily be concerned about local issues, they also exhibit considerable interest in wider political questions. A party in a marginal district draws upon a variegated population, and people with different backgrounds tend to nurture differing outlooks. The organization is made up of a good many working-class people who have been in the organization for a long time, and they may be impatient with newcomers and younger people; many of them have a keener interest in matters that directly affect their standard of living than in the 'far away' questions of colonialism and foreign policy. The party also recruits from segments of the middle class, and many of these people would rather spend their time debating issues than in discussing the humdrum tasks of administration. An organization in this setting usually manages to attract a group of zealots who are intent upon weighing every issue for its doctrinal purity. Activists of this type may be middle-class intellectuals who have had a comfortable upbringing but who have been forced into an idealistic position by an unyielding social conscience. They may be recent recruits into the middle class who have managed to ascend several steps of the social ladder but who have not

yet made it to the top and cannot forget the hardships of the climb. They may also be long-time socialists of working-class origin and status who believe that, despite the post-war gains, the class struggle still continues, though perhaps in disguised form.

(e) Owing to the party's heterogeneous composition, the internal divisions within the organization are more complex than those that arise in a safe district. The struggles are likely to be grounded on several important factors: personal allegiances; ideological differences; tensions between the oldtimers and the newcomers; and strains between the generations. Obviously, in some internal outbursts the factors become interlaced. Adding to these sources of disunity is the fact that competition usually arises for the posts that have to be filled. Not all of the aspirants can be elected to party office or serve on the GMC. Not all of the candidates for the borough council can stand in 'safe' wards; in contrast with a strong Labour area, some will have to take their chances in marginal or even less hopeful wards.

(f) Although the ingredients for internal disputes over policy questions are more abundant than in a safe district, observers and analysts often take the view that a Labour party in marginal territory will be more moderate than extreme in its doctrinal stance. The logic behind this position flows from two points: (1) Since electoral victory is possible, the militant elements have an opportunity to work off their frustrations in winnable campaigns, which require a measure of party unity and serve to integrate the organization. Then, when the more zealous types get elected to the borough council, they become deeply absorbed in the responsibilities of local government, putting aside or tempering their original ideological views. (2) An extremist party in a margnal district will offend some of the voters it has to win over if its campaigns is to be successful. This latter point is congenial with the proposition advanced by Anthony Downs: when two parties are well balanced, a movement of one of them away from the center in the distribution of attitudes means a gain in support for the other.[37]

(g) While apathy is always a problem for organizations, the malady is not so widespread in a marginal constituency. For those who are serious about politics, the pressure of the Tory opposition and the opportunities to gain political advancement operate to keep them reasonably active. A healthy organization, of course, has to give some attention to the social needs of its members. Here the party in a marginal constituency has some advantage over its counterpart in a safe district. The constituency is usually not such a tightly knit community, and the party does not have as many competitors for the time of the volunteers. Indeed, a party that operates in a district with a shifting population is in a position to attract new arrivals who may be interested in making social contacts.

(h) It takes little insight to observe that recruitment is less of a problem for an organization in politically marginal terrain. This is where the political excitement is, and party workers can quickly see the results of their efforts. Tory competition dictates a more complex party structure; with more tasks to be done, there are more posts to be filled. Moreover, to the extent that offices are competitive, the people who work the hardest may get the most rapid preferment. Mobility within the organization is also enhanced by the fact that, with some shifts in the population, replacements often have to be found for the party workers who move away.

(*i*) Political aspirations of Labour activists in a marginal domain are more of a 'mixed bag' than is the case in a safe, working-class district. Many of the workers, especially those in manual and conventional clerical occupations, opt for local positions. But since the party recruits its activists from a wider class spectrum, a higher proportion of them aspire to become M.P.s.

3. *The Party in an Urban Hopeless District*. (*a*) A local party that is destined to operate in a hostile environment has to be content with limited objectives. All that it can really hope to do is to 'show the flag' in its home territory and use its scanty resources to help the movement as a whole. This means that if the organization is active at all, it may try to spark a little interest by sponsoring open-air meetings in the marketplace or public meetings in the local library. At election time it will pull together a slate of nominal candidates for the borough council, mostly to tie the Conservatives down and force them to spend more money than would be case if no one filed against them. But the attention of most of the activists is directed toward helping the Labour cause in the marginals and in getting some political experience for themselves.

(*b*) Since there is no hope of winning the parliamentary seat, the local party is not overwhelmed with potential candidates. Trade unions are not inclined to pour their funds into hopeless territory, and the candidate usually has to be drawn from the 'B List', i.e., the non-trade union panel. The party may decide to select a local member who aspires to enter parliament and thus give him some campaign experience. But whether the candidate is a resident of the area or from another district, he has an incentive to run a respectable race; he will then be in a better position to be adopted for a later encounter in a constituency where the prospects are more favorable.

(*c*) The Labour party in a solid Tory environment is never faced with the problem of running the borough. If it has even a trickle of members on the council, however, it may need a liaison structure to link the party (or parties, if the borough embraces more than one constituency) with the Labour Group.

(*d*) The party's lack of influence in the borough council means that local issues command little more than peripheral interest among the activists. They place much greater emphasis upon the discussion of questions of national importance. This is understandable, given the social base of the district from which the local Labour party draws its members. Very few of the activists are the 'oppressed sons of toil', for working-class folk cannot afford to live in this high-rent area, and those who do reside there are not active in the Labour camp. The people who spend time in Labour's behalf are preponderantly from the middle class – those in professional, managerial, or intermediate clerical employment. Since the party rarely, if ever, schedules regular membership drives, the recruitment process tends to be highly selective: individual members encourage their friends to join.

(*e*) To be vigorous supporters of socialism in a 'blue-ribbon' residential area, where the overwhelming majority of the residents subscribe to conservative values and norms, requires a high measure of idealistic dedication and willingness to openly reject conformity and complacency. People who enlist for hopeless combat in a hostile arena do so because they are firmly committed to the movement and its doctrinal objectives, or because they believe that the experience will be personally beneficial. The social science literature indicates that middle-class activists who join 'left-of-center' movements are inclined to take a 'leftist' position on social and political issues. A local party that has to wrestle with long-term adversity usually enrolls a corps of articulate enthusiasts. As one observer puts it, they are 'deviants both within their social class and politically within the Labour Party'.[38] Some of these people are of middle-class lineage, but others have risen from working-class backgrounds and still protest against a system which, they feel, treated them shabbily during their formative years and continues to practice injustice upon the less fortunate. To these socially conscious people, the Labour program should read: 'full speed ahead to the new social order.' It is not coincidental that they want a full airing of ideological issues and foreign policy questions at their party meetings. Whereas party workers in safe and marginal districts have to be responsible for local government and can take out their muster on problems of immediate concern to them, the activists in a hopeless constituency stand little chance of being elected to the council or of participating in borough affairs in any meaningful way. Denied a normal political outlet for their frustrations and not having to be responsible for anything, they can afford to be flamboyant in their political utterances – behavior that sometimes brings them the publicity and visibility they seek. Some of the enthusiasts live in a state of chronic discontent, seizing every opportunity to raise awkward questions and to send forward critical resolutions, nearly all of which focus upon a speedier march to socialism or the remaking of the international order. In a sense, the passing of resolutions is the only channel they have to make their political views known.

(*f*) The factions that emerge in the local party tend to derive from clashing ideological positions. While personality conflicts are sometimes visible and occasionally become linked with issue orientations, the

controversies get played out in ideological terms. The selective recruitment process intensifies the struggles, as members of opposing factions seek to bring in their friends so as to increase their voting strength.
(g) As in the safe Labour districts, apathy among the voters and among potential workers is a disheartening problem for those who try to keep the organization alive. An alert party in 'blue-ribbon' territory has an opportunity to spark some life into its structure by organizing a program of social activities. After all, the local institutions are probably not well developed owing to the geographic space between home and work and the rapid shifts in population, which bring to the district a steady stream of newcomers, especially young people, who are looking for social ties. But the social conditions that provide the opportunity also have an adverse impact upon the party itself. The constant movement of people makes the composition of the organization unstable, affecting the continuity of leadership and the expansion of its resources. Under these circumstances, the local party is usually too weak to undertake attractive programs on a large scale and has to settle for smaller campaigns and social events on an infrequent basis.
(h) Two lines of development are open to a local Labour party in a hopeless constituency. One model is the *missionary organization*, which seeks to reach out and to link itself with the society at large. It carries on educational and propaganda campaigns and engages in proselytizing activities, attempting to win over 'souls' for the sake of the movement as a whole. To be effective at all, the 'missionaries' have to make their message relevant, and this often means that extremist views have to be modified and rigid positions tempered. The other model is the *political sect* which largely severs its connections with the world outside, being content to remain an exclusive group devoted almost entirely to the discussion of ideological matters, sometimes in esoteric form. The members of the sect make little attempt to expand its enrollment; the recruitment effort that does take place is highly personalized and contributes to the intellectual inbreeding. Reflections of both of these models are to be found among local Labour parties in Tory areas.
(i) One of the interesting things about such a party is that its political complexion can change within a short period of time because of population instability. An organization that has been under the control of 'militants' can quickly fall into more 'moderate' hands when the leadership corps is dispersed by changes in residence. New people, especially in the lower age brackets and with varying levels of political sophistication, are continually moving into the district — and some of them enter the political arena with starry-eyed enthusiasm and fresh ideas. Since the party has little 'organization memory' capable of retrieving constraining precedents, it is possible for the recently recruited activists to do some innovating — inside or outside the framework of Labour Party rules.

(j) The people who are involved in party work in hostile territory do not cast aside their political aspirations. A few of the newer, less seasoned recruits aim for seats on a local council so that they can gain some experience before going on further. Most of the middle-class activists, however, eagerly look forward to parliamentary careers in Westminster.

The reader may benefit from a summary of these constituency party profiles which appears in Table 1.1.

Table 1.1 Summary of party profiles

Dimensions of comparison	Safe area	Marginal area	Hostile area
Goals	Win elections in home territory and assist in marginal constituencies	Win elections in home territory	Assist in marginal constituencies
Manage the borough	All the time	Some of the time	Never
Issues commanding attention	Primarily local	Local and non-local	Non-local
Ideological posture	Wide agreement on 'traditional socialist' creed	Moderate	Often extremist
Bases of internal disagreements	Non-ideological	Ideological and non-ideological	Primarily ideological
Stability of membership and leadership	Highly stable	Less stable	Highly unstable
Political aspirations	Local	Local and parliamentary	Parliamentary

Hopefully, this discussion will have been useful, especially for the American audience, in describing the nature of a constituency Labour party — its structure, how it operates, and the problems it has to contend with. The information will be helpful in putting into perspective the study of the three local parties with which we are concerned. But before we turn to them, we need to examine briefly the larger framework of the Labour Party into which the local associations fit.

2 Labour Party Organization: a View from the Lower Tier

As we have seen, a local Labour party is the basic unit in a federated structure, which is organized nationally and which shapes and executes policy for the movement as a whole. As part of this larger framework, the constituency associations are naturally drawn into relationships with Labour Party organs that are higher in the organizational scheme and have responsibility for coordinating political activities over wider areas. The nature of these relationships depends to a considerable extent upon the type of constituency party (whether it operates in safe, marginal, or hostile territory and whether it is in a 'healthy' condition), and upon the organizational proximity of the Party organ to the local unit. Moreover, in some Party bodies rather than others, the constituency organizations have a more suitable forum for the articulation of their divergent views; this is true, for example, in the annual Party Conference.

METROPOLITAN UNITS

Until the recent reorganization of local government in Britain, a borough Labour party existed in nearly all of the major industrial centers. This unit was composed of all of the constituency parties within the borough, as well as the trade unions, the trades councils, and similar groups that were affiliated with the Labour Party at the city level. The borough party was organized along the same lines as a constituency association; the various federative components were represented on its management committee, which elected its own officers and an executive body. The original purpose of the organization on a borough-wide basis was to coordinate the activities of the constituency parties during elections for the local council and to handle policymaking and administrative work connected with borough council affairs.

Although in a few cities the borough party managed to keep the constituency party organizations fairly active, the forces for centralization were very strong and the locus of power shifted in varying degrees to the higher unit. The Labour activists became involved with the day-to-day problems of the borough, and their interest naturally centered around the party organization at that level, causing them to neglect party organization at the constituency and ward tiers. Located in positions of responsibility in the borough rather than in the constituency, local party leaders tended to promote an ideology of centralization. This was buttressed by financial power, since the borough party usually collected the affiliation fees of the unions – and in some instances the membership dues from the wards – reallocating some of the funds to the constituency parties but retaining the lion's share for the central treasury. Under these circumstances, the local parties within the borough often found it difficult to retain their experienced agents, and these units soon lost their vitality. This meant that they had to be rebuilt when a parliamentary election was in the offing, and usually there was not enough time to get the job done. As early as 1955, the Wilson Report on Party organization concluded that the dominant pattern of over-centralization was 'inimical to good constituency organization' – that the existence of top-heavy borough parties had led 'to a progressive withering away' of the constituency parties which seriously impaired Labour's 'efficiency as a machine for fighting parliamentary elections'.[1]

The situation was quite different in the London area, which embraced a number of separate metropolitan boroughs and forty-two parliamentary constituencies. Here the borough parties never developed strong roots. When a borough was divided into two parliamentary constituencies, each local party sent representatives to a coordinating or liaison committee which considered problems of mutual concern. When a municipal election was approaching, the General Management Committees of the two constituency parties might meet together (technically as a borough party), but once the election was over, the borough party structure disappeared except for the smaller liaison committee. The experience of the local parties in London had an important influence upon Labour Party leaders in 1974, when they reorganized the units of the party to fit the new pattern of local government.

The Labour leaders who studied the problem of local government reorganization sought to thwart the development of strong borough parties,[2] and the new organizational arrangement they adopted allows considerable flexibility, especially in the bases of representation for the affiliated units. In boroughs whose boundaries cut across two or more parliamentary constituencies, there is established a district party, which is one tier higher than a constituency unit. More than 400 of these organizations have been created, and they replace the 60 or 70 borough parties.

The purpose of the district Labour party is to deal with local government matters on a city-wide basis.[3] It coordinates election activities, formulates the election program, compiles a panel of borough council candidates, convenes the candidate-section meetings of the wards, endorses the candidates, and sends a specified number of delegates to meetings of the Labour Group in a consultative capacity. The district party may also coordinate other activities of the constituency parties within the area, such as the collection of affiliation fees for all of the units and the assignment of delegates from affiliated organizations to particular constituency parties. The district party has the same type of agencies and officer posts as a constituency unit, and its components send delegates to the management committee. The basis of representation, however, is left to the decision of the Labour people involved in the district organization, subject to the approval of the National Executive Committee. Liaison between the district party on the one hand and the Labour members of the district council and the constituency parties on the other is achieved by having the leader and secretary of the Labour Group serve as *ex officio* members with voting rights, and by having the full-time party agents in the district serve in the same capacity without the right to vote.

In London, the stand-in for the district party is the borough local government committee, which usually meets once every three months and confines its work to matters involving local government. It endorses the panel of borough council candidates and coordinates election activities. In the interval between elections, it formulates policies on local government affairs, which the Labour Group on the borough council is expected to implement. In line with these responsibilities, the committee serves as a forum for discussing reports by the chairmen of the various committees on the borough council. The local government committee is made up of representatives from the local constituency parties within the borough, usually a fixed proportion from the respective General Management Committees.

One of the basic features of local government reform in urban Britain was the establishment of metropolitan counties which include the boroughs that are components of a larger metropolitan area. Here again the Labour Party organizers were faced with a difficulty, for a county covers some parliamentary constituencies entirely and only parts of others.

To handle the problem of coordinating policy-formulation and election activities at this level, the Labour people have established the county party, which is organized along the lines of the coordinating committees that had been temporarily set up to handle matters at the county level.[4] The Management Committee of the county party is composed entirely of delegates from the GMCs of the constituency parties within the territory. The affiliated organizations secure representation through their GMC delegates who are chosen by and from among their sectional colleagues on the GMC. As in the case of the district parties, the leader and secretary of the Labour Group and the full-time party agents are *ex officio* members of the governing body (the latter without voting rights), and each constituency organization sends representatives to the Labour Group meetings for consultative purposes. The Labour Group on the county council appoints one of its members to attend the meetings of the county party in order to report on the work of the Labour councillors.

As can be seen from this discussion, the district and county parties are designed to coordinate the political activities of the various constituency parties within municipal areas. The aim is to avoid some of the problems occasioned by the old borough parties—to handle local affairs efficiently and effectively without cutting into the authority and power of the constituency units. The new organizational scheme has not been in operation long enough to exhibit particular problems. If problems emerge, however, they are likely to be clustered around two centers of conflict: (1) complaints by local activists that the various party committees endorsed certain candidates for the several councils who should not have been endorsed, or withheld endorsement from some who should have been approved; and (2) complaints by Labour stalwarts that Labour members on the respective councils are not carrying out their mandate to *implement* policies that have been *formulated* by the party organizations – the same type of complaint that flows from the relationship between the national Party Conference and the Parliamentary Labour Party.[5] Furthermore, the centralizing tendencies in the old borough parties may begin to afflict the new organizational framework unless more of the constituency parties are able to secure the services of full-time agents.

REGIONAL ORGANIZATION

While the district and country organizations we have just discussed primarily involve horizontal linkages among local constituency units, the Labour Party has established at the regional level a layer of administrative organization consisting of eleven units throughout the country. The main purpose of this structure is to provide a measure of vertical integration between the local parties and Labour's central headquarters in Transport House. It is largely through the mediating mechanism installed at the regional level that the Labour Party achieves a more centralized form than is true of American parties.

From the viewpoint of the constituencies, the regional organization can best be discussed under two headings: (1) the regional council, and (2) the regional administrative staff. The regional council, which meets annually, is composed of representatives from the local parties, the district and county parties, district councils of trade unions, separate unions that operate entirely within the region, and similar political groups. To be able to send delegates, all of these units, including the local parties, have to be affiliated with the council, and the number of delegate positions depends upon the size of the unit's membership. The total number of representatives varies from 250 to slightly more than 400, although in the case of London the figure jumps to more than 700. The regional council tends to be dominated by older Party members who have a keen interest in issues of local government, and some of the officers have served for long periods of time.

Each affiliated organization is entitled to submit a policy resolution to the annual meeting of the regional council, and these constitute a basis of discussion and debate. Although some council meetings may be influential on isolated issues, they are restricted in their policymaking function by a rule that they must confine the discussion to regional and local matters and avoid national or international questions. Indeed, they are not officially regarded as policymaking bodies.[6] Hence, in the plenary sessions, the delegates concern themselves with such issues as housing, welfare services, transportation, industrial relations, party organization, and related topics in so far as these matters are problems in the region.[7] Often the discussion is non-controversial and hence not very stimulating. The resolutions, however, do serve as an expression of local attitudes, and they may be transmitted to the appropriate minister, to the Parliamentary Labour Party, or to the National Executive Committee.

The delegates, of course, derive certain side-benefits from attending a regional council. A member of a local party may gain some personal recognition by presenting a resolution with vigor and wit. Opportunities are opened up for contacts among activists from various local parties, who compare experiences in informal conversation. The delegates are expected to pick up information, to assess trends, and to report back to their own organizations. Party members sometimes grow restive under the restrictions placed upon subject-matter to be debated, and they may seek to introduce a national issue under the guise of a local resolution. This happened, for example, at the 1962 conference of the London Labour Party, when a number of delegates sought to make a case for unilateral disarmament while debating resolutions on civil defense.[8] Despite requests for a wider discussion agenda, the national Party organization has resisted pressure to enlarge the policymaking role of the councils.

Responsibility for carrying on certain activities between council sessions falls upon the executive committee, which meets bi-monthly and on which each category of affiliated units has a proportioned assignment of seats. The members of the executive elect their own chairman, a vice-chairman, and a treasurer, but the secretary is the regional organizer who is responsible, not to the council, but to the National Agent's office in Transport House.

The administrative component of the regional organization is under the direction of the regional organizer. He is usually assisted by a women's officer, a youth organizer, and one or two other staff people. These professional organizers, working in behalf of their immediate superiors in Transport House and the National Executive Committee, engage in two types of activity: strengthening the organization of the constituency, district, and county parties; and coordinating the political work of the federated groups within the region.

When rank-and-file GMC members are asked to describe the connection or relationship between the regional organizer and their local party, most of them respond, 'Remote'. It is true that in many constitutencies the activists would see him only under special circumstances: he might conduct hearings on disciplinary matters, at the request of the NEC; he might investigate procedural irregularities; in the case of a parliamentary by-election, he will move into the constituency to supervise the campaign, normally serving as the candidate's agent; he will be present when the GMC selects its agent, making sure that the necessary financial arrangements are in order; and he is required to attend the meeting when the local party selects its parliamentary candidate, not to influence the choice, but to insure that the proper procedures are followed. Obviously, a strong constituency party does not need much assistance from the regional office, but the organizer is likely to be drawn into the affairs of a local party in a key area when it is poorly organized or is without the services of a regular agent.

The regional organizer and his staff will be active in a constituency during an election campaign, especially if the area is marginal politically or if the local party is in bad organizational shape. In such instances, the point of contact is the agent or other major officers, but the regional people will be much less visible to other activists. When the contest for a parliamentary seat threatens to be close, the organizer keeps in touch with the agent, checking the canvass returns from time to time, requesting information about voter reactions on the doorsteps, and offering advice on problems when they arise. It is the regional organizer who is likely to arrange for a well-known political figure to speak in the constituency, and it is he who plans the transfer of workers from safe districts to marginal areas.

The regional organizer and his staff also perform general services for the local parties within their domain, promoting activities that the units find difficult or impossible to carry out on their own. Since the contact is made through the agents, most of the GMC members may be unaware of these services or just take them for granted. In seeking to help the constituency parties, the regional officers sponsor a variety of training programs, in day or weekend schools or through correspondence, for the training of part-time agents, youth officers, candidates for local councils, and key election workers. Special attention has been given recently to the scheduling of special conferences for local parties that do not have full-time agents. The regional office also arranges seminars on policy questions for interested party activists, wcmen's sections, the Young Socialists, and similar groups. It also organizes membership drives, mass rallies and demonstrations, and caravan propaganda tours.

In their liaison and coordinating work with the elements of the federative structure, the regional officers try to foster united action on common problems, especially when groups with overlapping responsibilities have settled upon divergent policies. In a divided borough, for example, it is important for the Labour-dominated council to settle upon a single policy with respect to rents for publicly-owned housing. But the local parties within the borough may favor conflicting rent schemes – a confusing situation that can generate trouble during an election campaign. The regional staff also stimulate contact and consultation between local party officials, trade union leaders, and functionaries in the Co-operative Party.

The regional organizer enjoys little formal authority over the local parties, and how effective he will be in dealing with them depends upon the rapport he is able to establish with the agents and the executive officers. If he enjoys cordial relations with them, he may occasionally be able to make suggestions about the composition of the 'short list' at candidate-selection conferences, and to offer ideas on how to improve the organization and resolve other problems. The regional organizer, however, has more direct influence over the few constituency parties that have recently joined the partial National Agency Service.[9] Since Transport House pays a large portion of the agents' salaries in these areas, regional officials are in a position to require a schedule of results. The regional office issues detailed instructions to the agents, who are expected to turn in quarterly reports. But whether the local parties are directly tied to the central headquarters through the new agency scheme, or whether the linkage is more informal and personal – as is true in the majority of cases – the officials in Transport House regard the regional staff as an important mechanism for carrying out organizational and administrative tasks, which are involved in integrating the constituency parties with the national Party structure.

CENTRAL ADMINISTRATION: NATIONAL EXECUTIVE COMMITTEE AND TRANSPORT HOUSE

The work of the regional organizers is delegated to them by officials in the Organization Department of Transport House (the national Party headquarters, or Head Office), which operates under the authority of the National Executive Committee. The NEC is the instrument of the Party Conference, and the officials in Transport House are the servants of the NEC. The organizational flow-chart in the Head Office reveals a breakdown into departments corresponding with the NEC's committees – an organizational pattern that facilitates the supervision of the former by the latter. In this part of our discussion, we are concerned with the *administrative* roles of these two institutions, and in the next section we shall take note of their contribution to *policymaking* in the national Party.

The members of the National Executive Committee, who normally meet together once each month, are drawn from the several components of the federation.[10] Serving in an *ex officio* capacity are the Party Leader and his Deputy, who are elected by the Labour members of parliament. The other twenty-seven NEC members are chosen each year at the Party Conference. Twelve of the seats are filled by trade unionists, who are nominated and elected by the union delegates; since the general secretaries of the biggest unions serve on the Trades Union Congress General Council and are not permitted by the rules of their unions to become NEC members, these posts usually go to the assistant secretaries or other officials in the second echelon of leadership. The constituency party delegates are entitled to nominate and elect seven people to NEC membership, and they are often mandated by their home organizations to vote for particular candidates. One seat is reserved for a member nominated and elected by the socialist, co-operative, and professional societies, and one seat is allocated to the Young Socialists, which they fill by action of their own conference. Five positions are awarded to women members who may be nominated by any affiliated organization but who are voted upon by all of the Conference delegates. The universality of the women's election means that those who can secure enough support from the trade unions are successful in winning the seats, since the unions cast the lion's share of the Conference votes. Strong union backing is also important in the election of the Party Treasurer, who is chosen by the entire Conference and occupies an *ex officio* seat on the NEC. Thus, with their own twelve seats and Conference-wide selection of six others, a total of eighteen of the twenty-nine positions on the National Executive Committee are in the gift domain of the trade unions. While only a few of the trade union representatives on the NEC are M.P.s, nearly all of the rest of the members pursue parliamentary careers.

One of the important tasks of the National Executive Committee is to keep a watchful eye on the Party's organizational requirements throughout the country. This is done through a set of regular NEC committees: Organization, Press and Publicity, Finance and General Purposes, and Youth, as well as two advisory committees on women's organization and the Young Socialists. Its responsibilities for Party organization bring the NEC into contact, directly or indirectly, with virtually all of the local constituency units, although some activists, without realizing the resources that the NEC makes available to their organizations, are inclined to judge its work in terms of the watchdog and disciplinary actions which make the headlines.

The National Executive Committee, through the staff at Transport House, is not only concerned with the organizational health of the local parties, but it also supervises the selection of parliamentary candidates. It compiles lists of potential nominees for use by the constituency units, and it puts its seal of endorsement upon each person who is chosen. For more than a decade, it has taken steps to improve the quality of the candidate lists by having the aspirants interviewed to determine their suitability. When unique local conditions suggest the need for a relaxation of the ordinary rules, the NEC must place its stamp upon the modified regulations to insure that they do not contravene the spirit of Conference decisions or alter the standards of recruitment, the procedures for selecting candidates, or the relationship between the local party organizations and the national structure. In the case of parliamentary by-elections, the NEC takes a special interest in candidate selection (although it cannot impose its wishes upon a local party) and in the operation of the campaigns, even going so far as to approve the election addresses. As a matter of course, it sends out information to the constituency parties, drawing their attention to changes in the rules, special organizational or campaign activities, the time table for Conference resolutions, and the like. It also plans propaganda and advertising campaigns and supervises the preparation of literature to be sent to the local parties.

In line with its responsibilities for Party organization, the National Executive Committee is sometimes called upon to play a mediatory or even a disciplinary role. It is empowered to adjudicate disputes between Party units and the affiliated organizations, as well as between local parties and the regional administration. It is also vested with the authority to conduct 'inquiries' into alleged breaches of prescribed procedures or other constituency party affairs and to apply sanctions against disobedient groups or individuals. In exercising its disciplinary powers, it can 'take any action it deems necessary for such purpose, whether by way of disaffiliation of an organization or expulsion of an individual, or otherwise.'[11] The disaffiliation of a local Labour party is drastic punishment, for the organization can no longer depend upon trade union funds, and the NEC can take steps to form a new party in its place. At various times in the past, the Committee has instituted expulsion procedures against individual members of the Party, including several M.P.s. In pursuance of Conference decisions, the NEC has authority to 'proscribe' certain organizations whose objectives are regarded as being incompatible with those of the Labour Party, and, when this happens, individuals who are associated with the black-listed organization become ineligible for Labour Party membership. When the National Executive Committee takes disciplinary action — whether through disaffiliation or expulsion — it is required to make a report at the next annual Conference. Although the most publicized cases sometimes provoke discussion from the floor, the Conference delegates invariably support the NEC in the punishment it has meted out.[12]

The National Executive Committee also serves as the banker for the Labour Party. It watches over the general financial resources, and it establishes and maintains special funds to fight elections and for insuring the candidates against the forfeiture of their deposits. Recently the Party established a company to advise local parties on the management of their premises and the operation of their loan clubs and other financial schemes. The company has also acquired some properties which it rents to constituency organizations at nominal rates.

As we have noted, the NEC committees that are concerned with Party organization operate through the administrative staff at Transport House. Heading the staff is the General Secretary of the Labour Party, who is responsible to the National Executive Committee, not to the Party Leader in the House of Commons. As the highest administrative official in a large, complex Party, he plays an important coordinating and supervisory role for the entire organization outside of parliament. Included in his responsibilities are the general preparation of election campaigns, arrangements for the annual Conference, the administration of memorial funds and trusts, high-level meetings with leaders of the components within the Labour movement, liaison with socialist organizations in other countries, etc. Transport House divides its administrative labor among several departments which gear into the NEC's committee system — Organization, Press and Publicity, and Finance, as well as the General Secretary's section and the Research Department.[13] Since Transport House is inevitably called upon to deal with sensitive and controversial matters, it sometimes becomes the target of criticism for local activists who describe it as an 'intolerant, inefficient bureaucracy', threatening the autonomy of the constituency units. This is an extreme view, usually prompted by some sort of inquiry, and it overlooks the many services that the national headquarters performs for the local parties.

The Organization Department, directed by the National Agent, handles most of the local Party work which we examined in our discussion of regional administration — agents, candidacies, elections, conferences and training programs, and the like. It is responsible for managing the new National Agency Service, and it has recently established an administrative unit to promote political education in the constituency organizations. At election time, the Organization Department collaborates with the regional organizers in holding consultations with the candidates and agents from marginal constituencies, and it arranges subsidies for some local parties in need of funds. The Department also gets involved with the 'inquiries' conducted by the NEC into problems that have arisen in particular localities. These are usually concerned with violations of party discipline on local councils, the infiltration of constituency organizations by militant elements, and local party action against their parliamentary candidates or sitting M.P.s. As an outgrowth of some investigations, the officials in the Organization Department invite suggestions from the constituencies on how to handle certain problems or on what items to include in a code of conduct.

The constituency parties benefit directly from some of the work performed by the Research Department and the press section. The Research office supplies local Labour councillors with information about local government law and procedures, it provides materials for political education programs, and it publishes speakers' handbooks and subject-matter pamphlets for use by Labour candidates and other publicists during election campaigns. In seeking to mould a general 'image' of the Labour Party, the Press and Publicity Department arranges news conferences, prepares news releases for journalists and special broadcasts for radio and television, and conducts publicity campaigns through billboards and newspaper advertisements. Of more direct concern to the local districts, the Department publishes large quantities of pamphlets, leaflets, broad sheets, and posters for general distribution and for use by constituency organizations, making some of the literature available to parties in marginal areas at reduced rates. Since 1971, the national Party has sponsored a newspaper tabloid, *Labour Weekly*, vast numbers of which are distributed to local parties at election time. Through the publication of certain booklets – referred to as 'Green Papers' – the Press and Publicity section helps to launch discussion campaigns throughout the constituencies. It also provides local parties with special films and tapes. Recognizing the need to obliterate the 'depressed working-class' image of the Labour Party, the Department in recent years has sought to give a professional touch to its advertising campaigns by calling upon market research specialists and public relations experts for their advice. It has also sponsored conferences on publicity techniques for prospective candidates and their agents in marginal constituencies.

COLLECTIVE POLICYMAKING: TRANSPORT HOUSE, NATIONAL EXECUTIVE COMMITTEE, PARTY CONFERENCE, AND PARLIAMENTARY LABOUR PARTY

The Labour Party takes pride in the fact that it is a democratic organization, and both its leaders and its members are determined that the rank and file in the constituency units will have opportunities to become involved in the policymaking process. According to an official document, 'The right to a voice in determining policy is important to any member . . . and the Party provides a procedure for resolutions passed by members to be sent in for the Annual Party Conference agenda . . . The individual member has a chance to use the machinery of the Party to secure support for ideas on every aspect of Party policy.'[14] Many people in the constituency parties jealously guard their democratic rights and look upon themselves as the initiators of policy – not just the acquiescent recipients of decisions 'made from on high'. This long-standing commitment to the democratic ethic and the open channels which make democracy possible encourage issue-oriented individualists and the heterogeneous elements in the federation to compete in give-and-take struggles over policy issues. The open system, the 'looseness' of the federational structure, and the traditional respect for divergent viewpoints sometimes result in pitched battles during which the sharp divisions within the organization are exposed to public gaze. The participants in these encounters are often torn between their concern to keep the democratic machinery operating and their desire for Labour 'solidarity' in the trade union tradition.

The real problem in the collective decision-making process stems from the fact that the Labour Party has two important (and sometimes conflicting) centers of authority: the Conference, which speaks for the mass Party organization outside of Parliament, and the Parliamentary Labour Party (PLP), which represents a much broader clientele, namely the British electorate. This bifurcation of authority raises the controversial question as to how far the Labour M.P.s in the House of Commons are to be bound by Conference decisions of the external Party organization. The difficulty arises because the Labour Party was formed *outside of parliament* almost two decades before Labour became a parliamentary group of influential numerical strength at Westminster. The traditional policymaking arrangement, which followed the model of the Trades Union Congress, was especially called into question when Labour leaders assumed command of the government, for the Labour M.P.s could not, under the British constitution, be restricted by edicts issued by an outside body. The relationship between the Parliamentary Labour Party at Westminster and the Labour Party outside of parliament was never precisely hammered out, and the Party Constitution is ambiguous on the question as to which body takes precedence when their policies clash. Hence, the problem of how to link the two centers of power – the Party Conference and the Parliamentary Labour Party – has never been resolved in a way that is acceptable to all groups, especially the ideological enthusiasts in the constituency parties.[15]

In discussing policy formation in the Labour Party, we shall look first at how the leaders set about to solicit ideas and to survey opinions, especially in the ranks of the constituency organizations. Then we shall examine policymaking in the external organization through the mechanism of the Party Conference. Following this, we shall discuss the policy conflicts which can arise between the external Party and the Party in parliament.

Soliciting Ideas and Surveying Opinions

The National Executive Committee bears important responsibilities in the policymaking domain of the Labour Party outside of parliament. This is especially true when the Party is in opposition, for it is then that the external Party is searching for relevant and appealing issues for a long-range program, and the NEC does not have to compete with a Labour Cabinet. In preparing the groundwork for the issuance of policy statements and the publication of information papers, the NEC works through two of its committees – the International Committee and the Home Policy Committee. The International Committee is divided into specialized subcommittees and is responsible for drafting preliminary statements on foreign affairs. The Home Policy Committee, which includes two representatives from the Trades Union Congress, is assisted by subcommittees and *ad hoc* study groups which are made up of NEC members and coopted specialists from other parts of the Labour movement and from the universities. In recent years, the subcommittees have studied such subjects as finance and economic policy, agriculture, science and education, energy, human rights, and regional and local government. Special study groups and working parties have investigated problems of devolution, capital taxation, discrimination against women, aircraft, development land, Commonwealth immigration, penal reform, and similar topics. Prior to the 1964 election, the Party sponsored a series of beneficial conferences in London which were attended by the coopted members of the NEC's policy groups and a selection of business, industrial, and academic experts.[16] The International and Research Departments in Transport House spend a lot of time servicing the NEC's committees and subcommittees, and they also help to prepare the NEC's responses to Conference resolutions.[17] The Research Department, in addition to its information-gathering activities, undertakes some research on its own. Many of the studies carried out by the National Executive Committee and its subsidiary units result in the preparation of policy statements which are circulated among the various units of the Party for further discussion or are placed on the Conference agenda for debate and action.[18]

In an effort to assess the attitudes of local party people on an especially controversial question, the National Executive Committee occasionally summons a special conference of the Labour Party to discuss the issue. This happened, for example, in July 1971 when the NEC scheduled a one-day debate on the Common Market.[19] Despite the holiday season, the conference attracted 87 per cent of the delegates who were to attend the regular Conference three months later. In the course of the debate, a total of 49 delegates addressed the assembly, alternating on each side of the question.[20]

The National Executive Committee has also made more direct attempts to penetrate the local party organizations for the purpose of soliciting ideas and to tap rank-and-file opinions. This was done, for example, when the Simpson Committee conducted its two-year study of Party reorganization. The Committee members and their staff held consultations in 58 different areas of the country, interviewing 2700 activists from 570 local parties, as well as some trade union officials, regional organizers, officers in the Co-operative Party, and leaders in the women's organization. A preliminary draft of the report was sent to every constituency party for examination and discussion.[21]

A desire for wide consultation with grass roots membership on policy questions prompted the NEC to undertake an experiment in 1969 and 1972, copied from the Social Democratic Party in Sweden. The program was centered around two documents — *Participation '69* and *Participation '72*.[22] Both documents were designed to promote group discussions in the localities and to secure the opinions of the participants on specific issues and the order of priorities. After each discussion, the group leader completed a questionnaire on the attitudes of the members and sent it to the Research Department in Transport House. *Participation '69* dealt with two topics: women, and social security. The discussion of the topic on women was designed to solicit grass-roots reaction to the interim report of the NEC study group, and the discussion on social security, somewhat delayed, was to be used in preparation for the forthcoming parliamentary debates on the subject. *Participation '72* was focused on Labour's Party Program; its objective was to determine the subject matter of the draft statement and the rank-order of importance of the various issues. In the first phase of the experiment — *Participation '69* — a total of 2500 people took part in 200 discussion groups; the second campaign for mass party involvement in policymaking attracted about 10,000 members from 543 local discussion units.

These and other discussion activities sometimes provide the basis for the issuance of 'Green Papers' by Labour ministers. A Green Paper is a collection of ideas on a particular subject, which is presented to Party units for further discussion with no commitment on the part of the Labour Government. The discussions may take place at a regional conference, in the subject-group meetings of Labour M.P.s, or in the local parties. When a Green Paper is sent to a constituency organization, the General Management Committee holds a preliminary discussion, inviting its parliamentary candidate or the sitting M.P. After an initial debate, the GMC usually sets up an *ad hoc* committee to study the issue and present a report with a recommendation. The GMC members then consider the report and adopt a position on the question. A summary report is subsequently drawn up by the agent and submitted to the minister as evidence. It is possible for the discussion of a Green Paper to become the framework for a 'White Paper', which is a document prepared by the Government after it has made up its mind on the issue, before the introduction of a Bill into parliament. The Green Paper discussion process was inaugurated by the Party's national leaders when their proposals for trade union reform disappointed many local activists and split the organization.

An important mechanism for articulating the ideas and attitudes of the people in the localities is the solicitation of resolutions from the constituency parties. The members of a General Management Committee are entitled to submit a resolution to the national headquarters at any time, but the vast majority of them are drawn up in time for the annual Conference. Each local party and ancillary organization is authorized to submit one resolution on policy issues to the Conference, and, in every third year, when changes in the Party Constitution are scheduled for consideration, each unit may put forward an additional resolution concerned with the Party's rules. After the resolutions are sent to Transport House, they are circulated among the constituency parties and the affiliated groups, each of which has the right to draw up one amendment on policy questions and, when applicable, an additional amendment on resolutions pertaining to the Party Constitution.[23]

No systematic, *over-time* analysis has been made of resolutions submitted to the Conference. We do know that most of them come from the constituency parties, but that only slightly more than half of these parties seize the opportunity to express their views. When a given issue generates strong feelings among the activists, a sizeable number of the party resolutions will have identical or similar wording – a situation that suggests origin from a common source. Invariably some resolutions on policy matters are formulated in such a way as to constitute an attack on the Party leadership, and most of these come from local Labour parties in districts that have sent a Tory M.P. to Westminster, usually by a comfortable majority.[24] In 1962, for example, 79 per cent of the anti-leadership resolutions were submitted by Labour units in Tory-controlled areas – 40 per cent of them from parties in Conservative strongholds. On the other hand, the constituency organizations in Labour areas contributed only 21 per cent of the statements against the leadership, and some of them were undoubtedly infuenced by their left-wing M.P.s. Issues like defense, foreign policy, and the Common Market are conventional subjects for the anti-leadership resolutions sent in by Labour activists from Conservative districts, and the Party leaders have grown accustomed to the normal flow of such resolutions. But other sorts of issues – such as public ownership (Clause IV), trade union regulation, and the legal authority of the Party Conference – can precipitate resolutions from constituency units in Labour areas, and many of these may embody criticism of the leadership. When this development occurs, the Party leaders become much more sensitive to the moods and outlooks of the local activists than is the case when the hostile statements roll in largely from Tory districts. Although Hugh Gaitskell had to ward off attacks from parties in Labour territory on the public ownership issue, most of the time the majority of his adversaries were from Conservative districts, and they criticized him for his defense policy. Some of Harold Wilson's controversial domestic policies stimulated opposition in Labour areas, and this dissent was reflected in the resolutions sent forward by a good number of the local parties that ordinarily support the leadership.

The Labour Party's emphasis on democratic procedures has convinced most of the local activists that their resolutions can be effective under certain circumstances, and many of them use this channel of communication to the top leadership. The National Executive Committee and the officials in Transport House cannot afford to disregard them, especially when controversial issues are stirring the emotions of the local stalwarts. According to a former headquarters official, the NEC takes cognizance of the feelings within the Party and the probable reactions of Conference delegates when it draws up its proposals.[25] At any rate, the formulation of resolutions gives the local activists a sense of participation, and they tend to take the process seriously. Some of the more dedicated party workers entertain hopes that their statements will eventually become a segment of official Party policy. A ward club or a General Management Committee enjoys complete autonomy in formulating its resolutions. To deny the activists an opportunity to air their views, whether conformist or dissentient, would place a strain upon the organization, resulting in either rebellion or deadly disinterest.

For an illustration of a constituency organization that pushed a resolution to a succesful conclusion, one can turn to the Labour party in Chelsea, London. It had won a sum of money in a tote scheme, and, having to operate in a hopeless stockbrokers' preserve, it could not wisely expend its funds in electoral activities. Consequently, the GMC voted to use the money for a campaign in behalf of the 'young chronically sick' — youngsters with serious illness who were often confined in geriatric wards. The objective was to have the state provide the parents with financial assistance so that they could look after the children at home. In 1965, the Chelsea GMC drew up its resolution, produced an explanatory brochure, and solicited support for the idea among other constituency parties in London.[26] Thus, the Chelsea party had drummed up considerable support for its resolution before the Conference assembled. Although the NEC and the Conference accepted the resolution, the Labour Government took no immediate action. However, the Chelsea activists and their allies in other parts of London continued to campaign for the proposal through resolutions, and four years later they saw their proposed reform enacted into law.

Policymaking in the External Organization: The Party Conference

The Labour Party Conference usually meets each autumn at a seaside resort, where for five days the cool ocean breezes compete with the warmer political rhetoric. While polemical storms have raged for more than a decade over the question of whether the Conference or the Parliamentary Labour Party has the final say, there can be no doubt that the Conference is the authoritative body for the Labour Party as it operates *outside the chambers at Westminster*. The Conference has a mystique of its own which is rooted in the history of the Labour movement, and although its influence has fluctuated over time, it has always commanded prestige within the Party. Some local parties may encounter difficulty in securing delegates to represent them, but many activists eagerly look forward to the day when they can attend the Party Conference, even if they have to use their holiday time or forego their wages.

The Conference is a large body of about 1100 delegates from the constituency parties and the affiliated organizations.[27] The local parties are allocated one representative for every 5000 individual members or portion thereof. When the individual and affiliated women's membership exceeds 1500, a party may send an additional woman delegate, and when a local branch of the Young Socialists has a membership of 100 or more, an additional youth delegate may be appointed. Trade unions and other affiliated organizations are eligible to send one delegate for each 5000 affiliated members or part thereof. The members of the National Executive Committee, Labour M.P.s, Labour parliamentary candidates, and the General Secretary of the Party are *ex officio* members of the Conference without voting rights.

The agenda of the Party Conference consists of policy statements, the report of the Parliamentary Labour Party, a report on National Executive Committee activities, and the resolutions (and amendments to resolutions) sent forward by the constituency parties and the affiliated organizations. Of great significance are the policy statements and other proposals submitted by the NEC, which usually plays an important initiatory role in policymaking. The various resolutions, of course, take up a great deal of the Conference time. These are brought together and separated into subject-matter categories. The Conference officials attempt to reduce the number to manageable size and still insure that the divergent points of view will be presented for consideration by the delegates. By agreement of the interested spokesmen, some resolutions are left standing in their original form and the rest are either withdrawn or combined. The process of combining resolutions is called 'compositing', i.e., a number of resolutions bearing on the same topic are woven into a single statement containing the common elements. When an issue is controversial, Conference officials sometimes arrange to have two composite resolutions formulated with contrasting viewpoints so that both sides will have their chance at the rostrum. As already pointed out, it is possible for an individual to nurse his resolution through his ward, to push it through endorsement by his GMC, and to have it appear on the Conference agenda as an independent resolution or as one element in the composite design.

With the opening ceremonies out of the way, the Conference delegates begin to debate the policy statements and resolutions. The members of the National Executive Committee, including the Party Leader, sit on the platform for the duration of the conclave, listening to delegates who support or oppose their policy stands and to the 'stormy petrels' who delight in hurling political grenades at the Party's 'establishment'. The debate on each subject is usually opened by the mover of a resolution (if the proposal has been made by the NEC, a member of that body makes the opening statement), and the seconder follows with a short, supplementary talk. A general debate from the floor is then opened up, and the rank-and-file delegates air their views under a strict time-limit. The debate on each issue is concluded by a statement presented by an NEC member or someone else designated by that group – a national Party figure or, when Labour is in office, a minister. In summing up, the NEC spokesman may seek to avoid a Conference vote by accepting the resolution for consideration or implementation by the Committee or by requesting that it be withdrawn. But if the issue is important or controversial, some delegates will insist upon a formal vote, and the speaker who represents the NEC will urge the assembly either to support or to reject the resolution.

The size of the gathering, time-pressures, and the leaders' concern about the Party's 'image' on television place constraints upon the effectiveness of the Conference as genuine policymaking body. The agenda spans a wide range of subjects, with the result that the time allocated to the discussion of many issues is short.[28] It is difficult for an ordinary constituency delegate, even if he is lucky enough to be called to the podium, to make much of an impact in a three-minute speech unless he is a strong or flamboyant personality. Understandably, a sizeable portion of the Conference time is given over to speakers representing the National Executive Committee, who are responsible for introducing some of the issues and winding up all of the debates. Even so, the number of rank-and-file delegates who manage to get called to the rostrum is surprisingly large – in 1975, 133 of them were from the constituency parties, 73 were from the affiliated organizations, and 17 of the speakers were *ex officio* members.[29] Like political conventions in the United States, the Conference has some of the ethos of a 'pep rally' and is burdened with its share of evangelism and platitude-spinning. Factional differences over issues are often cast in ideological terms. But, unlike its American counterparts and distinctive in many respects from the Conservative Party meeting, the Labour Conference is characterized by a substantial amount of debate, planned and spontaneous, from the floor, and the clash of ideas is clearly evident. The speeches from the platform often resemble academic lectures in their cogency and the use of evidence – a characterization that can be made of some (but certainly not most) of the addresses delivered from the delegates' rostrum. The debates on controversial questions, however, are rarely dull, and occasionally a local party activist manages to sway the Conference by his sincerity, his courage, the persuasiveness of his argument, or his flourishes of picturesque prose. Speakers who displease the assembly may be heckled or subjected to the slow hand-clap. The delegates exhibit a remarkable capacity for political exchange, and when the daily sessions are over, they continue their debates at special teas and evening rallies and in the hotel lobbies.

In an overwhelming majority of the debates, the decisions are reached by voice vote or by show of hands. The delegates, however, are entitled to call for a 'card vote', and this is the voting procedure that is used in deciding the important, controversial questions. When a card vote is taken, it is *possible* for the local constituency parties to find themselves hopelessly outnumbered. (This assumes, of course, that the big unions and the local parties are solidly lined up against each other – a situation that rarely occurs.) The cards are the symbol of the block voting system, under which each unit – whether a trade union or a local party – is allocated voting strength in proportion to the number of Party-affiliated members in its organization. In specific terms, the delegates may hold up one voting card for every 1000 members, or part thereof, whom they represent. A constituency party with 1800 members, for example, is entitled to one delegate who is permitted to cast two votes. On the other hand, the largest trade union – the Transport and General Workers Union – which has about 1,000,000 affiliated members can claim 200 delegates who are eligible to cast 1000 votes. (The Transport Workers union actually sends only about 40 delegates.) At the 1974 Conference, the trade unions accounted for 89 per cent of the total votes,[30] and the proportion has increased as the number of individual Labour Party members has declined. Moreover, the trade union strength is concentrated in the six largest unions, the combined votes of which command an absolute majority.

It would be a mistake, however, to conclude that the unions are lined up against a united phalanx of constituency parties and act as a monolithic group to dominate the Conference proceedings and to determine policy by their massive voting strength.[31] The unions send forward only a fraction of the total number of resolutions submitted, and of those authored by unions many come from the small, leftist-oriented organizations. Moreover, as we have already seen, the trade union delegates do not consume as much debating time as do the enthusiasts from the constituency parties. Finally, the unions have been split among themselves on nearly every important question that has divided the Conference since the war, the size of the split varying according to the issues involved and the time period in which they have arisen. The voting behavior of the unions exhibited a noticeable lack of cohesion during the 'Bevanite period' in the 1950s, when they fell under heavy attack, and since 1960 the division within the trade union component has been made more dramatic as some of the larger unions – hitherto bastions of orthodoxy – have taken positions against the Party leadership on crucial issues. By the same token, the constituency parties do not function as a homogeneous element in their voting patterns, although a majority of them probably voted against NEC policy on German rearmament in 1954. Even when unilateral disarmament was winning the support of many local activists, a surprising number of constituency delegates appear to have supported Hugh Gaitskell at the 1960 and 1961 Conferences.[32]

Although the criticism of the unions by local party activists has been muffled since some of the labor organizations have drifted leftward, many constituency delegates have taken the view that the trade unions can use their block votes to 'steamroller' the Conference. This feeling was rooted in the fact that, while the unions were divided on most questions, some of the bigger labor organizations tended to support the orthodox leadership of the Party. As Martin Harrison pointed out, the balance of forces on a number of important issues was such that if one of these unions had decided to switch position, the voting outcome would have been different. Especially during the Bevanite period, the local party delegates complained that they scored the most points in the debates, that their position was usually supported in the show of hands, but that their cause defeated in the card vote.

Even today, many local party activists are persuaded that they, more than the trade union delegations, reflect the attitudes of the rank-and-file members of the Labour movement. They contend that some unions, which do not hold annual conferences, are not able to tap the opinions of their members on political issues before their delegates appear at the Party conclave, and that even when trade union conferences are held in advance, the agendas are so filled with industrial matters that little time is left for discussion of political and ideological issues. This difficulty, which worked to the advantage of the unilateralist militants in 1960, was pointed out by a leader of one of the big unions during the debate on unilateral disarmament: '. . . the tragedy is that some unions exercising large votes at this Conference reached binding decisions before the joint declaration [the NEC policy statement] was approved and circulated.'[33] In other words, the critics from the local parties grumble that some union leaders at the Labour Party Conference hold up voting cards in behalf of their members who may not have given a clear mandate on the issue being decided.

The constituency party delegates tend to regard themselves as being more in the 'spirit' of the political side of the movement than many of their trade union brothers. According to the argument, they and their colleagues on the GMC will have carefully weighed the arguments on the important issues to be debated at the Conference; indeed, on the significant questions to come before the assembly, many of the party delegates will have been instructed on how to cast their votes, and even if they have not been formally mandated, their political views were well known at the time they were selected to serve as delegates.[34] Thus, the representatives of the local parties make a special claim to political competence, often picturing themselves as reflecting the views of ordinary Party members, and they object to a voting system which, in their view, is heavily weighted against them.

The problem of how to allocate representation and voting power among the various elements, which sometimes have competing interests, is a serious problem for any federation, especially in a political organization whose power struggles are interlaced with ideological differences. Those who defend the block vote system not only point out that it is part of the traditional democratic procedures of British trade unionism,[35] but are quick to observe that its opponents do not condemn the union delegations when they hold up cards in support of a position taken by the local party activists. The proponents of card voting also call attention to the fact that the party delegates cast a block vote similar to that of the unions (only smaller), and that when they hold up their cards, they are speaking for the party members who were absent when the issues were being discussed. Indeed, the charge is often made that the resolutions adopted by many constituency parties were pushed through the GMC sessions by well-organized groups of militants whose outlooks are not representative of the clienteles for whom they presumably spoke.

Even though the debates are characteristically vigorous, the Conference delegates, in casting their votes, are willing to accept the recommendations of the National Executive Committee and other national leaders in the vast majority of the questions they are called upon to decide. The view is prevalent that challenges to the Party's leadership are less likely to occur when Labour is in power, since the delegates are reluctant to embarrass their Government or to present the image of a disunited organization. This conclusion may apply to the temper of the debates, but it does not hold up when we examine the voting tallies since the war.[36] In the Conferences between 1946 and 1951 (the period of the Attlee Government), the platform was defeated on four occasions – an average of 0.67 times per Conference. In the years of opposition – 1952–63 – it suffered only three voting defeats – an average of 0.25 per Conference. During the period of the Wilson Governments (1964–9, 1974–5), the leaders lost in twenty voting challenges – an average of 2.5 per Conference. And when the Party was in opposition during 1970–3, the leadership was defeated on seven issues – an average of 1.8 per Conference. If we combine this information, two conclusions appear to emerge: (1) the voting challenges to the leadership have been more frequent when Labour has been in power, an average of 1.7 issues per Conference, compared with an average of only 0.63 issues when it has been in opposition; and (2) the rejection of NEC recommendations was much higher when Harold Wilson served as Leader of the Party, both during periods of power and opposition, than it had been previously. That the Conference would be less amenable to leadership control when Labour is in power is understandable, because it is then that the Parliamentary Labour Party operates as a stronger center of decision-making and some of the policies it enacts into statute are likely to run counter to the feelings that the activists have expressed at the Party Conferences.

The National Executive Committee and the Party's key leaders naturally attempt to sidestep the awkward issues and to reduce the level of contention by striving for a wider consensus. The NEC tries to anticipate the currents of opinion within the Party and to shape its statements in such a way as to carry a majority of the Conference delegates along with it. As a steering committee, it succeeds amazingly well.

Despite the limitations of its policymaking role – weaknesses that are universal in legislative bodies of such size – the Labour Party Conference is an important mechanism in the national Party structure. It enables the national Party leaders and the local activists who helped to put them where they are to meet together for a few days of brisk exchange and social contact. Through the resolutions they send forward, in the debates from the floor, and through informal contacts in tea-rooms and bars, the local party workers have opportunities to express their opinions and to exert at least some influence on their national leaders, including a good number of M.P.s. For some of the fiery rebels, the Conference may perform a therapeutic function, for it enables them to work off their frustrations by taking pot-shots at established authority, and to derive satisfaction from the thought that they are hammering away at the power structure – a traditional phenomenon in a movement whose vociferous non-conformists tend to distrust leadership at every echelon. In this forum, the national leaders are able to sense the feelings that exist within the Party, to gauge the strength of the various factions, and to detect more realistically the causes of dissension. Moreover, the platform is available to the Party's dominant figures so that they can present their views and attempt to win the support of delegates who are among the influentials on the home ground. At the 1974 Conference, for example, Harold Wilson not only presented his parliamentary report to the delegates, but opened himself up to questions from the floor. To the extent that it serves to widen the area of consensus, the gathering helps to integrate the elements which make up the federation.

The Conference experience, of course, enables the delegates from the constituencies to look at the issues in a broader Party perspective and to carry back to their home units fresh outlooks on political and organizational matters which may have been given insufficient attention. When a delegate returns from the Conference to his local party, he will probably give a report to the GMC, which may become the basis for a policy discussion. He may also make the rounds of the ward clubs by invitation, and he might even appear before a local union branch or trades council.

Policy Conflicts: The NEC and the Party Conference versus the Parliamentary Labour Party

Most Conference delegates seem to be convinced that the machinery of the external Labour Party is democratic, but many of them believe that intra-Party democracy breaks down when the policymaking role of the Parliamentary Labour Party is taken into account. The PLP, which usually meets weekly or fortnightly, makes binding decisions on the policies and strategies to be followed by Labour M.P.s in their parliamentary encounters. When the Leader of the Party occupies the residence in Downing Street, he and his ministerial colleagues take the initiative in making parliamentary decisions, although they are naturally sensitive to the opinion currents on the back-benches. When Labour is in opposition, the Leader shares his executive duties in the PLP with the parliamentary committee ('Shadow Cabinet'), twelve members of which are elected annually by the Labour M.P.s.[37] The Parliamentary Labour Party also organizes itself into a set of subject-matter committees which discuss policy issues within their respective domains. These committees enable the back-benchers to air their views and to make recommendations to the parliamentary committee or even to the Labour meeting.[38]

Once the Labour Party caucus has reached a decision on an important policy question, each of the M.P.s is expected to march through the appropriate lobby when the division bell rings. An individual who nurtures a 'deeply held personal conscientious conviction' on an issue may abstain from voting, but this does not entitle him to vote *against* the Party's decision. The PLP has authority to withdraw the whip from a Labour member who refuses to conform to discipline, and it reports such action (which does not constitute expulsion from the Party) to the National Executive Committee.

In performing its policymaking role, the Parliamentary Labour Party sometimes adopts policies that are not in line with Conference decisions. Especially when there is a Labour Government, the decision-making power of the external Party Conference tends to be whittled down. Most of the Labour M.P.s are persuaded by the notion that parliament is sovereign; that they are to be legislators in the Burkean tradition, rather than mere delegates; and that a Conference instruction to vote on an issue in a way that contradicts the platform they were elected on would be a threat to the parliamentary system.[39]

The people who uphold the Conference as the final authority in policy matters also press their case with vehemence. They reject the notion that the Parliamentary Labour Party is autonomous, characterizing it as an arm of the external organization and hence subject to Conference decisions. The annual assembly, they argue, is not to be regarded 'merely as a ritual, tribal gathering' whose resolutions can simply be put aside by the PLP.[40] The depth of feeling was expressed by a delegate at the 1970 Conference: 'We, the grass roots, the rank and file, implore our leaders to heed us . . . and adhere to conference decisions.' On two occasions, the Conference has passed resolutions asserting the supremacy of the policymaking body of the external Party.

The ambiguity in the Party Constitution on the question of sovereignty was not really troublesome for the first decade of the post-war period. The PLP leadership had strong influence in the National Executive Committee through the constituency party representatives and the members elected with trade union support. In their struggles with the left during the Conference proceedings, the NEC and other Party figures could usually depend upon the allegiance and the block votes of the big trade unions.[41] The few decisions that were recorded against them were on relatively minor issues, and the PLP felt little pressure to compromise its perceived obligations in parliament.

In the 1950s, however, the solidarity of the PLP leadership began to erode as influential veterans died or retired and Hugh Gaitskell and Aneurin Bevan rivaled to succeed Clement Attlee as the Party Leader.[42] The disruption in the balance of forces was accompanied by sharp disagreements over domestic and foreign policy, and the Bevan group — only a minority in the parliamentary Party — sought to expand its influence by making inroads into the National Executive Committee and by taking its case to the floor of the Conference. In 1952, a majority of the constituency parties, in selecting their NEC representatives, began to reject orthodox political figures in favor of leftists in the Bevanite tradition, and, with few exceptions, this has continued to be their practice. Many local parties, even though they do not hew to a left-wing line, nevertheless mandate their delegates to vote for leftists for the NEC positions not only because they are prominent personalities but also because they serve as a 'ginger' counterweight against the more orthodox voices. The replacement of moderate M.P.s by members of the 'rebel left' tended to dilute the influence of the Party Leader and his colleagues on the NEC, making it one of the arenas of struggle over the leadership of the Party and its ideological orientation.[43] By 1960, the Committee was about evenly split between the two factions.

Even after Gaitskell had won the leadership post, disputes over defense policy and 'revisionist' doctrine continued to plague the Party. Gaitskell and his colleagues, however, did not suffer a formal defeat in Conference voting until 1960, when the delegates rejected the defense policy of the parliamentary leaders and committed the organization to a policy of unilateral disarmament. This shattering blow came about as the result of leadership changes and/or policy shifts in some of the large trade unions. From that time until the present, the PLP leadership has been unable to rely upon the huge card vote of the unions to sustain its position on the Conference floor.

The decision on unilateralism put the leaders of the Parliamentary Labour Party in an embarrassing position, for their opponents now carried the Conference endorsement of their views. Leftist M.P.s even tried to amend the PLP standing orders so that no Labour member could be disciplined for voting in accordance with Conference decisions. Most of Labour M.P.s, however, continued to stand with their Leader in support of their original defense policies, defying the Conference and agitating to get the unilateralist decision reversed, which they managed to do at the 1961 Conference by getting some of the unions to shift position. In short, the Parliamentary Labour Party was able to assert its autonomy, but the leaders felt so uncomfortable about being at odds with the Conference mandate that they set about making the policies of the two bodies congruent as soon as possible, though, of course, on their terms.

The Labour Party is still wrestling with the problem of divided sovereignty (currently dramatized by the sharp split over the Common Market).[44] Scholarly authority and precedent tend to support the view that the Parliamentary Labour Party is an autonomous body which cannot be subject to binding instructions by either the National Executive Committee or the Party Conference. The prevailing belief is that, while the Conference has the right to enunciate principles and to draw the broad outlines of policy for the Party as a whole, the PLP is entitled to interpret the policies and to determine the priorities and the timing at its own discretion. This is the view once expressed by Aneurin Bevan himself: 'It is quite impossible for a Conference of 1100 people, even if it were constitutionally proper, to determine the order in which the Parliamentary Labour Party and the Government introduce legislation into the House of Commons. It is for the Conference to lay down the policies of the Parliamentary Party, and for the Parliamentary Party to interpret these policies in the light of the Parliamentary system."[45]

No one would deny, however, that it would be unwise for the parliamentary leaders to detach their political antennae from the strong waves of opinion that are emitted by the delegates at Conference. These are the local activists who carry the main burden of political work in their home organizations. Sustained disagreement between them and their parliamentary leaders over policy issues and orbits of authority would disrupt the Party and endanger its electoral chances. For the Party machinery to operate smoothly, cordial relationships must exist between the PLP and the organizational structure outside of parliament.

Customarily, the linkage between the Party Conference and the Parliamentary Labour Party is achieved by joint consultation between the National Executive Committee and representatives of the PLP. The NEC, of course, has always had a large component of M.P.s – almost two-thirds of the Committee's membership in 1976 – although a good number of them do not always see eye to eye with the parliamentary leadership. In addition, the Party's General Secretary attends the meetings of the parliamentary committee, and the Chief Whip attends the meetings of the NEC. Occasionally, too, representatives from the parliamentary committees sit in on discussions conducted by the NEC policy groups. One of the most obvious occasions for consultation is in the preparation of the election manifesto, which is binding upon Labour M.P.s. Items to be included in the Party's program must be adopted by the Conference by a two-thirds vote. An initial draft of the platform is usually prepared by the Research Department in Transport House, and the precise wording is then hammered out by the NEC and representatives from the PLP, ordinarily the parliamentary committee when the Party is in opposition.[46]

In recent years, as the Party leadership has been challenged more frequently on the Conference floor, the National Executive Committee has tended to assert itself in behalf of the Conference and to exhibit concern about the alleged disregard of the assembly's decisions.[47] Indeed, the Committee has occasionally gone so far as to criticize policies of the Labour Government. The reconciliation of discordant viewpoints required special types of linkage mechanisms. During the early phase of the Wilson Government, the Labour people established a coordinating committee made up of seven NEC members and five representatives from the front bench, which became the main coupling between the two sources of authority. When it was perceived that the National Executive Committee was losing some of its power to the coordinating committee, the Prime Minister arranged a joint meeting of the NEC and the Cabinet for the discussion of long-range objectives. By late 1968, the NEC began the practice of inviting Labour ministers to their committee meetings to explain why some of their policies were not in tune with Conference decisions. Since 1971, NEC members and

Cabinet officials ('Shadow Cabinet' officials when the Party is not in power) have been holding joint meetings three times a year. In addition, the elected officers of the NEC, the Party's General Secretary, the Leader and Deputy Leader of the Party, and the Chief Whip meet in weekly sessions. These integrative mechanisms, however, have not achieved spectacular success in stilling the troubled waters, especially as the composition of the National Executive Committee has gradually taken on more of a 'leftist' hue. Policy differences between some members of the competing groups emerged during the preparation of the 1970 election manifesto, and in 1973 when pressures mounted to turn the Party toward the left, the NEC reportedly declined to meet with representatives of the Parliamentary Party in advance of the Annual Conference to discuss the watering down of some of the left-wing positions which were being formulated.[48]

Thus, the Labour Party has been unable so far to resolve the problem of divided power between the organization within parliament and the organization throughout the country. Nearly everyone recognizes the importance of strengthening the links and improving the relations between the national Party leadership and the agitated activists in the constituencies. But the split in Labour's organizational structure is reinforced to a great extent by basic policy disagreements over the Party's goals and strategies. Under these circumstances, it is difficult for political leaders to forge a consensus which would be both satisfying to the activists and attractive to the voters.

THE LABOUR M.P. AND HIS CONSTITUENCY PARTY

Apart from any influence they may have on the Labour Party by submitting and voting on resolutions, local parties in safe and marginal districts have an opportunity to influence the composition — and hence the ideological outlook — of the Parliamentary Labour Party through the selection and election of their Labour candidates. Selection is especially important in a safe constituency because the person chosen is likely to enjoy relatively long tenure in parliament; yet it is in such a constituency that the activists usually have the least experience in candidate-selection. Ironically, the people most skilled in choosing parliamentary candidates are those who work in hopeless territory, where a new candidate has to be selected each time a general election is called.

It is easy to conclude that political outlooks are the prime consideration in selecting candidates for parliamentary races. Occasionally, the party officers may be prompted to include a nominee on the short list (or to omit his name) because of his political orientation, and in any event the GMC members have an opportunity at the selection conference to investigate the policy stands of the various candidacy-seekers. When a government decides to cut back on the social services as an economy measure, a Labour selection conference may be attracted toward more 'militant' candidates. If the local party activists are in basic agreement on the major issues and they strongly desire to have a candidate whose outlook is congenial with theirs, they can usually choose such a person, for the local organization has virtually a free hand in selecting its parliamentary nominee. Observers can cite instances of left-wing parties choosing leftist candidates and of moderate parties selecting their nominees from the center or from the rightist side of Labour's political spectrum. Indeed, there have been times when both the left wing and the right wing have organized in an effort to influence candidate selection and ultimately the make-up of the Parliamentary Party.[49]

But the generalization that political preferences determine candidate selection oversimplifies the process. Professor Ranney's thorough study of candidate selection in the Labour Party between 1945 and 1964 indicated that most local parties, recognizing that the M.P. will be bound by Parliamentary Party discipline anyway, did not usually consider a nominee's views on particular issues to be crucial.[50] Non-ideological factors – such as the aspirant's place of residence, personal rivalries within the organization, sponsorship by a trade union, the need in the constituency for a candidate possessing certain personl qualities – may be of equal or greater importance to the selection conference delegates than the political views of the nominees. In fact, many of them may be primarily interested in evidence of the nominees' commitment to the Labour movement. It is not unusual to find leftist parties selecting center or right-wing candidates, or a General Management Committee made up almost entirely of working-class activists choosing a candidate with an affluent background and holding opposing views on significant issues. In the past few years, however, competition between the left and the right appears to have grown more intense, and stands on political issues may be more strategic in candidate selection now than they once were.

Even if the activists in a constituency party hold strong opinions on policy questions, their ability to influence the votes of their M.P. in the House of Commons is to a large extent circumscribed. The norms of the Labour Party encourage the 'Burkean approach' to local party pressures (but not to the promptings of the whips): the M.P. is not to act like a puppet responding to strings pulled by the constituency party leaders. Indeed, while still a candidate he will probably have been warned by the head office against making promises to special local groups or pledging himself to support policies not included in the official platform.[51] The Labour member will naturally consider the strong feelings of his local party when he has to decide his vote at meetings of the Parliamentary

Labour Party, but the outlooks of the home folk are only one of several factors that he must consider in reaching his decision. We have already noted that, once the PLP has taken a stand, the M.P. is ordinarily bound to support its policy; he gave this undertaking at the selection conference when he became a candidate. The local parties understand that they send their M.P.s to Westminster to become the members of a national team, and in most instances they do not require their representatives to become 'splitters' and endanger the position of the national Party merely because constituency interests happen to be involved. The local activists, to be sure, expect their M.P. to look out for constituency interests when he is not under orders from the leadership, but they can hardly expect him to run foul of the whips just for the sake of pressing a narrow constituency matter.

The normal relationships between the Labour M.P. and his constituency party are likely to become disturbed under three sets of circumstances: (1) when the constituency party feels that its member of parliament is for 'personal reasons' no longer equipped to do the job expected of him; (2) when the Labour member violates PLP discipline by 'jumping the whip' (just once on a major issue or on several occasions over a time-interval), thereby jeopardizing official policy and exhibiting disloyalty to the national leaders; and (3) when the political views of the local activists and their M.P. have become 'incompatible', even though the member has consistently supported the parliamentary leaders in the division lobbies. Actually, the *proportion* of known instances of constituency party conflict with the M.P. since 1945 is quite small. Some of the cases, however, have attracted publicity, and, as we shall see, the number of refusals to readopt the sitting Labour member has noticeably increased in recent years, especially since the 1970 change in the rules.

The GMC delegates in a local party may generate ripples of opposition against their parliamentary member when they fell that for some personal reason he is no longer suited to represent them effectively at Westminster. Excessive age, personal misconduct, eccentricities of one sort or another, unpopular business dealings, inattention to parliamentary duties, or neglect of service to the constituency are some of the 'failings' which, in the eyes of the activists, may render the M.P. unattractive for readoption. In his study, Ranney cites only four instances (in a twenty-year period) of M.P.s having been advised to retire by their local parties for personal reasons, and in each case Transport House acquiesced in the decision, even when there was strong suspicion that the ousting procedures had been somewhat irregular.[52] Dickson's more recent study of the period from 1948 to 1974 presents the following record: age of M.P., four cases; personal failings, four; neglect of parliamentary duties and lack of impact in parliament, two; and neglect of the constituency, seven.[53] When we take into account the total number of Labour M.P.s during this time-span, the number of cases of dissatisfaction on these grounds is remarkably limited; apparently not many Labour members are publicly accused of neglecting their parliamentary or constituency responsibilities.

The dissatisfaction becomes a bit more pronounced when we consider the M.P.s' political views as expressed in their parliamentary voting behavior and their public speeches. The constituency party may be represented by an M.P. who commits no serious indiscretions in a parliamentary setting but who occasionally makes an 'out-of-the-ordinary' statement in the House or at a public meeting which raises a question in the minds of the local activists. When this happens, the GMC may request an explanation and either let the matter drop or indicate their disapproval by taking 'full cognizance' of his utterances. During the Attlee era, for example, Raymond Blackburn was requested to appear before his local party to explain a remark he had made about the importance of private enterprise, and he received a vote of confidence.[54] In 1968, the constituency party summoned Brian Walden to defend his views on unemployment, and the borough party reprimanded him. More recently, John Robertson had to meet with the Executive Committee of his local party to explain his criticism of the Labour Government on devolution and other issues. And Maureen Colquhoun was called before her General Management Committee to justify her reaction to Enoch Powell's speech on immigration – behavior that resulted in a motion by the Young Socialists' branch that she be asked to retire at the next election.[55] A case with a more serious result was that of Mrs Margaret McKay, the Labour member for Clapham.[56] In 1969, the people in the local party became unhappy about her pro-Arab activities, and early in the next year they voted 21 to 14 to recommend that she not be re-endorsed. Prior to the 1970 election, the NEC authorized the party to begin formal dismissal procedures, but Mrs McKay decided not to go through the ordeal. A conventional method of rebuking its Labour member is for the GMC to send forward a resolution that runs counter to his position. At the time of the unilateralist controversy in 1960, at least fourteen of the unilateralist resolutions submitted to the Party Conference by local parties represented views at variance with those of their M.P.s.[57]

When a Member of Parliament makes a public statement in opposition to Party policy or engages in a 'floor rebellion' by defying the whip on a major policy question, the local party will sometimes take note of the action and request him to account for his behavior. The M.P. may even send a message of clarification to his constituency without having been asked to do so. Depending upon the issue, the M.P.'s standing in the local party and his explanation of the incident, the GMC or the Executive Committee may decide to express support or disapproval.

The activists in the home territory tend to become most disturbed when the M.P.'s defection in the voting lobbies puts him on the right wing of Labour's ideological spectrum, in close proximity to the 'left-wing' Tories. As Peter Richards has pointed out, 'The greatest crime a Member can commit in the eyes of his local constituency association is to appear to have some sympathy for the views of his political opponents.'[58] Woodrow Wyatt, for example, was requested by his local party to explain his opposition to the renationaliation of the steel companies and his support for an alliance with the Liberals.[59] Three other cases of 'right-wing deviation' provoked severe reprisals by the constituency organizations — action that won the approval, or at least the acquiescence, of national Party leaders. In 1948, the member for Middlesbrough East, Alfred Edwards, stood out against the Government's proposal to nationalize the steel industry.[60] Shortly after he had rung the tocsin of revolt, the members of the General Management Committee met in special session and voted overwhelmingly to request his retirement from the Labour seat. After summoning Edwards for an interview, the NEC endorsed the local party's action by expelling him from the Party. Another case of right-wing defection involved Stanley Evans, the member for Wednesbury.[61] Although early in his parliamentary career he had accompanied left-wing rebels into the opposition lobby,[62] he steadily moved toward a rightist course, and in 1950 he lost his post as a junior minister for opposing farm subsidies. Three years later, Evans argued against the Central African Federation, criticizing his own Party's stand during the debate.[63] Thereafter, his speeches in parliament and before business groups in his constituency emphasized the importance of British interests in the Middle East — views that were warmly received by some Conservatives. When the Suez action was being debated in the House in late 1956, Evans spoke against the Labour position and then abstained from the voting. This was the last straw for the Labour activists in Wednesbury, and after listening to his explanation they voted unanimously to request his resignation as their M.P. According to Epstein, the national authorities might have welcomed Evans' resistance to the GMC action, but before they could intervene, he gave up his seat. The third instance of censure for right-wing behavior concerned Alan Brown, the M.P. for Tottenham, who was invited by the local party in 1961 to resign his seat and stand in a by-election on the ground that he had been fellow-traveling with the Tories.[64] Brown's constituency organization took a strong unilateralist position on the defense question, while he opposed even the Gaitskell position as giving away too much. Professing 'contempt for the left-wing element', he resigned from the Labour Party and eventually joined the Conservatives.[65]

Occasionally, of course, a right-wing rebel commands such power in his constituency that he is able to carry his local party along with him. This happened in 1968 in the case of Desmond Donnelly (Pembrokeshire), a former Bevanite who gradually moved to the right, opposing such policies as the renationalization of steel, the withdrawal of British troops from 'East of Suez', and the withholding of arms shipments to South Africa.[66] Two months after resigning the Labour whip in parliament, he was expelled from the Party by the National Executive Committee. These developments created a serious situation for his local party, but after a stormy meeting from which the anti-Donnelly faction withdrew, a majority of the activists gave their M.P. a vote of confidence and took the unusual step of deciding to disaffiliate themselves from the national Party. At the next election, Donnelly stood under the sponsorship of his new party and lost the seat.

Local constituency parties are inclined to be more tolerant of rebellious spirit when their Members of Parliament, in challenging the national Party leadership, mark out a position on the left end of the policy continuum and can definitely not be regarded as a pale imitation of the Conservative outlook. Many of the left-wing dissidents enjoy the complete confidence of their local parties, and the national authorities are often reluctant to impose severe sanctions, not relishing embittered struggles with the constituency organizations. When Aneurin Bevan resigned from the Attlee Government in 1951, the GMC delegates in Ebbw Vale promptly called a special meeting, and after a period of hymn-singing voted unanimously to commend his action as being in the interest of the Labour movement.[67] When Bevan subsequently became involved in other rebellions, he could always count upon the support of the stalwarts in his local organization.[68] The Ebbw Vale party later transferred its loyalty to another rebel, Michael Foot, and in March 1961 it unanimously endorsed his dissident vote on the military budget, requesting that the whip be restored to him.[69] In similar fashion, the party in Bradford South upheld the position of its M.P., George Craddock, when on several occasions he dissented from Labour's foreign and defense policies; and the Jarrow party did the same for its member, Ernest Fernyhough.[70]

Even when some Labour M.P.s have drifted to an extreme leftist position, thereby inviting disciplinary action by the NEC, a number of them have managed to retain the loyalty of their constituency parties. In 1948, for example, on the eve of the Italian election, twenty-two Labour members signed a telegram to Pietro Nenni, leader of the left-wing Socialists, whose platform endorsed collaboration with the Communists – in opposition to the Saragat group, with which the Labour Party enjoyed a cordial relationship through the Socialist International. This action was officially interpreted as contradicting official policy, and the M.P.s who had signed the telegram were informed that unless they promised to avoid such conduct in the future, they would be subject to expulsion.[71] Nearly all of the offenders were called upon by their local parties to explain their behavior, and at least three of the constituency units repudiated the action of their parliamentary representatives.[72] On the other hand, at least seven M.P.s in the group received votes of confidence from their local organizations.[73] Other instances of local resistance to the disciplining of left-wing members occurred in 1949. At that time, the National Executive Committee not only refused to endorse for readoption, but also voted to expel three M.P.s of the far left — Lester J. Solley, Konni Zilliacus, and H. Lester Hutchinson — who had consistently attacked Labour's foreign policy, dramatizing their indignation on several occasions by marching into the opposition lobby. In each case, the local party tried to stand behind its member by protesting the NEC action, and the expulsions of Solley and Zilliacus were brought to the floor of the 1949 Conference, but with poor results.[74]

A constituency party may leap into action against a sitting member because, in remaining loyal to the parliamentary leaders, he has taken a position on controversial issues that was contrary to the strong views held by a majority of the local activists. In such cases, of course, the national Party leaders have sometimes intervened in an effort to assert their authority and to protect the loyal members from retaliation by local militants. This happened on several occasions prior to 1970, especially during the Bevan period. When Arthur Skeffington, the member for Hayes and Harlington, supported the Party leaders on the rearming of West Germany, his constituency organization was reluctant to readopt him, and he was able to retain the candidature because Transport House intervened in his behalf.[75] A much more publicized case was that of Mrs Elizabeth Braddock of Liverpool Exchange, a staunch supporter of the national leadership.[76] Her troubles began in 1952, when her local party fell under the domination of the Bevanites, with the encouragement of the agent. When she refused to be bound by the GMC mandate in her Conference voting, the local people declined to elect her as an official delegate to several conferences, and in June 1954 they took steps to unseat her. The attempt was unsuccessful because they failed to adhere to established procedures. As the 1955 election approached, the GMC members decided by a very close vote not to readopt Mrs Braddock. She appealed against the decision to the National Executive Committee, which conducted a second inquiry and eventually ruled in her favor. Under threat of disaffiliation and amid considerable tension, the local party yielded to pressure and accepted her candidacy. Another case of similar design concerned the member for Coventry South, Miss Elaine Burton, who had also been a firm supporter of the Party leadership.[77] She fell out of step with her local party when she voted to withdraw the whip from Aneurin Bevan and seven of his disciples after Attlee had made the issue a matter of confidence in his leadership. The next day the borough party passed a resolution of censure against her. But Transport House officials intervened to stop the cabal, indicating that the local party would not be allowed to depose Miss Burton, even if disaffiliation became necessary to enforce the decision.[78]

If the Parliamentary Labour Party demands disciplined loyalty from its members, the national Party organization has to give the M.P.s who are loyal some protection against whimsical action by local parties or cabals instituted by unrepresentative minorities which happen to be influential in the constituency units. The rules that Transport House is charged with enforcing are designed to make it difficult for a local party to deny a sitting M.P. another chance at his seat.[79] These rules provide that, in the case of a constituency party with a sitting M.P., the machinery for selecting the candidate will ordinarily *not* be set in motion 'until an election is imminent'. Thus, it is generally assumed that the incumbent, except in extraordinary circumstances, will be readopted; for a party to wait until the onset of a campaign before taking steps to choose a candidate does not allow sufficient time for the regular competitive selection procedures to become operative. Prior to 1970, even in extraordinary circumstances, a GMC that wished to terminate its relationship with the sitting M.P. was forced to go through an intricate process. Each ward unit and every affiliated organization in the constituency was required to hold meetings and to *mandate* delegates who would then attend a meeting of the General Management Committee where the problem of the M.P. was to be discussed and a resolution urging his retirement was to be voted on. Under this arrangement, preliminary bouts had to be fought out in each of the party's units before the main encounter could take place in the GMC, and in each contest the M.P. had the advantage of being considered without competition from known alternatives. If there had been a slip-up anywhere along the way, the NEC could intervene to influence the result.[80]

Since 1974, however, more Labour M.P.s have been confronted with readoption problems than ever before – a situation that is an outgrowth of several factors. In the first place, the National Executive Committee has stopped compiling a formal list of proscribed organizations, which makes it a bit easier for political extremists – who are still constitutionally ineligible for Party membership – to become active in some of the local organizations.[81] A second factor involves a modification of the rules, which was instituted by the 1970 Conference upon the recommendation of the NEC.[82] The rule change made no mention of the strict mandating procedure for the wards and the affiliated organizations. Opportunities for wide consultation, however, still exist. The General Management Committee holds an initial meeting to decide whether the machinery for replacing the M.P. should be put into operation. If the decision is in the affirmative, the people involved in local party affairs have a period of at least four weeks in which to discuss the issue, and then at a specially convened meeting the GMC delegates cast their votes on a resolution to request the M.P. to retire from the seat at the next election. Under the new rules, the M.P. who has suffered defeat at the GMC meeting has the right to appeal the decision to the entire membership of the National Executive Committee which has the authority 'to confirm, vary, or reverse' the local party's verdict.

Two other factors have merged with the two we have already mentioned to precipitate unrest in some of the constituencies and to create a measure of insecurity for the sitting M.P.s. Whereas in earlier times disputes between a local party and its parliamentary member were often ironed out through the informal mediation of the National Agent and the casualty list was small, these matters are now brought officially to the NEC, and its members have been inclined to consider only whether the stipulated *procedures* have been followed and not to look at the substantive issues involved. In other words, if the appeal to the NEC is to have a chance of success, there must be evidence to show that constitutional procedures have been violated. Under these circumstances, the NEC members have been less willing than previously to call for a reversal of local party action against their M.P.s in readoption cases. The NEC's approach to constituency party problems comes at a time when many activists on the local scene have grown unhappy about what they perceive to be the ignoring of Conference decisions by the Labour members of parliament. They feel that the M.P.s who have supported cuts in public expenditures and other anti-inflation measures of the Labour Government have violated Conference directives and sections of the Party Manifesto. The Labour members who have voted in favor of the Common Market have been special targets of criticism. So strong is the feeling among some party activists that proposals have been advanced to enable a local party to hold a selection conference during the lifetime of every parliament for the purpose of either endorsing the M.P.'s record or removing him from office.[83] As one delegate to the 1974 Conference put the matter, 'If the Parliamentarians are not going to take note of the Conference, then let us make them take note of the constituencies.'[84]

As a result of these developments, the local parties have attempted with much greater frequency either to bring their M.P.s to account or to try to unload them in time for the next election, and in a number of constituencies the struggle between the 'moderates' and the 'left' has been sharpened. It will be instructive to examine some of these cases briefly and to speculate about their implications in terms of an M.P.'s obligations to his local party and to the Party leaders in parliament.

The first case is of a special type and calls for little discussion in this context. On the eve of the election in February 1974, the local party at Blyth took steps to disown its sitting member, Edward J. Milne, on the ground that he had unfairly alleged corruption in Labour local government in the North-east region.[85] The M.P. and the local party officials, including the agent, had been battling for some time, and Transport House had conducted an inquiry in 1971. Just as the first 1974 election campaign was about to begin, the union that had sponsored Milne requested another inquiry, and in a series of quick actions the NEC officers authorized the Blyth party to go through the procedures for selecting a new candidate. Milne was invited to resubmit his name to a competitive selection conference, but he refused to do so. He fought and won the election as an independent candidate, but lost it the following October.

A different sort of complaint was lodged in 1974 against Edward Griffiths, the Labour member for Sheffield Brightside.[86] Some of the GMC members found his views to be too moderate and his life-style inappropriate for a Labour M.P. They also accused him of failing to keep his promise to move into the constituency and of being ineffective in parliament and inattentive to his responsibilities in Brightside. When the resolution went against him by a vote of 40 to 10, Griffiths turned the matter over to the NEC, which rejected his appeal for the reason that the procedures had not been violated. The GMC offered him the opportunity to be on the short list for the selection conference, but he declined. In his view, he was the victim of a coup engineered by extremists, and he fought the next election as an independent – unsuccessfully.

A more publicized case occurred in Lincoln, where Richard Taverne was the Labour member.[87] His difficulty with the local party started when he voted in parliament to support Britain's entry into the Common Market. According to some reports, the organization had fallen under the influence of left-wing activists, and the officers had urged him to abstain rather than vote with the Tories. After his defiance of the whips the GMC passed a no-confidence resolution against him by a vote of 54 to 50. An effort to carry the matter further resulted in a tied vote in an ambiguous GMC proceeding. At a special meeting in June 1972, however, the GMC delegates resolved by a vote of 75 to 50 to sack Taverne because, in the agent's words, he 'failed to take into account the views of the people who put him there as M.P.'. When he appealed against the decision to the National Executive Committee, the investigative team unanimously upheld the appeal because there had been inadequate 'consultation' among the Party members in the constituency. The full NEC, however, reversed the inquiry report, apparently contending that there had been no breach of the Party Constitution. Taverne then resigned his seat and precipitated a by-election, which he won. With the support of his 'Social Democratic Action', he managed to hold on to the seat in February 1974, but he lost it in the next election.

The M.P.s who jumped the whip in 1971 to support Britain's entry into the Common Market were in a difficult situation, for not only were they voting with the Tory Government, but they were also taking a position that was incongruent with a Conference decision. Efforts were reportedly made to whip up feelings in the constituencies against the pro-Market rebels, and several of them were haled before their local GMCs to explain their behavior.[88]

By all odds, the most celebrated case of a local party deposing an incumbent Member of Parliament was at Newham North-East, a declining urban area of London.[89] The M.P. was Reginald Prentice, who was also a member of the Labour Cabinet. Most of the criticisms made in the other dismissal proceedings could not be levelled against Prentice; apparently the most serious complaint that could be filed against him was his tendency to be a trifle blunt and persistent in his public utterances. He kicked up a storm when he warned the unions not to 'welch' on the social contract and later when he urged the 'moderates' to stand up and be counted in the struggle against the 'militants'.

The Newham party, operating in safe territory, suffered from some of the weaknesses that often afflict organizations in Labour strongholds. The individual membership had dwindled, and the activists had become engrossed in the affairs of the borough council to the neglect of their party work. By 1975, the constituency was in the throes of demographic change, as young people in white-collar occupations were moving into the district to take advantage of cheaper housing. Some of these newcomers — young teachers, technicians, students, and trade unionists — became involved in the work of the local party, and before long a core of young 'leftists' was pitted against the small band of elderly 'moderates'. An aging party with a tiny Labour membership is relatively easy to take over, and the newcomers quickly got control of several ward clubs and trade union branches. (A Conservative party in a safe Tory area is not so vulnerable to take over because it manages to keep a high number of active members.) According to Prentice, the small left-wing group was not representative of the Labour Party members in the constituency and it certainly did not speak for the massive army of Labour voters. In any event, the party decided to put the machinery for displacing M.P.s in motion.

The proposed action naturally attracted a great deal of attention throughout the country, not only because of Prentice's status, but also because of its political implications. In a communication to the Newham party, a national organization to promote Labour Party democracy expressed the view that an M.P. is responsible to the 'party organization which was instrumental to his selection and election'. Recognizing the potential ramifications of such an outlook for democracy in the wider national context, about half of the Cabinet officials and the other ministers and more than half of the back-benchers signed a letter to the local party in support of Prentice. Two days before the GMC meeting, the Prime Minister himself issued a statement in behalf of his Cabinet colleague.

On July 23, 1975, the GMC delegates rebuked Prentice by a vote of 29 to 19, suggesting that he step down at the next election. The case dragged on for several months, however, owing to questions about the voting eligibility of some GMC participants, NEC inquiry and mediation, an appeal to the Annual Conference, and even a court writ to halt the proceedings of one of the GMC meetings. During this time the M.P. tried to cultivate his grass-roots strength and to get his supporters elected to local party offices. This effort, however, was not successful, and the members of the General Management Committee reaffirmed its original decision and eventually received authorization to begin the process of selecting another candidate. In July 1977, the moderates, led by two young people, managed to take control with the aid of other judicial instruments. But this victory came too late to help Prentice retain the candidature, for he had already refused to countenance the use of the courts.

Reginald Prentice's inability to assert his political dominance quickly in Newham certainly did not discourage activists in other constituencies from trying to persuade their M.P.s to retire. Difficulties between the parliamentary representative and the local party were reported in such constituencies as Lambeth Vauxhall; Normanton; Nottingham East; Liverpool Toxteth; Manchester Blackley; Sheffield Attercliffe; Warley East; Islington North; Kettering; and Northampton North.[90] By mid-1977, grievances had been sharpened to such a degree in four other constituencies that the denial of readoption procedures were invoked. Some of the Party members in Hillingdon, Hayes and Harlington grew increasingly displeased with the political outlook of their member, Neville Sandelson, including his stand in favor of the Common Market and his failure to call for the release of the Shrewsbury pickets.[91] Sandelson had also been a leader in drumming up support for Reg Prentice, and this activity did not win him much support at his home base. He lost in the preliminary bouts, but managed to hang on to his seat by a narrow margin of 24 to 21 at the special meeting of his General Management Committee. A similar course of events transpired in Bradford West, where a core of activists sought to unseat Edward Lyons, reportedly for not taking part in an anti-fascist conference.[92] In the party election, however, the pro-Lyons people managed to retain most of the offices, and the censure motion was defeated 42 to 20.

The other two cases did not result in victories for the incumbents. In December 1971, the Edge Hill party in Liverpool decided by a vote of 11 to 9 to drop its member, Sir Arthur Irvine, who had represented the constituency since 1947.[93] This decision was later reversed by the National Executive Committee. Six years later, the local party decided to try again, giving as its reason 'inadequate representation of the constituency' as evidenced by failure to ask questions in the House of Commons and relatively poor attendance at roll calls. At the special GMC meeting held in May 1977, the delegates voted 37 to 3 to request him to relinquish the seat at the next election. The other victim at the hands of his local party was Frank Tomney of Hammersmith North, who had served the constituency since 1950.[94] Friction had been developing between him and some of the local activists for some time, and there had been several previous attempts to persuade him to step down. Although the formal complaint charged that he was not 'doing his job fully', Tomney's views on the Market, the Government's foreign policy, and capital punishment probably alienated some of the party workers. In any event, the GMC vote was 45 to 31 to urge him to retire, and he lost his appeal to the NEC.

A few of these cases involved M.P.s who had precipitated discontent in their parties which 'leftist' elements were able to exploit, and in some instances the difficulties eventually blew over. But what is noteworthy about these cases of disagreement between the M.P.s and their local parties is that a good number of the M.P.s were 'non-leftists' who had run into difficulty by voting their convictions on the Common Market and/or by supporting the Labour Government in the division lobbies on issues that were often unpopular at home and considered to be 'non-socialist'. At Westminster, the government whips were making traditional demands upon the Labour Member, and the constituency activists, in an effort to exhibit their hostility toward aspects of their Government's program, were attempting to impose a competing mandate upon him.

Some local Labour parties tried to insure accountability by exacting pledges from their prospective parliamentary candidates at the time of selection. Prior to getting on the short list, the aspirants for the seat at Lambeth, Vauxhall, for example, were asked to give a voluntary undertaking that they would offer themselves for competitive re-selection at the end of the third session of parliament, or earlier if the GMC so requested.[95] Under this arrangement, the local people could summon their M.P. to an accounting after any vote in the division lobbies that was not to their liking. The NEC's Organization Committee decided that attempts to secure such guarantees from would-be candidates went beyond constitutional limits. Along the same line, the GMC of the Kensington and Chelsea party reached an understanding with its candidate that she would stand aside at the next general election if her performance proved to be unsatisfactory to the delegates.[96] She would be free, however, to exercise her right of appeal to the National Executive Committee. She also agreed to abide by the *decisions of the GMC* with respect to the election of party officers and the *interpretation and implementation of Party policy* when applicable to the local scene. The pledge was designed to make possible 'redress' for parliamentary behavior that was antithetical to the program which the candidate had supported during the election campaign.

The Yorkshire area council of the National Union of Mineworkers also took steps to impose restrictions upon its trade union-sponsored M.P.s.[97] After censuring its Labour members who had opposed union policy by campaigning against Britain's withdrawal from the European Community at the time of the referendum, it established a set of guidelines for future parliamenatary behavior. Under this edict the Yorkshire mining M.P.s were to agree not to vote against trade union policy on any major issue; refusal to agree to or violation of the guidelines would result in the withdrawal of sponsorship. Later the Committee on Privileges of the House of Commons held that the resolution of the Yorkshire area council was a serious invasion of parliamentary privilege, and in any event the resolution was nullified by the governing body of the National Union of Mineworkers. The Yorkshire mining M.P.s ultimately received votes of confidence from their constituency parties.

The turmoil in the constituency parties since 1974 has been reflected to some degree in the division lobbies of the House of Commons. Compared with the intake of new M.P.s at other times, the newcomers to parliament in the two 1974 elections have exhibited a relatively high degree of dissidence. In seven major 'floor rebellions' during the Wilson tenure (between October 1974 and April 1976), the proportion of the 1974 first-timers who rebelled against the Party leadership in more than half of the divisions was 47 per cent – a rate of revolt that was more than twice as high as that of the other groups, except for the 1966 contingent (27 per cent).[98]

The developments we have seen – growing discord between the external Party and the majority of Labour M.P.s, more challenges to the Party leadership at the Conference, the transfer of factional disputes from the Conference to the Parliamentary Labour Party, and the increased tendency of local parties to attempt the unseating of their representatives – creates a serious problem for the Labour Party. Obviously, the selection of a parliamentary candidate should not constitute a life-time endorsement, nor is it desirable for a local party to retain an M.P. who has demonstrably lost the confidence of a large, *genuine* majority of its active members. But care must be taken to insure that the important decision to deny readoption is not made by a small clique which is unrepresentative of Labour opinion but which is able to manipulate the party machinery. For an M.P. to be displaced because he has been loyal to the national Party leadership he has pledged himself to support undermines Labour's discipline in the House of Commons. If Party solidarity is to be maintained in parliament, the M.P.s who are usually faithful to the whip, especially on issues that may be unpopular in certain constituencies, need to be assured of some protection against reprisals by local party activists. For a Member of Parliament to become *responsible*, in effect, to a thin majority of people in a local organization (which may quickly change from time to time) would require a reexamination of the traditional democratic underpinnings of the British political system.

A Member of Parliament, of course, can be most effective in his constituency when he is able to gain and sustain the confidence of the local activists. Mutual respect between the M.P. and his local party is especially important in the marginal districts, where the political stakes are on the line at every general election. A 'moderate' M.P. is often able to get along in a party of firebrands if he maintains an interest in its development and cultivates good personal relations. Even when the local enthusiasts disagree with him on major issues, their potentially hostile feelings are often dampened if they can view him as a 'good constituency man'. As one activist put the matter, 'So long as the M.P. keeps in touch with us and is attentive to our problems and concerns, we will put up with a great deal in terms of his personal stands on policies.'

The Member of Parliament is expected to do what he can to defend the interests of his constituency, usually on such questions as unemployment, foreign invasion of the cotton market, local government reform, or the disruption caused by highway construction. In the House of Commons, he might be able to advertise a local grievance through a Private Member's Bill (if he is lucky in the drawing) or by participating in a regular debate (if the issue appears on the Order Paper and he can 'catch the Speaker's eye'). But these are not the typical ways of pursuing constituency matters. More likely, he will put down a question for the Question Period, try to bring up the issue during the late evening debate on adjournment, or just 'have a word' with one of the Party leaders or ministers. Some local parties feel so strongly about constituency affairs that they prefer not to have an M.P. who might become a minister, since ministerial responsibilities might result in his neglect of the local scene. Some activists insist upon having a local man as their parliamentary representative – or someone who lives close by – so that he will be accessible to the people who require his services.[99]

Much of the work of the 'good constituency M.P.' takes place within the district. He makes an appearance at important community gatherings – prize-givings at local schools, special church services, sports contests, the dedication of public buildings, etc. Occasionally, a flamboyant member may attempt a publicity stunt in behalf of a constituency improvement, as organizing a 'demonstration' which holds up traffic during the rush hour. One of the time-consuming activities of a Labour M.P. is his regular 'surgery', which is usually scheduled weekly or fortnightly on a Friday evening or Saturday morning.[100] At his surgery, the Labour member holds individual conferences with local residents who are confronted with problems. Constituents solicit his help when they have difficulties with housing, when they have trouble getting their pensions or other benefits, when they wish to lodge complaints against local officials, or even when they are struggling with family problems. Here the M.P. performs in an expediting and 'Ombudsman' role. He is able to explain the administrative procedures to the constituent, assisting in the drawing up and filing of the complaint. If the borough officials or an officer in a national ministry are suspected of error, the M.P. will request them to investigate the matter promptly, though this will not entitle the complainant to any special consideration. Compared with borough council members, he has a more intimate knowledge of bureaucratic procedures and stands a better chance of commanding the attention of the administrative officials. In cases of great injustice (usually rare), the M.P. may be stimulated to request an interview with the minister, or even to raise a question in parliament. In this type of personal welfare work, however, the rules and administrative procedures may make it impossible for the M.P. to do much, except to lend a sympathetic ear and assist in drawing attention to the case. He probably does not gain many extra votes by helping people in difficulty, but he engages in this type of activity because he sees the need for it. As he renders assistance, the M.P. becomes more acutely aware of the problems confronting the inhabitants of his constituency, and he, along with other M.P.s who encounter similar problems of major significance, will relay this information to their parliamentary leaders.

The 'good constituency man' does not neglect his local party. He will try to attend its main social events, and whenever possible he will come to the meetings of the General Management Committee. In some parties, he gives a 'parliamentary report' as a regular item on the agenda. In any event, the GMC delegates relish the opportunity to chat with their M.P. and occasionally to turn over particular problems to him; it is a source of satisfaction when they are able to tell their work-mates the next day that the M.P. is 'looking into the matter'. Usually, however, the Labour member must be careful not to interfere in purely local affairs, especially borough council matters, for this would result in his 'taking sides' on some issues and thus alienating a segment of the activists and the voters. The member of parliament must carefully 'nurse' his constituency on a continuing basis – but judiciously; when he develops healthy attachments to his local party, he is in a better position to weather the storm when his views on national issues clash with those of his local supporters.

This completes our general discussion of Labour Party organization and how the local constituency parties fit into it. We shall now turn to the specific analysis of three of these parties, looking first at the contrasting 'environments' in which they are called upon to conduct their activities.

3 Socio-economic Settings in Three Constituencies

This study focuses upon three parliamentary constituencies in the London area during 1961–62: Bermondsey, whose adult citizens cast a heavy vote for the Labour Party; Fulham, which is usually classified as a 'Labour marginal', i.e., the voting is close, but it has a Labour Member of Parliament; and South Kensington, which is solid in its support for the Conservatives.[1] At the risk of flourishing the obvious, we should point out again that a constituency party has to make its way within a given 'socio-economic environment', and that this 'setting' will have a profound influence upon the organization and its tasks. The economic features of the area will determine in large measure the class structure of the community. The class structure will influence the political preferences of the adult citizens, and these in turn will affect the role and functions of the local party, its patterns of administration, and its reward structure. The industrial and demographic character of the district will determine the pool of potential recruits available to the party and will influence the nature and stability of the leadership, as well as the types of organizations that become affiliated with the local party and provide competing outlets for political activity.

In this chapter, we shall first draw separate sketches of the industrial and social development of the three constituencies – Bermondsey, Fulham, and South Kensington. With this preliminary work on the canvas, we can then look at the socio-economic profiles in a more comparative way. At this point, we are interested in examining the relationship of the respective settings to four elements of political life: (1) the political preferences of the voters; (2) the make-up of the leadership in the local party; (3) the stability of the party leadership; and (4) the role of affiliated organizations in the local party. While in terms of socio-economic features each constituency embraces areas that bear some resemblance to areas in the other two, we shall discover that as aggregate units the three constituencies are markedly different in most respects, and that the distinctive setting of each district helps to define the nature of the local party and the tasks it faces.

BERMONDSEY

Until shortly after World War II, the borough of Bermondsey was divided into two parliamentary constituencies — Bermondsey West and Rotherhithe. But, owing to the decline of population which had begun during the war, the two districts were amalgamated in 1949 to form the single parliamentary constituency of Bermondsey, whose boundaries coincided with the lines of the borough. Hence, in contrast with Fulham and South Kensington, to describe the Bermondsey constituency is to characterize the borough itself, whose long history and complex social structure should ignite the interest of more scholars.

A comparatively small area (1724 acres), Bermondsey is a riverside community, which is located along the south bank of the River Thames and stretches from the old location of London Bridge to the Surrey Docks. The best landmark for the foreign visitor is the Tower of London which lies just across the river to the north-west. From ancient times to the present, the Thames has helped to shape the character of the area. Early records show that what is now Bermondsey was once only a reach of marshland — Boermund's 'eye', or the island of Boermund, named after a Saxon lord.[2] A short distance up the river was 'rethra hythe' (the 'haven of sailors'), the Saxon name from which Rotherhithe is derived. Today the three and one-half miles of river frontage mark the boundary for two sides of the constituency and are the site for long lines of docks, wharves, and warehouses where ships from many lands discharge their cargoes and where thousands of Bermondsey people find employment.[3] Parts of the constituency are built upon reclaimed marshland, which is below sea-level. One section of the district is partially cut off by the river on one side and by the Surrey Docks on the other and has to be reached in places by small suspension bridges. Referred to by the natives as 'down-town', this cut-off area is vulnerable to occasional flooding at high tide, and the dwellings have to be of brick construction on raised levels.

Bermondsey figures in the early annals of English history when it was a rural village. Although its name appears in some ancient records and the area was the scene of important military engagements in olden times, Bermondsey was probably best known for its Abbey, founded as a Cluniac monastery in 1082. As a center of religious life and learning situated close by the Tower Bridge Road junction, the Abbey was the meeting-place for early parliaments, and it attracted royalty and other notables to its grounds. The Abbey began to decline in the fifteenth century, and all that remain today are fragments of walls — and a few street and place-names dedicated to its memory.

Some of the primitive industry, developed long before the industrial revolution, left its imprint upon the later economic life of Bermondsey. A tanning and leather industry, for example, was started in the fourteenth century, and this trade was expanded after 1560, with the arrival of the Huguenots. Although the leather crafts declined in importance in the nineteenth century, tanners were numerous in Bermondsey until 1940. Some Bermondsey people still make their living in the leather trade, and the leathermakers' union has its national headquarters in the constituency. Even today a leather market operates in Leathermarket Ward, and not far away Tanner Street, Morocco Street, and Lamb Walk are lingering testimony to a once-flourishing industry.

Other crafts besides leather-making had an early beginning in Bermondsey — brewing, carpentry, hatmaking, gunpowder manufacture, and goldsmith work. Refugee craftsmen who migrated from France and settled in the district helped to develop these new types of enterprise. Much of the craft work was carried on in people's homes or in tiny workshops employing local laborers. Some of these trades still exist, although they are not as conspicuous as the leather industry.

Despite the stirring of manufacturing enterprise, Bermondsey retained much of its rural character until the latter part of the eighteenth century, except for its expanding maritime activities. Especially in the Rotherhithe district, the building, repairing, and manning of wooden ships was an industry of growing importance and, as in modern times, many people were engaged in the loading and unloading of vessels which stopped at the local port on the Thames. In fact, Rotherhithe at this early stage had an indirect influence upon the course of American history; the *Mayflower* was built in Rotherhithe, its owners and crew were residents of the district, and the ship's master, Christopher Jones, is buried in the parish churchyard.

The outlines of a modern industrial complex were formed in Bermondsey during the latter part of the eighteenth century. Between 1750 and 1800, the first docks were constructed, in 1807 the great Commercial Dock was built, and during the following decades other companies moved into the waterfront to set up new facilities and expand the old ones. The economic patterns were filled out in the nineteenth century when entrepreneurs constructed railway lines and depots and established large factories and commercial houses. The building of Tower Bridge in 1886—94 provided an important radial connection with other parts of London, making it easier to transport the ship's cargoes which were unloaded in Bermondsey's docks.

These industrial developments increased the demand for manual labor — a feature of the Bermondsey economy that still persists. In the 1840s and 1850s, the supply of local manpower was insufficient to fill the need, and workers had to be brought in from the outside. Many of the new recruits came from Ireland; according to estimates, about one-third of Bermondsey's inhabitants during this period were Irish.[4] The Irish Catholic component of the population is still noticeable in the constituency, and many of these people work on the docks.

The rapid growth of shipping, railway transportation, and factory production brought with it the social problems that generally plagued Britain's urban industrial life.[5] The industrial revolution and the increase in population contributed to squalid living conditions. The prevailing picture was one of wretched, back-to-back houses with inadequate ventilation and unhealthy sanitation, as vividly portrayed by Charles Dickens in his description of Jacob's Island in *Oliver Twist*. Serious illness and disease were endemic in the area, and the rate of infant mortality was very high. These conditions, exacerbated by the uncertainty of employment for casual labor and the low wages paid to manual workers, marked Bermondsey as a 'depressed area', where some of Britain's worst poverty was to be found. Children had little choice but to leave school at an early age and take their places in the labor market. Young mothers were forced to go to work in factories and workshops, usually as sweated laborers in unskilled jobs. Some of the older Bermondsey folk who cooperated with the author in this study were victims of this impoverishment before and shortly after the turn of the century. Economic and social tragedy was reflected in some of their remarks on the questionnaires: 'I had to leave school at age nine to begin to help out', or 'There wasn't any time for leisure, what with the children and my work.'

In the closing decades of the nineteenth century, Bermondsey's plight became the subject of several official investigations, and religious and social workers became active in the area, distributing relief to the needy, carrying on mission activities, establishing settlement houses and schools for neglected children, and conducting education classes for working people. After 1900, the sordid conditions of life in industrial Britain captured the attention of national political leaders, and gradually the situation in Bermondsey began to show some signs of improvement. The trade unions gained in strength, and they exerted pressure for wage increases and improved working conditions in the factories. A series of parliamentary enactments, which were designed to better the position of Britain's working classes, reinforced the developments that were already under way in East London and in the region south of the Thames.

Not content to rely upon legislative action at Westminster, the citizens of Bermondsey took steps on their own to improve living conditions in the district, and the national press hailed their social program as a model for other communities.[6] Early in the century, the borough leaders began to tackle the problem of public health. In 1901, the council created the position of Public Health Officer on a full-time basis, and during the next three decades the community, under the imaginative leadership of Dr Alfred Salter,[7] pioneered in the establishment of a public health center, a sanatorium, a convalescent home for mothers and children, and several infant welfare centers. The Bermondsey council also embarked upon programs of slum clearance, and in the 1920s it became a leader in the construction of local public housing. Under wider powers granted by statute in 1930, it established a Building Works Department — a municipal construction agency with its own workshops and labor force — to tackle the job of transforming the slums. During this reform period, the council sought to brighten the grim industrial surroundings by converting an old workhouse into a recreation site, by building playgrounds, and by developing parks and gardens. One project called for the planting of trees along the streets — an innovation for industrial centers at the time — and today the visitor can walk for miles along the tree-lined streets of the constituency. By the time the depression struck, the council had improved the health of the community and the housing of its people, and had succeeded in bringing a little color and gaiety to the drab industrial setting.

The depression of the 1930s, of course, halted Bermondsey's progress and made the blemishes of poverty in the area more visible. A working-class district with a heavy component of casual and manual laborers was bound to be hit by the job shortage, and in 1932 the unemployment rate among the insured population was 17.8 per cent, compared with 13.5 per cent for London as a whole.[8] Many families became destitute, falling into dependence upon meager allotments from the 'dole' or the benefaction of private charity. Added to the woes of many people was the humiliation of being subjected to a 'means test' before they could receive food and clothing for their children. According to a local Labour party official, one of the reasons why the GMC members in Bermondsey did not return as many of their questionnaires in comparison with the other two constituencies was because some people were still suspicious of lengthy inquiry forms, having been forced to fill them out under trying conditions in the 1930s. One respondent, who had served on the Board of Guardians during the depression, recalled that she and her colleagues had been personally surcharged by the government for having included in the requests for food allowances some needy fathers who were not eligible under the strict terms of the law. Despite these difficulties, however, the Bermondsey council still managed to replace 3000 slum houses with 3500 new dwellings in the decade of the 1930s, providing modern accommodations for about 17,000 people.[9] But it was an era of severe economic struggle, and the hardships of the depression remain vivid in the recollections of many Bermondsey citizens.

Britain had not emerged from the depression when World War II broke out, and Bermondsey sustained some of the worst devastation of the conflict.[10] Its industrial area — with the valuable wharves, railways, and factories — was a primary target for the Nazis, who began to blast it in September 1940 and continued their destruction until the end of the war with a total of 1288 raids and 28 V-bombs. More than 900 people were killed and 3000 more were injured as a result of the Nazi attacks. Many of the docks and other industrial establishments were destroyed, and relatively few dwellings were left undamaged. The bombers did not spare much of the public housing or many of the welfare buildings which the borough council had worked so hard to construct. Widespread evacuation of Bermondsey's inhabitants reduced the population from 95,500 in 1939 to 45,440 in 1943.

After the war, Bermondsey turned to the difficult task of reconstruction – the rebuilding of the docks, the restoration of the factories, and the rehousing of its people. By 1946, the population of the borough had climbed to 56,320, rising to 60,661 in 1951, an increase that made the housing problem worse. To handle the problem, the council proceeded to convert bomb-sites and to requisition unfit properties, and by the end of 1962 it had erected 1923 new dwellings, in addition to repairing damaged ones, and had started construction on nearly 400 more. In the early 1950s the number of Bermondsey residents began to decline again, largely as a result of housing clearance and the resettlement of families outside the borough. By 1961, the population had settled at a figure of 51,860.

The Bermondsey Economy in the Post-war Era

As in past decades, the pattern of economic life in Bermondsey in the early 1960s was centered around the river and its wharf-lined banks. The constituency was an important landing-point for ships carrying foodstuffs, building materials, and other produce from Continental and Commonwealth ports, and several thousands of Bermondsey workers were employed along the river front, unloading cargoes on the docks and transporting them to other sections of London. Since food products constitute a high proportion of the imports, huge warehouses, food-processing factories, and refrigeration plants have been built close to the wharves, and these offer employment to large numbers of local residents, including many women. When foreign ships berth in Bermondsey's docks to discharge their freight, the distribution of the products requires the services of importers, shipping brokers, forwarding agents, and cargo superintendents – an important form of enterprise in the constituency. The import trade in food provisions is centered in a large exchange where the produce is graded and where buyers and sellers come together to negotiate their transactions.

In addition to food storage and processing, Bermondsey is the scene of other important manufacturing activities. These industries range from the making of biscuits, chocolates, jams, custards, rice products, and similar commodities to the manufacture of cardboard boxes, bags, paints, and glue. The constituency is dotted with machine-shops and engineering plants which turn out heating appliances, ventilating equipment, optical machinery, scientific instruments, etc. Several leathermaking and brewing firms, which were established in Bermondsey long ago, operate ancient trades in modern form. Local workers are also engaged in such enterprises as hatmaking, garment manufacture, printing, woodworking, grain milling, and related pursuits.

Bermondsey does not have any large shopping districts or many business office centers. Most of the shops and stores which cater to the daily needs of the residents are small concerns, owned and operated by individual tradesmen and their families. One of the largest shops in the constituency is the local Co-operative store. Many of the commercial firms involved in shipping have small offices in large buildings at the north-west corner of the district, near Tower Bridge and the old London Bridge site in Saints Ward. Here are located the dairy producers, a few solicitors, businessmen who mediate transactions between importers and wholesalers, and a scattering of other commercial specialists. Although these business and professional people have their offices in the constituency, very few of them live there.

Bermondsey, then, is an area of industrial concentration, with a heavy emphasis on shipping, truck and railway transport, and manufacturing. Partly because of its location, its association with the river, and its traditional economic patterns, most of the adult residents are employed as skilled and lesser skilled workers on the docks, in the factories, and in the trucking and railway yards. About 43 per cent of the labor force is employed in 'production' enterprises (as opposed to 'service' occupations), and nearly 18 per cent of these production workers are women, a much higher figure than in the other two constituencies.[11] Moreover, a relatively high proportion of Bermondsey's working people—45 per cent—find their employment within the confines of the constituency.

As we would anticipate, the workers in Bermondsey are well organized, and the trade unions command their support, even though they may not attend the branch meetings regularly. The unions are not as active in the Labour Party as they were in the immediate post-war years, but, as we shall see, they play a greater role in the affairs of the Bermondsey party than is the case in the other two constituencies. A total of forty-six trade union branches were affiliated with the constituency organization at the time of this study, and they were a cross-section of the industry of the district.[12] The Co-operative movement has also developed firm roots in Bermondsey, mainly represented by the Royal Arsenal Co-operative Society which has its strength in the region south of the Thames. The people associated with the co-operative had sizeable representation in the Bermondsey Labour party.

FULHAM

Like Bermondsey, the borough of Fulham used to embrace two parliamentary constituencies, Fulham East and Fulham West. In the 1954 reapportionment, however, the new constituency of Barons Court was carved out of the boroughs of Fulham and Hammersmith, and it included two wards from Fulham East and one ward from the West. The remainder of the borough of Fulham was designated as the parliamentary constituency of Fulham. Thus, in contrast with Bermondsey, the Fulham parliamentary district covers only a portion – though the largest part – of the borough of Fulham; the rest of the borough is in the Barons Court district. Such an arrangement creates problems for the political organizers, especially when the agents in two different constituencies are called upon to fight elections for the same borough council.

Fulham is also a riparian constituency, just across the river from Battersea and bordering along the north bank of the Thames from the Chelsea Basin upstream for about three miles. The foreign visitor can see Fulham when he arrives at the Hammersmith flyover on the way in from the airport. Unlike Bermondsey, Fulham is not cut off from its neighboring areas, having easy linkages by river bridges and arterial highways. Although the river has influenced the development of the district, it is too far inland to be an important landing area. Most of the wharves are small and are concentrated in Sands End Ward in the northeastern part of the constituency.

The history of Fulham goes back to the year 1691, when the Bishop of Hereford granted a manor to the Bishop of London.[13] The bestowal referred to the area as 'Fulanham', considered by some authorities to be the Saxon expression for 'place of fowls'. In one of their invasions, the Danes wintered in the district, using the sunken marshland as part of their defensive barrier. The Domesday Book, in which the name appears as 'Fuleham', refers to a hamlet and farmland. While some of the land was free, the Bishop of London in the early days had about fifty tenants. The little community centered around the church, and the vestry – a meeting of parishoners – became the unit of local government. It expanded to include both Fulham and Hammersmith, and they were not separated again until the seventeenth century.[14]

Since ancient times, Fulham Palace on the bank of the Thames has been the official residence of the Bishops of London. Members of royal families have been entertained in the Palace, and Fulham figures in some of the seventeenth-century struggles between the king and parliament. In bygone years, the district was something of a center for literature and the arts. Important personages resided in Parsons Green, the aristocratic part of the district – the novelists Samuel Richardson and Edward Bulwer-Lytton; Henry Hallam, the essayist; Sir Arthur Sullivan, the

Socio-economic Settings

composer; John Locke, the philosopher; Alexander Pope, the poet; and others, including several artists.

Despite the existence of a waterway, the pattern of economic development in Fulham was considerably different from that of Bermondsey. Until the middle of the nineteenth century, the area was distinctly rural and was famous for its market-gardens which were cultivated intensively and supplied vegetables, fruit, and flowers for Covent Garden, the principal clearing-house for produce in London. One of the first branches of the Union of Agricultural Workers was organized in Fulham. Although most of the people were engaged in these agricultural pursuits, some of the inhabitants were attracted to the pottery industry, which developed as early as the seventeenth century and continues to flourish. Other early crafts included the manufacture of patent casks, brick-making, and the weaving of luxury carpets and tapestries.

In the wake of the industrial revolution, the market-gardens were gradually taken over by the developers and the builders, and business men established some light industries which formed the base for Fulham's modern economic life — ironmongering, precision engineering, carpentry, contracting, the manufacture of bags and cartons, and similar lines of endeavor. Although by 1914 Fulham had a good number of small factories and workshops, many of them along the banks of the Thames, the area still had a lot of open space with patches of woodland and bridle paths. In the inter-war period, however, the district rapidly became 'built-up'. Construction companies erected terrace-type housing to accommodate the expanding population as people moved into the district to seek employment in the workshops and on the docks. By this time, parts of Fulham had taken on many of the features of a working-class community with drab, monotonous streets which were lined with houses already becoming dilapidated.

After World War I, the borough council began to recognize the urgency of the housing problem, and in the 1920s it undertook the building or purchase of some municipal dwellings. In the period from 1934 to 1939, however, the local authority began to tackle the problem with more vigor. Recognizing a particular need in the working-class districts of Sands End Ward and Walham Ward, it constructed such housing developments as Carnwarth House, John Dwight House, William Parnell House, and Fulham Court. The demands of the war halted the efforts to alleviate the housing problem, and the wartime destruction made the situation much more critical.

Although Fulham's fuel industry was a strategic target, the area suffered most of its damage from missiles that were overshooting or undershooting other marks. The worst bombing occurred in the areas of slum housing, which the borough council had already scheduled for demolition. When the European War ended, the Fulham council, like its counterpart in Bermondsey, turned to the task of reconstruction. Firms of builders formed themselves into a war-damage repair organization and placed their services at the disposal of the local authority. The council acquired bomb-sites and cleared them out, and it earmarked slum dwellings for removal. Large blocks of flats as well as single dwelling units began to emerge from the ruins and the dismantled slum streets. By 1960, more than 1500 buildings had been constructed, including a block of flats — Sulivan Court — which consists of 432 dwellings and four shops. Many more units had been repaired and brought back into occupation. Just as Bermondsey had done before the war, the Fulham councillors gave special attention to the landscaping of the estates and, in addition, to varied types of architecture. As a result of these efforts, what is now the Fulham constituency began to cast off its gloomy look and to take on a brighter appearance.

The Fulham Economy in the Post-war Era

Although the inhabitants of the Fulham constituency engage in a wide range of occupations, the district cannot be classified as heavily industrial. It is for the most part a dormitory area to which many people have moved in order to escape from the high rents being charged in the more fashionable residential centers of London. About 65 per cent of the people who reside in the constituency, including many factory workers, find employment outside the area.

Fulham, of course, does have an industrial core of its own, but the industrial complex is not as large or as significant as Bermondsey's. The biggest industry is oil refining and gas, which is centered in Sands End Ward and Walham Ward, where fuel is produced and distributed for a large part of the London region. Some Fulham citizens also find employment in shipping and transportation; the wharves, docks, and terminal depots are a noticeable feature of the economy. A large number of taximen live in the district, and two large taxi garages are located there. Although there are a few vehicle-building firms, most of the factories, workshops, and mills are comparatively small. These establishments produce such products as air-compressors, cisterns, hose fittings, paper bags, pneumatic tools, motor lubricants, and stoneware. The building construction industry is also an important local enterprise.

Large shopping establishments are few in number, and the daily needs of the residents are supplied largely by small-scale tradesmen who manage their shops in the main thoroughfares. A remnant of Fulham's agricultural past is the Saturday market at the North End Road on the border of the constituency. Here the barrow salesmen, whose stalls are lined up along one side of the street, display their garden produce and household wares, and crowds of local housewives stop by with their shopping bags to purchase their weekend supplies of vegetables and fruit.

The Fulham constituency, then, comes closer to being a microcosm of London than do either Bermondsey or South Kensington. Its variegated residential areas, as we shall see, draw from all socio-economic groups, and its inhabitants engage in all types of occupations, either within the district or in other parts of London. Local industry – fuel manufacture, shipping and transport, motor vehicle building and repairing, and factory production of light industrial items – provides employment for slightly more than one-third of the people. Whereas 43 per cent of Bermondsey's labor force are engaged in 'production' industries and 18 per cent of the workers are women, about 37 per cent of the Fulham workers are engaged in 'production' enterprises and 9 per cent of them are women.[15]

Although the trade unions in the Fulham constituency are not as numerous as they are in Bermondsey and tend to play a less active role in local Labour party affairs, they are nevertheless an important feature of the economic landscape. Some union branches – such as the National Union of General and Municipal Workers, which embraces the workers in the gas industry, and the National Union of Vehicle Builders – are strong enough to afford full-time secretaries and organizers. At the time of this study, a total of twenty-three trade union branches were associated with the local party, compared with forty-six in Bermondsey.[16] The Co-operative movement is also fairly strong in the constituency, and the Fulham Co-operative Party and a Women's Co-operative Guild are affiliated with the local Labour party.

SOUTH KENSINGTON

At the time of this study, the borough of Kensington was divided into two parliamentary constituencies – Kensington North and Kensington South. In its socio-economic and political complexion, North Kensington lies in sharp contrast with its neighbor to the south. Although clusters of elegant residences are plentiful, the district has large pockets of overcrowded tenements and deteriorated housing. It also has sites of small-scale industrial enterprise and streets of outdoor markets. Before the war, North Kensington was, like the rest of the borough, a safe Conservative preserve, though the residents of the slum areas exhibited signs of political unhappiness. In 1945, however, North Kensington sent the Labour candidate to parliament, and the Labour Party has continued to retain a marginal hold on the constituency in succeeding elections.

The constituency of South Kensington – a vastly different area – lies between Kensington Gardens (an extension of Hyde Park) and the

Fulham district. Holland Park Avenue and Notting Hill Gate separate it from North Kensington, and Fulham Road on the south marks its boundary with Chelsea. The River Thames is too far away to have had much influence, and radial thoroughfares provide easy linkages with other parts of the metropolis.

Like Bermondsey and Fulham, the South Kensington district is registered in the chronicles of ancient Britain.[17] Its name is derived from 'Cynesige', a Saxon family which settled there in early times. After the Norman Conquest, the area became a manor, with Aubrey de Vere as the 'tenant-in-chief' under the authority of the crown, and it remained with the family for generations. The original manorial court was at Earls Court, which in modern times became the name of one of the wards. The hamlet was centered around the church, and the area remained under vestry control until 1901, when Queen Victoria and King Edward VII made it a royal borough. The eastern edge of the constituency is the site of Kensington Palace, which was made a royal residence by William III, who sought clean air as relief for his asthma. At various times, later monarchs and the members of their families lived in the Palace, and Queen Victoria was born there. While it continues to provide accommodation for the relatives and friends of the sovereign, it also houses a museum which features exhibits of historical and contemporary life in London.

Less than two hundred years ago, Kensington was little more than a cluster of hamlets in a distinctly rural setting. Although large, luxurious residences were beginning to mark the landscape, what were to become blocks of residential housing and ribbons of pavement were then only grassland, vineyards, and fields devoted to animal husbandry, horticulture, and the cultivation of farm produce. In the nineteenth century, the South Kesington district grew into an exclusive residential area, attracting many upper-class families. As was to be expected, it became a center of intellectual and artistic life; such illustrious people as John Stuart Mill, Carlyle, Thackeray, and Macaulay were listed on the tax rolls. Parts of the constituency still retain their eighteenth-century character, and a few late Georgian survivals are to be found here and there. Some of the fine residences of older vintage on the edge of the constituency are now occupied by foreign embassies.

The industrial revolution brought no unsightly factories to the southern part of Kensington. In the decades prior to World War II, the district continued its development as a fashionable residential area characterized by stately homes, high rents, many beautiful gardens, some historic churches, and a few museums and exhibition halls. There were, to be sure, small pockets of working-class habitation, but even during the depression South Kensington did not bear the marks of poverty which were prevalent in most sections of London.

With the outbreak of the war, the constituency did not escape the bombing, but it was not much of a target compared with the more industrial parts of the metropolis. The area around Victoria Road and Kensington High Street suffered the most damage. Nevertheless, the task of reconstruction was costly, and since the end of the war South Kensington has been afflicted by a severe housing shortage. The borough council, however, has poured most of the money allocated for housing into North Kensington, where the need was perceived to be greater. The people seeking accommodation in South Kensington have had to depend largely upon private rentals, and many property-owners have subdivided their dwelling spaces in order to increase the number of tenants.

The South Kensington Economy in the Post-war Era

As is evident from what has already been said, South Kensington is for the most part a 'silk stocking' residential area. There are, however, large 'bed-sitter' sections which cater to the geographically mobile elements of the population. The smokestacks of factories are a rare sight in the constituency. Although there is a flourishing building trade, most of the companies are involved in 'servicing' types of business enterprise.

While small tradesmen operate their own grocery, tobacco, and produce shops on some of the main streets and entrepreneurs of a larger scale carry on their businesses in the recently developed section of Notting Hill Gate, the fashionable shopping and commercial center is on Kensington High Street. Here are located blocks of business and professional offices, some large department stores, furnishing and decorating firms, exclusive fashion shops, antique dealers, and similar establishments. Many of these have moved to South Kensington from sites in the center of London. The larger shopping areas are relatively few in number, and for the most part they cater to an affluent clientele.

Given the residential character of South Kensington, it should come as no surprise that slightly more than two-thirds of the inhabitants hold jobs beyond the boundaries of the Kensington area. Only 21 per cent of the labor force is engaged in production enterprise, and only 7 per cent of these workers are females. The overwhelming proportion of the employed adults—78 per cent—are engaged in service occupations.

Nor should it be surprising that the trade unions are not very active in South Kensington and that no union has its headquarters in the constituency. The unions that claim substantial membership reflect the socio-economic composition of the district—the Clerical and Administrative Workers Union, the National Union of Teachers, and the National Union of Journalists. At the time of this study, however, none of these unions was affiliated with the South Kensington Labour Party. Only three trade-union branches had entered into liaison with the constituency organization, each of them sending one delegate to the

General Management Committee: the National Union of Railwaymen, the Transport and General Workers Union, and the Association of Engineering and Shipbuilding Draughtsmen. In each of these cases of affiliation, the GMC member had exerted pressure on the branch to become associated with the party, and had taken the initiative to become the union delegate, even though the branches themselves were not very active in South Kensington. Needless to say, the Co-operative organizations were non-existent in the constituency.

SOCIO-ECONOMIC MAKE-UP OF THE CONSTITUENCIES

This brief glance at the historical development and economic structures of Bermondsey, Fulham, and South Kensington provides the background for a more detailed examination of the socio-economic composition of the three districts. The economic patterns of an area obviously have an important effect upon the social composition of the population and the 'social context' of the district. In this section we shall look at the general 'community' features of each constituency, and then examine its social configuration along specific dimensions.

General 'Community' Features

As the previous discussion suggests, Bermondsey represents a traditional, working-class community, whose inhabitants are overwhelmingly engaged in manual labor. Moreover, in comparison with the other two constituencies, its population is geographically stable. The census reports list only 6.5 per cent of the people as having recently moved from their domiciles, and nearly half of the 'mobiles' (2.7 per cent) merely changed their places of residence inside the constituency. In other words, less than 4 per cent of the inhabitants had moved to Bermondsey from other places. Unlike other sections of London, the area attracts very few transient workers who come to live in the constituency, although there is a movement of workers to and from the district each day to handle their job assignments. Most of the adult Bermondsians have lived in the community for long periods of time. Many of them were born there, they attended the local schools, they selected their marriage partners in the community, and they continue to live in close proximity to their kinship groups.

Bermondsey's isolated position on the riverside, the homogeneity of its social structure, the strong family linkages, and the shared experiences of hardship during the depression and the bombing have combined to weld it into a tightly-knit community with a distinctive character. You can detect a change in life-style as soon as you cross the Thames, and after a few visits you becomes aware of the working-class 'solidarity'. Compared with the other two constituencies, Bermondsey is more of a 'natural community'. A large proportion of the wage-earners hold jobs within a short distance from their homes, and the social life of most of the people is confined to local activities – bingo games, dances, sports events, weekend outings, variety programs sponsored by the borough council, and the entertainment provided by a large number of youth clubs.

In such a social environment, the radius of human relationships tends to be conspicuously localized. The people in Bermondsey are inclined to keep in close touch with the members of their extended families and to nurture intimate links of friendship with certain neighbors and with their work-mates. Within these networks of marital alliances and neighborhood friendships, there is a tradition of sharing and 'helping out'. In addition to being helpful in times of emergency, relatives and close friends assist each other in fixing up their homes, taking care of the children, and picking up groceries at the shop. Frequently, they lend each other household articles, and it is not unusual for them to share expenses on a joint holiday. Occasionally, they even lend each other money to help out in an emergency or to help to 'resist the tide' until payday.

Life in a relatively self-contained community has fostered sentiments of local loyalty and dignity among the Bermondsey people. They are proud of their style of living and their working-class values, and they regard manual labor, especially the work on the docks, as a prestigious calling. Many of the young men follow the careers of their fathers. The new council estates are a source of pride for Bermondsey's citizens who spend a lot of time arranging their flats or sprucing up their homes. To them Bermondsey is virtually native soil, and they are visibly pleased with their borough – its municipal housing, the public baths and the library, the schools and hospitals, and the recreation program. A feeling of community among the people was especially manifest during the wartime bombing attacks. A local tradesman described the solidarity of the Bermondsey inhabitants in this way: 'When we flocked into the air-raid shelters, we seemed to be like one big family. First, we would see to it that the old people, the women, and the children were comfortable. Then we would have some community singing, and sometimes we would act out little skits to take people's minds off the danger. In some ways, the war sort of brought us close together!' A sense of distinctive group spirit still lingers in Bermondsey.

As a marginal constituency, Fulham lies between Bermondsey and South Kensington on the socio-economic map. Parts of the constituency may easily be described as working-class, but there are also select, 'aristocratic' areas which contain some of the most costly housing in London. About 69 per cent of the occupied males are employed as skilled or lesser-skilled workers, but about 31 per cent of the male labor force are listed in non-manual occupations, large numbers of them in clerical work. In terms of demographic stability, Fulham's population is somewhat more mobile than Bermondsey's, but much less so than the population of South Kensington. According to the census figures, nearly 10 per cent of the Fulham people had recently changed domiciles — 4.5 per cent from inside the area and 5.3 per cent from other districts. Like Bermondsey to some extent, Fulham has many long-term residents — people who were born in the locality or who moved there when they were in their teens or as young adults.

Even though a stretch of the riverside defines part of the constituency boundary, Fulham is not 'self-contained' in the sense that Bermondsey is, and it cannot be described as a 'natural community'. The constituency is a blend of middle-class and working-class elements which produces a diversity of social and cultural interests. Easy access to the world outside, the large proportion of people who work outside the constituency boundaries, and the variegated structure of the population facilitate networks of social contacts that extend some distance beyond the confines of Fulham. Nevertheless, distinct traces of community consciousness can be detected in the constituency, especially among the residents of long standing and some of the young people. Fulham is the scene of many local activities, including a municipal open-air theater which offers a range of entertainment from Shakespearean drama and symphony performances to jazz concerts. As in Bermondsey, many of Fulham's residents take a special pride in the borough's progress.

South Kensington occupies a position on the opposite end of the socio-economic spectrum. An area of high rental property, it is distinctively middle-class in composition — the habitat of some retired people with respectable incomes, business executives, professional people, and intermediate and lower grades of office workers, most of whom travel back and forth to jobs outside the constituency. In sharp contrast with the other two districts, the population of South Kensington has a high rate of geographic mobility. Census reports indicate that as many as 25 per cent of the inhabitants are 'movers', and nearly 19 per cent of them have migrated from other boroughs to take up residence in the constituency. As we shall see, the population of South Kensington has a high component of single people, especially young women. The area also has a high proportion of students (7 per cent), many of whom live in the crowded bed-sitter section of Earls Court Ward.

South Kensington obviously lacks the ingredients that make Bermondsey — and Fulham to a lesser extent — a comparatively integrated community. The overwhelming majority of its residents were not born there, and intricate webs of relationships among family and neighborhood groups are extremely difficult to detect. The middle-class complexion of the district and easy access to urban pleasures help to nurture diverse interests among all sections of the population. There is little need for municipally-sponsored entertainment, even if the borough council had been inclined to provide it. Far from relying upon local facilities as the center of social life, the people of South Kensington — young and old alike — are attracted by the rich fare of activities and diversions to be found near the center of London.

To obtain a more exacting view of the socio-economic make-up of the three constituencies, it will be instructive to place the descriptive data in juxtaposition so that they can be seen in closer comparison. In this format, we shall examine the three areas on the basis of social class; distribution by age, marital status, sex, and national origin; and housing arrangements. This will provide us with a more complete view of the social contexts which influence the political life of the three constituencies.

Social Class

Although the term 'social class' is used frequently, scholars define it in so many different ways that its meaning is not always precise.[18] Implicit in its use is the assumption that recognizable social divisions exist in a given society — an assumption that has had ample empirical investigation in the case of Britain. Some form of stratification prevails in every social system, and in most instances the hierarchical structuring is related to the share of available wealth (goods and services) that particular groups are able to command. Distinctions based upon social class, then, involve the ordering of the population into categories based upon the differential capacity of various groups to control the resources of the larger community.

In their work on stratification in different societies, scholars have found that income and occupation are fairly sensitive measures of objective social class. Although the British census does not provide information on personal income, we can make use of occupation, with education as a supplementary measure. Both of these measures of social class have proved to be reliable in Great Britain, where social stratification has a decided impact upon political outlooks and behavior. An individual's occupation usually plays a crucial role in relating him to the social order; the job he works at involves an assignment in the stratification system. Usually a person's job is the main source of income, and it sets limits upon the supply of goods and services he is able to secure, as well as providing a type of association and experience which influences cognition. By the same token, the level of education attained is associated with the type of job held; indeed, education is one avenue of mobility through which people of working-class origin may be able to move to middle-class status.

The census reports give us a breakdown of occupations for employed males arranged in the following categories: (1) Professional people;

(2) Employers and managers; (3) Non-manual workers, largely in routine clerical posts; (4) Skilled manual workers; and (5) Lesser-skilled manual workers.[19] Thus, groups 1 and 2 represent 'middle-class' occupations, with group 3, which includes lower-grade office workers of various sorts, being peripherally connected with the 'middle-class' category but with many of its members being psychologically identified with the 'working class'. Categories 4 and 5 include the broad array of manual workers with different degrees of skill. Table 3.1 presents an occupational dissection of the gainfully employed males in the three constituencies under examination.

Table 3.1 Occupations of employed males

Occupation	London	Bermondsey	Fulham	South Kensington
Professional & managerial	*12.6%*	5.1	10.0	35.3
Non-manual	*21.3*	13.0	20.8	35.5
Skilled manual	*34.3*	36.8	37.7	12.2
Lesser-skilled	*31.9*	45.1	31.6	17.0

From this information, it is easy to see that Bermondsey, with 82 per cent of the employed males engaged in manual labor, is overwhelmingly a 'one-class' constituency. There are, to be sure, little hollows of difference scattered throughout the area, but only a small fraction of the male wage-earners are classified under the three non-manual categories, and most of these have jobs as clerks, receptionists, and other routine work. That Bermondsey is largely a homogeneous district can be seen from an analysis of social class composition in the thirteen wards. Here the proportion of occupied males who are employed in manual work ranges from 77 per cent to 87 per cent – and the ward with the lowest figure still contains more manual workers than the strongest working-class districts of Fulham. Only two wards – Saints and Dockyard – have as many as 10 per cent of the male workers in the professional/employer/manager category; comparable figures for the other units in Bermondsey vary from 2 per cent to 6 per cent. The largest spread among the wards – from 8 per cent to 18 per cent – occurs in the non-manual group, but even here the ward with the largest roster of non-manual employees is only slightly above the lowest of all the wards in the other two constituencies.

Table 3.1 shows a mixed configuration in Fulham–about 69 per cent of the employed males are in the manual worker class, while an additional 21 per cent are lower-grade office workers in the non-manual category, and 10 per cent are in the professional/managerial category. In three of the wards, manual workers comprise 70 per cent or more of the population, while in two wards—Town and Hurlingham—the proportion drops to 64 per cent and 60 per cent, respectively. The proportion of employed males in the non-manual category ranges from 18 per cent in Sands End Ward to 36 per cent in Hurlingham Ward. Although the number of male workers in the professional/managerial category is hardly sensational, it is still twice as large as Bermondsey's. In the two strongest Labour wards, it represents about 7 per cent of the employed male population, slightly more than 10 per cent in two other wards, and 16 per cent in Hurlingham Ward.

The data in Table 3.1 portray South Kensington as a constituency of an entirely different character. While it cannot be classified as 'solidly middle-class', large pockets of uniformly middle-class areas are easy to find, and the district as a whole comes closer to fitting the description than most places in London. More than one-third of the employed males hold professional and managerial jobs, and when the non-manual workers in group 2 are added to the roster, the size of the non-manual group increases to 71 per cent. We must point out, however, that South Kensington does not have the degree of social-class homogeneity on its side of the spectrum that Bermondsey has on the other side. The proportion of professional/managerial functionaries in the four wards ranges from 28 per cent to 45 per cent; and one ward—Redcliffe—registers only 59 per cent in the non-manual category, compared with more than 70 per cent in the other three wards. Similarly, while the range of manual workers in most of South Kensington is between 23 per cent and 29 per cent, the figure in Redcliffe Ward is 34 per cent.

Another useful index of social class is the level of education attained by various groups in the population. This can be measured in terms of the age at which people left school, and these data for the three constituencies are presented in Table 3.2.[20]

Table 3.2 Age at termination of formal education

School-leaving age	London	Bermondsey	Fulham	South Kensington
15 or under	78.1%	89.7	76.1	27.6
16–19	16.8	7.9	18.5	46.8
20 or later	4.6	1.0	2.3	18.4
Current students	0.5	1.4	3.0	7.2

The data on education predictably coincide with the data on male occupations. In Bermondsey, the proportion of citizens who terminated their education at age fifteen or earlier is more than 89 per cent in nine of the thirteen wards. The picture in Fulham is more uneven. In three of the wards, the percentage of early school-leavers ranges between 79 and 83 per cent, but in Town Ward it is only 69 per cent and in Hurlingham Ward it is about 65 per cent. Similarly, the proportion of Fulham people with advanced education is between 4 per cent and 6 per cent in Town and Hurlingham Wards, while the rest of the constituency hovers around the 1 per cent mark. Compared with Bermondsey and Fulham, the pattern is reversed in South Kensington, where the proportion of early school-leavers is only about 26 per cent, although in Redcliffe Ward the figure is 32 per cent. On the other hand, the proportion of South Kensington respondents who managed to remain in school beyond the age of twenty ranges from 17 per cent in Redcliffe Ward to slightly more than 21 per cent in Holland Ward.

Population Distribution by Age, Marital Status, Sex, and National Origin

On these dimensions, the population of South Kensington is markedly different from Bermondsey and Fulham, as we would expect from what we already know about the three constituencies. In general, the people of South Kensington are younger, fewer of them are married, females outnumber the males, and the constituency is much more cosmopolitan in terms of national origin.

In considering the age distribution, we can point out that while only about 26 per cent of the people in Bermondsey and Fulham who are of employable age (fifteen and above) are below the age of thirty-five, the figure for South Kensington is 41 per cent. This constituency also has the smallest number of 'pensioners'. Fulham has the largest number of people in the pensionable age bracket, with a proportion well above the norm for all of London.

South Kensington is also characterized by the relatively small number of ordinary family households. Whereas married couples constitute between 63 per cent and 65 per cent of the adult population in Bermondsey and Fulham, the figure is only 38 per cent in South Kensington. Indeed, more than one-half of the adult inhabitants are listed as living in 'no family' households. This demographic feature is reflected in the number of children below the age of fifteen as a proportion of the entire population: Bermondsey, nearly 25 per cent; Fulham 18 per cent; and South Kensington, 9.5 per cent (a figure far below the London norm). Slightly more than half of the adults in South Kensington are single, and single females comprise almost one-third of the adult population. While Bermondsey has only 81 single females for every 100 single males and Fulham has 97, South Kensington is a vividly contrasting haven for women, with a distribution of 159 single females for every 100 single males. When we combine the single people and the marrieds on the basis of every 100 males, the famale ratio for

Bermondsey is 108; Fulham, 113; and South Kensington, 144 (in the 15–24 age bracket the ratio is 167).

Urban Britain is characterized by a high degree of female employment in middle-class as well as working-class districts. The proportion of South Kensington women who work is 53 per cent, compared with 44 per cent in Bermondsey and 42 per cent in Fulham. Most of the women workers in South Kensington, however, are single, and many of them have recently migrated to the area from other parts of London or from other sections of Britain. The bulk of them are employed as clerical workers or are engaged in professional and technical work, especially as teachers, nurses, laboratory specialists, and the like.

In Bermondsey and Fulham, it is the 'non-single' women, largely those in the 'married' category, who constitute an important segment of the labor force and a very large proportion of the total women workers. Non-single women in Bermondsey and Fulham make up 27 per cent and 25 per cent, respectively, of the *total labor force*, while in South Kensington they comprise only 16 per cent. The figures for non-single women as a proportion of the *total women workers* are: Bermondsey, 68 per cent; Fulham, 66 per cent; and South Kensington, 32 per cent. Married women workers, then, are an important feature of the two most working-class constituencies, while single women workers characterize South Kensington.

The industrial setting in Bermondsey has traditionally attracted married women into the labor force on a full-time or part-time basis.[21] For the most part, they hold skilled or lesser-skilled jobs in the 'production' side of the economy – in the food-processing factories, the textile plants, and similar establishments. Fulham's industrial configuration, on the other hand, does not provide as many opportunities for married women to work near their homes, especially those who have manual skills. Fewer of the married women are engaged in strictly manufacturing enterprise, but they find employment in nearby shops, restaurants, and offices, while many of those with professional and clerical skills travel to work outside the constituency.

In reporting on ethnic composition, the census authorities work from data that are based entirely upon birthplace statistics, thus accounting for only first-generation immigrants from other countries. These data reveal marked social contrasts among the three constituencies in terms of national origin. According to the 1961 census, only 4 per cent of Bermondsey's inhabitants were born in other lands and 12 per cent of the Fulham people were non-natives; but the figure for South Kensington is 33 per cent.

Very few of the Bermondsey people were born in the newer Commonwealth nations or in other foreign countries, apart from Ireland. Only in one ward – Raymouth – do the non-Irish foreign-born comprise as much as 3 per cent of the population, and most of these people are immigrants from Cyprus. But the Irish do constitute an important segment of the population, the size of which is underestimated by the birth statistics of the census. Large clusters of Irish folk are to be found at each end of the constituency — along the river front to the north and west in Dockyard and Tunnel Wards, and farther up the river to the north-east and east in Saints, Leathermarket, and Southwest Wards. Two Roman Catholic churches in each of these locations serve the religious needs of the Irish community. Tunnel Ward has a large number of single women within its borders, and a sizeable percentage of these young ladies are Irish. As we have already noted, many of the Irish people in Bermondsey work as dockers, truck-drivers, construction workers, and general laborers, and the women find employment in the food-processing and clothing manufacturing establishments.

In Fulham, the non-Caucasian folk make up less than 3 per cent of the population, and they are clustered in three wards — Sands End, Town, and Hurlingham. Other foreign nationalities (apart from the Irish) comprise 4 per cent of the population, and they tend to live in the better residential wards, Town and Hurlingham. The Irish, listed at 5 per cent of the population, are fairly evenly scattered throughout the constituency, ranging in the five wards from 4 per cent to 6 per cent of the inhabitants. Five Roman Catholic churches minister to their religious interests.

In contrast with the other two constituencies, South Kensington is an extremely cosmopolitan area. The largest groups of non-Caucasians reside in Earls Court and Redcliffe Wards, where the proportions are 6 per cent and slightly more than 7 per cent, respectively. The other non-Irish nationalities (22 per cent of the total population) are to be found in sizeable numbers in all sections of the constituency, with the largest proportions living in Earls Court and Holland Wards, and the smallest concentration in Redcliffe Ward. Some nationalities tend to group in particular districts. A community of Polish people, for example, lives in the southern part of the constituency and extends into a portion of the Fulham area. The biggest concentration of Irish people, who make up slightly more than 5 per cent of the population, is in Redcliffe Ward, where many of them are employed as semi-skilled and lesser-skilled workers and in the catering trade and personal service. Three Roman Catholic churches — including Brompton Oratory, the largest church of its denomination apart from Westminster Cathedral — serve the religious needs of this community.

Housing Arrangements

Since housing has been a difficult problem in London since the war, becoming a dramatic political issue on many occasions, the housing conditions in the three constituencies represent an important part of their socio-economic setting. Moreover, studies have shown that the number of people living in council housing correlates significantly with the size of the Labour Party's vote. The data on housing tenure for the three districts is presented in Table 3.3.

Table 3.3 Type of housing tenure by household*

Housing Tenure	London	Bermondsey	Fulham	South Kensington
Owner-occupiers	15.6%	1.7	20.6	12.6
Council housing	21.2	48.8	9.3	1.8
Private rental	59.8	44.2	67.7	80.1

* The proportions do not add up to 100% because the housing that is rented as part of a job contract has been omitted.

The startling figures in Table 3.3 are the paucity of home owners in Bermondsey and the high proportion of people who live in council housing. In 1962, more than one-third of the residential property was owned by the borough, but the proportion of public housing was somewhat higher owing to a number of housing estates that had been built by the London County Council. The LCC units brought people from other parts of London into Bermondsey, and some of the 'newcomers' have experienced difficulty in fitting into the traditional community.

The Bermondsey statistics in Table 3.3, of course, hide some of the patterns of variation within the constituency. Raymouth Ward, which used to be a Liberal stronghold, has an owner-occupancy rate of 6.5 per cent, and in four of the wards – Tunnel, Dockyard, Abbey, and Neckinger – the proportion of households in council properties exceeds 70 per cent. By the same token, seven wards are above the constituency average in households that rent privately, and these range from 53 per cent to more than 70 per cent. Despite the completion of many council housing estates, the overall density of room occupation is the highest of the three constituencies – a situation that reflects the large number of children in family households and the absence of luxurious privately-owned homes and expensive private rentals. Moreover, the housing picture is still serious in parts of Bermondsey, especially in the wards with a relatively small amount of council housing and a high incidence of rented homes, flats, and rooms. In Central and Thorborn Wards, for example, the proportion of households sharing dwellings is approximately 63 per cent and 44 per cent (compared with a constituency average of 23.7 per cent). Similarly, the wards with fewer council estates and a large number of private rentals usually have a high concentration of households that do not have exclusive access to the basic conveniences.

Of the three constituencies, Fulham has the highest rate of owner-occupancy (nearly 21 per cent of the households). The most plush private homes are in Hurlingham Ward, where the celebrated polo grounds and other social attractions make the area a desirable residential neighborhood for upper-class groups. However, two other wards – Munster, which has a moderate number of people in middle-class occupations, and Sands End, which is heavily working-class – have an even higher rate of owner-occupancy, 24 per cent and 22 per cent. In these two wards, there are masses of terrace-type houses of uneven quality, some of which have long been earmarked for redevelopment. In Munster and Sands End particularly, one encounters large numbers of lower-grade office workers and skilled artisans who managed to purchase their own homes during the interwar years and who take pride in maintaining their property. Since the war, some workers have had to buy the homes they were renting in order to gain the security of tenure they desired, and in their spare time they try to improve their homes, painting the windows and doors with vivid colors to add a touch of individuality to the long rows of identical housing construction.

The housing problem in Fulham has been alleviated considerably by programs of municipal home construction and rehabilitation which, as we have seen, were begun in the mid-1930s.[22] While the average number of households in council housing is slightly below 10 per cent for the entire constituency, parts of the area have a much higher rate. About 20 per cent of the households in Walham Ward, for example, occupy council properties, and in Hurlingham Ward, where a new housing estate – Sulivan Court – accounts for a municipal housing rate of nearly 17 per cent, a 'blue' Conservative ward has been converted into a politically marginal area.

Apart from Hurlingham Ward, where Sulivan Court has reduced the proportion of private rentals to about 60 per cent, the number of Fulham households renting from private landlords ranges between 67 and 70 per cent. Some of this property, such as Rivermead Court in Hurlingham Ward, contains luxury flats which are within the grasp of only the high-income groups. The bulk of the private rentals, however, consists of uniform terrace houses, with a scattering of large, dingy buildings which have been broken up into small units. A large number of households in Fulham have fewer than 0.5 persons to a room; bringing up the percentage in this category are the households in Hurlingham Ward with its high-priced property and Munster Ward with its high incidence of owner-occupiers. The district of highest density of room occupation is Walham Ward, a working-class area with the largest number of youngsters. The degree of dwelling-sharing in Fulham is fairly uniform throughout the constituency (about 30 per cent). But when it comes to households having exclusive access to the basic amenities, Hurlingham Ward is well above the rest of the constituency with 63 per cent, and Town Ward with 50 per cent is better off than the three remaining wards, which vary from 40 per cent to 33 per cent.

While only about 13 per cent of the people in South Kensington households own and occupy their homes, the proportion is higher in the two high-income wards – Holland (18 per cent) and Queens Gate (15 per cent), which harbor some large, luxurious residences. As we have noted, the number of units of council housing is very small; the highest proportion of households living in such property is in Redcliffe Ward, and even there the council house occupancy rate is less than 4 per cent. The vast majority of South Kensington's population live in accommodations rented from private landlords, either individuals or large corporations. The constituency is peppered with huge apartment buildings, some of which contain luxury flats, some two- or three-room units, bed-sitter arrangements, or single rooms without cooking facilities and other conveniences. Some rented homes and apartments, especially in Holland and Queens Gate Wards, are extremely valuable properties, commanding rents that only tenants with good incomes can afford. Entire sections of South Kensington can be characterized as high-class neighborhoods, but it is not unusual to see a splendid home or a block of 'pricey' flats in a run-down district.

Two South Kensington wards – Redcliffe and Earls Court – have the highest proportion of private rentals, 82 per cent and 85 per cent, respectively. Here many people live in crowded quarters – in tiny flats and bed-sitter units – without adequate facilities. It is a common practice for property-owners to divide their houses or large apartments into smaller units so as to accommodate more tenants. In the constituency as a whole, about one-third of the households are in one-room units, the bulk of which are one-person households. In Earls Court Ward, however, nearly 44 per cent of all the households are confined to one-room accommodation. Of the three constituencies, South Kensington has the highest percentage of households with more than 1.5 persons per room, and the density of room occupancy is especially high in Earls Court. In Queens Gate Ward and Holland Ward, the proportion of households sharing dwellings is only 13 per cent and 23 per cent, but the figure rises to 33 per cent in Earls Court Ward and to 43 per cent in Redcliffe Ward. In terms of exclusive access to modern conveniences, the spread in South Kensington is from 82 per cent in Queens Gate Ward to 69 per cent in Redcliffe Ward.

CONTRASTING ENVIRONMENTS AND POLITICAL PATTERNS

Having viewed the socio-economic landscapes of Bermondsey, Fulham, and South Kensington, we are now in a position to add a political dimension to each of the three maps. Basically, we are interested in seeing how the socio-economic environment in each constituency influences some of the political configurations. We shall proceed by looking at the following matters: (1) Voting patterns; (2) types of borough council candidates selected; (3) the social composition of the General Management Committees; (4) the stability of GMC memberships; and (5) representation of trade unions and Co-operative societies.

Voting Patterns

We can get an overview of the voting patterns in the three constituencies by glancing at Table 3.4, which presents the range of the Labour Party vote in the parliamentary elections between 1955 and 1970, and in the elections for the London County Council between 1958 and 1961.

Table 3.4 Labour vote in parliamentary and London County Council Elections

Elections	Bermondsey	Fulham	South Kensington
Parliamentary elections, 1955–70*	77%–81%	54%–58%	13%–24%
LCC elections, 1958–61	82%–89%	55%–67%	7%–14%

* The peak election for Bermondsey and Fulham was in 1966; in South Kensington it was in 1970.

As one can surmise from the table, Bermondsey is one of the most important Labour strongholds in the London area. In fact, in the 1964 election it emerged as the most impregnable seat in London, with a majority of 59 per cent over the Conservatives.[23] Four wards –Abbey, Dockyard, Neckinger, and Southwest – are so solid for Labour that neither the Conservatives nor the Liberals bothered to put up candidates in the borough council elections after 1953, although the Communists entered one of their men in Abbey Ward in 1956. In the period from 1956 through 1962, the Tories regularly contested three wards – Central, Thorburn, and Tunnel – and they filed candidates in Saints Ward in 1962. The Liberals entered the field in Raymouth Ward in 1956 and 1959. But when polling day arrives, opposition candidates are lucky if they can pick up 175 votes in any of the wards. Bermondsey is indeed a safe Labour preserve.

Socio-economic Settings

Since its formation in 1955, Fulham has been a marginal seat in parliamentary elections. Only once — in 1966 — did the Labour majority exceed 5000 votes. The party, however, has customarily polled a bigger vote in the contests for the county and borough councils. For example, in the 1958 LCC election, when the Rent Act was an important local issue, the Labour vote jumped to 67 per cent, and in the borough council elections between 1956 and 1962, the Labour candidates usually garnered about 61–62 per cent of the vote.

Two of the Fulham wards — Sands End and Walham — are rock-ribbed Labour strongholds, and Munster Ward is safely Labour, though the degree of support is not as strong. Town Ward used to be marginal, but in the late 1950s it began to move over gradually into the Labour camp. The weakest Labour area in the Fulham constituency is Hurlingham Ward, which used to be a solid Conservative enclave, sometimes recording a poll of 90 per cent. However, a pocket of manual workers' residences in one corner of the ward and the construction of the Sulivan Court housing estate have cut into the Tory majorities. In 1959, the Labour party won one of the Hurlingham seats on the borough council by a handful of votes, and three years later it won two of the seats by wafer-thin margins. Thus, the population shift in Hurlingham Ward has moved it from the safe Conservative column into the marginal category, at least in local elections.

On the other side of the spectrum, South Kensington is an unassailable political fortress for the Tories. Not only is it the most invulnerable constituency in the London area, but it is also one of the safest seats in all of Britain. In a straight fight in the 1955 election, the South Kensington voters gave the Conservatives their largest majority in the country with 82 per cent of the ballots. The Tories' share of the votes is even higher in local elections, even when the Liberals enter the field. In a contest for seats on the old London County Council, it was not unusual for the Conservative candidates to win approval from more than 85 per cent of the interested electors, and in the borough council election in 1959 they managed to reach the 90 per cent mark. As we might expect from our discussion of the social composition of the constituency, the Labour Party is weakest in Holland and Queens Gate Wards, but draws a bit more support in the other two wards, Earls Court and Redcliffe.

In order to discern the socio-economic basis of Labour Party support in the three constituencies, we shall order the census data on social class (the occupations of employed males) in terms of the areas of Labour strength and weakness in each constituency. We know that Bermondsey is heavily Labour, and we would expect the strong Labour wards in Fulham to be a closer profile of Bermondsey than either the strongest Tory area in Fulham or the Conservative wards in South Kensington. By the same token, Earls Court and Redcliffe Wards in South Kensington should, in contrast with the rest of the constituency, bear at

Table 3.5 Occupations of employed males by political complexion of wards

Area	Professional managerial workers	Non-manual workers	Skilled manual workers	Lesser skilled workers	Total manual workers
South Kensington	35.3%	35.5%	12.2%	17.0%	29.2%
Holland-Queens Gate	42.2	31.9	10.5	15.4	25.9
Earls Court-Redcliffe	30.0	38.3	13.5	18.2	31.7
Fulham	10.0	20.8	37.7	31.6	69.3
Hurlingham	16.2	24.2	33.1	26.4	59.5
Town-Munster	10.9	21.1	37.6	30.3	67.9
Sands End-Walham	6.9	19.2	39.2	34.8	74.0
Bermondsey	5.1	13.0	36.8	45.1	81.9
Contested wards	5.7	12.2	39.2	42.9	82.1
Strong Labour wards	4.8	13.5	35.3	46.5	81.8

least some resemblance to a 'traditional' Labour district.

We present these data in Table 3.5. The format is arranged with South Kensington at the top, and with the two strongest Tory wards (Holland and Queens Gate) in juxtaposition with the other two wards (Earls Court and Redcliffe). Then we move to Fulham, comparing the wards in three groups: (1) Hurlingham Ward, where the Labour Party has its weakest roots; (2) Town and Munster Wards, where Labour is dominant but not so deeply entrenched as it is in the more working-class areas; and (3) Sands End and Walham Wards, the strongest Labour districts in Fulham. When we come to Bermondsey, the problem of differentiation grows a bit more tricky, since the Conservatives do not contest all of the wards. Besides, the comparative homogeneity of the constituency is likely to make the pockets of difference relatively slight. As a basis for differentiation, we have separated the five wards that the Conservatives and Liberals have seen fit to contest in the borough council elections between 1953 and 1962—Thorborn, Saints, Central, Tunnel, and Raymouth—from the other eight wards which never had to contend with opposition to Labour during that period.[24] For purposes of identification in the table, the two groups of Bermondsey wards are designated as 'Contested Wards' and 'Strong Labour'.

These data predictably show that the Labour Party has a consistently weaker hold in those areas where the proportion of professional and managerial people is the highest, and uniformly stronger roots in districts that include the highest numbers of manual workers. Although for reasons of space we shall not include the data, an even more uniform pattern emerges in the wards of the three constituencies when we analyze the educational levels of the electorate as an index of social class.

Table 3.6 Council tenancy and density of room occupancy by household

Area	Council tenants		1–2 person households in five or more rooms	
South Kensington	1.8%		7.5%	
Holland-Queens Gate		20.4		10.1
Earls Court-Redcliffe		79.6		5.6
Fulham	9.3%		6.1%	
Hurlingham		21.8		9.9
Town-Munster		30.4		6.5
Sands End-Walham		47.8		4.2
Bermondsey	48.8%		4.1%	
Contested wards		35.5		4.9
Strong Labour wards		64.6		3.6

Labour's Doorstep Politics in London

We can conclude this section on voting configurations by introducing a self-explanatory table on housing arrangements. Table 3.6 presents information on the distribution of council tenants (using the total number of council tenants households as the base figure) and the density of room occupancy expressed by the percentage of one- or two-person households in five or more rooms. The table shows that the Labour Party tends to pull more votes from districts with council housing and with relatively crowded living conditions.

Types of Borough Council Candidates

As we have already suggested, the social configuration of a constituency has an effect upon the sorts of people who are drawn into the activities of the local Labour party. We can see this in sharper focus if we look at the occupations of all of the borough council candidates who were nominated by the Labour Party and by the opposition Conservative and Liberal parties in the 1959 and 1962 elections. This information is presented in Table 3.7.

Table 3.7 Occupations of borough council candidates, 1959–62

Occupation	Bermondsey		Fulham		South Kensington	
	Labour	Conservative and Liberal	Labour	Conservative and Liberal	Labour	Conservative and Liberal
Professional & managerial	1.7%	–	30.3	29.8	38.8	71.7
Non-manual	37.3	50.0	54.6	48.9	44.9	13.3
Manual	54.2	21.4	15.2	8.5	8.2	1.7
Unclassified	6.8	28.6	–	12.8	8.2	13.3
N	(59)	(14)	(33)	(47)	(49)	(60)

The lopsided nature of Bermondsey's social structure is clearly evident in this table. More than most Labour parties in London, the Bermondsey organization drew its council candidates from the ranks of the manual workers. The Conservative and Liberal parties have also been affected by the Bermondsey environment. Although their small clientele may differ somewhat from the broad mass that supports Labour, they still have to draw their activists from the same homogeneous community. The number of Conservative and Liberal candidates was small, but they came largely from the non-manual, clerical group, with a scattering from the ranks of the skilled workers. None was registered as a representative of the professional/managerial class. In terms of the jobs they held, the opposition candidates bore some resemblance to their counterparts on the Labour side.

Fulham, the marginal constituency, drew only 15 per cent of its Labour candidates from the manual worker category. Crowding aside the working-class representatives were the candidates from the non-manual group — clerks, sales-persons, research workers, and lower-grade civil servants — and from the professional/managerial bracket, including several teachers. The Fulham party has had considerable success in local government elections, and the criteria for candidate recruitment are relatively high. For this reason, people with clerical and professional skills tended to do better in the selection conferences than did the aspirants who held manual jobs. It should be noted that the social make-up of the Labour candidates closely approximated that of the Conservative and Liberal candidates.

The middle-class complexion of the South Kensington constituency is reflected in the types of people who become closely enough identified with the local Labour party to be willing to stand as Labour candidates in a hopeless race for seats on the local council. No less than 39 per cent of them were recruited from the professional/managerial category, and a total of 84 per cent held non-manual positions. The opposition candidates, of course, were even more middle-class in terms of their occupational status, with nearly three-fourths of them being drawn from the professional/managerial group.

Composition of the General Management Committees

Having examined the influence of the constituency environment upon the types of people whom the various parties are able to recruit as borough council candidates, we now turn to the constituency influences upon the recruitment of local Labour activists who take their seats on the General Management Committees of the three parties. Here we are interested in seeing the extent to which the GMC membership reflects the composition of the general population, as well as the ways in which the local party is able to offset the limits of its environment by recruiting leaders from particular categories in the population, e.g., the younger people.

In assessing the class composition of the General Management Committees in the three constituencies, we shall rely upon the two indices employed in the descriptions of the constituencies themselves — occupation and level of formal education completed. The occupational description of the GMC membership is presented in Table 3.8, in juxtaposition with the percentage of employed males in each of the constituencies.

Table 3.8 Occupational description of population and GMC membership

Occupation	Bermondsey Employed Males	GMC	Fulham Employed Males	GMC	South Kensington Employed Males	GMC
Professional/managerial	5.1%	3.4	10.0%	28.3	35.3%	54.1
Non-manual	13.0	30.5	20.8	45.7	35.5	35.1
Manual	81.9	66.1	69.3	26.1	29.2	10.8

Data on social class as reflected in the level of formal education for each constituency population and its General Management Committee are given in Table 3.9.[25]

Table 3.9 Educational description of population and GMC membership

Educational Level	Bermondsey Population	GMC	Fulham Population	GMC	South Kensington Population	GMC
Elementary	89.7%	61.0	76.1%	39.1	27.6%	13.5
Secondary	7.9	39.0	18.5	50.0	46.8	48.7
University	1.0	–	2.3	10.9	18.4	37.9

In all three parties, the level of formal education achieved by the GMC delegates corresponds closely with the type of employment.[26] The university and training college people, as well as some with grammar school diplomas, tend to hold the professional and administrative positions; the intermediate non-manual jobs are held by some secondary school graduates and by some people with elementary schooling who have worked their way up by self-instruction and special adult classes; and the manual workers are for the most part individuals who were forced to leave school at age fifteen or earlier and who have sometimes managed to take technical training at evening school or in connection with their jobs.[27]

When we look at the class composition of the General Management Committees as revealed in Tables 3.8 and 3.9, several patterns immediately come into focus. As one would predict, Bermondsey recruits most of its GMC members from the ranks of the manual workers and from those who had to terminate their education at the elementary level. The Bermondsey party also brings a sizeable number of clerical, non-manual workers to the GMC, but the overwhelming majority of these people come from working-class homes and continue to identify with the working class.

It is not difficult to anticipate the social composition of the GMC in

South Kensington. The local party draws most of its GMC delegates from the professional/managerial category and from those who managed to complete secondary or university education. It also recruits people from the clerical, non-manual group, but most of these people, in contrast with Bermondsey, are of middle-class origin and identify with that class. The GMC members from South Kensington are the group with the highest level of formal education. In fact, about 22 per cent of them attended a 'public school', and 19 per cent of them graduated from Oxford or Cambridge. (Only one of the Fulham delegates attended a public school, and no one from Bermondsey was privileged to do so. Neither the Fulham nor the Bermondsey parties could claim any Oxbridge graduates as members of their Management Committees.)

Fulham follows a somewhat less predictable pattern than Bermondsey and South Kensington. Although a large working-class base exists in the Fulham constituency, the local party draws the largest portion of its GMC members from the clerical, non-manual group, pulling in smaller but relatively equal numbers from the professional/managerial group and from the manual workers. Similarly, most of the Fulham GMC members have completed the secondary educational level. The clerical/non-manual recruits, however, are people who come from working-class backgrounds.

What is clear from the two tables is that the GMC delegates in *all three parties* are recruited in disproportionate numbers from the non-manual and professional/managerial occupations and from corresponding educational backgrounds. Even in middle-class South Kensington, where the proportion of GMC delegates in clerical, non-manual work equals that of the general population, the party recruits in heavy measure from the professional and executive category. Manual workers with only elementary educational credentials are under-represented in all three constituencies.

It may be, of course, that the local parties feel a need for the skills of the people engaged in non-manual work and set about consciously to recruit them; one can find instances of such people becoming involved as a result of agents' efforts. Although all of the parties would suffer greatly without the services of stalwarts who never had the opportunity for advanced formal education but who nevertheless sharpened their skills through experience and self-study, the local officials welcome recruits from all social strata, including those whose formal educational attainments have prepared them for specialized work and the more sophisticated administrative tasks. Moreover, the people in non-manual occupations are often the ones who are fond of grappling with ideas or who become concerned about social reform. Given encouragement, they can be motivated to enter politics in Labour's behalf and to become increasingly engrossed in political work. In contrast, workers with manual skills are harder to recruit for jobs that have to be done after a day of strenuous labor, they are less interested in intellectual exchange, they are inclined to be somewhat apathetic about political affairs, or they are more atrracted to the 'bread-and-butter' objectives of the trade unions.

While the distribution of local party leaders on the basis of social class can be important in an ideological organization, the age profile of the leadership can be useful as an indicator of potential weaknesses in the recruitment patterns. We do not intend to discuss membership problems at this point, but we do want to glance briefly at the age distributions of GMC delegates in relationship with the age groupings of the adult population (age fifteen and over) in each constituency. This information is presented in Table 3.10.

Table 3.10 Age distribution of GMC delegates and constituency populations

Age Category	Bermondsey Population	GMC	Fulham Population	GMC	South Kensington Population	GMC
Under 45	52.4%	27.1	47.8%	43.4	60.1%	67.5
45–64	32.8	50.8	35.8	34.8	27.0	24.3
65 and over	14.8	22.0	16.3	21.7	12.9	8.1

In general, the age structure of the GMC in South Kensington is fairly similar to the age distribution in the entire constituency. As we have already observed, South Kensington is a relatively youthful district, and the bulk of the GMC delegates are drawn from the lower age bracket. The situation is that young people set about to recruit young people into the local party, and in a district that is characterized by geographic mobility, these recruits are not in residence long enough to enter the older delegate categories.

The age distribution of the GMC delegates in Fulham comes even closer to the age profile of the constituency as a whole. Especially distinctive is the recruitment of young people for GMC service in a constituency that has an aging population. The party has been somewhat less successful in recruiting from the 35–44 age bracket, but, as we shall see, the leaders were aware of this potential weakness and have tried to correct it.

The age distribution of Bermondsey's GMC members is the least representative of population in the constituency. In relative terms, the population is quite young; yet the local party recruits disproportionately few of its GMC delegates from the under-45 age group, and draws comparatively large numbers from the advanced age brackets. The problem of an aging leadership, of course, is often related to the stability of the leadership, which we shall now examine.

Stability of GMC Membership

The length of time that an individual has resided in a constituency is likely to have a close relationship to his tenure as a GMC delegate. Obviously, where the population is mobile and party members live in an area for only a limited period of time, the composition of the GMC will undergo more change than in a constituency in which long periods of residence are characteristic of the activists. Stability of GMC tenure may also mean that fewer opportunities are available for new and younger members to move into positions of responsibility in the local party. In this respect the three constituencies are quite different. In Bermondsey, 76 per cent of the GMC members had lived in the district for more than thirty years or since the age of five, while only 3 per cent had lived there for less than ten years. About 52 per cent of the Fulham GMC delegates had lived in the area for the lengthy time period and 13 per cent for less than a decade. The big difference, of course, is seen in South Kensington, where only 3 percent of the GMC members had lived there for at least thirty years or since early childhood, while no less than 60 per cent of them had been residents for ten years or less.

The same picture emerges when we look at the length of time that the activists had served on the GMC. In Bermondsey, 63 per cent of the delegates had been on the GMC for more than ten years, while only 19 per cent had served for three years or less. This stability can partly be accounted for by the paucity of contests for GMC posts. Fulham has a more balanced membership—41 per cent of them had been GMC delegates for more than a decade and 33 per cent had served for three years or less. A partial explanation lies in the relatively large intake of young people and in the active contests for seats on the GMC — sitting delegates are sometimes defeated in their bids for re-election, and some of them are content to nurse their wounds rather than to take the trouble to obtain credentials through other channels. In South Kensington, only 22 per cent of the GMC members had been in their posts for more than a decade, while 51 per cent of them had served for only three years or less. Competition for seats sometimes takes place in some of the wards, but others experience difficulty in filling their quotas because of the rapid turnover of membership. Despite the movement of people into and out of the South Kensington GMC, the composition of that body is more stable than is the rank and file of Party members in the wards. Many ordinary members decline to go on the GMC because they realize that they will not be living in the constituency for very long. This means that the GMC seats are occupied by people who have had longer residence in the area than most of the ward members, even though their period of residence is short by absolute standards.

We can view the relative stability of General Management Committee membership in the three parties even more vividly by comparing the rosters as they existed in 1962 with the delegate lists as they were at the time of the general election in 1964. In Bermondsey, 81 per cent of the 1962 GMC members were still serving, several of the older members having died or retired from active political work. The proportion for the Fulham GMC was 54 per cent. But in the case of South Kensington, only 38 per cent of the members still occupied seats two years later, and all of those who were replaced had moved out of the constituency, including the voluntary agent. (By 1970, the stability rate in South Kensington had been reduced to 18 per cent.)

Clearly, a measure of stability in GMC membership assures a continuity of party leaders who are conversant with the district and are aware of the problems of the organization. Too much stability, on the other hand, tends to diminish the excitement of the political battle and to curtail the possibility that young people will be able to rise in the party with sufficient speed. But the pattern of instability in South Kensington, reflecting as it does the nature of the constituency, presents difficult problems for a political organizer. When the agent and a few key workers move out of the district, the party organization loses much of its continuity and its management falls into the hands of inexperienced people, many of whom are not likely themselves to remain in the constituency for very long.

Trade Union and co-operative Affiliations

We have already made the obvious point that the economic character of a district affects the trade union and co-operative linkages with a local Labour party. In terms of *active* trade unionists who served on the General Management Committees in 1961–62, Bermondsey was far out in front with 48 per cent, Fulham had 26 per cent, and the South Kensington figure was 16 per cent.[28] When it comes to serving on the GMC as a trade-union representative, the breakdown was: Bermondsey, 27 per cent; Fulham, 22 per cent; and South Kensington, 5 per cent.[29]

In none of the parties did the co-operatives command as much support among the GMC delegates as did the trade unions. In terms of active co-operators, the Bermondsey GMC had 12 per cent, the Fulham GMC 15 per cent, and the South Kensington GMC had none. In the case of Bermondsey, 6 per cent of the GMC members owed their positions to Co-operative sponsorship, while in Fulham the proportion was 8 per cent.

This chapter has given us a glimpse of what the three constituencies are like – and how the varied environments make differential imprints upon voting patterns, the composition and stability of the activist corps, and the support base of the trade unions and co-operative organizations.

Socio-economic Settings

The next step in our investigation is to look at the goals and organizational structures of the three parties, and the people who occupy key roles within them.

4 The Constituency Parties: Goals, Organizational Structures, and Key Party Roles

The socio-economic setting of a constituency, within which a local Labour party is forced to perform, establishes the range of its potential achievements and sets an agenda of problems for it to wrestle with. Obviously, the social characteristics of the population influence the resource base from which the organization must draw active workers, as well as affecting the political preferences of voters from which the party must draw its electoral clientele. The nature of the district, in other words, determines the strength of Labour's opposition – an important factor in keeping a political association alive and in defining the type of activities upon which it can efficiently and effectively expend its limited resources.

The contrasting aggregate environments in Bermondsey, Fulham, and South Kensington have profoundly affected the goals, organizational structures, and patterns of operation of the Labour party in each of the constituencies. In this chapter we shall undertake a comparative examination of the three parties in terms of their objectives, their organizational structures and modes, and the people who occupy key roles.

PARTY GOALS

In a constituency like Bermondsey, where, according to a local Conservative, a Tory meeting has been known to attract only the candidate, the agent, two or three relentless supporters, and a policeman, the Conservative opposition offers Labour no more than token skirmishes for selected council seats [1] and is barely able to capture 20 per cent of the votes in a parliamentary election. The Labour party leaders, to be sure, keep raising the specter of Tory opposition (usually by suggesting in a general election that the Labour majority might suffer a decline, or in a local election by pointing out the marginality of Saints Ward), but for all practical purposes the Bermondsey party has 'no one to box with' — a situation that poses a challenge to the party managers who want to keep their organization alive and active.

In Bermondsey, the Labour activists are committed to three explicit goals: winning elections, helping the Labour movement as a whole, and doing a good job of running the borough. These objectives have remained steady in this stable Labour district, and many of the procedures have become routinized. The original objective of achieving electoral victory over a viable opposition has been transformed into one of keeping the Labour majority formidable enough for the party to retain its prestige, and some of the older party members are especially concerned about the local scene. One can detect no support for the argument, occasionally advanced by some leftists in other areas, that the Labour Party should return to its opposition role until the voters become educated in the virtues of pure socialism.

The Labour stalwarts in Bermondsey are also intent upon helping the cause of the Party on a wider scale. As soon as they have put their own electoral house in order, the party mobilizes experienced canvassers for work in one or more marginal constituencies nearby, transporting them in its station wagon. Usually enough volunteers are recruited for this outside work for six or seven evenings during the last fortnight of the campaign and on polling day. The Bermondsey party also performs a number of service assignments for the London Labour Party, whose chairman is the local Member of Parliament.

Since the Bermondsey organization holds all of the seats on the borough council, it is in full charge of local government affairs — a responsibility that consumes the energy of an important segment of the activists, deflecting their interests from exclusively party matters to a broader civic area. Indeed, the party's desire to turn in a good performance record and to resolve the local issues which are generated serve as a stimulus to the organization and help to keep the wheels turning.

The task of keeping the party's goals in sharp focus is not easy in an area where the electoral outcome is always a foregone conclusion. To persuade voters to go to the polls when many of them feel that their ballots will not affect the result requires a great deal of organizational effort. The job of combating apathy is rendered more difficult when challenging trade-union activity attracts potential leadership talent, when the activities of kinship and neighborhood groups absorb leisure time, and when so many youth clubs and settlement houses provide competing alternatives to political work.

In a constituency of this type, party leaders have to be concerned about the survival of the organization. As we shall see, they attempt to meet the problem by organizing membership drives and by trying to interest young people in party affairs. They also seek to hold the organization together by sponsoring a rich program of social events — evenings of bingo, dances, theater parties, day-long outings, a sports day for children, and activities for the older folk. In recent years, the Labour people have built an attractive social club in the party headquarters as a way of developing and sustaining interest in the party.

Political contests in Fulham create an atmosphere of urgency and excitement, because a Labour victory is never assured until all of the votes have been counted. The explicit goal of the local Labour party is to win elections; although some of the activists entertain 'left-wing' views, none of them would like to see either the national Party or the constituency party occupy an oppositional role for even a limited time. Operating in a marginal environment, the local party needs all of the workers it can mobilize at election time, and it cannot afford to dispatch any of them to the tighter races elsewhere, except in the case of by-elections. The party's spectacular success in local council elections has given its activists responsibility for managing the affairs of the borough, which they are forced to carry out under the critical glances of a Tory opposition. Thus, the constituency organization, like that in Bermondsey, has as one of its objectives effective performance in the area of local government. The political uncertainties inherent in their marginal position and the burdens of council responsibility in the face of a viable opposition mean that the interests of the activists are concentrated in the local arena rather than being deflected elsewhere. Indeed, as soon as one election is over, they begin to plan immediately for the next campaign.

While the electoral challenge and the press of borough activities serve to hold the party intact, the leaders are careful not to neglect the social side. The social program is not as varied or as complete as it is in Bermondsey, but the Fulham people manage to sponsor tombola sessions and to schedule an annual dinner, post-election parties, and similar events.

Holding the fort in a district where there is not a single street of Labour supporters, where the Tories have more than 2500 members in one ward alone, and where 50 residents move out of the constituency every day, the South Kensington party must necessarily live a different type of existence from its counterparts in Bermondsey and Fulham. Since electoral success is beyond even the faintest hope, it could, as we suggested in Chapter 1, opt to become a 'political sect', withdrawing from its hostile world and forming an exclusive club devoted to theological disputation over ideological matters; or it could choose to be a 'missionary organization', seeking to carry the socialist message to the world outside in the hope that the overall movement will be furthered by its activities.

The South Kensington activists selected the missionary model for their organization, and the overwhelming majority rejected the idea that the Labour Party should make a sojourn into the political wilderness until the voters called it back on its own terms. Recognizing that they were the leaders of a small, impoverished organization, the South Kensington people consciously marked out for themselves a realistic political goal—to further the progress of the Labour movement as a whole. Such an objective can hardly be immediate and the results are rarely visible, but the Labour members were nevertheless motivated to pursue it.

Their commitment to the goal of helping the Party nationally prompted the activists to contest every election, including all of the seats in local elections. The purpose of this was not only to 'display the Labour flag', but also to pin down at least some of the opposition's resources, thus forcing the Conservatives to go to the expense of providing committee rooms and campaign literature and at the same time preventing them from dispatching all of their available workers to marginal constituencies. The Labour people also felt that by garnering as large a vote as possible for their party they were helping to swell the Labour vote nationally and to make it possible for the Parliamentary Labour Party to claim a strong popular mandate.

In line with its nationally-oriented objective, the South Kensington party tried to make itself helpful in other constituencies. At election time, the activists recruited a brigade of canvassers to lend a hand in winnable districts. The party also made itself available to the regional organizer and to the London Labour Party for various types of service tasks, such as providing stewards for public meetings, speakers for outdoor gatherings, etc. Since a good number of activists resided in South Kensington for such a short time, the secretary sought to help the cause by passing their names along to the Labour organizers in the districts to which they were moving.

In the interim between elections, the people in the South Kensington party conceived of their role as one of political education and initial recruitment. From this objective flowed two types of activities: (1) a series of monthly public meetings in the local library on topics of current interest—forums that were conducted by 'name' speakers who usually attracted good crowds; and (2) weekly street-corner meetings on the Earls Court Road (which at times appeared to be another 'Speakers' Corner') for about six months of the year. The open-air meetings, which the party had instituted in 1959, relied at first on local speakers, but the burden of the schedule and the size of the audience (usually about 100–150) dictated the recruitment of a panel of speakers from other areas to help out. The assumption was that most of the listeners were not South Kensington residents but that the contact might set them to thinking and might even stimulate them to sign up for Party membership.

A party whose goal is fixed upon assisting other constituencies with the aim of benefiting the overall movement runs the risk that the political interests of its members will be deflected to other districts. South Kensington differs from other middle-class, bed-sitter constituencies—like Hampstead and Paddington South—in that there is not a Labour ward, not even a Labour street; hence, the South Kensington activists who aspired to become members of the borough council had to turn their attention to Kensington North, where the bases of Labour strength were. The Labour people in South Kensington would work hard in organizing a 'holding operation' in their home territory, but for more tangible results they had to travel to adjacent constituencies.

Cognizant of their problems, not the least of which was survival, the leaders of the South Kensington party sought to hold the organization together by keeping its activists as busy as possible. Some of the busy work involved politics—the open-air meetings, the public forums, the local elections, and the recruitment of workers for jobs in the marginals; but some of it was social—theater parties, the jumble sales, the annual dinner, and the Sunday rambles, all of which were usually well attended. One fruitful means of involvement was the sponsorship of an old folks' party, which came to be a party tradition. The activists sensed that the pensioners in their district were neglected, and they sought to provide a spot of cheer through a mid-winter supper and social gathering. They sent invitations to people whose names were solicited from the welfare office, and they arranged transportation for about one hundred guests who sat down to a fine meal and an entertainment program. The Labour people were proud of this service to the elderly, which they had performed for nearly a decade at some personal financial cost. They were careful, however, not to use the accumulated guest lists for political purposes. Involvement in this and other local activities, as well as a widespread recognition that their contribution had to be to the movement outside the constituency, helped to keep the party alive and worthy of membership, even though the roster of activists was in a continual state of flux.

PARTY STRUCTURES

Ward Organization

1. *Bermondsey.* The Bermondsey Labour party used to operate through thirteen ward organizations, but the decline in population—owing in part to slum-clearance programs—tended to make the wards too small for organizational purposes. According to the 1961 census, eight of the wards had fewer than 3000 persons above the age of fifteen, and the most populated ward contained only 4700 people in this age category. The outward migration of people, as well as the difficulty of sparking interest in safely Labour territories, prompted the suggestion that adjacent wards be amalgamated for purposes of party activities so that six 'areas

would replace the thirteen wards.[2] Although two wards—Central and Neckinger—resisted integration for several years after the plan was adopted, they were eventually fused in 1960. The combination of wards in five of the areas increased the population so that the range was 6400 to 8400; one area, however, embraced only Saints Ward, where the population was a mere 2300.

The welding of separate party structures into a new formation is a trying process for any organization, and it is especially difficult in a district where the activists are older and local allegiances are deeply rooted. The Bermondsey people had to grapple with the problem in 1949 when Rotherhithe and Bermondsey West were united to form a single constituency. People in both constituencies tended to resist the combination, and several years elapsed before they settled comfortably into the new mold. Even in 1961–62, when a controversial issue arose, it was not uncommon for some of the older members to refer in nostalgic terms to the days when the two constituencies were operating in different parts of the borough. The geographic division was reflected for a long time by the existence of two women's sections within the Bermondsey party.

The problem of selecting new officers and of transferring allegiances was almost as difficult when the wards were combined to form areas. In a district characterized by closely-knit primary associations, the disbanding of long-established political structures disturbs the traditional patterns, and the loyalties to the old ward system tended to linger for some years, although new personal linkages geared to the new structures eventually came into being.

Integration under the area arrangement was finally achieved by making concessions to a partially decentralized form of organization. This development was first evident in the realm of finance, and then, with adequate financial resources, the areas were in a better position to pursue activities and programs on their own. Collective effort at the area level in certain endeavors naturally had its carry-over into the realm of campaigning, where, as we shall see later, a decentralized pattern of administration was utilized.

Each of the old wards had enjoyed independent financial resources which tended to make the members vigilant of their autonomy. Following a practice established in nearby Woolwich, the wards were used to retaining one-fourth of the membership fees for their own coffers; a similar fraction was given to the paid collectors, and one-half was turned over to the treasurer of the constituency party. When the new area arrangement went into effect, the agent and other party leaders managed to persuade the activists in the subordinate units to hand over to the central headquarters all of the subscription money that remained after the collectors had been paid. In return, the party guaranteed to pay the administrative expenses of the areas. But these units were not left penniless, for they were able to claim some of the more lucrative profits from the weekly football pool which the party sponsored. This development came about as a result of pressure from the lower ranks. One of the old wards had been entrepreneuring a football 'tote' of its own, and it was more successful than the one sponsored by the party. The agent sought to combine the two enterprises, and as a concession to the areas it was agreed that revenue from the football pool earnings would be returned to them in proportion to the number of tickets they sold. As a consequence of this decision, the six areas all had funds in their treasuries, some of them rather large amounts. They used these resources to pay the expenses of their delegates to conferences and training schools, to underwrite their social activities, and to contribute to specific welfare programs. One of the areas, for example, gave Christmas gifts to more than ninety of its older members, some arranged outings and parties for the elderly, and nearly all of them contributed to the mayor's Christmas Parcel Fund.

Given the nature of the Bermondsey constituency, the area organizations carry the main burden of party activities in their respective territories. Although the chairman of an area may be the most prestigious officer, the main gear in the area machine is the secretary. He (or she) serves as a link between the central headquarters and the activists within the area, supervising and coordinating the political work. This is an arduous assignment in a constituency that has no threatening opposition, and the party often had to depend upon a few faithful veterans to carry the burden. Some of the area secretaries in Bermondsey had been at their posts for more than two decades, when the old wards were the units of organization. At the time of this study, two of the area secretaryships were held by older ladies who had served as ward secretaries for many years; one area was under the direction of a lady in her mid-fifties whose fine organizational skills had been rewarded by continuous re-election; two of the areas were in the charge of two men in their fifties who had been pressed into service when older veterans felt that they could no longer carry on; and the secretary of one area was a young lady in her early twenties who, after her marriage, was replaced by a young man in his early thirties. While the average age of the area chairmen was about fifty, the average age of the secretaries was about fifty-nine. At great personal cost, these area secretaries were carrying on with the work because they were devoted to a cause which meant a great deal to them. But the difficulty faced by the party in developing alternative leadership, especially among the younger people, meant that an area suffered some discontinuity when a seasoned stalwart stepped out of harness.

As was to be expected, the degree of organizational strength varied among the six areas and even between wards within an area. All of the units held regular meetings which always featured group discussion and sometimes scheduled live speakers or tape recordings of speakers, but the meetings were sparsely attended in three of them.[3] Some areas held their meetings in people's homes. The organizational health of an area seemed to depend more upon the leadership that was available than upon the political composition of the terrain. The two wards in which the Tories exhibited their greatest strength, for example, were among the weakest in terms of Labour party organization. One of these—Saints Ward—had lost about 1000 electors, most of them of Labour persuasion, through the clearance of over 400 flats—housing that would not be replaced, since the district had been zoned for industrial development. The other ward—Central—was on the verge of collapse until it was rejuvenated by Neckinger Ward, where the party organization was good, and merged into Area 2. In 1961–62, there was some competition for GMC seats in this Area, a sign of renewed political interest.

Two of the Areas appeared to be in very good condition. Both of them usually managed to secure live speakers for their meetings, and the average attendance ranged from 16 to 25. One of them recorded about 900 paid-up members on its rolls in 1961. Competition for places on the GMC was usual in these two organizations, and the defeated candidates often exhibited sufficient interest to get on the GMC by some other route, i.e., as representatives of the trade unions or the co-operative societies.

Although it did not record the highest membership, one of the units—Area 5—had an unusually large supply of local leaders. It sent the largest number of delegates to the GMC,[4] and it enrolled fourteen of the forty-five members of the borough council. A good number of the constituency party officials were also drawn from this Area. The Area secretary had been elected as party chairman or as one of the vice-chairmen for several terms, and her recognized leadership invariably received the endorsement of the activists from her Area. The GMC delegates from Area 5 had an attendance record of 80 per cent during 1961–62, and the component of council members included many who had been renominated and re-elected—a situation that indicates satisfaction with their performance. The Area secretary injected an element of competion into the political process by emphasizing in her reports the number of people from her district who were serving in an official capacity.

Although the performance record was not uniform, the evidence points to a considerable amount of social and charitable activity in all of the Areas, owing partly to the availability of funds, and to a good schedule of forums and discussions in about half of them. In 1961–62, the subordinate units in the Bermondsey party did not fit the general stereotype of an organization with a decayed infrastructure.

2. *Fulham.* When the 1954 distribution abolished the parliamentary constituencies of Fulham East and Fulham West and handed over a

portion of the Fulham borough to the new constituency of Barons Court, the task of picking up the remnants and of forming the new parliamentary unit of Fulham was as difficult as it had been in Bermondsey a few years earlier. Two wards from Fulham East — Sands End and Walham — had to be united with three wards from Fulham West — Hurlingham, Munster, and Town — and replacements had to be found for the party leaders who now resided in Barons Court. To add to the problem of fusion, the Fulham party and the Barons Court organization had to agree upon an equitable division of the assets, including the party premises, which had formerly belonged to the party in Fulham East — a distribution of property that involved delicate negotiations but was eventually carried out successfully.

It took nearly five years for the party leaders to get the restructured constituency operating as an integrated organization. Some of the women wanted to continue to meet in separate sections, but the General Management Committee intervened to prevent the formation of two groups. In the ward organizations, the loyalties to the old East and West units lived on for some time, but they gradually yielded to a new consensus as the older members, who had tended to resist the reorganization, retired from active political life. The people in the middle generation gradually accepted the inevitable, while the younger recruits grew up with the new arrangement. In rare instances during 1961–62, signs of the old East — West split emerged in the subtle criticism of a leader from one area by the older members of the other district, and occasionally an activist at a GMC meeting would get the floor to recall that 'in West Fulham we handled the problem this way.' But such occurrences were regarded as outmoded memories or mere statements of historical fact. The need for joint effort to meet contemporary election challenges and a string of successful victories at the polls have helped to eliminate the East — West feuds.

As in most integrative processes, the wards tended to cling to their autonomy for a sustained period. At the time this study was undertaken, they still jealously guarded their right to take a strong position on issues that agitated them, and they insisted upon their authority to select their candidates for the borough council. But they have gradually come to accept the fact that they are subordinate units in a larger party organization and that their functions are developed by the GMC on which they have prescribed representation. To a greater degree than in the other constituencies, nearly all of the wards have achieved the pattern of organization which is called for by the model rules, including the establishment of machinery at the polling-district level under the direction of a polling-district secretary, and some of the polling districts are even organized on a street or block basis.

Each of the five wards has the usual roster of offices, with the administrative burden falling largely upon the secretary. As is the case also with the ward chairmen, none of the secretaries has served for long stretches of time. This was true in some instances because an individual would serve his or her stint and then request a successor who could devote enough time to the job, and in other cases because there was competition for the post. On some occasions, the secretaryships have been held by activists whose work load on the borough council was so heavy that *de facto* administration of the ward was left to other workers; when this happened, the person who had assumed responsibility for organizing the ward sooner or later won the recognition of the members who then proceeded to elect him or her as secretary. In 1961–62 the average age of both the ward chairmen and the ward secretaries was about forty-five.

Although in a constituency like Fulham the party has to maintain strong ward organizations if it is to be effective, there is bound to be some variation among the wards. All of the wards held regular meetings, and the average attendance was about fifteen or sixteen members, with a range of five to forty. (The annual meetings and the meetings to select borough council candidates always attracted the largest crowds.) The ward secretaries often managed to secure some outside speakers or to call upon local members to present a point of view and lead the discussion. Occasionally, two wards would meet together to hear a speaker. As we shall observe later, the discussions in the wards sometimes led to the formulation of resolutions which were sent forward to the GMC.

In the 1961–62 period, the networks of organization were well developed in the two wards where the Conservative threat was the strongest – Town and Hurlingham. Here the party had a growing potential of Labour supporters as a result of public housing construction and an increase in the number of private landlords who had converted their premises into rentals. Moreover, the two ward organizations were endowed with some keen activists who were intent upon electoral victory. In Town Ward, where the party headquarters was located, there was a core of younger people who had been elected to ward offices and who generated some political excitement by disagreements among themselves and with their elders on the question of unilateral disarmament. Munster Ward, a large and populous area, was safely in the Labour column, and it enjoyed the services of a sizeable group of activists, several of whom carried responsibility on the borough council. The harnessing of Labour support in such a spacious ward was a challenge to their organizational efforts.

The two most solidly Labour wards – Walham and Sands End – presented a varying picture. Walham Ward was vulnerable to apathy, and at times it had trouble making its meetings attractive. But urban renewal had brought in an influx of traditional Labour voters, and a handful of party workers had devoted considerable effort to increasing the size of Labour's clientele. When an election was in the offing, the ward could be counted upon to carry its share of the load. In contrast with the other wards, the activists in Sands End were clustered in both the younger and the older age brackets (especially the latter), with only a few in the middle generation. This situation, combined with weak Tory opposition, made it somewhat more difficult to mobilize the ward's resources and to maintain a high level of political interest. During election campaigns, Sands End Ward sometimes had to be given assistance by workers from other parts of the constituency.

The Fulham constituency is distinctive in that all of the wards usually had competitors for the delegate seats on the General Management Committee. At least ten of the members, for example, had a break in their service between 1960 and 1962. As we have already indicated, however, a delegate who was not returned by his ward could still get the necessary credentials from a trade union or some other ancillary organization. The races for ward delegate posts nevertheless helped to stimulate an interest in ward affairs and were an important factor in the recruitment of younger people who perceived that the route to the GMC was open to them.

It should also be noted that in the Fulham party the activists in a single ward did not monopolize the major offices of the organization. This is significant in view of the size of Munster Ward, whose delegates could have become dominant if their ward loyalties had been deeply rooted and if they had been able to take a common stand on issues. A disproportionate number of GMC delegates from Munster did occupy seats on the borough council, but in the years since the constituency was formed the party's major officers have been drawn from nearly all of the wards. Although some ward rivalry can be detected, especially when a strong personality emerges within one of the units, the patterns of personal relationships and issue stands cut across the ward boundaries, thus diminishing the influence of a particular ward within the power structure of the party. The ward organizations in Fulham, to be sure, serve as useful centers of discussion, but they make their real contribution as essential units in a campaign machine which manages to win more than its share of contests in marginal territory.

3. *South Kensington*. Even though the ward boundaries had not been altered and the South Kensington party had not had to be restructured, the ward organizations were not characterized by long-established loyalties on the part of their members. The instability of the Labour membership in an area of shifting population did not permit such loyalties to solidify. Moreover, the wards did not have sufficient financial resources of their own to claim or to justify autonomy, and there was not as much social activity at the ward level as there was in Bermondsey. At times, of course, superficial attachment to a ward group

tended to develop, largely as an outgrowth of the rivalries among the members of the General Management Committee. But the high turnover of membership, as well as the changing lineup of factions according to the issues that emerged, prevented the competition among wards from becoming anything more than temporary. For this reason, loyalties tended to be transferred to particular groupings within the governing body of the party itself.

As in Bermondsey and Fulham, the most important ward officer in South Kensington was the secretary. What made the role particularly significant was the need for continuity of organization in a district where those who are recruited for Labour membership reside there for only short periods of time. The few activists who have lived in South Kensington since the end of the war had completed their servitude as ward secretaries long ago, and since then had had their interests turned to other parts of the Labour movement or to other constituencies, and they had withdrawn from party work at the ward level. Thus, the ward secretaryships tended to go to people whose residence in the area appeared to be fairly stable (i.e., they had lived there for about ten years) and who were interested enough to undertake the tasks of ward organization virtually on their own. Whereas the average age of the ward chairmen was about forty-two, the average age of the secretaries was slightly more than forty-six, almost ten years above the figure for the GMC as a whole.

Three of the four wards held regular meetings, with an average attendance of ten and a range of two to twenty-four. Two of the wards managed to schedule outside speakers for at least half of their meetings. As we shall see later, the ward meetings led to the formulation of a number of resolutions.

When this study was being conducted, the two wards with the largest Labour vote — Earls Court Ward and Redcliffe Ward — were reputed to be the best organized. Responsibility for the work in Earls Court rested upon a husband-and-wife team who served as chairman and secretary; they knew the district well, and were continually on the lookout for new members and for speakers to address the ward meetings. Redcliffe Ward was a special case. A sizeable group of the most influential and most active people in the local party resided in this ward, many of them in the same apartment building, and they systematically set about to make their influence felt by building up the ward organization. As a result, in 1961–62 nearly all of the major officers were elected from this group. In fact, the building in which the core of activists lived was jocularly referred to as the 'Transport House of South Kensington'. Eventually, competition developed for the GMC seats from Redcliffe Ward. When this happened, some of the members managed to get their trade unions to affiliate with the local party and to secure appointment to the GMC as union representatives. This move, of course, gave Redcliffe Ward more seats in the party's central organs and hence more power in the organization.

Holland Ward, which usually had the highest nominal membership, was literally held together by the secretary. In earlier years, it had had a stronger organization and was more inclined toward the 'left' than the other wards. Differences over ideological commitment, interlaced with personality conflicts, created difficulties within the ward, which became to some extent the basis of a factional struggle within the party. Over a period of years, however, the membership dwindled, and some of the influential members, who were more to the right in their political views, moved into Redcliffe Ward. This resulted in a shift of power from Holland Ward to Redcliffe. Before long, Holland Ward began to encounter difficulty in recruiting enough people to fill its quota of delegateships on the GMC.

Queens Gate Ward had the weakest ward organization in the South Kensington party. Its membership was very small — usually about 28 — and it had to be propped up by the party's secretary/agent, who also doubled as the ward secretary. Meetings were scheduled if a speaker had been engaged, or when conference resolutions of one sort or another had to be discussed. For nearly a decade after the war, the Queens Gate ward club had held joint meetings with Redcliffe Ward, but this practice was discontinued in the early 1950s; the activists in both wards resisted amalgamation, since each rival group would have had fewer delegates on the GMC.

Given the nature of the area, the ward organizations in the South Kensington party exhibited remarkable vitality, largely as a result of the initiative of the local officers. Each ward suffered, however, from a devastating turnover of members; its activists had to look to the intake of new members just to keep the membership at the same level — and the ward organization alive.

General Management Committees and Executive Committees

1. *Bermondsey.* In Bermondsey, the GMC delegateships for individual members were allocated to each area on the basis of the number of borough council members plus two delegates from each ward within the area. The trade unions qualified for one delegate for every one hundred affiliated members or part thereof. The affiliated unions, however, rarely sent all of the representatives to which they were entitled. The branches of the Transport and General Workers Union, for example, could have issued credentials to a total of 68 GMC members, but in fact they only appointed fifteen.[5] The labour organization with the best appointment record was the National Union of Public Employees, which sent along its full quota of six representatives. Some of the affiliated unions did not bother to appoint GMC delegates at all. The Co-operative organiz-

ations contributed their full component of GMC members who were conscientious representatives of their units and attended the meetings regularly. A final category of GMC members was the *ex officio* members who came to the policy-making body as borough councillors to observe the proceedings.

At the time this study was made, the General Management Committee of the Bermondsey party consisted of about 95 members,[6] and the average attendance was about 55 (58 per cent). This represented a decline from its strength in the 1950s, when the size of the GMC was about 170, although the rate of attendance was a bit lower at that time. As is true of most constituency parties, the delegates who were the least regular in their appearance at GMC meetings were the trade-union representatives, some of whom had conflicts with their branch meetings. It should also be observed that the number of active trade unionists on the Bermondsey GMC was much larger than the number of those who represented their unions, since many of them preferred to take their places on the GMC as representatives of party units.

The chairmanship of the party, which carried a two-year term, had been held by one individual for about a decade, but since 1956 this post and the offices of the vice-chairmen have usually been contested, although the person who stands for treasurer has an easy ride. At the time of the study, the median age of the major officers was fifty-five (compared with fifty-three in Fulham and thirty-nine in South Kensington), and all of them had lived more than 60 per cent of their adult lives in Bermondsey.[7]

An interesting feature of the GMC in Bermondsey was the extent of family involvement in local Labour politics. Active on the GMC were no fewer than ten husband-and-wife teams, as well as several father-and-son/daughter combinations. The potential complexity of these types of relationships can be illustrated by one case, even though it is probably located toward the extreme pole of the continuum. Mr A, one of the younger leaders of the Bermondsey party who had conscientiously worked his way up in the organization, indicated that kinship linkages had led him to become involved in political affairs. Mr A's grandfather, who had been active in local trade union affairs, became one of the first Labour councillors to be elected in Bermondsey. Mr A's father, originally a Liberal, was converted to the Labour cause by his mother, and he eventually played a major role in the Bermondsey party, succeeding his brother-in-law (a founding member of the Rotherhithe party) as treasurer and serving as mayor of the borough at the time of his death during the war. Mr A's mother was a leading light in the women's section of the party for many years, and she served as mayoress with her husband and later as mayoress for two other mayors. At the time of this study, Mr A's uncle was a borough councillor, as was his aunt who had once been a mayoress. Another aunt had rendered conspicuous service as a member of the borough council. A former councillor in the borough was related to Mr A by marriage, and all of his brothers and sisters were active in Labour party affairs in Bermondsey. Mr. A's remaining uncle was a trade unionist whose work had taken him to another part of London. Nearly all of these people had served on the GMC of the Bermondsey party at one time or another. The close connection between Mr A's family and the development of Bermondsey is an example of how familial relationships grow intertwined with Labour politics in the constituency.

The Executive Committee of the Bermondsey Labour party was a body of about thirty members, including ten to twelve seats for the area representatives, twelve posts for the trade unions, four delegates from the Co-operative groups, and one from the women's section. The attendance at Executive Committee meetings was about 55 per cent. Although some of the younger people from the areas and the unions had recently been placed on the Executive Committee, its membership included a sizeable core of party veterans. The four Co-operative delegates, for example, had an average length of Executive Committee service of more than thirty years, and about half of the entire Committee membership had performed in this role for more than a decade.

The task of the Executive Committee was to handle some of the party's housekeeping functions on behalf of the GMC and to make preliminary recommendations to the parent body. It also sent forward the names of people to serve on school and hospital boards, etc. Although it faithfully carried out these assignments, its responsibilities overlapped with those of the Action Committee, which was a unique body in the Bermondsey organization.

The Action Committee, established in 1951, was composed of representatives from each of the areas (usually the chairman and the secretary), seven members elected by the General Management Committee, and two delegates from the borough council who were to provide formal liaison between that body and the GMC. The Action Committee was assigned the job of studying the problems of the party and the borough and of making recommendations for improving Labour's performance in the constituency. That the Bermondsey party was willing to establish a mechanism for continual self-examination indicates that, unlike most other parties in Labour strongholds, it was aware of the need to identify problems and to appraise its programs and procedures. This scrutinizing operation involved a four-stage process: (1) the analysis of a problem and the hammering out of a recommendation by the members of the Action Committee; (2) referral of the matter to the Executive Committee for discussion and approval; (3) discussion, approval, and, when applicable, the implementation of the policy by the GMC; and (4) when applicable, sending the recommendation to the Labour Group on the borough council for discussion and possible implementation. Since many of the people who engaged in the discussions within the Action Committee, the executive, and the GMC, were also members of the Labour Group, ample opportunity was provided for deliberation on issues as the recommendations moved from one stage to another.

Since 1951, the Action Committee has considered a number of problems related to party organization and the running of the borough. It has studied ways to stimulate political interest at election time, to build up party membership, to develop a strong youth section, and to improve the political organization of women in the community. On a wider scale, it has made suggestions for helping the old-age pensioners and for adjusting borough council procedures so as to 'cut the red tape' and bring the council into more direct contact with ordinary citizens. The Action Committee has been a useful device for injecting new ideas into Labour organization and for generating discussion, but some of its proposals have been rejected by the General Management Committee, and others have been pushed aside by the Labour council.

An important function of the Action Committee was to examine the resolutions on the agendas of the Party Conference and the conference of the London Labour Party and to recommend a policy position on each controversial issue to the members of the GMC, who remained free to accept, modify, or reject it. In addition, the Action Committee arranged for the Bermondsey party to participate in various types of 'demonstrations', such as the May Day march and the mass protest against Suez. The fact that this group was smaller than the Executive Committee made it easier to go through conference agendas and to reach agreement on recommendations. The Action Committee has probably served a useful purpose in Bermondsey's organizational flowchart. If one assumes that self-appraisal and innovation are the price of a party's survival in a district of lagging political interest stemming from lack of Tory competition, it may be good strategy to set up a special organ which can attract people with broad perspectives and fresh outlooks, especially when existing agencies are composed of older people who may be reluctant to break with the past.

2. *Fulham.* Besides its secretary who served on the General Management Committee *ex officio*, each ward was entitled to a minimum of two delegates for a membership of 350 or less. The ward, however, could have an additional delegate for each fifty members or part thereof above the 350 figure, up to a maximum of ten members (including the secretary). Under this formula, four of the wards were each eligible to send three delegates in addition to the secretary, and Munster Ward was entitled to about twice that number of representatives.

The affiliated unions were permitted to have one GMC delegate for each fifty members of the branch (or part thereof) for whom affiliation fees had been paid. There was, however, a limit of five delegates from any one branch. Immediately after the war, trade-union delegates comprised nearly half of the GMC membership, and it was virtually impossible for any action to be taken unless the trade unionists approved. In the early 1950s, however, the union branches in Fulham began to lose interest in the political wing of the Labour movement, and in the 1960s some of them did not even bother to inform the party when they selected new secretaries. The lack of interest displayed by some union branches can be explained by their concern with 'bread-and-butter' matters, but some of the branches that were reluctant to work in harness with the party were those that had fallen under the control of 'extremist' leaders. When the extremist elements had been combed out of the unions, the branches changed their outlook and adopted a more co-operative attitude. As in the case of Bermondsey, the appointment of GMC delegates by the affiliated unions was spotted. Seven branches in four of the unions filled their quotas, and branches of three other unions appointed delegates for some of their entitled seats, but the branches of six unions sent no representatives. Some of the trade-union delegates on the GMC had taken the initiative in securing their credentials so that they could occupy seats on that body, although many of these people were also interested in having their union branches represented.

The Fulham party rules authorized representation for special sections of the organization and for other types of affiliated groups. The Women's Section, for example, was entitled to two seats on the GMC. In 1961–62, however, the party had organized a new form of women's organization as an experiment, and after a controversy in the Executive Committee over the constitutional question of GMC representation, the 'Women's Advisory Committee' was granted one delegateship. The Young Socialists were awarded two positions on the GMC, and the party's youth officer was permitted to attend its meetings without voting rights. The co-operative organizations, including the Fulham Co-operative Party, had five GMC representatives; the recently organized Fulham-Hammersmith branch of the Fabian Society placed one delegate; and one GMC member secured delegate credentials from the Socialist Medical Association.

In 1961–62, the General Management Committee had about fifty members, and the average attendance was approximately 60 per cent. As in Bermondsey, the absentee rate was highest among the trade-union delegates, especially those who had not taken steps themselves to get on the GMC by the union route. Many GMC members, of course, were active in the affairs of their trade unions, but they preferred to gain their seats through their wards.

An analysis of ward residence of all GMC delegates, regardless of whom they represented, reveals a preponderance from the large Munster Ward; the other four wards had about equal strength. In contrast with the other two constituencies, however, the Fulham party did not have one or two geographic districts that were able to wield dominant influence in the politics of the organization, largely because the cores of factional groupings that were formed around ideological issues and the defense question were not confined to particular wards.

The Executive Committee of the Fulham Labour party was composed of twenty-two members, as well as the Education Officer and the Youth Officer who served *ex officio* without the right to vote unless they had been elected as regular members in some other capacity. The voting members of the executive included the major party officers, ten members elected by the ward delegates, five chosen by the trade-union representatives, and one each from the Women's Section, the Young Socialists, the Co-operatives, and the socialist societies. Since the Executive Committee was an important locus of power in the party, there was vigorous competition for these posts, especially for the seats to be filled by the ward delegates. In fact, even the trade-union seats were usually contested, since some of the union representatives were really party activists who had obtained credentials from their union branches so that they could be politically involved. The attendance at meetings of the executive averaged about 80 per cent—a record that would have been even higher were it not for some of the trade union people who managed to be present about half of the time.

The largest group of Executive Committee members came from Munster Ward, but the figure is somewhat misleading, since a fairly large number of trade union delegates resided in that ward. A more realistic view of the lineup of political forces can be seen in the voting for 'individual members' (ward delegates) who were to be seated on the executive in 1962. The activists from Munster and Town Wards secured the election of three members from each district, and Hurlingham and Sands End Wards each won two places. At this time, the question of unilateral disarmament was agitating the party, and all of the winners from Munster and Town took a unilateralist position, while those from Hurlingham and Sands End took an opposing stand.

The Executive Committee was an influential body in the Fulham party, and some of the struggles over issues initially took place in its meetings. It not only dealt with financial matters and problems involving the premises, but it also considered other important business in a preliminary way (including resolutions), making recommendations to the General Management Committee. Once the members of the executive had discussed an issue and reached agreement by majority vote, the entire group became collectively responsible for the decision and each individual was expected to support it when the matter was turned over to the GMC. This rule naturally made the Executive Committee an important arena for discussion and decision-making when controversial issues appeared on the agenda.

3. *South Kensington.* The seats on the General Management Committee in the South Kensington party were allocated to each ward on the basis of four delegates for the first forty members or part thereof and another slot for each additional group of ten members. The ward secretary automatically became a GMC member with the right to vote. The allocations for wards were more liberal than in most constituency parties because of the need to keep the GMC as large as possible in an organization of small membership. The leaders hoped that, with these rules, preferment would be rapid enough to attract workers who would help to keep the party moving along.

Any union branches that affiliated with the party were entitled to one delegate for every fifty members or part thereof, but, as we have already observed, only a tiny number of unions was associated with the organization, and the delegates concerned had taken the initiative in securing the affiliations. The Young Socialists were entitled to two GMC delegates for every twenty-five members or part thereof, and two additional seats for the next bloc of twenty-five. During the 1961–62 period, the two Young Socialist representatives were a young husband-and-wife team – the secretary and assistant secretary – who lived in 'Transport House' in Redcliffe Ward. One GMC member, who was active in the Central London Fabian Society, had secured an extra seat for Redcliffe Ward by representing the Fabian Society.

In 1961–62, the South Kensington GMC consisted of about thirty members, whose attendance record averaged about 75 per cent.[8] This relatively high attendance rate is somewhat surprising in view of the competing activities in which the members – overwhelmingly middle-class in occupational background – were engaged. Those who were the least regular in their GMC attendance were some members of the 'left', whose interest sagged a bit when they discovered that the party had fallen into the hands of their 'rightist' colleagues.

The strength of Redcliffe Ward is indicated by the fact that during 1961–62 it had a total of twelve representatives on the GMC, ten of whom served for the entire period. Holland Ward had twelve delegates, but several of them moved out of the constituency, and only five members were continuous in their participation. Earls Court Ward and Queens Gate Ward could lay claim to twelve and eight delegates, respectively, but only about half of them served complete terms. The disappearance of old faces and the emergence of new ones reflected life in a high-rent constituency inhabited by rootless flat-dwellers and bed-sitter tenants who would eventually be forced to search for new living quarters elsewhere.

In 1961–62, the Executive Committee of the South Kensington party consisted of fifteen members – six GMC officials,[9] four from the wards, two from the unions, one from the Young Socialists, and one from the Fabian Society. Here again the size of the Redcliffe contingent surpassed that of any other ward, accounting for about half of the executive's membership.

The Executive Committee in South Kensington was much less influential than it was in the other two constituencies. It did not meet regularly, usually about once in every two or three months. In 1961–62, its most important accomplishments were recommendations for revision of the party's constitution and on procedures for waging election campaigns. More than had been the case in the early post-war years, the political antennae of the party officers were attuned to the dominant and conflicting points of view within the GMC, and since it was a small body, the members of the executive were usually willing to let it wrestle with the issues and make the necessary decisions without a prior recommendation.

Special Sections

1. *Bermondsey*. The women in Bermondsey have a long and splendid history of political activity. Before World War II, the Women's Section in Bermondsey West was strong enough to have a professional organizer of its own. Reflecting a national trend, however, the women's organization has suffered a decline in recent years, and in the early 1960s the enrollment in the Women's Section was about thirty. In an effort to stimulate more interest among the women, the Action Committee made plans to redecorate some of the rooms in the headquarters so that the ladies would have a more comfortable place to meet. The Committee also secured agreement on the holding of sherry parties which would feature prominent personalities, films, and discussions of interesting topics as means for attracting more women into the organization.

Even though the women's organization in the Bermondsey party was small, it was more active than its counterpart in other local Labour parties. Meeting once a week, the women usually had outside speakers and spent some time discussing topics of national and local interest. They sent delegates to national and regional conferences and participated in various political training programs. The Bermondsey women have been especially active in the women's organizations in south-east London and in the London-Middlesex area, their delegates occasionally serving as officials on the executive bodies. The Women's Section was an important recruiting-ground for workers at election time, and many of its members had civic responsibilities on the council, school management boards, and the like. The women were kept informed about the party's policies and activities through a monthly report on the GMC meeting, and occasionally they instructed their delegates to present their views to the party's governing body. Each year they made financial contributions to welfare work in the community. The Women's society also had its social side, sponsoring theater parties, teas, and all-day outings.

The Bermondsey party has been less successful in recruiting people for its youth organization. In the early 1950s, the youth movement had about twenty members who met each week for political discussion and scheduled a full program of social activities. However, inadequate premises at the time and failure to replace members who had passed the age limit resulted in a decline in the young people's section. It was brought to life again in 1958, and in the following year, when the party moved into new premises, the membership jumped to thirty-six. But many of the young people seemed to be more interested in the social side than in intellectual pursuits, and the youngsters who were concerned with politics grew discouraged. This conflict resulted in a decision to separate the two types of activities, with the social affairs being held in a public hall and a small, more select group being scheduled for political discussion in the party headquarters.

Although many constituency parties in the early 1960s were being faced with the problem of left-wing extremists infiltrating their youth sections, this was not the case in Bermondsey. The question was whether the party should be content merely with a 'social club' which might attract young people who were not seriously interested in political work, or foster the development of a smaller group who would become active in the party. Most constituency parties have not succeeded very well in nurturing youth sections which would support and feed into the parent organization. But the problem is especially difficult in Bermondsey for two reasons: (1) On the social side, the party had trouble competing with the more than twenty-five youth clubs in the borough. Many of these clubs had been established by social reformers in the inter-war years when Bermondsey was a depressed area, and they still flourished, offering the young people excellent recreational programs. (2) On the political side, the local party, despite the valiant efforts of some of its managers, was an aging organization with relatively stable leadership and was unable to offer the rapid promotions which many young people desire. Moreover, it was possible for the younger generation to benefit from many party-sponsored social activities – bingo games and public entertainmant – without having to suffer the drudgery of doorstep work, a great deal of which is required before an individual is able to rise to major positions of responsibility.

2. *Fulham*. The women in the Fulham party experienced a little difficulty in adjusting to the formation of the new constituency, and they had to be persuaded, with the help of the London women's organizer, not to continue with two sections, each going its own way. Even when this problem was resolved, the organization remained small and continued to operate on a centralized basis instead of breaking up into ward units, which the party leaders felt would be more effective in

recruitment. In the following years, the Women's Section struggled along with a small membership, meeting each month in the party headquarters for discussion and social interchange. The annual dinner usually attracted good attendance. The women took an active part in the Christmas Fair and Bazaar, and they always made a significant contribution during election campaigns.

The Fulham officers were convinced that the party should be making a bigger impact on married women in their twenties and thirties. They felt that the women in this age bracket, even when they came from working-class backgrounds, tended to fall victim to Conservative propaganda and to associate material affluence with Tory government. It was essential, they believed, for Labour to make a positive appeal to these women and to try to bring them into the orbit of party activities, especially since the demographic trend was toward a larger proportion of females in the constituency.

Looking upon the recruitment of women as the responsibility of the entire party and not just the Women's Section, the Labour people decided in 1962 to embark upon an experiment in recruitment. The focal organization in this campaign was the Women's Advisory Committee under the leadership of a young lady—a part-time employee in the central headquarters—who served as the women's officer. The program called for a series of open receptions featuring a prominent speaker, a discussion period, and an informal coffee or sherry session. The hostess was responsible for inviting women in the neighborhood and other guests. It was hoped that eventually this type of activity might be scheduled in each polling district. The receptions got off to a good start with Mrs Gaitskell as the honored guest; about fifty women came to greet her and to discuss some of the problems of the day. While spectacular results were neither anticipated nor achieved, a number of new women members were brought into the party, and they soon became involved in its activities, especially the fund-raising bazaars. This experiment represented a determined effort by the Fulham party to diagnose in local terms a problem that confronted the Labour Party in the country, and to attempt to alleviate it.

Compared with the youth groups in other urban settings, the Young Socialists in Fulham were a relatively large organization with a membership varying from twenty-five to thirty-two and an average attendance of about thirteen at the weekly meetings. The approximate figures for other London branches were twenty members and an average attendance of nine. The membership of the Fulham group naturally fluctuated as a result of people moving away, but a solid core of earnest young people provided adequate continuity for the organization. The Young Socialists developed a good program of weekly discussions—often with speakers; they participated in speaking contests and training schools; and they engaged in a variety of social activities.

That the youth section was successful may be attributed to the fact that it was regarded as an integral part of the local constituency organization, responsible to the General Management Committee which appointed a youth officer to supervise its operation. Although some friction occasionally developed between individual young people and a few members of the adult party, the Fulham party generally welcomed young people into its ranks and gave them encouragement. At one point in 1961, six Young Socialists held some type of office in the local party, and three of them were officers in their trade unions.

At a time when the national and regional youth organizations were afflicted by schisms generated by extremists whose loyalty was not fixed upon the Labour Party, the Young Socialists in Fulham pursued a moderate course, helping at times to counter the subversive elements in the federations with which they were affiliated. Rather than being seduced by diversionary tactics, they centered their attention upon the local party, devoting their energy to concrete organizational activity. They participated enthusiastically in election campaigns, they canvassed new voters with a view to soliciting their support for Labour and trying to recruit them into the Young Socialists branch, they helped to decorate the party premises, and they conducted a public opinion survey on the borough council's recreational program. Compared with the other two constituencies, the Young Socialists in Fulham managed to achieve greater stability of leadership and to play a more effective role within the local party.

3. *South Kensington.* The young ladies in the South Kensington party were very much involved in the work of their wards and the constituency organization, and a women's section was not attractive to them. Hence the only ancillary organization was the Young Socialists. At the time of this study, it was a small group of about ten members, most of whom attended the meetings regularly. The weekly discussions usually took place in the secretary's apartment, since the party had no facilities of its own. Members of the Young Socialists branch helped the party with its election activities, and they developed a calendar of social events.

The Young Socialists in South Kensington adopted the same moderate outlook as their colleagues in Fulham, except that most of them renounced unilateral disarmament. They sided with the Fulham people in fighting the subversive groups in their federation, and, like Fulham, they eventually broke their affiliation with it. When the secretary of the Young Socialists won his election to the borough council, the administrative work was handed over to several successors, each of whom moved out of the constituency after a short period of residence. Lack of continuity in leadership resulted in the youth section becoming defunct in 1963, and after a year's lapse it was reorganized and continued to struggle for life in an adverse environment.

KEY PARTY ROLES

In describing the organization of the three constituency parties, we have not mentioned two roles that are of crucial importance in the operation of a local Labour party—the secretary/agent and the Member of Parliament.[10] We have already considered these roles in a general way, but we need at this point to look at them again in terms of the personalities who occupied them in the three districts. We shall also refer to them from time to time when we examine the functions of the three units.

A local party depends upon the willing participation of volunteers who are free to drop out of the organization when they grow dissatisfied. This means that the power of sanction for unsatisfactory performance cannot really be exercised. A Labour party, to be sure, has the authority to expel a member, but such drastic punishment is reserved for only the most serious cases of violations of discipline. Political work involves certain costs for the participants in terms of monetary contributions, lost wages or holidays, leisure time sacrificed, and home life neglected. For people to be willing to pay these costs, they have to be motivated in some way—they have to derive some personal 'satisfactions' or 'rewards' from their political activities which they consider to be worthwhile. Since material rewards are virtually absent in a local Labour party, the benefits to be derived from political effort must necessarily take other forms: a political career at the national or local levels, the prestige of party office, social interaction with friends and associates, popular recognition, satisfaction derived from party work, gratification of a sense of responsibility, fulfilling a commitment to a cause, or just pleasure flowing from a love of politics.[11] A party flourishes when the motivations of individuals are closely linked with its goals, i.e, when the achievement of the party's objectives enhances the goals of the people who are associated with it.

Although some of these rewards and satisfactions may be distributed by the party managers over a period of time, most of them are usually under the control of the group. The General Management Committee, for example, decides who its leaders will be, and a ward unit has a strong voice in the selection of its borough council candidates. This means that the party organizers are responsible for directing and coordinating the work of the volunteers and they need to have people comply with their requests and instructions, but they have only limited control over the incentive system. Under these circumstances, the political leaders have to define organizational tasks, some of which are arduous, and to recruit people to carry them out, but at the same time they have to ensure that the party atmosphere remains friendly and the morale of the workers does not sag.

Given the paucity of rewards at the command of the managers, how do they get the party work done with a minimum of tension and interpersonal conflict? One possible clue is given by Professors Thibaut and Kelley in their studies of small groups.[12] They distinguish between the role of a 'task leader' and the role of a 'maintenance leader'. According to their analysis, a social group that is confronted by a particular task or problem requires a 'task leader' who initiates the 'task-related interactions', which usually involve increased personal costs to the individual members. Unless the task assignment 'quickly brings compensating rewards', the group members begin to evaluate the relationship as unsatisfactory from their point of view – a perception that encourages them to direct their resentment against the task leader who issued the orders. If the situation worsens, the ratio of costs to rewards becomes so imbalanced that the group may break up. The job of the maintenance leader is to prevent the group from reaching such a stage. 'His contribution is to increase the rewards to members, by warm supportive behavior toward them, and/or to reduce their costs, by such behavior as making jokes that release tension and, in general, by reducing their anxieties.' Thibaut and Kelley suggest that it is better for the two roles to be performed by the two different people, since they require different skills which one individual is not likely to have. Moreover, the roles tend to be incompatible; one is concerned with urging the members to get on with their jobs, while the other is interested in their becoming somewhat more relaxed about their work. Then, too, the orders of the task leader tend to generate feelings of hostility, while the maintenance leader stimulates positive feelings of support; hence, if a single individual were to occupy both roles, the group members would probably be ambivalent towards him, and his effectiveness in one or both of the roles would be diminished. One would anticipate that in a constituency party the secretary/agent would ordinarily perform as a task leader, and that the Member of Parliament would operate in the role of maintenance leader.

The Secretary/Agent and the Member of Parliament

1. *Bermondsey*. The agent in Bermondsy was Mr John R. Thomas – a local man, the son of a docker, who had been selected for the post in 1947. He also served as one of the elected representatives of the London County Council. He was a professional in every way and he had won the respect of the Bermondsey activists for his organizational ability.
   Thomas did not face the problem of having to build the party in the midst of vigorous competition from other political groups. He had inherited an organization that had already won its battles and had annihilated the opposition. At the time of this study, he was the manager of a party that was akin to an established firm with a monopoly of the electoral market. This monopoly involved full responsibility for running

the borough; it required an alert party which could identify local problems and resolve them. Thomas' main task was to make sure that the party remained alert and that its machinery was kept running effectively, as it had in the past.

To keep the party running smoothly in a safe area like Bermondsey was a challenging assignment. The voters knew in which column to mark their ballots; it was a question of convincing many of them that trips to the polling stations would make any difference. Moreover, the party itself was made up of many Labour veterans whose roles had become stabilized over the years and who were wedded to traditional outlooks and procedures. As seasoned foot-soldiers in the long struggle for socialism, the older party members were influential on the GMC and on the borough council, and their splendid record of achievement was plainly visible; even their Conservative opponents somewhat grudgingly admitted that their governance had been of generally high quality. Party workers of this type naturally tend to cling to practices that have worked well in the past and with which they are familiar. If the agent were to advocate change with a view toward modernizing the party's procedures as it confronted new problems and faced new tasks, he would have to make a persuasive case which would be attractive to the older members whose views were highly respected. He would also have to utilize his knowledge of human relations. The members of the GMC – the vast majority of whom proudly identified with the working class – were independent of mind, especially when it came to local affairs, and were sensitively aware of their power in a democratic organization. They would listen to and consider suggestions, but they would not be dictated to, whether the commands were to come from the agent or from Transport House. The agent was expected to lead, and he could encourage and try to persuade. But it was unwise for him to issue instructions in the form of edicts. As a native of Bermondsey, Mr Thomas had a deep understanding of these problems, and he was the type of agent who could perform well in that environment.

John Thomas had a clear image of what he wanted his role to be. Since Labour was completely responsible for borough affairs, he sought to integrate the party into the life of the community. Election majorities, he felt, were really compiled between campaigns because people's attitudes are formed as a result of the day-to-day administration of local affairs. For this reason he tried to detect areas in which the party was not as influential as it might be, and he encouraged the party people to involve themselves in as many organizations as possible within the constituency. The aim of such activity was not only to improve the party's image as a dynamic force in civic affairs, but also to insure that these organizations would not fall under the domination of elements that did not have the interests of the Labour party and the borough at heart.

The agent was also interested in recruiting more people for work in the party and as borough council candidates. The party's responsibility for its own administration and for borough affairs necessitated a heavy commitment of manpower so that administrative burdens needed to be spread among more people. When the most conscientious activists became overloaded, he felt, the quality of the work is threatened. He was continually on the lookout for promising individuals who might be persuaded to become involved in party endeavors. He was especially concerned about drawing young people into the organization, for he realized that if the party were to remain effective in the future, replacements would have to be found for the older people who would be retiring.

Acutely sensitive to the hazards that a party without competition faced, Thomas tried to be innovative, continually pointing out new challenges and injecting new ideas into the organization. He was inclined to the view that during election campaigns the party should pay less attention to its home ground and pour more of its resources into the marginal districts. Undisputed control over a constituency needed, in effect, to generate its own opposition; in the absence of a threat from outside the organization, it was likely to develop internal rivalries within its own camp. Self-evaluation, in his view, could function as a surrogate opposition. This was the rationale behind the establishment of the Action Committee. As we shall note, the Bermondsey activists always listened carefully to the suggestions for change, but they did not always accept them.

The Bermondsey agent cannot be clearly fitted into the role of a task leader. If he could, perhaps a few more of his suggestions might have been tried. Many of the tasks had become routinized, and the people in the wards seemed to carry them out according to their own schemes. As he sought to guide, he was called upon to persuade, to mediate personal disagreements, and to induce people to cooperate. His role shaded into that of a maintenance leader, as he sought to encourage, commend, and support.

The Member of Parliament for Bermondsey was the Rt Hon. Robert J. Mellish, who had represented Rotherhithe from 1946 to 1950 and was adopted as the candidate for the new Bermondsey constituency in 1950, winning the seat in that election and easily retaining it in subsequent contests. Born the son of a docker in nearby Deptford, Mellish left school at the age of fourteen to work on the docks. His recognized ability soon brought him into trade union work, and for many years he was employed as an organizer for the Transport and General Workers Union. He joined the Labour Party in 1927. During the war he served with an engineering battalion of dock workers, and after demobilization he began his parliamentary career under the sponsorship of the Transport and General Workers Union. The hope of the Bermondsey people that their children might have opportunities which were denied to them was realized in the case of Mr and Mrs Mellish. Their eldest son was admitted to Cambridge University where he took a degree in English and became a grammar school teacher.

Few trade union M.P.s from solid Labour constituencies rise to positions of prominence in the British Parliament, but Bob Mellish is a notable exception. He has compiled a distinguished record at Westminster and at Whitehall, and has won the respect of his colleagues on both sides of the House. When the Labour Party was in opposition prior to 1964, he was a dogged front-bench spokesman on transport problems, and when Harold Wilson became Prime Minister in 1964, Mellish was appointed Joint Parliamentary Secretary in the Ministry of Housing and Local Government, with special responsibility for housing in London. Here his work with the London Labour Party – he had been chairman since 1961 – served him in good stead, for he was effective in dealing with Labour groups on the borough councils. In 1967, he became Minister of Public Building and Works, and two years later the Prime Minister appointed him to the post of Chief Whip.[13] In this capacity he eventually occupied a seat in the Cabinet.

Despite his responsibilities in parliament and the demands placed upon him by the national Party and the regional organization, Robert Mellish devoted a great deal of time to the people of Bermondsey while this study was under way. He served as chairman of the board for a group of Bermondsey and Southwark hospitals and was a governor of Guy's Hospital and of several secondary schools. He was an active supporter of local community projects, and regularly attended community functions. As we shall see, he conducted a weekly advice bureau, where constituents could come to talk with him about their problems. He was widely recognized as being a 'fine constituency man.' He enjoyed the confidence of the Bermondsey folk, and many of them referred to the party headquarters as 'Mellish's place'. While as a Roman Catholic who was made a Knight Commander of St. Gregory by Pope John he was understandably popular among the Catholic segments of the population, he had also gained widespread support from other religious groups in the constituency.

The member for Bermondsey played an important role in his local party. He was keenly aware of the long-term problems which the party faced, and he helped the agent by personally participating in membership drives and by encouraging particular individuals to become active in party work. He appeared at nearly every meeting of the General Management Committee, presenting a detailed report on the issues before parliament. As a former docker and union organizer and a long-time participant in working-class politics, Mr Mellish understood the balance of forces within the party and the borough council and was often able to anticipate problems (usually of a factional sort) before they arose. As we shall note in more detail later, the Bermondsey activists tended to take their cues on foreign policy questions from their M.P., but when a divisive issue arose — such as German rearmament and the Common Market — Mellish was careful to present the arguments on both sides and then indicate the position he took and the reasons for it. Nearly always he managed to keep himself above the factional disturbances in a way that the agent, from the nature of his job, could not, and because of the prestige he commanded, he was in a position to act as an integrating force when division threatened.

Bob Mellish definitely served as a maintenance leader for the Bermondsey party, and, as we have already indicated, John Thomas' role was a fusion of task and maintenance. Given the nature of a safe Labour constituency — with its long-established traditions, the relative shortage of activists in all age brackets and a consequent lack of competition for party posts, and the presence of older, experienced people who are used to handling their jobs in their own way — one might hypothesize that neither the agent nor any of his colleagues can really occupy the role of task leader, and that this situation tends to create organizational ambiguity within the unit.

2. *Fulham.* The secretary/agent in Fulham was Mr Leslie Hilliard, who was born near London of working-class parents. In addition to holding a regular job, his father was a Nonconformist lay preacher. Hilliard was trained to be an electrical engineer, but a love for politics and a fervent belief in the Labour cause prompted him to abandon his engineering career to enter the agency service as a professional organizer. He returned from military service in 1945 in order to take over as the agent for Fulham West, and after the 1954 redistribution he was chosen to be the agent in the new Fulham constituency. He also served for a number of years as the secretary of the Labour Agents trade union. As the senior practicing constituency agent in the entire Labour Party, he was widely recognized for his professional competence and his long list of election victories. He won enviable acknowledgement in June 1967, when his name appeared on the Queen's Honours List and he was made a Commander of the British Empire for his service to the community in the field of local government.

When Mr. Hilliard first took over as agent in the Fulham area, his role was considerably different from what it later became. At that time he had to lay the foundation for a new Labour party in a frosty political environment. His first task was to recruit a set of cadres to whom the organizational and agitational work would be delegated and around whom the ward structures could be built. The job of recruiting was difficult because the prospect of electoral success was grim; only dedicated idealists who had faith in the movement's 'ultimate victory' were willing to brave the chilly winds of ridicule and apathy. Hilliard and his tiny band of partisans were forced to spend much of their time in inspirational and propaganda work in their efforts to recruit party members and to persuade reluctant voters to move into the Labour camp. Furthermore, it was a struggle to scrape together enough money to keep the fledgling party alive. Under these conditions, the desk work of the agent was much less important than leg work.

Political success over the years significantly changed the nature of the Fulham party and the agent's role in it. Marginal districts tend to produce political organizations with more complex administrative structures, and Hilliard's tasks as an organizer gradually yielded to those of a political manager. But it was not the management of a party that enjoyed a monopoly, as in Bermondsey; it was the management of an organization that was continually under political and economic pressure. Every ward had to be combed at every general election, and even in local contests nothing could be taken for granted. Moreover, the party leaders had to keep a watchful eye on finances, for the Member of Parliament was not sponsored by a trade union.

Leslie Hilliard had his mind fixed upon the future of the Labour party in Fulham. He felt that, given the marginal nature of the district, it was important to build a modern, streamlined organization whose activities were planned according to the imperatives of changing times and which was capable of meeting contemporary challenges. In line with this objective, he sought to impress upon the party the need to develop a balanced leadership core in terms of age distributions and to expand the organization's general membership. In his view, formal party membership was merely a by-product of extensive party activities. He thought in terms of *all* Labour supporters, and he was concerned about linking them and their families to the party through some form of direct or indirect participation. An initial contact might be made, for example, through the party-sponsored lotteries, and the people who displayed interest might be drawn into closer association with the party through related forms of activity.

Hilliard's futuristic outlook was clearly evident in his interest in census data and voting statistics. He was aware of the changing demographic features of the constituency. The patterns of change convinced him of the party's need to make a greater impact upon the women, to appeal to people in the 30–40 age-bracket, and, in an area with an aging population, to direct a flow of younger people into the organization. He kept detailed statistical records of political allegiances and voter participation, which would quickly capture the interest of any political scientist. He used the data as a basis for current campaign strategy and long-term planning.

Current and future objectives require some division of labor, with responsibility being delegated and the party's efforts being coordinated within a pattern of planned development. These efforts included the managing of borough affairs in a district in which an alert opposition was always a threat. Some of the old-timers in the party, of course, were inclined to take a dim view of the development of a 'modern' party organization. Recalling the loose structure of amateurs in the 'old days', they nurtured a distrust of 'professional bureaucracy' which they saw ensconced in the local headquarters. Occasionally, one of them would remark, 'Let the staff do it; that is what they are paid for!' They failed to appreciate the problem of having to defeat an opposition party that could afford and did not hesitate to employ up-to-date methods. Hilliard knew that he, like all party managers, was dependent upon voluntary workers, and he sought to patch up discords and to smooth over personal differences. As an expert political craftsman, he knew the importance of good morale in an organization that has to fight close elections, and he would compliment his colleagues for their fine performance and comfort them when they made mistakes. In this sense, he was carrying out 'maintenance' activities that every successful agent has to do. To be able to lead and direct a party through its struggles and crises, the agent has to be able to carry most of the activists along with him. Unless consensus has been fostered in the period between elections, he will not be able to secure compliance with his directives without injuring personal feelings.

Although Leslie Hilliard did not neglect the maintenance side, he can accurately be classified as a task leader, and his record is testimony to his success. As the manager and tactical leader of a well-organized party, he often found it necessary, especially during political campaigns, to make administrative decisions and to issue orders in the form of nicely worded 'commands'. In some parties in marginal districts (as, for example, the one in Barons Court in the 1960s),[14] the agent may opt to be a maintenance leader and issue instructions in the form of suggestions. But when this happens, other leaders in the campaign team — such as the canvassing officer or the ward secretaries — have to take over the task function. In Fulham, however, Mr Hilliard had a keen perception of the problems the party was facing, and he kept this role for himself. His colleagues agreed that no one else could have handled it.

The role of task leader is not easy in any organization, but it appears to be especially difficult in a party that has to operate in a marginal, competitive environment. The probability is that the organization will be potentially schismatic because of the heterogeneity of the population from which it draws its activists. It will not only have the personal rivalries which plague all local parties, but it will also encounter differences in viewpoint between the working-class and the middle-class elements which may take on an ideological coloration. The situation is likely to be complicated by generational discords that arise if efforts are made to bring young people into the organization in order to expand the manpower pool and groom new leaders for the future. In other words, more of the ingredients for controversy may be latent in a marginally-based party, and if contention is permitted to hamper efficiency, the electoral consequences are serious by virtue of the fact that the constituency is marginal.

At the time of the study, the Fulham party was tormented by the unilateralist controversy, and the line-up of forces was more delicately balanced than it was in the other two parties. Since there was little room for compromise on an issue of this sort, the activists on both sides found it almost impossible to hammer out a consensus. The agent was convinced that unilateralist sentiment was a passing phase in the party's evolutionary development and would ultimately serve as a lesson in political judgment for the younger activists. But he could hardly afford to ignore the divisive effect of the issue upon the party, and he was fearful that it might adversely influence the voters in this 'swing' constitency at election time. For these reasons, he chose to intervene in the controversy, though he was careful at all times to bow to the decisions reached through the democratic machinery. The agent also played an active role in several party discussions of other issues, developing a persuasive brief when he thought that the GMC might follow an unwise course and sometimes suggesting alternative routes if he thought that compromise was possible. The activist side of his role was also noticeable in the council chamber, where he served as a Labour councillor.

In some constituency parties, the overt involvement of the agent in political as well as organizational affairs is considered to be hazardous, since it often results in his 'taking sides', possibly weakening the organization though the alienation of some of the volunteers who are important to it. But this was not the case in the Fulham party. Even though some activists might disagree with the agent's views on some matters, they invariably agreed with him on other issues. Besides, they all respected him for his long record of successful leadership; they all recognized and applauded his outstanding managerial and tactical ability. The fabric of consensus was usually repaired by election time, and virtually all of the dissidents were willing to forget about any recent disagreements and were disposed to carry out, usually with cheerful smiles, the tasks which the agent assigned to them during the campaign. The fact that time often proved that the agent had been right helped to reinforce the loyalty to him and to tighten once again the sinews of cohesion within the organization.

One important reason why the Fulham party enjoyed its reputation for being a strong organization was because Mr Hilliard continually stressed the importance of winning elections, and he laid out an agenda of essentials for such victories. The party, in his view, was strengthened when it focused upon the problems of the borough affairs. The voters, he felt, were primarily concerned about local issues; they did not worry as much about tribal politics in Africa as they did about getting their rubbish hauled away regularly. Put another way, when Labour did a good job in the daily administration of the borough, it was developing a wide basis of support, not only for its council candidates, but also for its parliamentary candidate in the infrequent general elections. The Labour activists in Fulham busied themselves with their civic responsibilities, and this tended to siphon off discontent and blunt the impact of ideological issues upon the party's internal harmony. Such involvement naturally increased the number of party tasks and made Mr Hillard's role as a task leader even more necessary.

The Member of Parliament for Fulham was the Rt Hon. Michael Stewart, who represented Fulham East from 1945 until the redistribution in 1954 and then became the Labour candidate in the new Fulham constituency. He won the seat in the 1955 election and retained it in subsequent contests.

Born in London, the son of a writer on scientific subjects, Stewart was educated at Oxford University, where he took an M.A. degree. After completing his education, he became a school teacher, eventually winning appointments as assistant master at the Merchant Taylors' and the Coopers' Company schools. He had joined the Labour Party in 1922, at the age of sixteen. He suspended his teaching career to join the army for service in the Middle East, and after demobilization he entered Parliament. He was the author of two well-known books on politics.

In his long years of service in the House of Commons and as a government minister, Mr Stewart had an enviable record of achievement, and had won the respect of his Labour colleagues and his political opponents alike for his ability and integrity. After serving as a government whip from 1945 to 1947, he was appointed Under-Secretary of State for War and subsequently Parliamentary Secretary in the Ministry of Supply. When the Labour Party moved into the Opposition benches after its defeat in 1951, Stewart became the front-bench spokesman on education and later on housing and local government, and in handling these assignments he developed a reputation for painstakingly collecting the facts and then launching devastating attacks upon the government. When Harold Wilson moved into No. 10 Downing Street in October 1964, he initially appointed Michael Stewart as the Minister for Science and Education but shifted him a few weeks later to the post of Foreign Secretary. He held this position until 1970, except for a period in 1966–8 when he served as Secretary of State for Economic Affairs, being responsibile for executing Cabinet policies designed to get Britain back on her economic feet. In recent years he has served as leader of the British delegation to the European Parliament. On several occasions, he was one of a small group of Labour figures who had been mentioned as potential leaders of the Parliamentary Labour Party.

Mr Stewart never referred to his own political accomplishments. He was quiet, almost shy, in manner, and his modesty prompted him to shun publicity and self-advertisement. Yet when he appeared on a public platform, he engaged his audience with a fluent, machine-gun style of delivery without raising his voice; hecklers had a difficult time with him because they were never quick enough to intervene.

Despite the heavy burden of parliamentary duties and a speaking schedule that took him to all parts of the country and quite frequently abroad, Michael Stewart managed to devote a considerable amount of time to the affairs of his constituency. He maintained a full calender of engagements at community functions – civic celebrations, prize-givings, school events, and the like. He was always willing to head a Fulham deputation to see a minister about some local problem. As we shall see later, he also conducted an advice bureau to help Fulham citizens with their problems. When the Labour Government took an unpopular turn, people, especially the elderly, could occasionally be heard to express the view: 'The Government is a bit of a nuisance, but Mr Stewart is a fine man.' In his constituency work, he was ably assisted by his wife, who usually accompanied him when he attended community affairs and who served on a board of school managers, a hospital board, and other civic groups.

Like Robert Mellish of Bermondsey, Michael Stewart of Fulham played an active role in local party affairs. His frequent contacts with the Labour activists made them aware of his sincere interest in their work and of his appreciation for their efforts. Many a party worker was encouraged by his warm greeting and his kind word of thanks. He was regular in his attendance at GMC meetings, where he presented a report on the policy stands and strategies of the Parliamentary Labour Party. He also attended some of the ward meetings when his schedule permitted, and at these gatherings he had the rare ability to present complex, sophisticated ideas in an unpatronizing way by bringing his listeners up to his level. If he thought they might be helpful, he would send documents to the ward secretaries. Most important of all, he took his turn at the open-air meetings, and he and Mrs Stewart could be seen on the doorsteps every day during an election campaign, especially in the marginal wards, whether the election was for the parliamentary seat, the borough council, or the London County Council.

Although he always made his views on controversial issues known to the people in the party and some would disagree with them, his quiet style and his acknowledged sincerity helped him to keep above the factional encounters. By remaining aloof from the party's smoldering disagreements, he was often able to act as a unifying force within the organization. His integrative role can be partly explained by the fact that, while his 'conservative' approach to questions of foreign policy and national defense might be contrary to the mood of some activists, none of the Labour people in Fulham could find fault with his strong positions on domestic and local issues, with which most of them were preoccupied. Since he did not appear as a 'controversial figure' and was not swept up in the tides of dispute, he was able to wield informal influence in the direction of unity. 'He is loyal to us', some activists would say, 'so we should be loyal to him.'

Michael Stewart easily met the criteria of a maintenance leader. By his close association with the local party people, by his personal commendations for their work, and by his willingness to do his share of the doorstep activity and speaking 'on the stump', he had won the affection of the Labour stalwarts, and these cordial relationships enabled him to be of assistance to the agent in making the party a vital organization. Indeed, he reinforced the agent in the role of task leader by his own example. When he would come into the party headquarters to begin his day's work in the campaign, he would invariably ask the question: 'Les, what assignments do you have for me today?'

3. *South Kensington.* The hopelessness of the Labour cause in South Kensington and the lack of financial resources dictated that the job of secretary/agent be voluntary and part-time. In 1961–62, the position was held by Mr Maurice Barber, a solicitor's clerk in Gray's Inn. He had lived in the constituency for about ten years, and for more than five years he had carried on as the voluntary agent. In addition, he represented one of the North Kensington wards on the borough council.

Needless to say, Barber's post in the South Kensington party was an extremely difficult assignment. A good number of the volunteer workers he had to rely on were in the constituency for only a short time; indeed, some campaign workers who may have been lined up six weeks in advance would have moved out of the district by polling day. The size of his general staff at election time – the people who knew the area well and were in a position to exercise delegated authority – was very small because this type of responsibility required activists who had been associated with the party for a comparatively long period of time. Furthermore, it was difficult to entice workers to stuff envelopes and deliver literature on behalf of candidates who could not win, and then at a strategic moment urge them to desert their own candidates and transfer their activities to a neighboring area so that they could begin their work for someone else. Such circumstances often made the secretary/agent's problems appear to be overwhelming, and he was expected to resolve them in his 'spare time' without financial recompense.

At the time of this study, Maurice Barber was the main prop for a party with tender and shallow roots. Without his competent services, the organization would probably have fallen apart. At election time, of course, he performed the usual executive tasks of an agent, supervising candidate selection, worker recruitment, envelope addressing, etc. (In borough council elections, he served as the South Kensington agent while campaigning himself to retain his council seat in North Kensington.) But the crucial task of the secretary/agent was not the management of election campaigns. Given the South Kensington environment and its effect upon the local party, the central challenge was to make certain that the organization held together in the period between elections. It was in meeting this challenge that Maurice Barber performed an indispensable service for Labour in South Kensington.

Earlier on, we suggested that the secretary/agent, in directing a party's operations, runs the risk of wounding people's sensitivities when he issues the necessary instructions or of becoming involved in conflict when disputes rock the organization. Special dangers lurk when the Labour party is largely made up of middle-class adherents who may not be used to taking orders and who are inclined to line themselves up on almost every political issue. The situation may be alleviated somewhat if there is someone in the organization who keeps himself above controversy and is thus in a position to encourage, to console, and to administer to the wounded on both sides. As we indicated, the M.P. is a logical person to fill this maintenance role.

But the party in South Kensington did not have a member of parliament, and the chances of its electing an M.P. were only slightly better than the probability of Switzerland launching a successful military invasion of Britain. The mediatory role had to be played either by the secretary or by the chairman. Although the chairman had won election because people in rival groups felt that he would be impartial in his rulings (an expectation that he lived up to), he was a member of the 'Redcliffe wing', which tended to dominate the organization. While he was not conspicuously identified as a ringleader, his views were well known. For this reason, the task of integrating the party between elections fell largely to the secretary/agent. To some extent, his assumption of this role was an outgrowth of his ordinary administrative duties. Even more important, his personality and temperament fitted him for this type of maintenance endeavor; he would have been less happy as an overt leader of a faction or as a participant in ideological rivalries. While he had his own views on issues, he did not press them ostentatiously in public, and his avoidance of contentious involvement provided him with political currency which could be used in eliciting help from some of his colleagues.

Concentrating on the maintenance role, Maurice Barber did not really subscribe to the requirements of a task leader. He did not take the initiative in delegating authority very often; it was a rare thing for him to issue assignments by direct order. As a rule, he preferred to have people volunteer to help him. Once the General Management Committee had decided to follow a course of action or to embark upon a special project, it was up to the other activists in the organization to offer their assistance in implementing the decision. At times, of course, not enough assistance was forthcoming, and the burden fell too heavily upon the secretary/agent and his wife. As a matter of fact, his party responsibilities and his work on the council took up most of his free evenings and were carried out at the expense of time he was able to devote to his family. But he derived personal satisfaction from his involvement with the party, and he was proud of the fact that it was active and playing a distinctive role, despite the unfavorable political setting.

A constituency party operating in hopeless territory has need for a task leader because the interests of its members are split between internal responsibilities and work in other districts, requiring an efficient marshalling of scarce human resources and coordination of work efforts. It also requires a maintenance leader because of the inertia against edicts and the probable existence of ideological factions. Because the activists are few in number, the leaders have to be careful that their enthusiasm does not wear thin. But there is no M.P. to occupy the maintenance role, and both types of leadership have to be taken over by the voluntary secretary/agent or shared with someone else. This presents difficulties, of course, because the party membership is small and no one works for the party on a full-time basis. The situation might be improved somewhat if the job of election agent and the secretaryship were handled by two people. This would enable the agent to handle the concentrated part of the task leadership which occurs during campaigns and enable the secretary to conserve his resources for the job of keeping the party intact between elections.

Now that we have a clear idea about the goals, organizational structures, and key roles in the three constituency parties, we turn next to an examination of these units in action, observing how they carried out their party functions in their respective environments.

5 Constituency Parties in Action

Our purpose in this chapter is to examine the three constituency Labour parties in terms of the functions and 'operational objectives' set forth in Chapter 1. The reader will recall that, for the vast majority of activists, the primary goal is to have the local party win its elections and to be as influential as possible in exerting an impact upon the community. This goal requires certain secondary or operational objectives, and these will command our attention in this chapter. The operational objectives we shall be concerned with are: (1) Recruitment of party members and workers; (2) Education and training of party workers; (3) Coordination of workers' activities; (4) Policymaking; (5) Conduct of election campaigns; (6) Management of local affairs; (7) Liaison between public officials and ordinary citizens; and (8) Finance of the organization. Since comparative data are available on three of the topics, we shall, whenever possible, contrast each constituency party with other equivalent parties in the Greater London area.[1]

RECRUITMENT OF MEMBERS AND WORKERS

As we have already observed, the mobilization of manpower resources is important for any local party which is interested in realizing its goals. Rank-and-file members not only provide the talent pool from which the activists, including candidates for the borough council, are drawn, but they are also a source of financial support through their subscriptions (or dues). While the recruitment of new members would obviously help to relieve the burden upon existing workers in all three parties, the membership dues as a source of revenue are particularly important in Fulham and South Kensington. We hardly need to mention that the enlistment of potential members/activists will be limited by the size of Labour's support in a district—it is easier to recruit in Bermondsey and Fulham than it is in South Kensington. Recruitment is also influenced by the competition of other activities for a person's time. The party's competitors in Bermondsey were the trade unions and the social clubs, while in South Kensington the competition came from the intellectual and social allurements of London's West End and from other welfare 'causes' like racial injustice, anti-colonialism, and improved housing in

London. Probably the Fulham party was able to secure the biggest hold on a person's time because it was in a more favorable competitive situation. Not only did it have different incentives to offer, but it had fewer unions and hardly any social clubs to contend with, and the glamor of the West End was not so attractive to its people. We have already noted that individual membership of the national Party has been eroding since 1952. This means that an examination of the recruitment performance of a given party involves a determination of how well it resisted the national tide. Effective recruitment, of course, really depends upon the guidance of the party leaders and upon the willingness of the workers to 'bear the heat and burden of the day' on the doorsteps. Compared with roughly equivalent parties in their respective categories, Bermondsey and Fulham came off very well, but South Kensington encountered trouble, as we would expect.[2]

Bermondsey. Both the agent and the Member of Parliament were aware of the need to expand the membership of the Bermondsey party, and they worked closely with the collectors and canvassers to help make this possible. On appointed days, the workers would swarm through a neighborhood, while the M.P. would work from the sound truck. Mr Thomas and Mr Mellish were especially interested in bringing more young people into the organization, and the agent kept a sharp lookout for promising individuals to perform party assignments and to stand as candidates for the borough council. When competent incumbents were tempted to give up their posts because of competing pressures, he urged them to reconsider, or if they decided to drop out for a time, he would try to persuade them to return. In the recruitment work, the hard core of activists cooperated with their leaders. Nearly all of the the areas did interim canvassing, and several wards within the areas were quite active in membership drives, one of them picking up about one hundred members during a campaign in 1961. In the spring of 1962, Transport House organized a national membership campaign, and the Bermondsey people responded appropriately. The agent set a target for each area, and he organized a central team to assist workers in designated wards. To help make the drive attractive, the party offered a prize to the group recruiting the largest number of new members. By the end of the year, the Bermondsey party had recorded a 7.5 per cent increase in paid-up members.

Bermondsey's membership peaked at 4715 members in 1954. The following year it was recorded at 4031 and by 1962 it had fallen to 2980. For purposes of comparison with fourteen other London parties operating in strong Labour territory, we shall have to be content with the 1955 membership figures.[3] At that time the average membership of these parties was 2345, and the figure for Bermondsey was 72 per cent above the average; the Bermondsey party was in third place in terms of total members, behind Woolwich East and Barking. This ranking continues to hold when the size of the membership is related to the size of the Labour vote in parliamentary elections. The reader will recall that, according to the officials in Transport House, a desirable membership target is 10 per cent of the Labour strength in a general elecion. Bermondsey exceeded the target in both the 1959 election (14 per cent) and the election in 1964 (17 per cent).

The Bermondsey party, however, experienced some difficulty in converting its members into active workers. Out of a total membership of 2980 in 1962, for example, only about one hundred (3.4 per cent) were active. The hard core of this activist group numbered about twenty-five. In light of these facts, it is not hard to understand why the party leaders were interested in recruiting more activists and in encouraging young people to become involved.

Fulham. The Fulham agent was very concerned about the party's membership, and in his annual reports to the General Management Committee he kept stressing the need for the recruitment of new members. He was always on the watch for new people, especially those with special skills, who might be of use to the organization. The establishment of the Women's Advisory Committee was an attempt to bring more women into the party. The ward leaders, under the agent's direction, embarked upon sporadic recruitment drives, and the Young Socialists usually picked up a few members when they canvassed the young voters' list. Although the membership began to improve in 1961 when the party employed a part-time field worker to help with the canvassing, the really systematic recruitment drive took place in the spring of 1962. Transport House had set a target of 476 new members for the Fulham party, but the Executive Committee was sufficiently caught up in the enthusiasm to raise the figure to 500. The thirteen-week campaign was highly organized; target figures were established for the wards and the Young Socialists, and, as in election campaigns, the work was centrally directed but carried out by wards. The ward officers met with the regional organizer to receive an orientation toward their responsibilities. Canvassing centers were set up in members' homes, from which the canvassers moved along designated roads and streets. When the results were reported to him, the agent sent his customary letter of welcome to each new recruit. In line with the experience in most parties, the attempt to expand the membership rolls by bringing in new people was a difficult undertaking. But the Fulham party managed to register a 2.7 per cent increase.

Just prior to the 1954 redistribution, the combined membership of Fulham East and Fulham West was 6577. After the reorganization, the membership roll of the new Fulham party listed 3510 names, and in 1962 the total was 2442. The Fulham membership compared favorably with the other fourteen Labour marginals; their average was 2261 in 1954, and the Fulham party exceeded it by 55 per cent. In terms of total members, the Fulham party was in second place, behind Lewisham South, a larger constituency. The membership figure at the time of the 1959 election represented 12.8 per cent of the Labour vote, and in the 1964 election it was 10.5 per cent.

The Fulham party had a reputation for bringing a good proportion of its members into active involvement. At the time of this study, it was estimated that, out of a membership of 2442, about 175 (7.2 per cent) were activists, and of this group about 100 were regarded as 'hard core' activists.

South Kensington. With a turnover rate of about 30 per cent each year, the South Kensington party had to 'run fast' in its recruitment program just to 'stay in the same place' in terms of numbers. A few members were picked up at the open-air meetings, and six people were registered after one of the public meetings with a 'name' speaker. But the party did not undertake a systematic membership drive. In a realistic sense, many of the South Kensington members were self-recruited. When a person moved into the district and decided that he wanted to join the party, he would have to get in touch with Transport House because the organization had no premises and was not listed in the telephone directory. Transport House, of course, would put him in touch with the secretary/agent. For an individual to persist under these circumstances, he had to have considerable interest to start with. Some recruitment also took place as a result of the initiative of particular ward officials. The husband-and-wife officers in Earls Court Ward, for example, took pride in building up their organization, and were always watching for new recruits. Efforts to enlist additional members in some wards stemmed in part from a desire to offset the power of Redcliffe Ward. Although the instability of the membership tended to disrupt social ties and weaken cohesion, it was not entirely a negative factor. The influx of new members often brought in enthusiastic young people with fresh ideas, and since they knew little about the history of the organization, they were less bound by the rigidities of precedent.

As we would expect, the membership of the South Kensington party fluctuated considerably, ranging from an official listing of 388 in 1954 to 217 in 1956 and about 250 in 1962. Compared with other parties in strong Conservative districts, South Kensington ranked next to the bottom, just slightly ahead of Chelsea. The average membership of the other fourteen parties was 1139 and it ranked about 66 per cent below this mark. The party's membership in 1959 constituted 4.8 per cent of the Labour vote, and in 1964 the proportion increased to 5.5 per cent.

Given the nature of the district, however, South Kensington people were able to do quite well in persuading their members to become activists. The total number of active members was 20, or 8 per cent of the membership, a figure that looks respectable largely because of the narrowness of the base.

Perceptions of the Recruitment Problem

A section of the questionnaire invited each GMC member to list in open-ended fashion the most serious problems confronting his or her party. Of the 132 people who responded to the question, 78 (59 per cent) mentioned recruitment in such terms as 'we need more new members' or 'more active workers'. The distribution of responses by constituency was: South Kensington, 71 per cent; Fulham, 66 per cent; and Bermondsey, 45 per cent.

The most important influence on the GMC members' perceptions of recruitment as a problem was the class factor. In terms of occupation, the professional/managerial group was the most concerned about recruitment (77 per cent) and the people in routine, clerical jobs exhibited slightly less concern (65 per cent), while the manual workers displayed the least concern about the problem (40 percent).[4] The pattern becomes more refined when we look at objective/subjective self-placement according to social class. The group most preoccupied with the recruitment problem was that of professionals and managerials who considered themselves to be working-class and those individuals who refused to recognize the existence of social class, i.e., those who were sensitive about their working-class ties and were somewhat inclined to evangelical, ideological outlooks (85 per cent). Grouped closely together were the professional/managerial/clerical people who identified with the middle class (69 per cent) and those engaged in clerical work who listed themselves as members of the working class (63 per cent). Again, those portraying the least concern for recruitment were the manual workers who proclaimed their affinity with their own class (38 per cent).[5] We should also observe that 75 per cent of the respondents who had spent less than three-fourths of their adult lives in the district recognized the need for systematic recruitment, compared with 46 per cent who had spent most (75 per cent or more) of their adult lives in the area.[6]

One might have expected the party officers to be sufficiently aware of the recruitment problem to list it on the questionnaire. The major officers at the constituency level were concerned about it, but there was no difference between the ward officers and the non-officeholders. A somewhat clearer distinction emerged, however, between the concern expressed by the people who had served on the Executive Committee and those who had never served on this body.[7] In the South Kensington party, the more involved the GMC members, the more concerned they were about recruitment.[8]

In elaborating on the recruitment problem, 27 respondents (20 per cent) pointed out the need to bring young people into the party. Although the number is small, the important observation to be made is that Bermondsey, where the problem was the most serious, was the most cognizant of it (26 per cent). On the question of recruiting young people, Fulham and South Kensington recorded 18 per cent and 14 per cent, respectively.

Slightly more than half of the respondents emphasized the need to improve their party's image through better publicity and more imaginative appeals to potential recruits. Here again occupation was the most significant factor. About 80 per cent of the activists in professional and managerial jobs were concerned about the 'image' problem, and 60 per cent of those in manual positions felt that better publicity would be beneficial. The group that exhibited the least interest in this matter was the routine clericals (35 per cent), many of whom had a 'traditional socialist' outlook and were distrustful of modern 'public relations' techniques, preferring to rely upon the power of socialist argument.[9]

EDUCATION AND TRAINING OF PARTY MEMBERS

An alert constituency party needs to be concerned about the level of political sophistication of its members, who usually have contact with other voters. A political education program is important, of course, for the new members who require knowledge about the ideology and the way the organization operates. But such a program is also useful for party members of longer standing, who need to be kept abreast of new issues and recent developments as they unfold. Programs of political education may be carried out in ward meetings, in the GMC's policy discussions, or in special forums.

In addition to its political education activities, a constituency party has to provide training for its activists who are called upon to occupy special roles. Probably all of these people require a modicum of training; but, beyond this minimum, the amount needed will depend upon the level of expertise they have already achieved. A district in which Labour is entrenched has, comparatively speaking, more offices to be filled, and yet proportionately fewer of the activists wll have had the advantage of advanced formal education and daily administrative experience on their jobs as, for example, the activists in a more middle-class area. This does *not* mean that the people in middle-class constituencies are more intelligent. In fact, the education of the activists in a working-class district usually did not stop when they left school, and eventually they more than make up what they lack in formal education by self-instruction, special adult education courses, and practical civic and political experience. But, compared with a clerical worker who has learned certain skills in secondary school or at the university and who has sharpened these skills through his occupation, the manual worker usually has not developed clerical expertise to such a degree in his elementary schooling, and his job on the docks or in the factory does not give him much administrative experience. Party-sponsored training programs enable these people to develop the skills needed to carry out specialized assignments, and many of them find their political roles challenging – a welcome relief from the monotony of their regular work. The training programs are usually conducted at special day or week-end 'schools' or as a series of meetings scheduled over a period of weeks. Some of the training schools, as we have already seen, are sponsored by regional organizers.

Bermondsey. We have already observed that the Bermondsey party was concerned about the political education of its members and sought to develop interesting programs in the area meetings, although the response varied among the areas. The party's young political education officer took his responsibilities seriously and collaborated with the area secretaries in suggesting speakers and in making tapes and discussion materials available. At one time the party experimented with a series of public meetings devoted to special issues discussed by invited speakers, but these were discontinued after a year. Some political education took place in the meetings of the General Management Committee, especially when the Member of Parliament explained the complexity of certain divisive issues. When, for example, a discussion of the Common Market erupted in one of the GMC meetings, the M.P. addressed himself to the question in a general way, and the delegates decided to schedule a special discussion session which would be primarily devoted to the issue. In suggesting the meetings, several GMC members expressed a desire to learn more about the Market and Britain's potential role in it. When the meeting was convened, Mr Mellish opened the discussion by presenting the major arguments for and against Britain's entry.

Since most of the election activities were carried out through the area organizations under the leadership of knowledgeable secretaries, there was no attempt to set up a training program for campaign workers. In1962, the party, however, did sponsor a series of three meetings on the problems of local governmet for the benefit of new candidates for the borough council – a program that was well attended.

Fulham. The activists in the Fulham party were seriously interested in elevating the level of political knowledge in their organization. The political education officer cooperated with the ward secretaries in arranging educational components for some of the ward meetings. In 1961–62, the party also sponsored a series of special forums oriented around certain themes in the Labour policy document *Signposts for the Sixties* and led by outside speakers; the meetings on education and immigration were particularly fruitful.

In the training of party workers, the Fulham party was especially active. In 1955, when the new constituency was being organized, it participated in a week-end school sponsored by the regional organizer for the training of election workers for the coming borough council elections. In preparation for the local election in 1962, the agent himself prepared a syllabus and conducted a one-day training course for campaign workers. At the same time, the political education officer arranged a special thirteen-meeting program for twenty new candidates for the borough council. The detailed syllabus included a treatment of the obligations of borough councillors, the mechanics of local government, town and country planning, the reorganization of local government, and the fine points of the law as they related to London boroughs. Each meeting featured a specialist on the subject under discussion, including Members of Parliament and representatives from the London County Council. After each lecture, designated Fulham councillors who had had considerable experience in local government made appropriate comments. This training program, which was successful on all scores, provided a thorough orientation for the new people who were likely to assume a role in borough council affairs.

South Kensington. As we have already seen, all but one of the ward organizations in the South Kensington party attempted to inject elements of political education into their meetings. Political education was also one of the objectives of the open-air meetings on the Earls Court Road. The educational component of the GMC meetings was not strong, largely because the party sought to achieve this objective through their monthly public meetings. Ordinarily, it is difficult for a constituency party in Conservative territory to secure 'name speakers' for meetings of this type, but South Kensington was a distinctive exception. Residing in the constituency were nine Members of Parliament, two former Members, and about a dozen prospective candidates, several of whom were willing to speak at these gatherings. In addition, an energetic public meetings officer button-holed other M.P.s and subject-matter experts to appear at the forums. During 1961–62, the speakers handled discussions on such topics as Nigeria, capital punishment, the social services, education, housing in London, and the Common Market. The party spent quite a lot of money in advertising the forums, and they were usually well attended. The South Kensington people were proud of their public meetings, and they continued to sponsor the project until the mid-1960s.

Since the party had very few borough councillors and since it did not conduct campaigns on the home ground with in-depth thoroughness, it had little need for training schools. The one person who needed to be informed about party organization was the secretary/agent, and he had taken advantage of two week-end schools on the management of election campaigns, which were sponsored by the regional office. He had also enrolled in the postal course for Labour Party agents and was proud of his first-class pass certificate.

COORDINATION OF PARTY ACTIVITIES

A constituency party is concerned not only with the mobilization and training of individual activists, but also with the coordination of their efforts in order to achieve particular objectives. The fact that the organization is composed of free-wheeling volunteers makes the task of coordination more imperative and, in the absence of material incentives, more difficult. At all times the coordinating effort is centered in the secretary/agent, who is the official point of contact with Transport House, the regional office, and other constituency parties. This is especially true at election time, since the agent is the officer who bears legal responsibility. Moreover, it is during political campaigns that the party usually develops a primitive division of labor based upon specified purposes, and the specialization of tasks generates a measure of interdependence which makes the coordination of individual efforts even more necessary.

In examining the coordination of party activities, we shall discuss the effect of a party headquarters upon the party's operation, the diffusion of information through the communications system, and the party's contact with outside units.

Party Premises

The existence and location of a party headquarters may appear at first glance to be a trifling matter, but further reflection shows that they can have an important effect upon the operation of a political organization. If a party does not have central premises, it has to pay rental on halls for its meetings and for its election campaign headquarters – a drain on limited financial resources, especially at election time when a ceiling is placed upon campaign expenditures. Even when the party can afford its own premises, they may be too small to accommodate large groups of activists. When this is the case, the agent is forced to decentralize the party operations through the wards or other subordinate units. This makes it imperative for him to recruit competent people to supervise political activities away from the center and to develop an efficient system of communication so that the work of the entire organization can be properly integrated.

When a constituency party has grown strong enough to establish a permanent, centrally located headquarters, its identity becomes mmre visible and its ability to function as an organization is enhanced. The existence of adequate premises gives the leaders the option of developing a centralized pattern of operation if they perceive advantages to be gained. Moreover, the headquarters, strategically located, provide a central meeting place for the activists as a *group*, widening the orbit of potential interaction and weakening narrow parochialism. With adequate facilities of its own, the party can develop a calendar of social activities which are helpful in the recruitment and retention of members.

The problem of securing adequate premises in a central location has been difficult for the Bermondsey party, partly because two different districts covering a wide area have been fused into a single constituency. The old headquarters in Rotherhithe and Bermondsey West were badly damaged during the blitz, and for a number of years after the war the party had its headquarters at No. 5 Storks Road in the north-central sector of the constituency, only a short distance from the river. This had been the residence of Dr Salter, who had done so much for the party and the borough, and the Labour people had an emotional attachment to the building. These premises, however, proved to be inadequate for the organization's activities, and this limitation, together with the uncertainty of the party's tenure under projected housing plans, made it necessary for the Labour people to negotiate for more suitable quarters. In 1958, the Bermondsey party bought the residence of Dr Gillison, a long-time partner of Dr Salter, for the sum of £5000, borrowing a portion of the funds from the Transport and General Workers Union. Some party members looked upon this move with apprehension stemming from nostalgia and financial concern. The loan, however, was repaid in short order, and the upstairs rooms were decorated and rented to the hospital for use by nurses.

The new headquarters are located in the south-eastern corner of the constituency, close by the Surrey Docks. While the premises are excellent for small conferences, for a social club, and for housing the offices of the agent and the M.P., they cannot accommodate large groups of people. This is one of the reasons – though not the most important – why so much of the party work was carried out through the area organizations under the agent's direction. The GMC meetings required a fairly large room, and the party had to rent accommodations in the library or the town hall, both of which were in a more central location than the headquarters. By the same token, facilities had to be rented for the large social events (such as the bingo sessions). Although the headquarters were remodeled to provide an attractive setting for a social club which the activists enjoy, its small size and the location limited the patterns of potential interaction among members as they engaged in party work and tended to reinforce loyalties at a subordinate level.

After the war, the Labour party in Fulham West was badly in need of premises, for few suitable places for meetings existed in the constituency. Moreover, the cost of hall rentals for an organization in which one or another of the units was holding a meeting every evening was virtually prohibitive. The agent and his colleagues urged the party to consider purchasing a site and erecting a headquarters. The idea was approved by the Executive Committee and the GMC in a close vote, and this action resulted in the construction of Harold Laski House, which became the Labour party premises in the new constituency of Fulham after the 1954 redistribution.

Responsibility for the management of the property was eventually vested in an organization known as 'Fulham Labour Premises, Ltd.,' which was composed of a few party leaders respected by their colleagues for their long experience and wisdom. The composition of the General Management Committee may change rapidly, but this arrangement not only provided for continuity of control over the premises, but also enabled the party to obtain certain benefits, including tax relief, which derive from the corporate ownership of property.

The Labour premises in Fulham proved to be a valuable asset for the party. In addition to the agent's office, a central typing and duplicating facility, and a reception area, the building could accommodate large groups of people in its main halls and enabled the agent to designate sections of it for the performance of specialized activities during campaigns. Thus the headquarters permitted the agent to introduce centralized patterns of administration when he felt that it was wise to do so. Moreover, the relatively central location of the premises made it easier for party members to work with colleagues from other wards or just to drop by for a cup of tea and a chat. In addition, the party was able to obtain revenue from the lease of flats on the top floor and from the rental of halls for trade union meetings, wedding receptions, private parties, etc.

The lack of a permanent headquarters put the South Kensington Labour party at a decided disadvantge. Anyone seeking to contact the organization experienced some difficulty because there was no listing in the telephone directory. For several years, the party was administered from the basement of a member's home in the Earls Court district. When this site was no longer available, the meetings of the General Management Committee were held in people's home – an arrangement that presented scheduling problems since only a few members had flats large enough to accommodate thirty people. In 1961–62, the secretary/agent's apartment in Queens Gate Ward served as the party's central headquarters, and the records and mimeograph machine were kept in the sitting-room. All of the ward meetings were held in people's homes, and there was no regular meeting place for the activists to come together as a group. For the GMC meetings, the party hired a room in the new library building near the town hall, which was a fairly central location. The lack of facilities meant that the secretary/agent had to rely upon the ward officers for some of the jobs that would ordinarily be done in a central headquarters. The absence of premises also meant that the GMC became an important agency for the dissemination of information.

Diffusion of Information

In a federated structure comprising ward organizations, trade union branches, Co-operative societies and parties, women's sections, and youth groups, the coordination of activities requires a two-way flow of communications. Through their representatives and other channels the various units are able to bring before the party's governing body those matters that are of concern to them. Similarly, the delegates who represent these units receive the decisions of the collectivity and relay them to their respective clienteles. At the GMC meetings they also receive the information that the secretary/agent has collected from Transport House, the regional organizer, and other constituency parties, and they make this information available to the rank-and-file members of the units they represent. In 1961–62, the Fulham party used a quarterly newsletter, *Focus*, to disseminate some of its information to all individual members and affiliated units, and the organization in South Kensington published a monthly *Labour Report* for the same purpose. But all three of the constituency parties made use of the GMC meetings for the transfer of information to and from their component units.

In the meetings of the General Management Committee in Bermondsey, about 15 per cent of the meeting-time was devoted to the flow of information.[10] On many occasions, the chairman would order certain information to be circulated among the area organizations, and often the appointment of delegates to particular conferences would be delayed until the next GMC meeting so that the components of the federation would have an opportunity to submit names for consideration. The GMC delegates always insisted that the people who had been chosen to attend conferences and special meetings be present to defend the party's interests, and they expected these representatives to present detailed reports at the next GMC meeting. Individuals who failed to live up to expectations were unlikely to be selected again for other meetings. Complete reports of the GMC meetings were presented at the meetings of area organizations.

In the Fulham party, nearly 20 per cent of the GMC meeting time was given to the diffusion of information, even though detailed reports by the Executive Committee enabled the delegates to dispense with some minor announcements. Like the Bermondsey folk, the activists in Fulham insisted upon reports from the people who had attended special meetings and conferences, and they spent considerable time discussing and providing information about membership drives, the recruitment of women, and the integration of the Young Socialists into the adult party. Often these reports were written out and circulated among the GMC delegates for their comments and questions. At one conference on the reorganization of local government in London, the two delegates disagreed on the conclusions to be drawn, and they both submitted separate reports for discussion. Since the pattern of organization tended to be a bit more centralized than in many local parties, it was important for the two-way communications flow to operate so that the outlying wards would be properly integrated into the system.

Of the three constituency paries, the South Kensington GMC spent the most time – about 34 per cent – in collecting and distributing information within the organization. Although the monthly newsletter was useful in supplying the rank-and-file members with some information, the GMC became the real clearing-house for this purpose, largely because the party was operating without a regular headquarters. At every GMC meeting, each ward secretary and the representatives of every affiliated organization presented reports; without these, the GMC delegates, including the secretary/agent, would not have been able to get an adequate view of what was happening in the party. With the announcement of a forthcoming conference, a discussion often bordering on 'policy' would arise over the question of whether the GMC should be represented; but if representation was sanctioned, the delegates to particular gatherings were expected to present oral reports, which usually precipitated discussions of policy issues. While the GMC members in South Kensington were more inclined to list policy discussion rather than the representation/information function among the reasons why they were willing to serve on the GMC – probably because they did not feel so much pressure from their units, given the nature of their party – they nevertheless devoted a substantial portion of their meeting time to the exchange of information.

The need for communication was recognized by the GMC delegates themselves, especially in Bermondsey and Fulham. In these two parties, the subordinate units were more variegated than they were in South Kensington, and the activists were somewhat more dependent upon the GMC meetings for the information about what was happening in the national organization. In Bermondsey, for example, 20 per cent of the GMC members who responded to the motivational section of the questionnaire indicated that they were prompted to serve on the GMC so that they could represent the interests of their clienteles and carry the necessary information back to them. Awareness of the representative/communications role was even more pronounced among the Fulham activists, 44 per cent of whom listed it as one of the motivations for GMC membership. The comparable figure for the South Kensington people was only 14 per cent; as we have noted, they spent a lot of time performing the information/representative function, but their concern for policy discussion eclipsed it when they were asked why their GMC service was necessary.

The recognition on the part of GMC delegates of the need to represent and to report back to their units appears in a clearer light when we combine the responses of all three parties on the basis of the groups they represented on the GMC. Those who were the most inclined to list the representative/information function as an important motivation for GMC service were the trade union delegates (57 per cent); next in line (42 per cent) was a heterogeneous group of delegates representing other units – the Co-operatives, women's sections, Young Socialists, etc. The least motivated by the need for representation and communication were the ward delegates (14 per cent).[11]

Contacts with Outside Units

Each of the three constituency parties had relationships with external units – more than the activists realized – and in each instance the key person involved was the secretary/agent. He, of course, was the only point of contact with Transport House and the regional office; but he was also responsible for the coordination of effort that was needed when his party engaged in joint programs with other constituency parties.

The Labour party in Bermondsey had only minimal contacts with the regional organizer. Occasionally he or one of his representatives would make a routine appearance at candidate selection meetings to insure that the correct procedures were being followed, and sometimes the Bermondsey agent would contact the regional organizer for advice on how to handle a particular problem. But as a practical matter the regional organizer, realizing that the Bermondsey organization had close ties with the London Labour Party through its chairman, Mr Mellish, often delegated its formal supervisory tasks to the London Labour Party staff. As traditional working-class socialists who were independent in outlook, some of the Bermondsey folk were inclined to resist administrative edicts from Tranport House, where the regional office was located. For this reason they were more favorably disposed toward the requests and instructions that were issued from the separate headquarters of the London Labour Party, which, after all, was headed by 'Bob'. In fact, the Bermondsey party often directed its requests for information and assistance to the London organization rather than to the regional office. As we have already seen, the Bermondsey party carried out a large number of service assignments in behalf of the London Party; the fact that it was one of the few parties with a van of its own made it an easy target for service requests.

Since the constituency boundaries were coterminous with those of the borough, the Bermondsey party did not have the problem of establishing liaison with a neighboring party in order to handle council affairs. Apart from association with other delegations at various conferences, the main contact that the Bermondsey activists had with other constituency parties was through canvassing and other campaign activities at election time. Their assignment to work in one or more marginal constituencies was usually made through the London Labour Party, although occasionally a representative from the regional office would issue the request. Sometimes the Bermondsey party was urged to disperse its workers into several districts, as in the 1955 general election when activists were sent to Putney, Battersea North, and Brentford and Chiswick. But usually it was requested to concentrate its efforts in one marginal constituency; in 1959, it was one of the Wandsworth districts, and in 1964 it was Dulwich. The activists in Bermondsey preferred to give their support to constituencies in south London where they were familiar with the terrain and had previously-established contacts. A favorite area for the Bermondsey people was Lewisham, although Woolwich was a frequent recipient of their aid.

The Bermondsey activists were compulsive about their help to other districts, and they were pleased when the leaders of the recipient parties were so well organized that the canvassing materials were ready when they arrived and they could immediately get on with the job. But when the campaign officers of the host party were inefficient and the Bermondsey workers had to waste time in getting their assignments, the experience was mentally recorded and the Bermondsey agent usually encountered difficulty in recruiting workers to return to that district. On one occasion when a group of Bermondsians traveled to another London borough to help in a council by-election, only to discover that the campaign was poorly organized and that they had wasted part of their effort in duplicated canvassing, they dispatched a letter of complaint to the London Labour Party.

As in Bermondsey, the Fulham party was well organized and required little supervision by the London Labour Party or the regional organizer, and since it jealously guarded its autonomy, it was not inclined to encourage intervention. The Fulham party's relationships with the regional agencies largely involved consultation about general problems. At various times, the secretary of the London Labour Party, the women's organizer, and the regional officer were invited to attend the GMC meetings to discuss organizational matters. The regional organizer assisted the parties in Fulham and Barons Court in working out a liaison arrangement for joint action in borough affairs. He was also brought into consultation with the Fulham party on the question of reorganizing London government.

The Fulham party cooperated with a number of adjacent constituency parties on several ventures. At election time, for example, the party usually joined with sister organizations in sponsoring a huge public rally; in several campaigns Harold Wilson was the featured speaker. When the plan for reorganizing local government in London was being considered, the Fulham leaders consulted with the officials from Barons Court and Hammersmith North in order to study the possible effects of the plan upon their organizations. Fulham was also a leading organizer of and participant in the West London Labour Supporters Society, an organization of several constituency parties which sponsored fundraising lotteries.

In the 1960s, at the suggestion of the regional organizer and with the consent of the Fulham GMC, the services of the agent, Mr Hilliard, were made available to a marginal constituency during election campaigns. In 1966, for example, a mutual-aid arrangement was made with the party in Eton and Slough, under which Hilliard directed the campaign at the same time that he was managing the Labour campaign in Fulham. This was made possible by the employment of a sub-agent in each of the constituencies under the financial auspices of Transport House. Mr Hilliard delegated responsibility to the sub-agents and supervised their work. The scheme enabled the two constituency parties to have the benefit of experienced management while the sub-agents were gaining practical experience in political organization. During the period of this study, the Fulham party, at the suggestion of the regional organizer, took on a trainee agent who received instruction from Hilliard.

The Fulham party, however, had its most sustained contacts with the Labour organization in Barons Court, since it bore joint responsibility with three of the Barons Court wards for the management of the borough. Their alliance for purposes of Fulham council work meant that the two groups had to reach agreement on such matters as a rental policy for council properties, even though their approach to the problem might differ from that taken by the other four wards in Barons Court, which fell under the jurisdiction of Hammersmith. The activities of the people in the Fulham party and their comrades in the three wards of Barons Court had to be especially well coordinated when borough council elections were scheduled. Some of the Barons Court activists competed for candidatures in the Fulham wards. The people from both groups had to work out an election manifesto and appropriate campaign strategies.

Even in the interim between elections, the Fulham and Barons Court parties worked in close harness on matters of mutual concern. In 1962, for example, they prepared a memorandum on hospital services in West London and sent it to the Parliamentary Labour Party. They also organized joint campaigns against the British action in Suez and against the Rent Act which had been sponsored by the Conservative Government.

At times a certain amount of tension naturally developed between the activists in Fulham and Barons Court. After all, the people in Barons Court had their interests deflected in two different directions, and those who lived in the three wards which were tacked on to Fulham only for certain purposes had associational loyalties that were different from those of the Fulham activists. Local rivalries could sometimes be discerned in the selection of borough council candidates, the election of people to the aldermanic bench, and the conduct of campaign activities

Constituency Parties in Action

As a rule, however, the relations between the two parties were cordial. The activists on both sides realized that they were operating in marginal territory and that disunity would impair their political effectiveness. Although the two agents had contrasting managerial styles, their common interests and their respect for each other stimulated them to work together and to provide a good measure of integration on joint endeavors.

For a local Labour party in a hopeless area, the organization in South Kensington had a considerable amount of communication with the London Labour Party and the regional organizer. One reason for this was the attitude of the secretary/agent, who wanted the party to be of service to the wider movement and was a willing point of contact. The officials in the London Labour Party and in the regional office were aware of the potential resources which could be tapped in South Kensington, and they frequently issued requests for assistance at public meetings, for canvassers in by-elections, etc. They also designated the marginal districts in which the South Kensington activists were expected to work in regular elections. In addition, the higher authorities sometimes called upon the South Kensington party to advise and train people from other districts who were also trying to cultivate barren Labour soil. Unlike many constituency parties operating in Tory belts, the South Kensington organization had a secretary/agent who had been at his post for a comparatively long period of time, and he was cooperative in making his experience available to other parties which were facing similar problems. The regional organizer knew that he could rely upon the South Kensington party, and he wanted to see it flourish. He helped the activists revise their constitution so that they would not be bound by the regular norms of representation for GMC positions, and the special set of rules was approved by the National Executive Committee. He also consulted with the officers of the South Kensington and North Kensington parties in working out procedures for the selection of borough council candidates.

We have already noted that the Labour people in South Kensington recognized their obligation to help in marginal constituencies. When a by-election was under way, it was a common sight to see two or three carloads of young canvassers heading for the battlefield on Saturdays and Sundays – a source of manpower that the officials in the London Party and the regional office always welcomed. At one point, an attempt was made to develop some form of coordination among the London constituency parties in hopeless districts – South Kensington, Chelsea, Paddington South, and other organizations. The scheme was dropped, however, because the parties had serious ideological disagreements and could not agree on a central meeting place.

Although the South Kensington party developed a personal interest in the Barons Court constituency because one of its leaders was adopted as the prospective candidate in 1961 and later became the M.P., its closest relationships were with the party in Kensington North. Kensington was a divided borough, and it was necessary for the component parties to maintain liaison so that the attack upon the opposition at the borough level would be properly coordinated. In order to achieve continuing contact, two GMC delegates from each party attended the meetings of the other. The arrangement, however, turned out to be a one-sided affair; the delegates from South Kensington were rarely invited to join in the discussions at the North Kensington meetings, while at the South Kensington GMC the guests from the North actively participated in the proceedings, occasionally informing the group that the North Kensington people might object to a particular line of action.

The relations between the two Kensington parties were often less than cordial, although the full-time agent in North Kensington, recognizing the difficulties between the two areas and wanting to help cultivate interest in the neighboring constituency so that his job would be easier, was always courteous and obliging to his voluntary counterpart in the South. The young people from South Kensington helped to establish a branch of the Young Socialists in North Kensington and they spent countless hours in canvassing on North Kensington doorsteps. But many of them felt that their work was not appreciated. Some of them perceived that while they were tramping the streets to help the North Kensington party, some of the local activists were engaged in recreation or were listening to speakers at public meetings. One did not have to penetrate very far beneath the surface to get at the root of the problem. The South Kensington activists who aspired to become realistic candidates for the borough council naturally cast their eyes upon some of the wards in the northern constituency, and they spent their time on the doorsteps in those areas. The activists in North Kensington, on the other hand, tended to be suspicious of South Kensington people who seemed to exhibit an interest in their political affairs and who might be aspiring to candidacies in the North Kensington preserve.

In the immediate post-war years when North Kensington had established its Labour majority, the South Kensington party would submit the names of potential borough councillors for possible invitation to the selection conferences in wards most likely to elect Labour people. The candidates on this list were usually the settled activists who, it was felt, would make a contribution to the council and had no other way of obtaining seats. At one point, about 25 per cent of the Labour representatives on the Kensington borough council were members of the South Kensington party.

When the North Kensington people began to object to this procedure a new arrangement had to be worked out. Instead of having the South Kensington organization prepare the list of possible candidates, a delegation from the North would come to the South to inquire whether particular individuals would accept nomination for council seats. This practice did not lead to a great reduction in the proportion of South Kensington members representing North Kensington wards, but it did signify the difficulty that the North Kensington party had in recruiting enough suitable candidates from its own ranks.

The resentment of the North Kensington activists toward their sister party was not softened in 1962 when six people from South Kensington were adopted as council candidates in North Kensington wards, and three of them were elected. Despite these rivalries, however, the North Kensington party was the beneficiary of most of the assistance which the South Kensington stalwarts offered in their effort to improve the fortunes of the Labour Party outside of their own territory.

POLICYMAKING

In his classic study of the German socialist party, Michels advanced the proposition that oligarchy inevitably develops in large-scale political organizations — that power is turned over to a few leaders who become detached and aloof from the ordinary members, who grow more conservative in outlook, and who appoint themselves as guardians of the gateway to power, keeping the 'undesirables' out of the important offices.[12] Recently some scholars and publicists interested in Labour Party organization have rediscovered Michels and are wondering whether his analysis applies to the operation of the local constituency parties.[13]

It is true, of course, that the local Labour parties, many of which have had to contend in the past with extremist elements, have developed certain rules and operating procedures to protect the leaders who are responsible for the health and development of their organizations. For example, the standing orders which establish time limits for GMC meetings are designed to minimize the effect of unanticipated behavior on the part of dissidents. Similarly, the rule that all Executive Committee members are bound by majority decisions may be used to strengthen the hand of the leadership when it takes a controversial issue to the GMC for approval. As the reader will recall, the organization comes closer to the oligarchical model during election campaigns when the party is temporarily disbanded and a more visible division of labor is established under the direction of the agent, although he may be called to account when the GMC reappears.

But our study of three constituency parties offers little support, at the lower tier of organization, for the Michels thesis. Far from being remote from the rank-and-file GMC members, the officers were very much aware of the delegates' views and occasionally tailored their pronouncements to make them acceptable. In fact, as we shall see later, there was no significant difference in outlook between the officers and non-officers on many contemporary issues, and on a few of the controversial questions some of the leaders, instead of trying to impose their views, were reluctant even to take a position. Also acting as a curb upon oligarchical encroachment was the system of open elections. In Bermondsey, for example, the GMC members voted to replace a chairman who had held office for about a decade; in Fulham, a sizeable group of unilateralist rebels was elected to the Executive Committee at one stroke, and some of them later became party officers as a result of the competitive elections; and in South Kensington, the situation was so fluid that a majority on one side or the other of a given issue often depended upon which delegates happened to appear at the GMC meetings. Finally, oligarchical tendencies were arrested owing to the fact that the local activists were concerned about policymaking in their parties, they perceived that they were making the real decisions in their GMC meetings, and they were sensitively jealous of their prerogatives. At some time during 1961–62, each of the three General Management Committees rejected a recommendation made by the leaders, the Executive Committee, or, in the case of Bermondsey, the Action Committee. Small wonder that each of the agents was always interested in seeing what his new General Management Committee would look like.

Many of the activists who responded to the questionnaire exhibited an interest in the discussion of issues and expressed the view that the GMC was the decision-making body. When asked why they were willing to serve on their General Management Committees, a total of 52 per cent of the respondents from the three parties indicated that the GMC was the place where the issues were thrashed out and decisions made. This outlook, however, was primarily a class phenomenon, with occupation being the most ineresting and the most important predictor. The occupational distribution was as follows: the top professional/managerial group, 44 per cent; middle-range professional and supervisory, 81 per cent; routine clerical, 63 per cent; skilled manual, 35 per cent; and semi-skilled manual, 7 per cent.[14] The relationship is curvilinear, with the second and third tiers of middle-class respondents being the most concerned with the airing of issues and the determination of policy.

Even if Michels' formulation on oligarchical control held relevance for the national Party, it is probably not applicable at the constituency party level for several reasons. First, the degree of specialization (division of labor) in the organizational structure is too small to foster the growth of oligarchy, and usually the party leaders are not financially autonomous.[15] Second, if they are to be successful, the leaders have to be concerned about the enrollment of new members, and this requires them to be sensitive to the outlooks of potential recruits. Third, the leadership at the local level has to work closely with party members and GMC delegates at the grass roots, and the interaction prevents them from becoming isolated from the viewpoints of other activists. Fourth, the local parties operate under a system of norms which emphasize democracy and place structural restraints upon the leaders; the non-officers have access to mechanisms that can stop the party machinery, and the fact that such blockage is possible, even though it may rarely happen, tends to keep the leaders in check.

If Michels' 'iron law' were operative at all among local parties, we would venture the statement that it would be least applicable in Labour organizations in marginal districts. Although the division of labor is more visible, recruitment is more of a necessity, the views of the recruits and veteran members tend to be more heterogeneous, and the internal elections are more competitive – all of which operate to thwart oligarchical tendencies. Slightly more vulnerable to domination by leaders are the parties in safe Labour areas and the parties in Tory strongholds that follow the 'sect' rather than the 'missionary' model. Here the organizations are more homogeneous in outlook, the lack of competition promotes apathy and slows down recruitment, and the parties often experience difficulty in filling their elective positions.

In a constituency Labour party, the discussion of issues and the formation of policy on the issues usually occur as an outgrowth of the M.P.'s report or as a result of resolutions sent forward by the party's sub-units. The opportunity for rank-and-file members to draw up resolutions for consideration by the appropriate bodies and, if they are approved at each echelon, by the Party's leaders is an important feature of the democratic process in the Labour organization. The procedures for handling resolutions not only enable the local members to express their views but also provide the leaders with a crude index of the sentiments of activists who have succeeded in guiding their resolutions to the pinnacle. Action through resolutions at the local level may be taken in three types of situations: (1) A ward organization, a trade union branch, or some other unit of the local party may send forward a resolution through regular channels to the GMC at any time, or it can draw up an emergency resolution for the GMC to consider; if the GMC delegates give their approval, the resolution will be sent on to an appropriate destination – the National Executive Committee, the regional organization, a ministry, or some other agency. (2) The local units may draw up resolutions for an annual conference, such as the regional Party conference, the Party's Annual Conference, or an annual women's conference, and these resolutions too must win approval from the GMC before they can be sent to a higher echelon. (3) When a Party conference publishes the resolutions that are on the agenda, the GMC of the local party may discuss them in advance, perhaps mandating the conference delegate on some of them or authorizing him to use discretion when he listens to the debates.[16]

Before we turn to policymaking in each of the constituency parties which concern us, it will be useful to get an overview of the amount of time devoted to particular types of subject matter in the three General Management Committees. This breakdown is given Table 5.1.[17]

Table 5.1 Proportion of time devoted to agenda items at GMC meetings

Category of GMC business	Bermondsey		Fulham		South Kensington	
Policy matters	49.6%		30.6%		29.2%	
National affairs/foreign policy		46.5		26.1		25.0
Borough affairs		3.1		4.5		4.2
Party housekeeping	26.1		47.5		22.1	
Election of party officers		6.9		20.6		6.5
Party finance		9.9		13.6		9.3
Miscellaneous		9.3		13.3		6.3
Information exchange	14.8		19.5		33.8	
Elections	7.0		1.0		13.0	
Social affairs	1.4		1.5		1.0	
Party welfare activities	1.0		0.0		0.8	

A local Labour party attracts people who are issue-oriented and who derive pleasure from the discussion of issues that are of intellectual and personal concern. In listing the reasons why they were prompted to serve on the GMC, the largest proportion of the delegates cited policy discussion most frequently – 37 per cent in Bermondsey, 58 per cent in Fulham, and 67 per cent in South Kensington. Apart from the discussion of borough affairs (which occupied between 3 per cent and 4.5 per cent of the agenda time), the GMC delegates devoted a great deal of attention to issues of national concern, including domestic affairs, defense, and foreign policy. The distribution of time spent on the major issues of the day was as follows:

Bermondsey		Fulham		South Kensington	
London reorganization	36.8%	Immigration	25.0%	Common Market	24.4%
Common Market	22.9	London reorganization	22.3	Education	10.8
Housing and rents	10.2	Industrial relations	13.1	Housing and rents	10.7
Immigration	5.4	Common Market	3.9	London reorganization	10.0
Transport	5.1	Other foreign poicy	2.5	Defense	7.0
Defense	4.1	Miscellaneous	33.2	Immigration	3.4
Miscellaneous	15.5			Colonialism	1.8
				Miscellaneous	32.0

With this comparative description of the content of the GMC meetings, we can now move to a discussion of policymaking in each of the constituency parties.

Bermondsey. As Table 5.1 shows, the GMC of the Bermondsey party spent the largest proportion of its meeting time in the discussion of policy matters. For many of the delegates, the GMC was the place where they came into salient contact with the issues of the day, and they looked forward to the discussions. When the constituent elements of the local party submitted resolutions to the GMC, the delegates discussed them thoroughly. Similarly, when the printed resolutions to be considered by the Conference of the London Labour Party were presented for consideration, the Action Committee made its recommendation on each item, but the GMC delegates discussed all of the major issues, sometimes modifying the position taken by the Action Committee and usually mandating their representatives to the Conference. Again, when the Women's Section had taken action on the resolutions which were on the agenda of their annual conference, the ladies submitted their views to the GMC and the delegates went over every item carefully. As we have already recorded, Robert Mellish always presented his parliamentary report, which usually set the stage for policy discussions. Sometimes these discussions turned out to be lively affairs. We noted earlier that on one occasion, when the M.P. had mentioned the Common Market in his report, the GMC members seized the opportunity to discuss the controversial issue but soon discovered that the question was too complex to be handled in the limited time available that evening. They therefore resolved to spend the next GMC meeting on that issue alone, after the routine business was out of the way.

One reason why the Bermondsey activists were concerned about policy during the period of this study was because several of the issues directly affected their lives, and all of the substantive resolutions they adopted were focused upon these issues. They were especially perturbed by the Conservatives' plan to reorganize local government in London. Under the proposed arrangement, Bermondsey would cease to exist as an entity of local government, being fused with Camberwell and Southwark to form a new borough. About 95 per cent of the Bermondsey respondents to the questionnaire expressed vigorous opposition to the reorganization proposal. But more than this, 57 per cent of them were opposd to the adoption of any scheme which might be proposed within the next five or ten years. The reasons for the resistance of the Bermondsey people to the proposed reform are not difficult to find. For one thing, they did not relish the thought of their self-contained community being destroyed by amalgamation with other districts. For another, they had sacrificed to improve the housing conditions of their own people, and they naturally raised this question: Why should the inhabitants of Bermondsey inherit the housing problems of other communities where the local councils had not been so conscientious and foresighted? The Bermondsey activists were also fearful that in a new, enlarged borough with more inhabitants the local councillors would not be able to develop personal relationships with their constituents, which had been a feature of local government in their community for so many years. Nor did they overlook the fact that, with the council members in the new borough being drawn from several communities, some of the incumbent Bermondsey councillors would not be chosen to serve on the new authority. The Bermondsians were proud of their housing estates, their health facilities, their parks, and their programs of local entertainment, and they were united against any perceived threat to these achievements. For these reasons, the Labour activists in Bermondsey were willing to pass resolutions and organize demonstrations against a plan which had been introduced by 'the Tory Government'. Indeed, some of them saw the reorganization issue as a vehicle for breaking down some of the political apathy in the district and rejuvenating interest in the party — a development that had not occurred with the Rent Act in 1958 because so many of the Bermondsey people lived in council housing and had not been affected.

A second issue of concern to the GMC delegates in Bermondsey was the Common Market. One might have expected that the activists in a parochial, working-class district would have been overwhelmingly opposed to Britain's entry, but this was not the case in Bermondsey. Although 49 per cent of the delegates expressed their opposition to Britain joining the Common Market, about one-third of them indicated their approval; another 15 per cent were undecided (the official position of the national Party at the time). Two trips to the docks uncovered the reason why some of the Bermondsey workers were favorably disposed toward Britain's entry. Many of the people whose economic future was tied to the river were growing alarmed by what they perceived to be the declining position of manual labor and the specter of unemployment. They had begun to wonder why so many more ships were discharging only some of their cargoes in Bermondsey and transporting the rest to the continent. And to France, of all places! If the Market could pull France up. perhaps Britain's entry would not be bad policy. Britain's economic future — either in or out of the Market arrangement — was of great concern to Bermondsey's inhabitants, and the GMC delegates devoted a large amount of time to discussions of the issue. The fact that they were more divided on the Common Market than on any other question helped to keep the issue smoldering.

The problem of restricting immigrants from the newer Commonwealth countries also generated anxiety in the Bermondsey party. In 1961–62, only a few of these people worked in the district and none lived there, but the GMC members were distressed by the influx of immigrants into the country, about two-thirds of the GMC respondents favoring restrictions beyond medical checks. Several factors help to explain this attitude. In the nearby borough of Deptford (the home of Bermondsey's M.P.), the immigrants constituted a sizeable component of the population and were not very well integrated with the rest of the community. The Labour activists in Bermondsey were fearful that a similar problem might arise to disturb the tranquility of their district. In addition, many of the GMC members regarded the immigrants as a potential threat to the jobs of native Britishers and a strain on scarce housing resources. During the GMC discussions, several delegates pointed out that these strangers were using Health Service facilities which the British were paying for. They were also concerned about the inadequacy of medical checks for immigrants, especially after an outbreak of smallpox, since the dockers were vulnerable to health hazards deriving from contacts with foreign vessels.

Although the question of nuclear weapons was still bothersome in some sections of the Bermondsey party—about 24 per cent of the respondents listed themselves as unilateralists—the defense issue did not take up much of the policy discussion time. The party's stand on defense had been hammered out at two GMC meetings in 1960. At the first meeting, when the attendance was poor and the M.P. was absent, some of the pacifists made a strong case for unilateralism, and the GMC delegates voted to support the unilateralist position by a margin of two votes. At the next GMC meeting, however, Mr Mellish presented the brief for the multilateralist viewpoint, and the delegates voted to reverse their previous decision by a majority of 48 to 6. The M.P. was extremely effective in summing up the arguments for and against a given policy and then stating his own position and his reasons for it. While the GMC members were vocal on local and domestic issues, they were usually willing to accept the M.P.'s lead on matters of defense and foreign policy.

Contrary to the stereotype of Labour parties in safe territory, the Bermondsey organization devoted a respectable amount of agenda time to the discussion of resolutions. In contrast with the other two parties in the period of this study, the GMC delegates gave careful advance consideration to the resolutions that were to be voted on at the London Labour Party Conference and at the women's annual conference. In addition, the GMC considered six ordinary resolutions submitted by party units, five from the areas and one from a trade union branch. Three of the area resolutions expressed opposition to the reorganization of local government in London; one called attention to a local traffic problem, and one objected to prescription charges in the National Health Service. The trade union resolution, submitted by the Public Employees' union, indicated concern for evictions under the Rent Act. All of these statements were approved by the GMC and sent forward to the appropriate authorities.

When the time arrived for the Bermondsey activists to decide whether they wanted to send a resolution to the 1962 Annual Conference, two of the area units submitted statements to the GMC opposing the reorganization of London. The GMC delegates decided to combine the best parts of each statement which they sent to the National Executive Committee to be included in the Conference listing.

In the years 1955 and 1959–62, the Bermondsey party submitted four resolutions to the Annual Conference: one reaffirming the party's commitment to a planned socialist economy and greater control over the private sector (1955); one urging the national Party to improve its publicity through the use of modern media and techniques (1959); another calling for the regulation of immigrants entering the country (1961); and one opposing the Government's plan to reorganize London local government (1962).[18] None of the statements deviated from what one might expect a local party in a safe Labour area in London to propose. The resolutions in 1961 and 1962 – on immigration control and local government reform – dealt with issues that not only generated the most concern among the Bermondsey activists but also commanded the highest degree of consensus. The immigration resolution, which the Conference had remitted to the National Executive Committee for consideration, was returned to the Bermondsey party by the NEC a few months later. In their letter, the NEC members presented an account of how the Parliamentary Labour Party had consistently opposed immigration controls except for health checks, and they indicated their endorsement of that position. They also disagreed with the Bermondsey view that overcrowding in Britain was the result of 'unchecked immigration'. After discussing the NEC's rejection of their resolution at a subsequent GMC meeting, the delegates decided to let the issue simmer; two years later, in 1963, the Parliamentary Labour Party moved closer to the Bermondsey position, urging immigration controls until an agreement could be negotiated with the Commonwealth countries. The resolution of the Bermondsey party expressing concern about the reorganization of London's local government articulated the sentiments of nearly all of the other Labour parties in the London region, but the Conservative Government nevertheless went ahead with its plan.

Fulham. The amount of time devoted to policy discussion by the Fulham party was somewhat distorted by the fact that it scheduled fewer GMC meetings and had to handle proportionately more 'housekeeping' matters at each session. This was especially true of the annual meeting, where the election of officers and committees required a large allocation of time because most of the posts were vigorously contested. Although some deliberation on issues arose from reports on conferences or on the work of local civic committees, most of the policy discussions were an outgrowth of the M.P.'s parliamentary report; very little discussion was generated by the introduction of resolutions. To a great extent, the issues seized upon by the GMC delegates were those that Mr Stewart had introduced or referred to in his remarks. Mr Stewart, however, did not lead the discussion of policy as Mr Mellish did, and the Fulham activists were not as inclined to follow the cues of their M.P. as were the people in Bermondsey.

It was from the parliamentary report that the question of restricting the entrance of immigrants came to occupy such a high place on the discussion timetable of the Fulham GMC. While slightly more than two-thirds of the respondents opposed restrictions (apart from medical checks), about one-fourth of them favored more stringent controls. More immigrants were living in Fulham than in Bermondsey, and some delegates expressed concern about the lack of integration, the exacerbation of the housing problem, potential competition on the job market, the effect of immigration on the crime rate, etc. The discussion of this sensitive issue tended to take the form of questioning, partly because the proponents of controls realized that they were in the minority. For this reason, the lines of the argument were not clearly drawn, and a number of people who supported restrictions did not participate in the clash of viewpoints.

Another problem to which the Fulham delegates devoted considerable time was that of reorganizing local government in London. From the beginning of the controversy, the Fulham council had been unique among Labour-controlled authorities in recognizing the difficulty of governing a sprawling metropolitan area with an outmoded governmental structure. Many of the local political leaders felt that reform was long overdue, and that the transfer of some responsibilities from the county level to viable borough units might help to generate more interest in local affairs. The party's stand on local government reform had already been formulated before this study was undertaken, and the Labour-dominated council had already presented its testimony to the Royal Commission.

By 1961–62, however, the reorganization plan had taken concrete form, and with most of the other local parties as well as the London Labour Party having come out in vocal opposition to the scheme, the Fulham activists were left standing in the corner by themselves. Most of the GMC discussion of the issue grew out of a report by the M.P. and the report of a regional conference which several Fulham people had attended. Since the delegates to the conference disagreed in their interpretations of the results, they drew up individual reports which were mimeographed and sent to the GMC delegates so that they could study them in advance of the meeting. Some GMC delegates were disturbed by three recent developments: (1) parts of the Government's White Paper, in their view, made inadequate provision for education, housing, and child welfare services; (2) they had heard the case against reorganization, and they had an uncomfortable feeling that their party was out of step with the rest of the movement; and (3) they were worried lest their own M.P., as the front-bench spokesman for Housing and Local Government, would be expected to make the case against reorganization in the House of Commons.

In terms of individual attitudes, the party's leading officers were the most favorably inclined toward the reorganization (75 per cent), while only 18 per cent of the ward officials and 19 per cent of the non-officers took this view. During the discussion of the issue, the agent and the central officers, who had been influential in the party and the borough council when Fulham's original policy stand had been decided, took special pains to outline the history of the question for the benefit of the new GMC members and to impress upon them the need for rationalizing local government and the obligation to present constructive options. The questionnaire results indicate that they were only partially successful. It should be observed, however, that about 87 per cent of the Fulham activists realized that some form of reorganization would have to be instituted during the next few years.

The question of an incomes policy for industry was a matter of grave concern for most of the Fulham delegates, and a discussion of this issue blossomed as a result of the M.P.'s criticism of the Tory 'pay pause' at one of the meetings. On this problem, however, no difference of opinion emerged. During one of his reports, the Member of Parliament also introduced the question of the Common Market, but the issue did not provoke much discussion among the GMC members. The disinclination to tackle the question may have stemmed from the fact that the M.P. favored Britain's entry, while 83 per cent of the activists either opposed or were uncertain about such a policy.

It is interesting to note that the Fulham GMC, which was about equally divided between unilateralists and multilateralists, did not devote any of its policy discussion time to a direct treatment of the defense issue. Unilateralism had sparked controversy in the party the year before (1960–61), and in a number of heated discussions the majority had kept shifting from one side to the other, usually by slender margins. The GMC had eventually resolved the matter by sending a unilateralist delegate to the 1960 Party Conference with a mandate to vote for the multilateralist position.

During the 1961–62 period, the unilateralists were still very active in the Campaign for Nuclear Disarmament, and they operated as a visible faction within the Fulham party. For the most part, however, the people who were deeply involved on either side of the question maintained cordial relations with each other and were seriously interested in fostering unity in the organization, especially since the borough council elections were approaching. This was the main reason why the defense issue was not taken to the floor in a direct way. But it did engage the GMC members indirectly at one of their meetings. During the election campaign for the brough council, some of the unilateralists distributed a letter urging the voters to support candidates who espoused their views. This action produced an immediate response from the opposition camp on two grounds: the voters were being asked to support only a *selected* list of Labour candidates; and the appeal was illegal since printed communication with electors during a campaign must go through the agent and be included in the schedule of campaign expenses. As a counter-move, the agent – with the approval of the party chairman – distributed an article from the *Daily Herald* on the disruptive activities of the unilateralists. The issue came to a head in a subsequent GMC meeting when some of the unilateralist delegates asked whether the expenditure of funds for the circulation of the *Daily Herald* article had been properly authorized. The inexperienced dissidents, however, had not raised their objection through the established procedures, and after a vigorous exchange of views the matter was dropped.

Although unilateralism was a divisive issue for the Fulham party, the activists were noticeably organization-oriented, and were much more concerned about winning elections than they were about introducing and debating resolutions. During the period under examination, the wards and other party units submitted a total of five resolutions: three dealt with local party organization, one concerned the housing problem, and one expressed opposition to an alliance with the Liberals.[19] In the spring of 1962, when the time arrived for the formulation of a resolution for the Party Conference, the Fulham people were so absorbed in local party matters and in campaigning for borough council seats that they forgot about it. They became aware of the oversight late in the political season, and at the next GMC meeting they decided that the subject matter of the resolution should be the hospital and welfare services, and they authorized the officers to draw it up in proper form. When the officers carried out their instructions, the delegates promptly voted approval.

In the years 1955 and 1959–62, the Fulham party submitted only three resolutions to the Annual Conference: one urging the Government to provide the local authorities with more funds and to channel to the public the increased wealth accruing from inflated land values (1960); one pointing out the need for the coordinated development of pipeline transport under public ownership (1961); and the other rejecting the Conservative health plan and calling for a revitalization of the health service (1962). All of these issues were of vital interest to the citizens of Fulham, and the resolutions reflected the long-held positions of the Labour organization in that community.

South Kensington. Like its sister organization in Fulham but in contrast with Bermondsey, the South Kensington party spent relatively little time in policy discussion at its GMC meetings. This is an unexpected finding in view of the fact that the GMC was overwhelmingly middle-class in composition and a large proportion of the delegates indicated that the discussion of issues was one of the main reasons why they decided to serve on the party's governing body. One explanation for the comparatively small proportion of time given over to policy questions was the need of the party, lacking premises and a centralized communications system, to spend time on housekeeping matters and the diffusion of information. Besides this, the party did not have a Member of Parliament to present a report, which usually served as a catalyst for discussion in the other two organizations. Moreover, the monthly public meetings provided some opportunity for the airing of policy questions, although the number of GMC delegates who attended these gatherings varied considerably. Then, too, many of the South Kensington activists traveled in intellectual circles and did not have to rely upon the GMC meetings as a source of information about the issues that were engaging the national Party and the organizations in other constituencies.

Most of the policy discussion in South Kensington grew out of the resolutions submitted by the wards and the reports of the delegates who had been sent to regional and local conferences. Occasionally policy debates would also arise from the handling of matters that would ordinarily be regarded as routine. For example, the question of whether the party should send representatives to a conference on colonialism in which some left-wing 'extremists' were involved gave rise to a lively confrontation. On another occasion a policy discussion was provoked by the question of whether the *Labour Report* should be edited by a single individual or by a three-person board. In light of such spontaneous outbursts, it was surprising that the South Kensington GMC decided, without discussing any of the issues, to give its delegates to the London Labour Party Conference a free hand in voting on the Conference resolutions.

In handling the policy questions, the South Kensington activists tended to discuss them in somewhat theoretical and abstract terms — without the awareness of a personal stake in the outcome which seemed to characterize the discussions in Bermondsey. The issue which attracted the most attention and triggered the greatest discord was that of the Common Market. About two-thirds of the delegates favored Britain's entry into the European arrangement, while one-third of them were vehement in their opposition. As a rule, those who were hostile toward the Market were linked with the unilateralist faction, and they based their arguments on the ideological premise that the new European Community was really a capitalist enterprise which would perpetuate the split between East and West.

Another item of concern to the GMC members was education, especially the need for comprehensive schools; they devoted a good deal of time to the issue even though it produced little disagreement. Nor were they divided on the question of housing and rents, about which all of the GMC members nurtured strong feelings. On the issue of London reorganization, the suggested legislation attracted as much support in South Kensington as it did in Fulham, but the supporters of the reform, in contrast with the Fulham officers, had not been publicly active. In fact, there was no real policy discussion of the issue in the South Kensington party. When the matter was taken up, it was considered largely in terms of how it could best be handled in the election address during the borough council campaign.

Although one-third of the GMC members in South Kensington were professed unilateralists, the question of defense policy ranked below these other issues in the breakdown of discussion time. As was the case with the other two parties, the activists in South Kensington had fought the issue out a year or so before this study was undertaken. In 1960, the GMC had been equally divided into distinct unilateralist and multilateralist wings. The delegates would pass a resolution at one meeting by a razor-thin majority, and then at the next session, after the opposition had done the necessary spadework, they would reverse their stand.[20] Following the unilateralist victory at the Annual Conference in 1960, however, a group of six determined multilateralists in South Kensington set about to mobilize support among the GMC delegates for the position taken by Hugh Gaitskell. In private discussions, they decided which candidates they would support for the various party offices, and by voting as a solidly organized core and by attracting scattered votes from other GMC members, they were able to get their people elected. As a result of this strategy, the multilateralists by 1961 had achieved a strong grip on the organization, and the unilateralist controversy tended to die down. In the meantime, however, some of the people who held to the unilateralist position became dissidents on other controversial issues, such as the Common Market.

As might have been expected, the South Kensington activists were more addicted to the introducing and debating of resolutions than were the other two constituency parties, and foreign policy commanded more of their attention. In the 1961-62 period, the party's units submitted a total of ten resolutions to the General Management Committee. These resolutions dealt with such subjects as the Common Market, the use of United Nations forces rather than SEATO troops in policing the border between Laos and China; multilateralism; education; housing in London; publicity for the Youth Committee of the Kensington borough council; and a condemnation of the Labour Party's attitude toward Bertrand Russell.[21] All of the wards, as well as the branch of the Young Socialists, sent forward at least one resolution during the period under study, but the most active resolution-producing unit was Earls Court Ward, which included a number of people of left-wing persuasion. Several of its statements, however, were introduced as emergency measures and failed to garner the necessary two-thirds majority. It is interesting to note that, in addition to the statement submitted to the Annual Conference, four other resolutions were approved by the GMC and sent to the designated recipients.

The South Kensington people always submitted a resolution to the Annual Conference during the years 1955 and 1959–62. These resolutions did not fit the stereotype of a Labour party operating in Tory territory. They called for: an investigation of the building industry with a view toward reducing building costs and increasing housing construction (1955); an investigation of the advertising industry (1959); the investment of Labour Party funds in equity shares (1960); an examination of all possible forms of public ownership so that the alternatives to nationalization might be considered (1961); and an increase in the number of places for students in higher education (1962). The 1962 resolution on education had an interesting origin and was not without some impact. For this reason it merits a brief treatment.

The Evolution of a Resolution

The author of this study realized that the most lively struggles over resolutions to the Annual Conference were likely to arise in the South Kensington party, and he decided to follow developments in that organization as closely as possible. In retrospect, this was a wise decision: there was a fairly wide range of resolutions from which to choose; the discussions were lively; in the crucial stages the voting was close; and the resolution adopted by the South Kensington activists became an important element in the composite resolution debated at the Conference and eventually found its way into the Labour Party's manifesto in 1964. It will be fruitful, therefore, to trace the evolution of a resolution from its emergence in a ward organization through to its adoption by the delegates to the Annual Conference and its placement in the Labour platform. An examination of this process not only reveals the line-up of political forces in the constituency party, but it also shows how the roles of particular types of activists were crucial to the outcome.

The opening scenes in the drama take place in the Labour party in South Kensington. During the period of this study, the activists in Earls Court Ward were the most prone to the writing and passing of resolutions, and it was natural that the investigator's attention would initially be focused on that unit. Eleven members of the ward organization assembled to consider the adoption of a potential conference resolution. Two statements were proposed: the first was in opposition to Britain joining any alignment of world powers, since such action would further polarize the Eastern and Western blocs, and the second, which was introduced by the secretary, was unilateralist in design and urged that NATO be equipped with conventional forces. The members then had to choose between these two propositions. When they balloted to determine whether the first resolution should be considered, the vote was tied. The chairman, who favored the unilateralist statement of the secretary, nevertheless felt compelled to cast a deciding vote so that the resolution could be discussed. Several objections were levelled against it in the course of the debate, and in the final balloting it was overwhelmingly defeated.

This action left only the unilateralist resolution on the agenda. It attracted considerable discussion, including one amendment, but when the ballot was taken, it too was defeated. This meant that under the procedural rules the ward was unable to send any resolution forward to the GMC. The supporters of each of the two propositions had been so geared up to their own statement and were so confident of its adoption that the need for negotiation and compromise was never taken into account. Before anyone realized what was happening, the second resolution had suffered the same fate as the first statement, and no procedural way was open to the members to reconsider their action. The Earls Court people would thus enter the GMC meeting without a resolution of their own; the only position upon which they could agree was in opposition to the Common Market – a collective attitude that was to be influential in the final action taken by the GMC.

In Redcliffe Ward, ten activists met to consider submitting a resolution to the GMC. Three propositions were placed on the agenda: the first advocated the municipalization of housing; the second welcomed the opportunity for contact with continental socialists which Britain's entry into the Common Market would provide – a special twist designed to make entry more palatable to the left-wing opposition; and the third was an outright demand that Britain take the initiative in entering into relationships with the Market countries. The second and third resolutions were composited into a single statement before the discussion began.

In weighing the merits of municipalized housing and the Common Market as subject-matter areas for a potential resolution, one local party official supported the housing topic for the reason that the Common Market issue might split the national Party when it was still nursing wounds from the struggle over unilateralism. This view was countered by the argument that a large number of anti-Market resolutions were bound to be pressed upon the Conference and that a few resolutions in favor of Britain's entry would provide needed balance, supplying Party leaders with evidence that there was strength on both sides of the question and that the delegates should refrain from taking premature action. When the ward members called for the question, three of them voted for the housing resolution, and six of them supported the proposition on the Common Market. They then proceeded to tidy the wording on the Market statement, which was sent to the GMC in the following form:

> This Conference welcomes the prospect of Britain's entry into the European Economic Community and urges the National Executive Committee to take the initiative in working with the democratic-socialist-based political and economic Community in Europe.

The people in Redcliffe Ward knew that their resolution would encounter some opposition from Earls Court Ward and from a few of the activists in Holland Ward, although they hoped the wording with respect to contact with other socialist parties would soften the sting for some of the people. The Redcliffe contingent, however, counted on the support of the Queens Gate organization, and they anticipated that competing resolutions might split their opposition with the result that their resolution could survive the struggle.

The people in Holland Ward assumed that a resolution from Earls Court Ward would be congenial with their views, so they decided not to transmit a resolution of their own. The only organization left, then, was Queens Gate Ward, which did not meet regularly and which was a nesting-ground for multilateralist outlooks. But the action of this party unit turned out to be strategic, and the story largely centers around one individual who had been a member of the South Kensington party for only a few weeks.

This young man — from a large, working-class family in the north — had managed to obtain a grammar school education and was working on a degree in physics at the Imperial College. Aware of the advantages that education can bring to an individual and sensitive to the need for trained people if the British economy was to expand, he was disturbed by the small numbers of places in higher education available to qualified students. His views had been shaped by a reading program on the subject and by a year's visit to the United States. His concern about the narrow range of opportunity in British higher education was reinforced through association with a former grammar school classmate with whom he shared a 'flatlet' in South Kensington.

The two chaps were unhappy about the 'lack of thought and action' within the Labour Party with respect to the Tory Government's attitude toward higher education. In pursuing the matter, they arranged a meeting with a young M.P. who had recently won a seat in the House of Commons and who encouraged them by articulating their feelings in a more 'elegant' way. Walking back from the meeting, the young physicist and his colleague determined to do something concrete about the problem if they could, and the thought occurred to them that they might lay down a resolution at the next ward meeting.

The two men had no knowledge about the rules of the ward club. They thought that the ward could submit more than one resolution to the

GMC, and on the day before the ward meeting they set about to draw up five of them. The first of these – influenced by their conversation with the M.P. – called upon the Government to make places available in higher education for 'all who desire it' and, as a first step, for at least 400,000 students by 1970. The next two resolutions – one in support of the Common Market and the other a pro-NATO statement – were prompted by their sincere interest, but the phrasing was carefully planned so as to produce a minimum of hostile reaction. The fourth and fifth resolutions called for urban renewal on a massive scale and for full mortgage guarantees at low interest for young married couples who wished to purchase their own homes. Although these two statements reflected the views of the authors, they were largely designed to be 'stoppers' to prevent the adoption of extremist resolutions against the Common Market and against NATO.

When the physicist and his colleague arrived at the ward meeting in Queens Gate, they joined seven other members in the gathering. Three members of the group were university students who shared a flat and who had joined the Labour Party that evening. When the resolutions item appeared on the agenda, an older member offered a strong unilateralist motion. The two activists who had the five resolutions in their pockets were still under the impression that the ward could send forward more than one policy resolution, and they did not put up much resistance at first. But when they were informed that only a single resolution could prevail, they unlocked their verbal artillery and aimed it at unilateralism. To offset the unilateralist statement, the young physicist introduced his pro-NATO resolution, at the same time informing the group that he had another resolution on education which he preferred to offer.

When the unilateralist and NATO statements were set aside, the ward members turned to an examination of the statement on education. A 'near-the-knuckle' encounter broke out over the phrase 'for all who desire it', and the two authors of the resolution peppered the discussion with facts they had been gathering for several weeks. An attempt to modify the 'desire' section of the statement resulted in a garbled amendment which the members rejected. After nearly an hour of debate, the resolution on education was carried by a vote of five to four, with the proposer of the unilateral statement and the three new members joining in opposition.

The two authors of the statement on education had done their homework, and by careful planning and persistence they were able to fill the vacuum created by the defeat of the unilateralist motion. Their resolution as adopted by the Queens Gate unit read as follows:

This Conference deplores the Government's inadequate plans for expansion in higher education and strongly recommends, as a first step to the provision of free higher education of the student's choice for all desiring it, the forming of plans to provide places in higher education for at least 400,000 students by 1970.

They knew that the next step was to get their resolution accepted by the GMC delegates. But as they thought about the matter, they became more confident about its passage. The people on the GMC, they felt, usually think in terms of 'left' and 'right', and the resolution that is the hardest to fit into these categories is likely to attract the strongest support. Their only concern was that another ward might have formulated a unilateralist or anti-Market resolution in such moderate phraseology that it would draw enough support to pass. When they learned that the only competing resolution was one favorable to Britain's entry into the Market, they grew more confident of success, optimistically predicting that their statement would pass by a solid majority. Their forecast of victory proved to be accurate, but they misjudged the margin.

The General Management Committee of the South Kensington party was convened in June to consider, among other things, the resolution to be transmitted to the Annual Conference. On the agenda were the two resolutions from the wards – one from Redcliffe urging Britain's entry into the Common Market, and the other from Queens Gate on the expansion of opportunities for higher education. Six delegates – four multilateralists and two unilateralists – were absent, each having sent his or her apologies.

The Queens Gate resolution on higher education was the first item of business. In making his case, the young physicist listed the objections which had been raised at the ward meeting and then presented a statistical indictment of the British higher educational system for its inadequacies, defending in anticipatory argument the phrase 'for all desiring it'. In a procedural vote, the GMC delegates decided to consider the Queens Gate statement as a possible resolution for the party, with one member opposed. The person who had been largely responsible for the Common Market resolution from Redcliffe Ward then introduced the statement, and the GMC members voted to consider it. This action opened the gate for a debate on the merits of the two propositions.

As the discussion moved along, it became focused upon the question of the Common Market, with the delegates from Earls Court Ward leading the attack. At one point, an Earls Court representative tried to amend the resolution by substituting the word 'regrets' for 'welcomes' – a move that was ruled out of order since it changed the substance of the original statement. Most of the opposition to Britain's entry into the Market came from the unilateralists (almost coincident with the 'left'), although a few of the orthodox 'rightists' could not bring themselves to support a pro-Market resolution until they knew the negotiated terms.

This was a policy debate of fine quality – the longest and liveliest which occurred in the South Kensington party during the period of this study.

When the delegates voted to terminate the debate (13 to 6), the spokesman for each resolution summed up the discussion and made a final plea. In the balloting which followed, eleven delegates voted for the resolution on education, and ten supported the statement on the Common Market. Included in the one-vote majority were the delegates from Queens Gate Ward, most of the unilateralists (especially those from Earls Court Ward), the Young Socialists, and one multilateralist who was worried about the terms for entry into the Common Market. Once the decision had been reached, the delegates began to examine the wording of the resolution carefully. After some discussion, they authorized the young physicist and the party officers to 'work it over' so that the figures would be 'realistic' and the language appropriate. When the statement was sent forward to the Annual Conference, however, its wording was the same as when it was introduced at the meeting of the GMC.

The South Kensington party selected the chairman, a representative from Redcliffe Ward, to be its delegate to the Annual Conference. When the NEC published the list of resolutions, the local activists noted that twenty-six of them dealt with education, and they assumed that this would be the subject of an important debate at the Conference. They knew that their resolution would be composited with others of a similar nature, but they hoped that their delegate would be lucky enough to be called to the debating rostrum and cast a beam of glory upon the South Kensington organization. Their hope was realized, for the delegate used his initiative to carve out an important role in dealing with the subject of education at the Conference.

Shortly after arriving at Brighton, the delegate from South Kensington began to study the twenty-six resolutions on education with an eye toward fitting them into a single statement which could be handled efficiently in a Conference debate. He knew that the framework of the South Kensington resolution could stand a better chance of being preserved if he had a hand in drafting the composite statement. After considerable effort, he managed to formulate a composite resolution which embraced no fewer than twenty-two of the original twenty-six statements, and he took the draft to the chairman of the compositing committee who was relieved to see a preliminary summary of the resolutions in such complete form. When the representatives of the resolution-sponsoring organizations assembled for the compositing, the Scottish delegates insisted upon adding a statement concerning the need for another university in Scotland, and this problem was resolved by a general remark about the 'just needs of Scotland'. After having taken care of the substantive aspects of the composite resolution, the interested parties had to decide who would move and who would second the resolution from the floor. Since the delegate from South Kensington had done nearly all of the work on the resolution on education, his colleagues on the compositing committee felt duty-bound to invite him to be the main spokesman during the Conference session. The problem of deciding who should second the resolution was a bit more difficult, since the Scottish delegates wanted to make sure that their point of view was adequately presented. Under a compromise agreement, one of the seconding positions was allocated to a Scotsman and the other to an English delegate.

When the resolution on education was taken to the Conference floor, it was listed as Composite No. 16.[22] The section that was influenced by the South Kensington motion assumed this form:

> The Conference deplores the Government's neglect and lack of foresight in the field of education and reaffirms that Labour will accord it the highest priority.
>
> It calls upon the National Executive Committee to draw up an emergency programme designed to provide in the shortest possible time:
>
> (a) places in universities and other institutions of higher education (including training colleges) for all possessing the necessary qualifications. Due regard should be paid to geographic distribution, including the just needs of Scotland; . . .

The debate on education came late in the afternoon, after lengthy discussions of transport policy and housing, and time pressures dictated that it be short. This was not a serious limitation because the feelings of the Conference delegates on the subject of education made the composite statement relatively non-controversial. The Scottish 'seconder' seized the opportunity to point out how his region was being subordinated to England in the allocation of educational resources and to make a case for the establishment of a sixth university in Scotland. The speaker who closed the discussion in behalf of the National Executive Committee indicated a willingness to accept the composite resolution, provided that it be read in conjunction with the statements on education which had appeared in the official policy document, *Signposts for the Sixties*. The Conference then approved the composite resolution.

The debate on education at the Party Conference a year later (1963) was a bit longer and covered some of the same ground, but did not touch the subject-matter of the South Kensington resolution of the previous year.[23] The general subject of education had been debated at Party Conferences on many occasions, and certain basic reforms commanded a wide base of support. It was to be expected that the essential elements of these reforms upon which there was broad agreement would attract

Constituency Parties in Action

the attention of the Labour Party leaders as they proceeded to formulate the education section of their 1964 election manifesto. The essence of the resolution of the South Kensington party in 1962 was reflected in the Party platform as follows:

> Our country's 'investment in people' is still tragically inadequate. The nation needs and Labour will carry through a revolution in our educational system . . .
>
> (v) Labour will carry out a programme of massive expansion in higher, further and university education. To stop the 'brain drain' Labour will grant to the universities and colleges of advanced technology the funds necessary for maintaining research standards in a period of rapid student expansion.[24]

The complete statement on education in the manifesto, upon which the Labour Party made its educational appeal to the electorate, had long been in the making. It reflected the findings of special study groups, as well as the views of Labour activists expressed in resolutions submitted to the Conference at various times. One element in the Party's educational policy reflected the sentiments expressed in the resolution of the South Kensington party two years earlier. This resolution had been pushed through a ward meeting and taken to the GMC by two young men who were sensitively concerned about the need to expand opportunities for students in Britain's higher educational establishment.

Conference Resolutions: A 'pilot' analysis

Standing by themselves, the Conference resolutions in the three constituency parties in 1955 and 1959–62 do not tell us much: Bermondsey submitted four out of five possible statements, all of them dealing with domestic or local affairs and one of them (on immigration) challenging what was the Party's official position at the time; the Fulham people sent forward three out of five possible resolutions, all of them touching upon local problems; and the South Kensington party exercised all of its 'resolution prerogatives', but none was a 'radical' pronouncement – the activists seemed to be striving for unity in the organization and settled upon relatively non-controversial items. Since these sets of resolutions, viewed in isolation, are not very meaningful, we decided to try to put them in a broader context.

Conventional wisdom suggests that constituency parties in safe Labour areas do not send in as many resolutions as their counterpart organizations in other districts, and that the statements they do submit deal largely with 'bread-and-butter' issues and tend to be supportive of the leadership. Labour parties in the 'hopeless' areas, on the other hand, are much more entranced by the resolution process and devote a lot of time to the spinning out of statements on defense and foreign policy. In line with these views, we hypothesized that, in sets of constituency parties based upon the size of the Labour Party's majority, as the Labour strength diminished there would be an increase in: (1) the number of resolutions submitted; (2) the number of resolutions dealing with defense and foreign policy; and (3) the number of resolutions incongruent with the position of the national leadership and/or the Party's official position. We divided the constituency parties in the Greater London area into five groups: Group I – impregnable Labour (19 cases); Group II – moderate to marginal Labour with a sitting M.P. (23 cases); Group III – alternating between Labour and the opposition (23 cases); Group IV – moderate to marginal Conservative with a sitting Tory M.P. (17 cases); and Group V – impregnable Conservative (20 cases).[25] The resolutions we used were those submitted to the Annual Conference in 1955, 1959, 1960, 1961, and 1962.

The data indicate that as Labour's strength diminished, the average number of all resolutions sent to the Conference went up: Group I, 3.1; Group II, 3.7; Group III, 4.0; Group IV, 4.2; and Group V, 4.3. The data on the subject matter of the resolutions also show that defense and foreign policy issues became more conspicuous as Labour's electoral chances declined.

Category	Defense/ Foreign Policy	Domestic Policy/ Miscellaneous	Party Matters*	No.
Group I	20.4%	75.9%	3.7%	54
Group II	29.6	63.0	7.4	81
Group III	46.5	45.4	8.1	86
Group IV	52.3	42.0	5.8	69
Group V	50.0	41.0	9.0	78

* Important resolutions dealing with Party matters – such as the locus of power in the Conference, the restoration of the Labour whip to rebel M.P.s, the need to cease personal attacks, etc. – are included here. Resolutions dealing with more routine Party affairs – such as the need for more agents, better propaganda, improved organization, etc. – have been eliminated in this table. The number of the latter resolutions, however, is relatively small, and their elimination does not affect the results.

In similar vein, the incidence of resolutions that ran counter to the position taken by the national leadership and/or the Party's official position tended to increase in the categories in which Labour's voting strength was attenuated. The figures are: Group I, 11.1 per cent; Group II, 29.6 per cent; Group III, 40.7 per cent; Group IV, 36.2 per cent; and Group V, 47.4 per cent.[26]

One of the interesting findings to emerge from this analysis is that the constituency parties in Group III – those that were in power by only a slender margin or were within striking distance of winning power – were conspicuous in their concentration on defense and foreign policy questions and were near the top in their emphasis upon policy stands that ran counter to the leadership and the official posture of the national organization. This is another way of saying that, contrary to what some of the literature tell us, local parties in marginal districts were not espousing 'moderate' policies.

Coming back to the three constituency parties with which this study is concerned, we see that Bermondsey submitted an above-the-average number of resolutions in Group I (4.0 as opposed to 3.1 for the category), but it followed the group in emphasizing domestic concerns. The Fulham party, on the other hand, was below the Group II average in resolution submissions (3.0, in contrast with 3.8 for the category), but its resolutions did not reflect any of the defense and foreign policy issues which were of interest to some of the other parties in its group. South Kensington's resolutions record was higher than the Goup V average (5.0, compared with 4.3), but this party too did not send forward any of the defense and foreign policy statements that were so prominent in the resolutions of its sister organizations in the category.

CONDUCT OF ELECTION CAMPAIGNS

The other functions of a local constituency party are largely oriented around its primary task: organizing campaigns to win elections. Political campaigns supply the party with a set of concrete objectives, and since some people make their initial appearance during these periods, party organizers have an opportunity to capture their interest so that they will remain involved. Local elections, scheduled on a regular basis, are an important stimulus for the constituency organization. Sometimes they appear on the calendar shortly after a parliamentary contest, serving to keep the party out of its post-election doldrums. Although the question of how much the 'quality of organization' affects the outcome in general elections is unsettled, there is a probability that organization is a strategic factor in local elections, especially in marginal wards, since the voter turnout is smaller.[27]

In considering the management of election campaigns in the three constituencies, we shall be primarily concerned with the borough council election in 1962 and the parliamentary election of 1964.[28] Our examination will focus upon the method of selecting candidates, the organization and activities of the campaigns, and the voting results.

Selecting the Candidates

Parliamentary elections. The activists in a local Labour party usually take the selection of their parliamentary candidate very seriously, and the process is designed to be thorough. To begin with, the party can draw its potential nominees from two lists of approved candidates. 'List A' is a roster of people who have been officially placed on the 'panels' of most of the trade unions; this means that they will be 'sponsored' by and receive financial assistance from their trade unions if they are selected by a local party. The 'B List' is a register of 'unsponsored' aspirants whose names have been sent forward to the National Executive Committee by action of a person's General Management Committee. The usual way for an individual to get his name attached to the B List is to get one of the wards, often the one he resides in, to nominate him. He then presents himself to the GMC, making a statement about his background and qualifications and answering questions posed by the GMC members. After the GMC has approved a nomination, it sends the aspirant's name to the National Executive Committee, and he then fills out an application form and lists as references two 'well-known members of the Labour Party'. At the time of this study he was requested to appear for an interview before a few members of the NEC's Organization Committee who passed upon his 'suitability' as a possible candidate.

When a local party begins the task of searching for a prospective candidate, it may decide to request the NEC to send either the A list or the B List, or both, and it authorizes the wards and the affiliated organizations to make specific nominations. After all of the nominations have seen submitted, the Executive Committee of the local party picks out about six or eight nominees – a group that constitutes the 'short list'. This list of names is then presented to the General Management Committee for its approval. The GMC delegates are entitled to revise the list if they desire, dropping some people and adding others.

Once the 'short list' has been decided upon, the GMC and the regional organizer set the date for the 'selection conference', which is another name for a special meeting of the GMC. At this conference each aspirant is given time to make a short speech and to answer questions. After all of the candidates have 'performed', the delegates proceed to the voting without discussing the merits of the several nominees. The voting is the 'exhaustive ballot', i.e., the delegates keep voting by secret ballot until one person has a clear majority, the candidate with the smallest number of votes being dropped each time.[29]

No systematic study has been made of selection conferences for parliamentary candidates to determine what factors are strategic in certain types of situations.[30] For such an analysis to be most useful, several factors that might influence selection would have to be taken into account. (1) The political views of the GMC delegates and the aspiring nominees; (2) The socio-economic composition of the electorate and the perceived qualifications of the candidates to 'fit the bill'; (3) The trade union or cooperative affiliations of the GMC members and the appropriate sponsorship of the potential candidates; (4) The presence of local candidates among the nominees, and information about their involvement in local conflicts; (5) The behind-the-scenes suggestions of the agent, the regional organizer, or the retiring M.P.; (6) The performance of the candidates at the selection conference; (7) The element of 'chance' – in a case that has been called to the author's attention, the friend of one of the candidates had to leave the conference before the balloting was completed, and if he had left one ballot earlier, the eventual winner would have been dropped from the running because of the close vote.

In Bermondsey, Robert Mellish's formal association with the local party began in 1946 when a by-election was scheduled in Rotherhithe because the sitting Member of Parliament had left the House of Commons to take an executive post with the National Coal Board. Mellish, who was sponsored by his union, the Transport and General Workers Union, was one of eight people on the 'short list'. He managed to secure the candidature largely because his exceptional ability enabled him to perform well at the conference, and also because some of the union branches which were affiliated with the party but had not appointed delegates to the GMC decided to fill the vacant slots in accordance with the legal prescriptions.[31] When the two Bermondsey constituencies were amalgamated in 1950, Mellish and his colleague from Bermondsey West, who was also a Transport and General Workers Union M.P., found themselves competing for the candidacy. Mellish, who was a much younger man and whose record as an M.P. had already attracted attention, won the selection easily. He experienced no difficulty in securing readoption in subsequent elections. The author attended the readoption meeting in 1964, and he observed the enthusiastic response which Mr Mellish received from the GMC delegates.

When the redistribution created the new Fulham constituency in 1954, Michael Stewart and Dr Edith Summerskill, who had represented Fulham East and Fulham West, faced each other in the selection conference. It was a difficult decision, for both of these people had been good Members of Parliament and were respected for their service. One might have expected Dr Summerskill to emerge the victor, since most of her wards were included in the new constituency, while some of Mr Stewart's wards had been shifted to Barons Court. In a situation like this, however, it is possible for certain value preferences to tilt the balance. Dr Summerskill had expressed her opposition to boxing without distinguishing between the amateur and professional brands; she was a strong advocate of women's rights, which was no longer an issue in the party; and she was active in the birth control movement which was not popular among religious groups in the area. In any event, Michael Stewart won the candidature by a narrow margin, and in subsequent elections, including another redistribution in 1971, he was readopted without difficulty.

As residents in a Tory area, the GMC members in the South Kensington party are called upon to select a new parliamentary candidate for each election. They usually follow the practice of selecting a local person – a neophyte who has never stood for election before. They regard South Kensington as a training ground for parliamentary aspirants who desire campaign experience and are willing to pioneer in the wilderness.

In 1962, the South Kensington party prepared to select its prospective candidate for the next election – the contest that was eventually scheduled for 1964. The Executive Committee recommended that each ward interview several candidates and that no ward should nominate any candidate who was being considered by any of the other units. The General Management Committee endorsed the recommendation, but only Redcliffe Ward carried out the plan of interviewing several people, and it voted to nominate Mr Barrie Stead, a solicitor's clerk. Holland Ward decided to nominate one of its members whose potential candidacy had recently been approved for the B List. Earls Court Ward also nominated one of its members. A member from Redcliffe Ward arranged to have her trade union branch submit a nomination, but the individual who was chosen decided to work with Ivor Richard in the Barons Court constituency. The union branch then turned to another South Kensington activist, but he withdrew because he was sitting for his doctoral examinations. Another Redcliffe Ward member persuaded the Central London Fabian Society to make a nomination. When all of the arrangements had been completed, the party had four nominees: one each from Redcliffe, Holland, and Earls Court Wards, and one from the Fabian Society in Central London. The Executive Committee decided that the four people would constitute the 'short list', and the GMC endorsed it.

The party encountered difficulty in scheduling the selection conference. On the appointed day, the Fabian Society nominee could not attend for personal reasons, and the Earls Court nominee was in Africa. Their inability to be present resulted in a postponement. The conference was finally held in December in the flat of the chairman of Earls Court Ward. The nominee from that Ward was still in Africa, however, and he submitted a letter of protest. Twenty-one GMC members attended the conference. Each of the three nominees was allotted fifteen minutes to present his speech and fifteen minutes for questioning. The people from Redcliffe Ward were not mandated, but the Earls Court members voted as a group for the Fabian Society nominee. The Redcliffe nominee, Mr Stead, was just short of a majority on the first ballot, and in the next round he managed to win by a narrow margin.

Borough council candidates. In preparing for borough council elections

Constituency Parties in Action 201

the party solicits nominations, and the General Management Committee approves the panel of nominees. This endorsement procedure is to insure that 'undesirables' do not get their names on the list. The members of each organization determine which people they wish to interview, although they are required to interview the incumbents who desire to stand again. The Executive Committee may also decide to send potential candidates to be interviewed by a ward. A selection conference is composed of the ward members and the members of the Executive Committee, who are also entitled to vote if they do not have a conflict of interest. The Executive Committee members are obligated to vote for the recommended nominees decided upon by the majority.

In the 1962 borough council election, the Bermondsey party needed to select forty-five candidates from the various wards. At the appropriate time, the General Management Committee invited the party units, including the affiliated organizations, to submit nominations, and it subsequently approved a panel of fifty-five nominees, a larger number than in the previous contest. The potential candidates were asked to indicate the wards they would like to stand in, but some expressed no preference. Although all Executive Committee members were entitled to attend the ward selection conferences, the Bermondsey party followed the practice of sending only five representatives. The Executive Committee made no recommendations to the wards. The Bermondsey people have a reputation for taking their candidate-selection responsibilities seriously, insisting that their council members maintain good attendance records in the council chamber and show an interest in the wards they represent. They usually choose their candidates from among the party activists. In 1962, all but six of the candidates were in this category, and five of the people who were not active in the party were involved in trade union work. Fourteen of the succesful candidates were not members of the retiring council. Two incumbents were not chosen to stand again.[32]

Since Fulham is a marginal area, the party is faced with the problem of distributing its candidates among the safe wards in order to insure a 'good council' and a balanced ticket. In 1962, the Fulham people had the additional problem of placing two sitting members who had been moved out of the Barons Court wards. They needed twenty-four candidates for the Fulham part of the borough, and they had twenty-nine names on the approved panel.

The selection machinery was put into operation when the Executive Committee met to examine the records of the nominees carefully and to outline the rules to be followed. The members realized that they were engaged in a sensitive undertaking, for personal feelings can be injured in the selection process. But they recognized that they had to act with integrity; it was their responsibility to see that the interests of the entire party were not neglected and to be on guard against nepotism. At this meeting, they discussed a 'code of understanding' which was said to be a summary of the principles that had guided past selections.[33]

At the ward meeting prior to the selection conference, the secretary presented background information on the candidates who were to be interviewed. The members of the Executive Committee met before each adoption meeting to determine which nominees they should recommend to the ward. The party chairman was the presiding officer at each conference. After the meeting opened, each aspirant in alphabetical order presented a three-minute statement, which was followed by five minutes of questioning. The questions were designed to probe the nominees' ideas on housing, London reorganization, the civic theater's programs, improvements in the library, how to assist the old people, and how to improve the efficiency of the borough. Most of the candidates were asked about the committees they would like to serve on, and some were queried about their willingness to work in the ward. When the interviews were completed, the conference members proceeded to vote without further discussion. Only those who had been present during the entire meeting were permitted to mark their ballots. The author was informed that in some instances the attendance of council members at ward meetings was taken into account.

The first selection conference — held in Walham Ward, a safe area — was the most difficult because the Executive Committee members were all potential nominees and could not attend the proceedings. The meeting was conducted by the party chairman, and the agent was present, but they could not participate in the discussion or the balloting. After the first selection meeting, however, the Executive Committee members who had been selected as candidates could participate in the conferences. As more selections were made, the representatives of the Executive Committee usually outnumbered the ward members, and their recommendations were carried without much difficulty. The candidates are usually chosen from the ranks of the party activists, but those who are not are drawn into the circle once they get on the council. Out of a total of twenty-four candidatures, seventeen went to incumbent members of the council, while seven went to newcomers. Five aspirants were not selected, including three who had previously occupied council seats.

The South Kensington party ran into problems in selecting its full slate of borough council candidates. The GMC decided to run candidates in every ward on the assumption that if any areas were left uncontested, the Conservatives would have surplus workers to send elsewhere. This meant that thirty-six candidates had to be lined up, and this was a struggle because the group of activists was small to begin with and six of them were standing in North Kensington wards. The Executive Committee had decided that the ward secretaries would participate in the allocation of the candidacies, but the agent did not have time to schedule a meeting of the ward leaders. At one of the GMC meetings, he had to ask for volunteers, and he did the allocating himself, assigning the candidates to their own wards whenever possible and trying to strike a balance between men and women. When he thought that he had a complete list, he discovered that three of the candidates had already moved out of the constituency. By the time the ballots were printed, the Labour candidates for the South Kensington wards included seventeen GMC members, five who were fairly active in the wards but were not on the GMC, five who were not active and not on the GMC, and nine volunteers from North Kensington.

Campaign Organization and Activities

As we have already indicated, effective campaigning is an ongoing activity. A flourishing party keeps its election register up to date by frequent canvassing and maintains its visibility through local press coverage. The agent attempts to keep the Labour M.P. or the prospective candidate in the public eye by having him attend civic gatherings in order to meet voters and get his name in the local paper. As the election campaign begins, these sorts of activities are stepped up and others are undertaken. In examining electoral activities of the three parties, we shall be concerned with the pattern of campaign organization and the forms of electioneering, focusing upon the 1964 parliamentary election and the 1962 borough council election in each constituency.

Bermondsey. In carrying out its election tasks, the Bermondsey party used a decentralized pattern of organization. This was to be expected in view of the relative autonomy of the ward/area units and the fact that the activists in the units tended to be older people who had a lifelong familiarity with the political terrain. Each area kept its own election registers and canvassing reports, and the agent relied upon the secretary to assign workers to the various tasks and to coordinate the campaign effort within his or her jurisdiction. The agent, of course, was in daily contact with the secretaries, keeping track of the progress and handling problems as they were reported. The only activity carried out from the central headquarters was the allocation of motor cars on polling day.

The main issues to emerge in the 1964 parliamentary campaign were housing, the cost of living, the price tag for social reforms, and immigration. The latter issue was not a matter of contention between the two parties, but it was a question often asked on the doorstep and at public meetings. By this time about fifty immigrant families had moved into Bermondsey, and many more came there each day to work. Some of the Labour voters in the constituency were unhappy about this situation, and while they would not consider voting for the Conservatives, they threatened to abstain. The voting result tempts one to consider the probability that several hundred Labour supporters stayed away from the polls.[34]

During the campaign, the party fielded a total of 250 volunteer workers, about 100 of whom were 'core' people who appeared for duty regularly. Using about 50 of the volunteers, the party managed to canvass nearly 75 per cent of the voters; the canvassers were requested to report any local problems they encountered and any grievances expressed by the residents. The Labour activists took the matter of postal votes seriously for the first time, processing about 370 of them, as well as handling about 200 internal removals — about half of the total. The party also dispatched 12 experienced canvassers to a nearby marginal constituency each night, and it sent 20 workers there on polling day.

Although the Labour candidate, Robert Mellish, was much in demand as a speaker in other constituencies, he nevertheless devoted considerable attention to Bermondsey. He worked with the agent in preparing the election address, and he frequently went out with the van to address the voters through the loudspeaker. Recognizing the difficulty of sustaining interest over a three-week period, he preferred to make the 'big push' during the last three or four days. He covered all of the constituency once, and then went over parts of it a second time. He also accompanied the canvassers in several areas, attended some bingo sessions, and appeared before a number of trade union branches. In addition to debating the Tory candidate at a church gathering, Mellish conducted a number of outdoor meetings, and he appeared at two indoor rallies, one at each end of the constituency.[35] Before the campaign was over, he had reportedly won the support of three local churches — Catholic, Methodist, and Church of England.

For a safe Labour district, the Bermondsey party was well organized during the campaign and on polling day. While the polling stations were open, about 75 volunteers worked at the task of rounding up the voters. Although twenty cars were available to transport elderly and incapacitated people to the polls, ten more could have been used. The Bermondsey activists were greatly absorbed in the campaign work within their constituency; they could easily have won even if more of their resources had been deployed to marginal districts. But the party leaders found it difficult to persuade the older veterans of the wisdom of the marginal strategy.[36]

In borough council elections, the Bermondsey Tories try to contest as many wards as possible so as to pin down Labour workers and thus prevent the party from sending so many to help in the neighboring boroughs. This nuisance strategy, according to the Labour people, does serve to tie up some of the party's resources which could be profitably used in outside areas. The number of wards the Tories are able to contest, of course, depends upon how many candidates they are able to recruit; not all of the Conservative supporters are willing to carry the banner in public view.

In 1962, the Conservatives decided to challenge Labour in only four of the thirteen wards, and in two of them they were unable to field a complete slate of candidates. This meant that the Labour party had to prepare and distribute a leaflet informing the voters in the uncontested wards why the polling stations would not be open to them.

The main campaign issue was education, and the Labour party wounded their opponents by distributing a leaflet on the break-up of the London County Council and the reorganization plan and its potential impact upon the schools. The Labour activists supplemented this attack upon the Conservatives by some hard work in the four wards. Residents of the uncontested districts were requested to help in Saints Ward, the most marginal area, and a heavy canvassing target was set. The Labour people virtually completed their canvass of two wards (including Saints) and made good progress in the other two. They traced nearly 400 removals in the four wards and made four deliveries of literature. The M.P. visited on the doorstep with many new people who had just moved into council flats. In addition to these activities, about ten veteran activists gave three evenings of work to Lewisham. Although we shall discuss electoral performance in the next section, it is worth noting that the Labour strategy had its payoff. Saints Ward had a voter turnout of more than 35 per cent (compared with the overall average of 29 per cent), and the Bermondsey party scored on about 76 per cent of the ballot papers issued. The ward was no longer marginal!

Fulham. The agent operates on the assumption that every political campaign is different and hence the organization and strategies must be fitted to the circumstances. Generally, he employs a centralized pattern organization, especially in parliamentary elections. (More work is done through the ward units in borough council campaigns.) In his view, the primary focus must be upon the outcome in the entire constituency or the borough rather than in any of the subordinate areas. This means that the organization should be flexible enough to permit workers to be easily shifted about when the agent decides that the transfers are necessary. In parliamentary contests, the committee rooms in the wards are usually not set up until the latter part of the campaign. If the nineteen committee rooms were put into operation any earlier, staff resources would have to be taken away from the canvassing effort.

In anticipation of the campaign, the agent and the executive officers collaborate in the selection of people to occupy key roles in the headquarters organization, and each role has clear-cut responsibility: Personnel; Canvassing; Records; Window Bill Publicity; Press and Public Relations; Postal Votes and Internal Removals; Materials Preparation; Election Address Mailing; Literature and Election Messages Distribution; Trade Union Liaison; Youth Liaison; Outdoor

Activities and Public Meetings; Work Supervision; Transportation; and Candidate's Aide. At the outset, the key workers are fully informed about the campaign plan and how their assignments fit into it. The agent sends detailed instructions to the canvassers, the heads of the committee rooms, the party's representatives at the 'count', and other campaign volunteers. In borough council elections, similar instructions are sent to the candidates. There can be no doubt that the key workers in the Fulham campaigns are fully informed about their responsibilities.

The central headquarters is organized so that particular rooms (or parts of the largest room) are devoted to specialized activities. Key workers appear at the appropriate place for their materials and any last-minute instructions, and the charts on the wall indicate the progress which has been made and what remains to be done. The canvassing activities, which are supervised from the center by the canvassing officer, are carried out on a ward basis by the ward leaders who form their own teams. These are reinforced by surplus workers allocated from the central headquarters. The agent and the canvassing officer also assign additional personnel to areas that fall behind in their targets. The canvassing reports are drawn up after each evening's work and are examined by the agent the next morning. When he compiles the lists, he is able to see what the situation is in each polling district, each ward, and the constituency as a whole. The organizational patterns at the central headquarters are designed for specialization of function, and the elaborate reporting system enables the agent to detect weak spots and to take quick remedial action.

The agent regarded Fulham as a marginal constituency, and by the autumn of 1964 he had the Labour machine in full gear, ready for the parliamentary election. As the campaign moved along, the Labour candidate, Michael Stewart, became the main target of the opposition and sharp clashes erupted. Besides defending the Government's record the Tory candidate (whose first name was also 'Michael') sought to present the image of a 'younger Michael' by employing the slogan 'ring out the old, bring in the new'. He alleged that the Labour Party's position on the bomb would leave Britain 'defenseless', and he accused Mr Stewart of having voted against immigration controls when the issue was before the House of Commons. From time to time, Labour canvassers had to field questions about immigration on the doorstep but the Conservative challenger was never able to develop the issue into a significant point of contention. The Labour people attacked the Government's record on housing and rents, education, pensions, and the general state of the economy, taking pains to relate these problems to the Fulham scene. They featured Michael Stewart as the 'shadow minister' of Housing and Local Government and hence well qualified to deal with them.

The party employed the services of nearly 300 people during the course of the campaign, and it had street captains in nearly every row.[37] About 50 or 60 of these workers were involved in the canvassing effort, which was carried out selectively. The important thing, in the agent's view, was the *repeat* of voting record, i.e., the identification of voters who over a long time-period had indicated to the canvassers a sympathetic attitude to Labour or to the Conservatives. As the election approached, the party mounted a blanket canvass on forms that were not marked from previous surveys; in this way the canvassers would have to make an independent judgment. This canvass would pick up newly qualified voters and those who had moved into the constituency since the last election. As the results poured in, they were collated with the reports from the previous election. The registration numbers of the 'repeating' Conservatives were then dropped, and the registration numbers of the consistent Labour supporters were ticked with a red pencil mark. (On polling day, the mark would be extended to a red line through the number when it was known that that person had voted.) Thereafter the experienced canvassers would concentrate on the 'doubtfuls', which were later sorted into 'Labour doubtful' and 'Tory doubtful'. Note was taken of any peculiar movements of voter reactions, and these were checked to see whether they resulted from inexperienced canvassing or from a shift in support which needed further investigation. The usual procedure was to schedule a literature distribution in a particular area, followed by the loudspeaker and a canvassing team. A mass canvass was held on Sundays. Under the leadership of the agent's wife, the party also tackled the problem of about 5000 removals, which involved a heavy processing of postal votes.

The campaign leaders organized an extensive distribution of literature and letter appeals to target groups in the constituency. Ordinarily, the distribution of literature to Labour members and supporters was carried out by one worker in each polling district. When this burden was too heavy in a large district, the central headquarters sent workers to handle the deliveries in certain streets, and it would assign a section of the area to the regular polling district worker. The distributors were given notice of the forthcoming delivery, and a deadline was usually set. Selective appeals – letters dispatched under the candidate's signature – were made to women, first-time voters, and old-age pensioners.

The agent kept a watchful eye on the display of window bills. When these were distributed in a strong Labour area, he was interested in seeing how many would be displayed almost as soon as they were received. The spontaneous posting of window bills he interpreted as a sign of enthusiastic support among the faithful – a phenomenon that would be disconcerting to the opposition. If the window displays were below his expectation, he assumed that there was disaffection in the Labour camp.

Although public meetings have trouble competing with television, the

Fulham party scheduled four of them, with prominent M.P.s speaking in behalf of Mr Stewart. The big event, however, was a huge rally during the last week of the campaign which featured Harold Wilson as the main speaker. Fulham collaborated with ten other constituency parties in sponsoring the meeting, and the Fulham workers had distributed 9000 handbills to advertize it within their territory. The gathering was reportedly the largest in the London area in more than a decade.

As a leader in the national Party, Michael Stewart had a heavy speaking schedule in marginal constituencies and on television during the earlier part of the campaign. For the last ten days, however, he confined his external commitments to the London area so that he could spend more time in his own constituency. Nearly every morning and afternoon, Mrs Stewart and he did a lot of street-by-street calling in districts marked out by the agent or the canvassing officer. The candidate also helped to get some local newspaper coverage by holding a press conference every Friday morning.

Polling day was an exciting event in Fulham. Every worker was at his assigned post early in the morning, and new volunteers appeared during the day to lend a hand. An efficient transfer of information took place between the number-takers outside the polling stations, and this enabled the committee room clerks to keep up-to-date records of the Labour supporters who had already voted and those who had yet to be contacted. The agent also kept an account at two-hour intervals of the number of voters who had cast ballots in each polling district. By comparing the turnout rates with previous elections, he was able to gauge whether the Labour vote or the Tory vote was up or down in particular areas of strength. When it appeared that the balloting in two or three Labour polling districts was below his expectations, he transferred seasoned leaders, workers, and loudspeakers into the slack areas from districts that were less important to the outcome. The fact that about half of Labour's promised vote had to be gathered in after 6.00 in the evening placed a heavy burden upon the organizational machinery, but it was efficient enough to carry the load. The agent ventured that his candidate would win by a majority of 5500; the official return put it at 4946. A day or so after the election, Mr Stewart toured the constituency to thank the voters.

As prelude to the borough council campaign in 1962, the agent scheduled a conference of the candidates and key party workers. The candidates also received a briefing sheet about the accomplishments of the Labour-controlled council which had been drawn up jointly by Fulham and Barons Court. One instruction leaflet requested them to get lapsed party memberships reactivated, and offered some hints about how to meet the voters. It also warned them against making promises they might not be able to keep, and called important features of the election law to their attention. Another document listed some Conservative arguments with suggestions on how to meet them.

The campaign received an official send-off immediately after the GMC annual meeting, when Hugh Gaitskell was the honored guest. He introduced all of the candidates,[38] after which the agent outlined the strategy to be employed in the campaign.

The Labour appeals were oriented around the theme of the 'new Fulham', pointing out that change was in prospect as a result of the proposal for the reorganization of London and that there was a need to plan for the transition. The party literature also attacked the Conservative Government because of the housing situation which had recently been dramatized by the number of 'homeless' people in London. Special letter appeals were sent to council tenants; to homeowners because property taxes were rising; and to would-be homeowners because of the paucity of mortgage financing.

The pattern of campaign organization was a bit more decentralized than in parliamentary contests. The candidates operated as teams from the central headquarters, but some committee rooms were set up at the outset of the campaign to distribute the workers and to handle some of the canvassing. About 60 activists carried the burden of the campaign, but about 200 additional people worked at some stage of the effort, especially on polling day. The party managed to complete a 75 per cent canvass of the Fulham sector of the borough. Town Ward presented a special problem because more than 1000 new voters had moved into the district. About two hours before the polls closed on election day, the agent studied his records and decided to shift a brigade of workers into Town and Hurlingham Wards, which were the most marginal. This strategy apparently had a beneficial effect because Labour won all but one of the seats, and the single loss was only by six votes.

South Kensington. The South Kensington party started preparing for the 1964 election about eighteen months ahead of time, with the candidate, Barrie Stead, and the agent, Maurice Barber, giving the lead. The ward secretaries assumed responsibility for having the necessary envelopes addressed. Workers were recruited for Sunday morning canvasses – the first real attempt at voter identification – and by the official opening of the campaign the activists had made about 6000 contacts, mostly in Redcliffe and Earls Court Wards. This effort produced 1000 'promises' and twenty new members. When the workers discovered any removals, they passed the information along to the London Labour Party.

By the time the election was called, Maurice Barber had left the constituency, and Mr Harry Ellis, a GMC member of two-year's standing who had served as assistant election agent in Barnet in 1959, became the volunteer agent, devoting a great deal of time to the task. He recruited a skeleton staff to be responsible for such matters as preparing the election address; printing the election address, handbills, and posters; finishing the envelopes; organizing the public and outdoor meetings; handling press coverage; and recruiting volunteers for work in marginal constituencies. The party set up only one committee room, and each ward secretary was expected to round up the necessary workers within his or her area. About fifty South Kensington people were involved in the party's activities during the campaign, the most important of which was aiding the effort in adjacent marginal constituencies.

The South Kensington workers, to be sure, carried on some activities within their own bailiwick. They sent out election addresses by free post; they distributed 8000 Transport House leaflets on housing and education: they mailed a special appeal to 700 young voters whom they had identified; and they held two large public meetings, with prominent speakers, and two smaller indoor meetings and several open-air gatherings which they conducted on their own.[39] Any canvassing that was done during the campaign, however, was handled by the candidate himself. On the doorstep and in his public messages, he emphasized the problem of housing, contending that it was the source of other social ills.

When the campaign began, the South Kensington activists divided their efforts between Barons Court and North Kensington. Early on, the people in North Kensington had said that they did not need any help, but they soon discovered that 10,000 voters had moved out of the constituency, thus creating a difficult removals and postal vote problem. When they appealed to the London Labour Party for assistance, the London officials asked the South Kensington party to respond. On polling day its efforts were entirely directed toward the sister organization. At least thirty South Kensington people showed up for their assignments and they made twenty automobiles available to the transport officer. Even the South Kensington candidate, who concluded that he had been working hard for two years in his own constituency and additional effort on polling day would not be of much benefit, decided to set an example for his co-workers by moving in to North Kensington to help achieve victory there. For an individual to spend virtually all of his spare time for nearly two years in hopeless territory, realizing that when the campaign really starts his organization will be transferred to more fertile terrain, is a real test of loyalty.[40]

In the 1962 borough council election, the South Kensington activists wanted to give the appearance of activity in their wards, but they did not wish to become so involved that an optimal number of workers would be denied to North Kensington. The agent was called upon to direct the campaign in South Kensington while defending his own seat at the other end of the borough. The South Kensington people did no canvassing in their own wards. Although they could have used a standard election address, the agent and two of the other officers designed their own, making arrangements to have 13,000 of them printed and then delivered in selected areas by some of the candidates. They also scheduled one public meeting with a prominent speaker, whose views were of little

concern to them so long as he drew a crowd of about sixty people. The
aim of the South Kensington GMC was to make only a token effort; its
primary strategy was to get the workers to the North Kensington wards
which were being contested by South Kensington people.

Electoral Performance

It would be nice if we had sensitive measures of the organizational
'efficiency' and 'effectiveness' of the three constituency parties. This,
however, would require simultaneous studies of the organizations of
other Labour parties along specified dimensions.[41] Since we do not have
the necessary data, we shall have to be content with an analysis of the
voting results in comparison with previous elections. These balloting
returns, of course, are influenced by other factors besides local
organization, and they cannot be used as a valid measure of organizational efficiency and effectiveness. In the case of the parliamentary
election. we shall make a rough comparison of the voting results in 1959
and 1964 in each of the three constituencies with the returns in
comparable constituencies in the Greater London Area.[42] When it
comes to the 1962 borough council election, we can do no more than
look at the voting result in terms of the previous local elections in 1959.

Bermondsey. The voter turnout in Britain in 1964 was down 1.8 per cent
from the level of participation in 1959, and this was reflected in
London's safe Labour areas that featured straight fights between the
two major parties. The Bermondsey party, however, managed to stem
the tide better than most of its sister organizations. Of the eight
constituencies in the safe Labour category, Bermondsey ranked second
in voter turnout in 1959 (70.5 per cent), and it remained in second place
in 1964 (63.3 per cent), behind Woolwich East both times. In terms of the
size of the Labour majority, however, the Bermondsey party improved
its position, rising from second place with a 53.6 per cent margin in 1959
to first place and a 58.6 per cent edge in 1964. The Bermondsey activists
were understandably delighted by their success, but a few of them
wondered whether the Labour cause might have been better served by a
smaller majority and more work outside the constituency, especially
since the Labour Party won office by such a slim margin of seats.

In the 1962 borough council elections, the rate of voter participation,
compared with the previous local election, was increased in the four
contested wards.[43] This apparently worked to the advantage of the
Labour party, for its vote was augmented in each instance.[44]

Fulham. The size of the poll in Fulham in the 1959 parliamentary
election had been 77 per cent, the second highest in the Labour marginal,
straight-fight group; the turnout in 1964 was 73.2 per cent, which
represented a tie for first place with Hayes and Harlington. In the 1959

election, the Labour majority in Fulham was 7.3 per cent, and the shift to the Tories was less than that in any of the other constituencies. The 1964 election brought a majority of 14 per cent, but the shift against the Tories was less than in the other districts in the group because of Fulham's noticeable resistance to the Conservative sweep in 1959.

As in Bermondsey, the voter turnout in Fulham at the 1962 council election increased over the previous local contest in every ward.[45] This was translated into an expansion of the Labour vote in three of the wards, including the two most marginal areas. In Sands End Ward and Munster Ward, however, the Labour vote was down 2.2 per cent and 3.8 per cent respectively.

South Kensington. The party in South Kensington significantly improved its position in the 1964 general election. Compared with 1959, its vote increased by 17 per cent, removing the Liberals from second place.[46] In terms of percentage differences in the size of the Labour vote between the 1959 and the 1964 elections, South Kensington ranked in seventh place, out of a possible eleven. This success, of course, probably represents more of an anti-Conservative reaction than a significant increase in Labour's organizational efficiency. It is true that, prior to the official opening of the campaign, the activists worked harder than they ever had before, but, as we have seen, they diverted their resources to the marginals at the strategic moment, and this would obviously have some effect upon the result in their own constituency.

The returns from the South Kensington wards in the 1962 borough council election are of little use from an organizational point of view. The Labour vote was diminished in all of the wards, largely because of the intervention of Liberal candidates. Had the activists taken the local campaign more seriously, it would probably have been at the expense of the result in North Kensington, which was much more important for the larger movement and for the South Kensington activists who were trying to get on the council from North Kensington wards.

MANAGEMENT OF LOCAL AFFAIRS

A constituency party's main instrument for influencing the management of local affairs is the borough council. This is the body that deals with such matters as council housing, library services, parks and playgrounds, refuse disposal, education, local tax rates, some aspects of social work, and the like. The council, of course, must operate within the framework of the legislation enacted by parliament, but at times it may seek to exert pressure on the bureaucracies in Whitehall. To whatever degree its authority may be limited by the edicts of the central government, however, its deliberations and administrative activities have an important effect upon the daily lives of the citizens.

Labour party activists can hardly avoid taking an interest in the council. Their involvement in party affairs soon puts them in touch with the council's activities as they listen to the councillors' reports at party meetings and as they participate in borough council campaigns. Before very long they begin to see what can be done to improve the conditions of life in the locality and what personal benefits they can gain from service on the council. Council membership bestows status upon a person which an ordinary GMC delegate cannot claim. For many people, especially those from the working class, a seat on the local council represents the zenith of their political ambitions.

People in local parties often complain about the quality of borough councillors, emphasizing the need to recruit able candidates who will be diligent in carrying out their responsibilities. Council service involves some personal sacrifice — always in terms of leisure time and frequently in terms of reduced income, as when a person selected as mayor is forced to curtail the working hours on his regular job, or when a worker on the night shift is prompted to mark up an absence so that he can attend the council meeting. Some people who might serve with distinction are reluctant to face the uncertainties of the hustings. After they have managed to survive the ballot count, some council members find the work too demanding, or become so involved with their borough responsibilities that they tend to loose touch with the GMC and the wards they represent.

The Labour members of the borough council (the 'Labour Group') are, of course, organically linked with the local Labour party. In fact, the relationship between the Group and the GMC bears some resemblance to that of the Parliamentary Labour Party and the Annual Conference. The Labour members of the council are bound by the platform which the party has formulated, but they have some discretion in assigning priorities. The leader of the Group is a dominant political figure whose role is similar to that of the Party Leader in the House of Commons. The chairmen of the council committees exercise important power and function as small-scale ministers, becoming dependent upon the civil service staff in the town hall and having to learn about how the various departments are run. Sometimes a determined chairman may be tempted to follow an independent course somewhat at variance with the local party people or even his colleagues in the Group. When the Labour members constitute a majority on the council, they make the strategic decisions in the caucus meeting and then 'put the whip on'. This means that the votes in the council chamber are merely ratifications of earlier decisions which have been reached in private sessions.

The heavy demands upon many council members — and the fact that they are set apart, bound by rules and routinized procedures — often make them prone to losing touch with the local party, which was the initial source of their power. In order to surmount this problem, the party and the Group need to develop effective channels of communication, as well as some mechanisms for rendering the council members accountable to the party. The communication function may be performed in several ways. First, the borough council members are usually drawn from the ranks of the party activists, many of them continuing to hold their credentials as GMC members; this means that they can carry the ideas of their party colleagues to the Group meetings and also transmit relevant information about the council to the GMC. By the same token, Labour members of the council are expected to attend their ward meetings, which provide opportunities for listening to complaints and for explaining policies. Second, the party and the Group may establish formal liaison mechanisms through which representatives of each organization can meet together for the exchange of ideas. Third, citizens' grievances may be detected by ward secretaries or by canvassers and dues collectors on the doorstep, and these are then relayed to the appropriate council members. When it comes to establishing the accountability of the Labour people on the council, we hardly need to point out that the opportunities for communication also provide opportunities for confrontation which help to keep the incumbents aware of the feelings within the party. Furthermore, the party has the ultimate sanction at its command – refusal to adopt recalcitrant councillors at the next election.

Bermondsey. In 1962, Bermondsey was one of five metropolitan boroughs (out of a total of 28) in the County of London in which the Labour party held every council seat. It was also unique in having such a high proportion of manual workers, especially dockers, taking their places in the council chamber. As we have already noted, the Bermondsey activists were proud of their borough and took pride in the council's achievements. At one point in their history, they were reluctant to participate in a program to distribute tax revenues taken from the wealthier areas to the poorer boroughs on the ground that there might be strings attached.

The Labour Group on the Bermondsey council had close linkages with the local party. As had been the case in recent years, all of the council members served simultaneously as delegates on the party's General Management Committee, most of them as regular members and the rest as *ex officio* members. The fact that each councillor wore two hats meant that he or she had ample opportunity to examine issues both within a party setting and within the framework of the Group meetings. (It also meant that personal and factional competition was sometimes transferred from one arena to the other.) During the period covered by this study, specific local grievances, such as leaking roofs in council flats, were sometimes brought to the attention of councillors at ward meetings, and GMC delegates discussed such matters as poor lighting on particular streets and a bomb-site that was hazardous to children.⁴⁷

The leaders of the Bermondsey party were aware of the problems that arise when an organization has a monopoly of political power in the community.⁴⁸ They recognized that the lack of an effective opposition might weaken the internal cohesion of the party and that the recruitment of forty-five council members of uniformly high caliber would tax the strength of any organization. For this reason they sought to inject fresh blood into the council by persuading individuals who displayed the necessary qualifications to offer their names for the candidates' panel. In addition, the people in the wards expected conscientious performance from their representatives, reporting instances of neglect of duty to the Executive Committe or applying the sanction of not reselecting them when they failed to measure up to expectations.

One way in which the Bermondsey party attempted to subject itself to evaluation in the absence of a viable opposition was through the Action Committee.⁴⁹ Cognizant of the fact actual decision-making in the Labour Group meetings tended to make the formal sessions of the council stereotyped and dull, some Action Committee members wanted to see more 'clash' and debate in the council chamber. They believed that even if some of the questions asked had been planted in advance, the confrontation in public view would generate greater interest in the proceedings and council activities would gain wider publicity. They also suggested that some of the committee meetings be opened up on an experimental basis, particularly those that were already composed of some lay members. The GMC was receptive to the idea, but for various reasons the councillors insisted upon keeping the doors of the committee rooms closed. The council also resisted a proposal to coopt one or two Conservatives for service in the chamber, largely on the ground that little would be gained by their presence. Through the Action Committee mechanism, however, the party was able to help some of the council committees to get through to the public a little better. The housing committee, for example, was prevailed upon to prune and up-date the regulations for council tenants, and several other borough council units were shown how they could improve their services to local citizens. In these and other ways the Labour leaders in Bermondsey attempted to nurture institutional devices for self-examination as a partial substitute for an opposition.

On the most important issues, the main linkages between the party and the Labour Group on the council developed from the overlapping memberships. A GMC resolution on local matters could hardly be ignored by the Labour-dominated council. Then, too, when a controversial issue arose (such as rent increases for public housing), the leaders of the Labour Group usually followed the practice of trying to win the support of the GMC delegates before officially taking the matter to the Labour councillors. Policy decisions hammered out in the GMC proceedings would carry weight in the Group meetings, since many of its members would already have been committed. Prior GMC approval for a decision that the Labour council would have to take anyway made the political ground a bit firmer for the councillors to stand on because the reasons for their action would be transmitted through the party's communication system from the GMC to the wards and the affiliated organizations. Effective liaison and cooperation between the GMC and the Labour Group were essential for the building of consensus and the smooth passage of prickly local measures.

The Labour party was interested in maintaining visibility in the constituency, and it sought to extend its influence beyond the ordinary activities of the borough council. Whenever new organizations were formed, the Labour people tried to become involved; even the tennis clubs attracted their attention. The party enjoyed good relations with the local churches and even with the Chamber of Commerce. When civic leaders wanted something done, they naturally turned to the Labour party which usually attempted to be of assistance. Even the local Conservatives admitted that the Labour people 'ran the borough pretty well'.

Fulham. The development of effective liaison between the Fulham Labour party and the Labour members of the borough council was difficult owing to the fact that the borough of Fulham embraced the constituency of Fulham and three of the seven wards in the constituency of Barons Court. This meant that in borough council affairs the Fulham party had to establish a good working relationship with a segment of the Labour organization in Barons Court.

At the time of this study, there were forty seats on the Fulham council, twenty-four of which were the political property of the wards in the Fulham constituency. Labour dominated the council; the Conservatives held seven of the seats, only one on the Fulham side (Hurlingham Ward) and six from a single ward in Barons Court. This line-up of forces meant that a large number of activists from two constituency parties were interested in standing for the rest of the seats in six safe or reasonably safe Labour wards, all but two of which were in the Fulham constituency. Needless to say, there was lively competition for the candidacies in the Fulham wards, and some of the competitors resided in Barons Court territory. The adoption of some candidates and the rejection of others led to some turnover of council members from one election to the next, and while this competition helped to energize the party, it also resulted in disappointment for some activists. The problem was alleviated to some extent by the willingness of a few older council members to step aside and make room for younger aspirants or for party stalwarts in the sister organization next door. The situation was helped, too, by the practice of electing some people who had failed to get on the council through regular channels to vacant aldermanic posts. As we have already seen, the Fulham party made room for two Barons Court people in the 1962 election; no Fulham activists were selected as candidates in any of the Barons Court wards.

For several years the divided borough and the lack of institutional links between the Fulham and Barons Court parties made the establishment of an effective relationship between the General Management Committees and the Labour Group on the council a troublesome problem. Apart from the fact that members from the two GMCs occupied seats on the council, the lines of communication were not tightly joined; the local parties had no official representatives at the Labour Group meetings. Besides, the members of the Group tended to regard themselves as components of an autonomous body and jealously guarded their authority. In 1960, however, the relationship between the Labour members of the council and their sponsoring organizations was clarified when the Group adopted a written constitution and a set of standing orders. These rules established formal channels of communication between the Fulham party and the Barons Court wards and between the two constituency organizations and the Labour Group.

Contact between the Fulham party and its counterpart in Barons Court on borough matters was provided by two separate but intermeshed mechanisms.[50] The first of these was the joint meeting of the GMC delegates of the two parties which was held at least once a year, more frequently when an election was in the offing. (When sitting in joint session, this group was technically known as the Borough Election Committee.) Since this body was large and unwieldy, it was authorized to set up a second mechanism – the Liaison Committee – composed of one representative from each of the five Fulham wards and from each of the three wards in Barons Court, together with a scattering of trade union delegates from the Barons Court GMC who resided in the borough of Fulham. The Liaison Committee members served for a three-year term, to correspond with the tenure of the councillors. The rules stipulated that the Committee should meet at least four times a year to discuss policy matters and that it should issue a report to the two parent bodies at their annual meetings.

Besides establishing a linkage between the two constituency parties, the new arrangement provided for regularized communication between the two parties and the Labour members of the borough council. The Liaison Committee was authorized to meet with and to take its views to the Labour Group at least twice a year, usually in June and December. An additional point of contact between the parties and the Group was established by allowing the agents from the Fulham and Barons Court organizations to attend all Group meetings in an advisory capacity. The accountability of the Labour Group to the constituency parties was further achieved through the requirement that the leader or deputy leader appear before the GMCs of the two organizations at least once a quarter. Furthermore, the Labour Group was directed to prepare an annual report of its activities to be presented at the joint session of the two General Management Committees, with the leader of the Group answering questions on the report.

How was policy on borough affairs shaped through this complicated machinery? When a problem arose, the Executive Committee of the Fulham party would discuss the matter and reach a decision. The decision might take the form of a resolution to be sent to the GMC, or it might be a recommendation to one of the wards or a trade union branch to table a resolution for consideration by the Executive Commitee and then the GMC. Sometimes the wards or the affiliated organizations would initiate and discuss suggestions on their own and send their views through the appropriate channels to the GMC. A resolution adopted by the General Management Committee was then passed on to the Liaison Committee which solicited the views of the component units. After having discussed and approved the resolution, the members of the Liaison Committee would talk the matter over with the officers and other councillors on the Labour Group. If the suggested course of action was acceptable to the Group, the appropriate legislation would be drawn up and sent to the council for debate and approval or rejection. The Fulham GMC was in a position to follow through on its proposals by requesting reports from its members on the Liaison Committee, by the presence of its agent at the Group meetings, and by contact with the Group officers during their quarterly appearances at GMC meetings and at the meeting of the Borough Election Committee. It was understood that the authority of the Labour party organizations was instructive in policy matters, and that the Group had the upper hand in administrative matters, including the timing of proposed legislation; in cases of dispute between the two spheres of authority, the conflict was to be resolved by the National Executive Committee.

Informal contact between the Fulham party and its representatives on the borough council was maintained in the ordinary ways. The councillors, for example, were expected to attend the party meetings in the wards they represented. This was not a serious problem in the Fulham Labour party, since all but five of the borough council members resided in the wards that had sent them to the council chamber and they were active politically in those districts. As in the case of Bermondsey, the ward secretaries and the canvassers would inform the councillors about the problems they had encountered, and local grievances were sometimes brought to councillors' attention at ward and GMC meetings.

The Fulham party, too, was concerned about increasing its visibility and becoming an integral part of the life of the community. Scores of its activists served as school managers and governors; as committee members of voluntary welfare organizations, hospital boards, and insurance tribunals; as magistrates, etc. In 1962, some of the GMC members still managed to weave borough council affairs into their hectic schedules during the last week of the election campaign. As one of the Tory councillors observed, the Labour party got itself 'seen' by 'being in everything'. Its people, he said, were the 'leading lights' of the community and the local citizens knew them. Besides, he grudgingly conceded, they were 'not doing a poor job!'

South Kensington. When this study was undertaken, the Labour representation on the Kensington borough council was very small, and all of the Labour councillors represented wards in North Kensington. In 1961, the South Kensington party claimed only two council members (the secretary/agent and one of the vice-presidents who was the oldest GMC member), but three additional South Kensington people suceeded in getting on the council from a North Kensington ward in the 1962 election. The migrant councillors from South Kensington managed to keep their colleagues on the GMC informed about the activities of the Labour Group, and they were in a position to reflect the views of the GMC at the Group meetings. An additional point of contact between the South Kensington party and the Labour councillors was provided by a two-member committee, elected by the GMC, whose purpose was to keep its eye on the Labour Group. The committee members reported to the GMC on the matters being considered by the Labour councillors and the actions taken by them, and they were authorized to carry suggestions from the GMC to the Group.

Labour had little influence in the borough of Kensington, and within the small nucleus of Labour councillors the South Kensington party carried little weight. It had no areas in its district that could be worked to Labour's advantage, and its inroads into the North Kensington wards were viewed with suspicion. Apart from the party, the South Kensington activists engaged in some civic and welfare activities, including the annual party for the old folks and aid to London's homeless. But a small political party with such little support among the voters and with no firm roots in the borough council was hardly equipped to address the local problems which it saw emerging.

LIAISON BETWEEN PUBLIC OFFICIALS AND ORDINARY CITIZENS

In the last section we noted that the local councillors had specific problems pointed out to them at meetings of the wards and the General Management Committee, and that in carrying out their assignments the ward secretaries and the canvassers would sometimes encounter grievances and hardship cases and would transmit this information to their local representatives on the council. This type of 'problem surveillance', however, was informal, and much of it dealt with matters relating to property or civic improvements, such as the upkeep of council housing or poor street lighting; the personal problems confronting local citizens would not ordinarily be brought to light through this process.

The wartime devastation and the problems of reconstruction in the post-war years complicated the lives of many ordinary citizens, and most Labour parties felt the need to establish regular procedures by which people experiencing personal difficulties could seek advice from their borough councillors or their Member of Parliament in private meetings. The institutions for such a purpose are the 'advice bureau' which is usually operated by the councillors and the 'surgery' which is held by the M.P.[51] At these personal conferences, the elected officials are requested to help people with such problems as inadequate living quarters, pension claims, family disruptions, and the like. This personal assistance to constituents is really a form of social or welfare work. By taking his turn in an advice bureau or by holding his surgery, the elected official is to some extent 'nursing' his constituency. But when a researcher observes some of these conferences, he soon realizes that the political aspect is dwarfed by other considerations. The clients are ordinary people who are beset by personal difficulties, and the elected officials respond from feelings of sympathy and concern for the welfare of the more unfortunate among their constituents. Work in the advice bureaus and surgeries over long periods of time gives them a dramatic view of what the problems in the locality really are.

The people who come to the local party headquarters for assistance often express their desire to speak with the Member of Parliament rather than the local councillors, largely because he may be more visible to them and because they think that he has more influence. Such an outlook places an excessive burden upon the M.P. and may cause him to become involved in local politics in a way that will antagonize people on the council. When this danger arises, the sagacious M.P. will divide his cases into two areas of jurisdiction and refer some of them to the local councillors.

In many instances, there is nothing that either the councillors or the M.P. can do, but they must nevertheless make an effort so that the citizen can at least get his case considered. This may require that the Member of Parliament write a letter to a minister, the staff at the town hall, or some department at the county level. He may also put his constituent in touch with specialists who can give legal advice, if he is not qualified to give it himself. When a serious case of hardship is brought to his attention, the M.P. may decide to submit a question for Question Time in the House of Commons or to deliver a speech on the motion to adjourn. He cannot plan to raise the matter during a regular debate, since the opportunity for a backbencher to be recognized by the Speaker at an appropriate time is very slim.

Bermondsey. Every Thursday evening, the Bermondsey party conducted an advice bureau which was staffed by the local councillors, four at a time. For the most part, their cases involved the allocation and upkeep of council housing and problems growing out of council action. In 1957, their agenda became crowded with cases arising from the Rent Act, and the party eventually relieved the pressure by distributing 10,000 handbills on the legal implications of the Act for Bermondsey citizens.

The heaviest burden of assisting ordinary citizens with their personal problems naturally fell upon the M.P., Robert Mellish, who was well known and respected for the attention that he gave to such cases. He conducted his surgery every Friday evening for about three hours. Usually he held twenty or thirty conferences at each surgery, virtually all of them with working-class people. (He set a record in 1957 by handling fifty-four cases in one session of his surgery.) The overwhelming number of people who came for help were trying to find adequate living quarters; at first they were people of all ages, but in 1961–62 they were mostly young folk. Immediately after the war, pension claims were also a conspicuous part of each surgery, and the M.P. and the agent made representations to the tribunals. Pension rights and other forms of supplementary assistance were still problems for many people in the early 1960s. The M.P. also gave advice and administrative help to individuals who experienced difficulties with their neighbors, school administrators, hire-purchase (instalment buying), legal controversies, family break-ups, etc. Mr. Mellish's mail flow was about 120 letters per week – a heavy burden owing to the fact that he could claim the services of a secretary for only an hour each week. This meant that he had to answer about 100 of them by hand; his work was cut out for him every Saturday morning.

Fulham. Much of what we have said about Bermondsey also applies to Fulham. The party offered a legal advice service twice a month, and it set up a program of having the borough councillors visit housing estates regularly to listen to complaints and to relay them to the town hall. Every Friday evening the Labour people sponsored an advice bureau, which was staffed by London County councillors on two Friday evenings each month and which became the M.P.'s surgery during the other two Friday nights. Here again the agenda of personal conferences was always filled, and most of those who took advantage of these services were working-class people. While their problems ranged over a wide spectrum, most of them involved housing, pensions, divorce, and race relations. Mr Stewart, the M.P., worked hard to help these people resolve their difficulties, and often he was able to 'unclog the wheels' when people had become embroiled in bureaucratic mix-ups. His reputation as a sympathetic confidant meant that he too had a lot of letters to answer every week.

South Kensington. Since the South Kensington party did not have a Member of Parliament and none of its wards had Labour councillors, there was nothing like an advice bureau or a surgery. Several of the South Kensington people who represented North Kensington wards on the council, however, took their turns in staffing the advice bureaus there.

FINANCE OF THE ORGANIZATION

Compared with the Conservatives, the Labour Party appeals to a less pecunious clientele and is unable to depend upon large donations from business concerns and private individuals. The national Party, however, is able to draw large sums from the trade unions. The source of these funds is the political levy upon trade union members who do not take the initiative to cancel their assessments. A local Labour party may be the direct recipient of trade union money when the parliamentary candidate is sponsored by a union and when union branches decide to affiliate with it. A local organization may receive financial support indirectly from the unions when Transport House or the regional units provide literature at low cost, make subsidies available for special purposes, or contribute to its campaign fund. An active Labour party, however, usually faces the problem of increased political burdens in the face of limited financial resources, and unless it has a good number of trade union branches in the district and enjoys good relations with them, it has to cast its net about for a variety of revenue sources. Traditionally, the constituency parties have relied upon membership subscriptions, but since the early 1950s, these have proved to be inadequate because of the inefficient methods of collection and the declining population in many areas.

In searching for supplementary means of support, many local parties have organized loan and holiday clubs and have sponsored bingo games, 'bring and buy' sales, and similar fund-raisers. Even more important, they have taken advantage of the British proclivity for small-scale gambling by sponsoring raffles, sweepstakes, and lotteries within the rules laid down by the Small Betting and Lotteries Act.[52] As we have already observed, some of the parties in an area collaborate in administering football pools or 'draws'. The idea is to encourage people to take out membership in a club or association, pay them benefits when they hold the lucky numbers, retrieve the administrative costs, and derive a gain from the profits. Organizational effort along these lines, of course, tends to detract from regular politcal work, but some Labour organizations try to use the tote membership lists as a pool from which to draw more volunteers into their orthodox activities and to utilize the collectors for distributing literature and reporting any citizens' complaints they might encounter. In any event, these new forms of revenue are crucial items in the budgets of local Labour parties.

The Labour organization in Bermondsey was, comparatively speaking, financially secure, but the Fulham and South Kensington parties had to struggle in order to keep their budgets in balance. When we posed the question of what were the most serious problems the local party faced, only three of the Bermondsey respondents listed finance, while 41 per cent of the Fulham people and 37 per cent of the South Kensington folk mentioned the difficulty of raising funds. When we examined the Fulham and South Kensington data, we found that, as expected, those who were the most involved in party affairs were the most conscious of the financial problem. In the two constituencies together, 60 per cent of the highly involved activists mentioned and discussed it, 47 per cent of the moderately involved were concerned about it; and only 12.5 per cent of the people with low involvement were attentive to the matter.

It is difficult to make an accurate comparison of the ledgers of the three constituency parties because the categories were not standardized and the headquarters accounts in the Bermondsey party did not include the revenue that was taken in by the area organizations. The rough distribution of income is nevertheless presented as follows:[53]

INCOME

Item	Bermondsey	Fulham	South Kensington
Balance brought forward	$ 219.41	–	–
Membership dues	828.45	1,319.80	301.14
Affiliated organizations dues	459.67	166.92	17.36
Grant from trade union	980.00	–	–
M.P.'s donation	–	140.00	–
Social functions*	1,820.00	3,416.43†	350.86
Rental of rooms	1,725.50	5,074.44	–
Other donations	7.53	743.18	–
Sale of land	7,000.00	–	–
Bank interest	11.18	45.89	1.61
Miscellaneous	–	174.38	–
TOTAL	13,051.74	11,081.04	670.97

* Includes dances, fairs, raffles, and lotteries.
† The breakdown for Fulham was: West London Supporters Society, $1,714.91; Sweepstakes, etc., $1,304.01; Christmas Fair, $397.51.

It is worth noting that party membership dues were not the major source of income for any of the parties. Bermondsey relied heavily upon social functions and lotteries, the rental of rooms at the party headquarters, and a grant from the M.P.'s trade union. The rental of rooms was the biggest income producer for the Fulham party, and it too derived important monetary benefit from social functions and lotteries. The social functions in South Kensington largely consisted of dances, jumble sales, and the annual dinner; the raffles and draws were less conspicuous in the reports of its treasurer.

The expenditures of the three parties were as follows:

EXPENDITURES

Item	Bermondsey	Fulham	South Kensington
Office Management			
Staff salaries and travel	3,203.07	3,710.75	–
Stationery, printing, publicity	585.81	650.65	155.37
Telephone, postage	346.76	339.28	123.92
Bank charges	28.60	15.74	1.23
Accounting and legal fees	92.01	35.28	–
Premises			
Upkeep	1,829.58	3,395.16	20.38
Amortization	1,974.00	1,741.05	–
Political			
Affiliation fees	430.50	495.60	126.98
Collection expenses	–	221.73	–
Room hire	106.19	35.34	96.60
Conferences, delegates' fees	82.25	272.75	68.66
Elections	594.52	1,259.31	–
Donations	43.26	43.40	57.26
Miscellaneous	2.80	29.12	–
TOTAL EXPENDITURES	$ 9,319.35	$12,245.16	$ 650.40
INCOME ABOVE OR BELOW EXPENDITURES:	$ +3,732.39	$ −1,164.12	$ +20.57

Of the three parties, Bermondsey was in the best financial position. The area organizations had surpluses in their treasuries, and the agent indicated that the party was operating with a favorable balance even before the sale of its land. South Kensington was forced to pay affiliation fees on 800 members when it had less than half of that number, and it barely managed to balance its accounts. The organization in Fulham was forced to end its fiscal year with a deficit, but it sought additional revenue from loyal members who were willing to pay more than the regular subscription fees.

In light of continuing financial struggle, how did the three parties finance their political campaigns? Bermondsey experienced the least difficulty The M.P.'s trade union paid 80 per cent of the cost of the general election campaign. For the borough council election, the agent made a special appeal to the trade unions which had members standing as candidates, and he urged other unions and the areas and wards to contribute to the election fund. Usually there was no need to dip into the general fund; at times the party even made a profit on its election activities. The election for seats on the London County Council was the most costly, and the party had to bear the brunt of the expenses for this endeavor.

Elections were harder to finance in Fulham since the M.P. did not have trade union sponsorship. The agent and the party treasurer tried to set up a reserve before the onset of an election, and when the campaign got under way letters appealing for funds were sent to the unions and their branches and to other affiliated organizations, as well as to individual members. In borough council elections the party leaders made an effort to get contributions from the unions whose members were competing for council seats. The difference between the amount collected and the sum expended was taken from the party's general funds.

As a small party operating in territory where people were reluctant to invest in a hopeless cause, the South Kensington party had to piece together small sums for its election campaigns. The secretary/agent and the treasurer tried to set up a modest election fund in advance of a parliamentary contest, but they made no effort to do this for local elections. Whatever the nature of the election, they made an appeal to party members and the affiliated organizations, sometimes sending as many as four letters to those who did not respond. The few GMC delegates with trade union connections tried to solicit some funds from their unions. In addition to these sources, the party was usually able to get a small grant from Transport House. Even after these efforts had been made, the South Kensington people always had a campaign deficit which they erased by using regular party funds or by transferring receipts from dances.

Now that we have examined the structures of the three constituency parties, the composition of their leadership, and their 'operational objectives' and how they set about to achieve them, we can move on to a markedly different phase of this study. Several scholars have pointed out that we know very little about the political attitudes of Labour activists at the 'grass roots'. We must bear in mind, of course, that we are definitely limited by the small size of the activist group, but the data nevertheless permit us to say something about the outlooks of the GMC delegates.

6 Outlooks of the Activists

Besides collecting data on the demographic features of the three constituencies, the organizational patterns and activities of their Labour parties, and the backgrounds of the delegates who comprised the General Management Committees, the author sought to probe the opinions and attitudes of the activists on certain issues. This should interest the readers of this volume for at least two reasons. First, as we have just stated, the research cupboards are virtually bare when it comes to knowledge about the political outlooks of the people who do the doorstep work for their local parties. Second, the attitudinal patterns we shall be examining are based upon the issues that generated controversy at GMC meetings during the period of this study. This will enable us to see the general line-up of forces on these divisive questions in each of the three parties and to note the impact of certain socio-economic factors upon issue stands. The issues we shall be considering are: unilateral disarmament, support for the leadership of the national Party, the Anglo-American 'alliance', the relevance of traditional socialist doctrine, Clause IV (nationalization), the possibility of cooperating with the Tories, the Common Market, the restriction of immigration, the abolition of capital punishment, limitations on the Communist Party, and the reorganization of London government. The Labour Party is still wrestling with many of these issues today. Before we proceed any further, however, we need to offer a brief explanation of the procedures followed in this analysis.

A NOTE ABOUT THE TECHNIQUES OF ANALYSIS

Most of the dependent variables used in this study were dichotomous. Although some of the independent variables were continuous (some of the temporal factors, for example), they were usually of a nominal or ordinal nature. But in the case of the nominal variables, a judgment was always made with respect to the ordering of the categories.[1] In making this analysis, we used the regression routines in the Statistical Package for the Social Sciences (SPSS).[2] The author realizes that the use of nominal and ordinal data in regression analysis violates an assumption of the statistical model: the level of measurement must be at least interval. Since the model also assumes linearity of data relationships, the use of the data with unequal intervals introduces a form of measurement error, which results in biased estimates of the regression parameters and correlation coefficients. Most social science studies face these problems, but in many cases the reader's attention is not called to them.

Despite the fact that much of the data in this study is not coded with equal intervals, their analysis through regression techniques permits a more sophisticated examination than is possible through reliance upon techniques specifically designed for nominal and ordinal data. Moreover, some studies have shown that the degree of error introduced in this way is usually not very great unless the intervals are vastly unequal, which is not the case in this study.[3] Correlation and multiple correlation coefficients are usually conservative estimates, while regression coefficients may be biased in either direction, although as a rule not very much. Under these conditions, standardized regression coefficients are generally more stable than unstandardized coefficients. Since the size of the error by using regression analysis does not appear to be great and since the ordinary techniques for the processing of nominal and ordinal data do not permit refined analysis, we decided that the benefits of regression techniques far outweighed the disadvantages. The aims of the analyses in this chapter are modestly descriptive, and, given the intercorrelations among some of the variables, especially those tapping social class factors, we were more interested in the regression program as a *variable-sorting mechanism* than we were in the regression results *per se*.

Since class factors are salient in the analysis of many political issues in Britain, the problem of multicollinearity is a disturbing one. We knew that some independent variables would tap the same empirical domain; for example, age, period of entry into the Party, and length of Party membership were all measuring a time dimension. Though we were constrained by the size of the population (142 respondents), we sought as best we could to capture important relationships in complex, class-based data. This meant that we had to combine and restructure variables in the analysis of most of the issues, thus in effect creating a new variable. We speculated that a given attitude was not randomly distributed throughout a group, but that it may be differentially distributed among clusters of people with similar traits within the larger grouping. A simple category of, say, education might reveal stronger relationships when, for example, the subgroups are combined with occupational breakdowns. In other words, a group of people who have completed secondary school may display different outlooks if we separate the manual workers from the routine clerical personnel. Thus an attempt was made to construct the best variable possible from a combination of other variables which would reveal distinctive outlooks among subgroups.[4] When using the regression, we were looking for differences within the population we were working with; since it was a population, we did not have the problem of sampling error.

The restructured variables in this study were developed through the following procedures. (1) Considerable thought had been given to particular factors expected to be influential as a result of observations during the research or findings in the literature. (2) We examined the intercorrelations among the important single variables as they appeared in the original rank order. (3) The bivariate cross-tabulations were examined and note was taken of the appropriate significance tests, especially the Cramers V. (4) We subjected the data to the Automatic Interaction Detection and the Multiple Classification Analysis routines, although the results were used only for advisory purposes. (5) An initial run with the single variables was made on the SPSS regression program, and attention was paid to the changes in the Bs and Betas. (6) A theoretically interesting combination of single variables was tested on the SPSS program. (7) Other competing combinations of variables were tested to insure that the ones selected were not suppressing other variables or potential combinations of greater strength. All of the single variables that were high in the rank order of simple correlations, the Cramers V scores, and the initial SPSS run were tested against each other, and on some issues we tried fifty or more combinations. (8) We have been careful to report the single variables and restructured variables that were significant but were pushed aside in the computer runs owing to the fact that a competitor with a slightly higher F score was chosen – a feature of the SPSS program. As we have already mentioned, the main purpose of the regression analysis in this study was to facilitate the most judicious selection of variables from among a variety of factors which were often highly correlated.

Before we proceed any farther, we must offer a word of caution. This study was designed principally as a comparison of three local Labour parties at the same point in time. The constituencies were selected so that there would be variation in party types – and the fact that they were all in the London area means that the case studies are regionally skewed. The author was naturally interested in tapping the attitudes of the respondents, but the fact that the research was centered upon GMC delegates in only three districts meant that the number of people in the entire group would be small – a situation that was beyond the control of the investigator. In other words, the analysis of attitudes is a 'side-benefit' flowing from the main research thrust. The data do, of course, permit us to say something about the attitudes of the activists in the three parties. In the case of some phenomena – such as the impact of social class upon certain outlooks – the associations are so strong that we can be fairly confident about the findings. In other cases, however, some of the refined points in the patterns cannot be accepted as being anything more than suggestive owing to the small number of responses we had to work with. The reader must be continually aware of these limitations.

It was anticipated that social class would be a salient influence in some of the responses to the controversial issues that arose in the GMC meetings. For this reason, the last item in the questionnaire invited the respondents to indicate what they perceived their own class status to be, i.e., whether they located themselves in the working class or in the middle class. We shall turn now to an analysis of this class self-placement. Following this, we shall examine the relationships between certain socio-economic factors and the positions taken by the respondents on the contentious questions listed on the first page of this chapter.

ATTITUDES TOWARD SOCIAL CLASS

While social class or status groupings are an importat variable in the study of any society, the class factor is especially significant in British politics. Professor Alford has pointed out that class voting in the decade from 1952 to 1962 was consistently higher in Great Britain than it was in Australia, Canada, and the United States.[5] The delineation and analysis of social class is, of course, a tricky exercise. We can place individuals into particular class categories, but we cannot assume in the absence of empirical studies that the people assigned to a given status necessarily share the same outlooks or display mutual feelings of 'class consciousness'. In this section of the study we shall be concerned with how the respondents *classified themselves* — how they perceived their class identity according to their own mapping.[6]

In this endeavor, we have some general guides to go by. In various British surveys, according to Mark Abrams, about one-fourth of the adult population in non-manual occupations listed themselves as working-class, while about 35 per cent of the people in manual jobs described themselves as middle-class.[7] When we consider the GMC delegates in the three constituencies as a group, a slightly different picture comes into focus. About 45 per cent of the activists in non-manual positions identified with the working class and only about 7 per cent of those in manual occupations recognized any affinity with the middle class.[8] The other surveys dealt with electors in the general population; it is not particularly startling to find a different set of outlooks among activists in ideological, working-class parties.

As we anticipated, the overwhelmingly important predictor of class self-identification was constituency.[9] In other words, the social class with which the activists identified varied according to the social composition of the community in which they resided:

Class self-identification	Bermondsey	Fulham	South Kensington
Working class	96.4%	68.3%	17.2%
Middle class	3.6	31.7	82.8
	(N=55)	(N=41)	(N=29)

(Cramers V, 0.66)

All of the manual workers in Bermondsey placed themselves in the working class, while 89 per cent of those in non-manual occupations listed themselves with the workers. In Fulham, 75 per cent of the manual workers indicated an identification with the working class and 66 per cent of the non-manuals located themselves there. In South Kensington, on the other hand, two manual workers would not commit themselves, and one of the remaining two listed himself with the workers and the other registered himself with the middle class; of the people in non-manual occupations, only 14 per cent claimed affiliation with the working class. The reader will recall that the GMCs in Bermondsey and Fulham embraced a good number of people in routine clerical jobs, and the gap between them and the manual workers was narrow. When we separated the non-manuals into 'clerical' and 'professional' groups, the former tended to identify much more with the working class than did the latter (72 per cent to 26 per cent). In Bermondsey and Fulham, however, even the professional people (though few in number) exhibited a tendency to identify with the workers, while in South Kensington both groups overwhelmingly located themselves in the middle class.

Several studies of much wider populations – voters rather than just activists – point up the tendency of people to identify with the social elements that are dominant in a community. Whereas only 13 per cent of the working-class respondents in the Labour stronghold of Dagenham rated themselves as middle class, the comparative figure in the Tory base at Woodford was 34 per cent.[10] The research of Michael Young and Peter Willmott in East London indicates that working-class people were disposed to elevate, in comparison with the rankings of the Hall-Jones scale, the more skilled manual occupations and to underrate the non-manual positions.[11] As in Bermondsey, the working-class folk regarded manual labor as more important to society than non-manual endeavors.

Although constituency was the strongest factor in class self-designation, education could not be overlooked; the two variables were highly correlated. For this reason, we dropped constituency out of the analysis in order to assess the importance of the education variable. It turned out to be the only remaining factor of any significance – a finding that was reinforced when separate regressions were computed for Fulham and South Kensington.[12] The influence of education upon the respondents' assignments to social class is readily noticeable:

Class self-identification	Elementary	Secondary	University
Working class	94.6%	62.7%	5.6%
Middle class	5.4	37.3	94.4
	(N=56)	(N=51)	(N=18)

(Cramers V, 0.64)

The pattern was almost identical when we made a separate analysis of the people in non-manual occupations.

Thus, in their own assignments to places in the class structure, the activists moved in the same direction as the general populations studied in other research — but they went much farther. Class self-placement by the GMC delegates was determined largely by the type of community in which they resided; after that, the level of education was the strategic consideration.

INTERLACING OF ISSUES

When this study was being carried out, the Labour Party was in turmoil over the issue of unilateral disarmament. The supporters of unilateralism naturally called into question Britain's 'special relationship' with the United States, the world power that had been the main instigator of the NATO pact. In some respects, however, these defense questions were a reflection of the basic struggle within the Party over 'revisionism' — a controversy that had resulted in a defeat for the Gaitskell forces in 1959 when they introduced their proposal to revise Clause IV (nationalization) of the Party's Constitution.[13] Perturbed by Gaitskell's attempt to modify the long-term objectives of the organization, many supporters of principled socialism lined themselves against their leader on the unilateralist issue and vigorously challenged him for disregarding the Conference decision in 1960. When the Gaitskell group managed to get the Conference to reverse itself on unilateralism a year later, many left-wing activists turned their attention to the Common Market, registering their opposition to Britain's entry.

The interlacing of these and other issues is noticeable in the attitude responses given by the activists in the three constituencies.[14] Detailed information is presented in Table 6.1.

The relationships tend to cluster in three groups. The first cluster of issues consists of unilateralism, the national Party leaders, and the Anglo-American Alliance. Here the supporters of the unilateralist position were the most hostile to Gaitskell and his colleagues, and they exhibited the most opposition to the Alliance. The non-unilateralists, on the other hand, strongly supported the leadership and were much more favorable to Britain's liaison with the United States. The Common

Table 6.1 Interlacing of issues

	Leadership			Alliance			Clause IV	
	Vs	For	Abandon	Loosen	Favorable	Retain	Revise
For unilateralism	44.9%	55.1	(49)	35.4%	39.6	25.0	(48)	87.2%	12.8	(47)
Vs. unilateralism	5.0	95.0	(80)	2.6	31.6	65.8	(76)	50.7	49.3	(73)

	Doctrine		Cooperation with Tories			Market	
	For	Vs.	Not at all	Hardly	Some	Vs.	For
For unilateralism	72.9%	27.1	(48)	39.6%	35.4	25.0	(48)	76.0%	24.0	(50)
Vs. unilateralism	46.3	53.8	(80)	29.5	19.2	51.3	(78)	53.8	46.3	(80)

	Doctrine		Cooperation with Tories			Market	
	For	Vs.	Not at all	Hardly	Some	Vs.	For
Retain Clause IV	72.8%	27.2	(81)	44.4%	25.9	29.6	(81)	72.8%	27.2	(81)
Revise Clause IV	33.3	66.7	(42)	22.0	22.0	56.1	(41)	46.5	53.5	(43)

	Capital punishment		Communist Party		London reorganization later		Current London reorganization	
	Retain	Abolish	Restrict	Not Restrict	Vs.	For	Vs.	For
For curbing immigration	43.6%	56.4	(55)	35.2%	64.8	(54)	46.4%	53.6	(56)	92.6%	7.4	(54)
Vs. curbing immigration	11.8	88.2	(76)	12.2	87.8	(74)	19.7	80.3	(76)	76.3	23.7	(76)

Market stands as an issue apart from the other three. In their study of the general population, Butler and Stokes point out that the opposition to Britain's entry into Europe came from a wider group than the ordinary 'left-wing' contingent.[15] This pattern was repeated in our research on local Labour activists. Note in Table 6.1 that the differences between the unilateralists and the non-unilateralists were not so striking on the Market question.

The second cluster of issues is made up of Clause IV, traditional doctrine, and the notion of cooperation with the Conservatives. To be sure, the unilateralists gave strong support to the retention of Clause IV and to traditional doctrine, and they rejected the thought of cooperating with the political opposition. But the relationships on these issues are less strong than they are in the other cluster. In other words, the sanctity of Clause IV and traditional doctrine and continued hostility to the Tories constitute more of a 'traditional socialist' grouping which attracted significant support from the people in the non-unilateralist camp.

The third cluster of issues embraces immigration, capital punishment, the Communist Party, and the reorganization of London government. The activists who favored restrictions upon the intake of immigrants also tended to support the death penalty and stricter regulation of the Communist Party, and they stood in firm opposition to London reorganization under any conditions.

It is to each of these issues that we now turn our attention.

UNILATERAL DISARMAMENT

The Labour Party, a protest movement itself, has always been vulnerable to special 'causes' and 'protests' within its ranks. The cause that triggered the fiercest controversy during this study was that being pursued by the Campaign for Nuclear Disarmament (CND). This movement, which began in 1957 and did not wind down until the mid-1960s, fought with religious zeal against the manufacture, testing, and use of nuclear weapons by Britain and demanded that foreign missile bases be removed from British soil. The country would be better off, the disarmers argued, if it were to renounce the possession and the use of nuclear weapons unilaterally and unconditionally, thus providing a 'moral lead' for the rest of the world. Although the unilateralist camp eventually attracted a varied assortment of people whose protests were about more than just the bombs, it is fair to say that the CND views struck melodious notes for many Labour stalwarts who interpreted the socialist scriptures to mean hostility to all forms of arms build-up and support for a 'neutralist' stance in foreign policy. Moreover, unilateralism was a non-bargaining type of issue – it was a black vs. white question which could not be reworked into shades of grey. Small wonder that most of the constituency parties were tormented by the fury of the debate.

As already mentioned, the unilateralist controversy moved into the three parties which engage our study. The impact was not so severe in Bermondsey and South Kensington, where only about one-third of the GMC delegates were professed nuclear disarmers. In Fulham, however, the line-up of forces was much more delicately balanced, with the unilateralists having a slight lead (51 per cent).[16]

The best study of the Campaign for Nuclear Disarmament has been made by Professor Frank Parkin, who drew his sample from CND supporters who actually participated in the 1965 Easter march. He concluded that the movement was a middle-class phenomenon. Our study, however, is concerned with local Labour party activists, a good number of whom identified with the goals of the CND movement but only a few of whom had joined the marches.

In analyzing the GMC sessions of the three parties and in observing a number of other Party meetings and conferences at which the unilateralist issue was injected into the discussions, the author noted the concern that many activists had lest their party organizations be torn apart by the bitterness of the debate. After a number of interviews, he began to suspect that the people who were the most involved in party work and had relatively long records of service would be the most likely to take a stand against the nuclear disarmers. This was the hypothesis of major concern when we began the analysis, although we were alert to the possibility that support for unilateralism might be a middle-class or younger age-bracket phenomenon.

This involvement hypothesis survived the initial screening, for the rank order of simple correlations gave us three factors: period of entry into the Labour Party,[17] the officers' length of service, and length of membership on the GMC. In the original computer run, the first two variables were retained, but objective/subjective social class replaced GMC tenure.[18] In examining period of entry into the Labour Party, we observed that only about 19 per cent of the people who were recruited prior to 1935 were unilateralists, compared with 41 per cent of those who entered after World War II. But the most interesting discovery was the high level of unilateralist sentiment (73 per cent) among the *small* group who joined the organization during the period 1935-44, especially during the time when the peace issue generated such controversy within the Party.[19] When it came to length of officers' tenure, all but one of those who had served for three or more years were opposed to the disarmament position (96 per cent). These two groups, then – people who had enrolled in 1935-44 and the officers with the longest tenure – were comparatively distinctive and stood on opposite sides of the question. The residue group, we suspected, would reveal some variation if we analyzed it in terms of other variables that ranked high in the simple correlations but were pushed aside in the computer run, probably because of intercorrelation. Hence, we set about to construct a new variable which was basically a combination of period of entry into the Labour Party, length of officers' tenure, and length of service on the GMC. The results are recorded in Table 6.2, where for simplicity and economy of space we report just the proportions in opposition to unilateralism.

Table 6.2 Officers' tenure, recruitment period, GMC tenure, and trade union activity: Unilateralism

	Opposes	N
Officers serving 3 or more years	95.8%	(24)
Non-officers and Officers serving less than 3 years		
Recruited into Party other than during 1935–1944		
On GMC more than 10 years	83.9	(31)
On GMC 10 years or less		
Trade Union: Inactives and non-members	54.5	(33)
Actives and quasi-actives	36.7	(30)
Recruited into Party 1935–1944	16.7	(12)

[Cramers V, 0.54; Kendall's Tau-b, −0.49]

The table is really not as complicated as it looks. It is divided into two basic groups – the officers who had served for three or more years (a group we have already mentioned) and the rest of the respondents. This latter group also has two basic divisions: those who were recruited *except* during the period 1935–44, and the 1935–44 recruits (a small aggregate we have already singled out). Among the activists not recruited in 1935–44, length of GMC service reveals some difference, with those who have been on the GMC for more than a decade expressing the higher note of opposition to unilateralism. Of those who had served on the GMC for a lesser period, trade union activity was a distinguishing factor; the non-members and the inactives were less enthusiastic about unilateralism than were the active and quasi-active trade unionists.[20] Thus, it would appear that the people who were involved in party affairs over a comparatively long time-span were more inclined to oppose unilateralism than were the rest of their colleagues. Among those who carried less responsibility and/or were involved for a shorter time, the unilateralist position was most attractive to active trade unionists and the people who had joined the party during 1935–44, the era characterized by ideological militancy.[21]

Unilateralist sympathy was not primarily a middle-class phenomenon in this study. The people in non-manual occupations who placed themselves in the middle class included the smallest group of nuclear disarmers (29 per cent, $N=35$). Next in line were the clericals who identified with the working class (32 per cent, $N=28$), followed by the manual workers who subjectively assigned themselves to their own class (38 per cent, $N=42$). The group that exhibited the greatest sympathy with the unilateralist cause was an aggregation of deviants from their objective status (60 per cent, $N=25$) – professional and managerial people who located themselves in the working class, those who refused to commit themselves on social class, and a tiny band of manuals who opted for the middle-class category.

So far as this study is concerned, then, the greatest resistance to the unilateralist movement tended to come from the activists with the greatest and longest involvement with the local party. Within the less involved category, active trade unionists tended to give unilateralism some support, as did the small group of people who had joined the Labour Party during the era when the peace issue was prominent. In terms of social class, the only really distinctive group of unilateralists was made up largely of middle-class activists whose subjective class mapping deviated from their objective status. The rest of the categories are fairly well grouped together, although it should be noted that, comparatively speaking, manual workers who identified with their own class expressed a surprisingly high preference for the unilateralist position. The class phenomenon was certainly influential in the unilateralist controversy, but the degree of commitment to the local party is worthy of further investigation.

NATIONAL PARTY LEADERSHIP

As the leader of the national Party, Hugh Gaitskell became the target of the unilateralists. Some people who were chronic opponents of the leadership 'establishment' seized upon the unilateralist question as a means of voicing their wrath. Feelings against Gaitskell ran high in many constituencies, and some of his public meetings were disrupted.

In order to assess the degree of support for or hostility toward Gaitskell in the three constituency parties, we asked the respondents whether, in general, they supported the policies of the national leadership, and we offered them an open-ended space which enabled them to list the policies with which they disagreed the most.[22] Recognizing the trade union emphasis on 'solidarity' and the tendency of working-class folk to be loyal to their leaders, we expected to find that the people who had had the longest exposure to working-class norms – through such socializing experiences as elementary education, manual labor, and lengthy residence in the area – would tend to be the most supportive of the Party's leadership.

The analysis of the leadership problem presented some difficulties. In the first place, the number of negative responses was very small (26 cases), which would not encourage us to expect much variation.[23] Second, the relationships in two of the variables—education and occupation—were curvilinear. The respondents who had had secondary education were more opposed to the leadership than were the activists with elementary and university training.[24] Similarly, the people employed in routine clerical posts and in the less established professions (teaching, journalism, social work, etc., as contrasted with law and medicine) were more hostile to the leadership than were the manual workers and the people in the more traditional professions. Third, the strongest variables appearing in the analysis were intercorrelated and seemed to be tapping the same thing, thus making it difficult to determine the individual contributions of the several factors.

The expectation that the nature of the community environment would influence the support accorded to the Party leaders can be seen in the breakdown by constituency: Bermondsey, 93 per cent; Fulham, 80 per cent; and South Kensington, 65 per cent.[25] Besides constituency, the main variables emerging from the preliminary analysis were proportion of adult life spent in the community, objective/subjective class, and social mobility.

In the initial computer run, length of residence and constituency retained their positions, objective/subjective class indicated an influence upon residence, and social mobility, which had a high correlation with the other two variables, was suppressed in the regression. For this reason it will be useful to glance at the social mobility classification: stationary manual, 94 per cent; mobiles to white-collar positions, 72 per cent; mobiles to professional/managerial status, 93 per cent; and stationary middle, 68 per cent.[26] Thus, the greatest support for the leadership came from the manual group and from those who had made the most advancement from manual status; those who had moved from the working class into clerical posts offered less support to the leaders, but the stationary middle-class group indicated the weakest support.

Significantly enough, the proportion of adult life spent in a community proved to be the strongest single variable in all tests. The distribution in terms of leadership support was: residence for 75 per cent or more of adult life, 92 per cent ($N=73$); for less than 75 per cent, 69 per cent ($N=64$).[27] In many ways, the category of residence in a community for 75 per cent or more of adult life captures the geographically stable activists who have had the most exposure to working-class socialization processes.[28]

When it came to analyzing the geographically mobile elements— those who had lived in their districts for less than three-fourths of their adult lives—the task was more difficult, largely because of the heavy representation from South Kensington. The latter constituency party had only a tiny band of manual workers, and the number of people with elementary education was small. Moreover, it was in the South Kensington group that the curvilinear relationship in education emerged. It will be recalled, too, that in the South Kensington organization a group of young newcomers, supporters of Gaitskell's policies, had wrested control from the older veterans who had served longer in the Party and on the GMC. For these reasons the numbers of respondents in most of the 'working-class boxes' made it impossible to study the exposure of the geographically mobile people to working-class socialization processes in a satisfactory way.

The best predictor on opinions with respect to the national Party leadership was a combination of length of residence, education, and objective/subjective class. This new variable, along with constituency, survived the final regression run.[29] We have already examined the constituency results. The data for residence and objective/subjective class are presented in Table 6.3.

Table 6.3 Residence, education, and objective/subjective class: National Party Leadership

	Supports	N
Adult life in community: 75% or more		
Education: elementary	97.7%	(43)
post-elementary	83.3	(30)
Adult life in community: less than 75%		
Manual identifying working class and non-manual identifying middle class	75.0	(40)
White-collar and professional/managerial identifying working class and won't commit	58.3	(24)

[Cramers V, 0.35; Kendall's Tau-b, 0.33]

This table hardly needs explanation. Those who were subjected to the most sustained exposure to working-class norms as indicated by long residence in the community and elementary education (they were also the people with manual jobs) were the most supportive of the national leaders. Among those who had moved into their communities more recently (in the case of South Kensington the norms were not working-class), the people whose subjective assessment of their class status matched the objective situation were more favorably inclined toward the leadership than were those whose middle-class occupations were incongruent with their working-class identification and those who refused to make a judgment about their class status.

ANGLO-AMERICAN ALLIANCE

As mentioned earlier, the campaign against nuclear weapons clashed with Britain's traditional relationship with the United States, a nuclear power which had military bases on British soil. The unilateralists vigorously opposed the NATO pact – a position that had some attraction for non-unilateralists who nurtured distrust of Germany. While most of the nuclear disarmers lined themselves up in opposition to the alliance, one could hardly expect an identical breakdown in the analysis. For many Labour people, the two issues were separate; an emotional sympathy for neutrality between the United States and the Soviet Union and an uneasiness about having to be linked with West Germany through the American connection were sufficient reasons for them to entertain doubts about the Anglo-American arrangement.

In order to gauge the sentiments of the activists in the three parties, we asked them whether they thought that the 'alliance' should be strengthened, remain in its current form, be loosened, or be abandoned.[30] Since the alliance question was tied to unilateralism, we expected some of the basic findings to be similar: opposition to the alliance among people who had been recruited in 1935–44 and in the decade of the 1950s; among activists who were sensitive about their class status as reflected in their subjective assessment; and among the respondents whose involvement in the party had been comparatively limited and relatively short. But we were alert to the probability that other facets of the alliance question, especially the appeals to neutralist sentiments and to anti-German feeling, would disturb the predicted patterns when a concrete alliance structure was up for consideration. Since the question dealt with Britain's relations with the United States, however, we speculated that activists with the greatest exposure to a working-class milieu would be conspicuously supportive of the arrangement, largely on the ground that the intricate relationships among foreign policy issues would not capture their interest and that favorable attitudes toward American policies in the immediate post-war years still lingered among ordinary British people.

When the pointer turned to the three constituency parties, Bermondsey was the most favorably disposed to the alliance (Favorable, 65 per cent; Loosen, 29 per cent; Abandon, 6 per cent). South Kensington was next, with a bunching in the middle category: Favorable, 29 per cent; Loosen, 52 per cent; Abandon, 19 per cent. The greatest amount of dissent came from Fulham, where the comparable figures were: Favorable, 56 per cent; Loosen, 22 per cent; Abandon, 22 per cent.[31] Though all the simple correlations and Cramers scores were suprisingly low, proportion of adult life spent in the constituency and objective/subjective class were ranked at the top, followed by constituency. Other variables that appeared to be influential were education and several party factors – office-holding, period of entry into the Party, and length of service on the Executive Committee. In the initial regression, length of residence remained the leading variable, but education and objective/subjective class were left below the tolerance level. We proceeded, therefore, to restructure the variables.

The most powerful predictor was a combination of adult residence and objective/subjective class, as seen in Table 6.4. Just as they were the most ardent supporters of unilateralism and the severest critics of the national leadership, the activists whose class self-rating was incongruent with their objective positions or who refused to commit themselves on social class were the most hostile to the Anglo-American alliance. The rest of the respondents were divided into two groups according to the proportion of their adult lives spent in their communities. Among the geographically mobile, the white-collar workers who identified with the working class were the most critical of the alliance, followed by the manual workers who linked themselves to the working class, and then by the non-manuals who assigned themselves to the middle class. When it comes to the geographically stable – those who had lived in their communities for 75 per cent or more of their adult lives – the middle-class element was more suspicious of the alliance than was the working-class group.

The second restructured variable is composed of period of entry into the Party, trade union activity, and length of service on the Executive Committee. This variable, which bears some resemblance to that recorded in Table 6.2, is explained in Table 6.5. Among the GMC delegates who entered the Party during the peace struggle in the middle and late 1930s and during the ideological fervor of the 1950s, the people most active in their trade unions registered the most opposition to the Anglo-American alliance. For those who were recruited at other times, association with the party made some difference, with those having served on the Executive Committee for a longer period being more disposed toward the arrangement with America than were those who had served a shorter time. (The same pattern obtained when we compared the opinions of the officers and non-officers in each constituency; the officers were much more supportive of the alliance.)[32] In the eyes of some of these 'involved' activists, the unilateralists were seizing upon the issue of the alliance to disrupt the party, and they refused to adopt an extreme position.

The third factor that appeared in the regression was education. Here again the relationship was curvilinear, as seen by the following scores: university, 1.53; secondary+, 2.16; secondary, 1.67; and elementary, 1.47. The scores in the secondary categories reflected the deviancy of a segment of the middle class (objectively determined) which has already emerged on other issues. In order to assess more fully the impact of education in the regression, we took steps to straighten out the curve.[33]

Table 6.4 Objective/subjective class and residence: Alliance

	Favorable	Loosen	Abandon	Score	N
Prof./mgr. identifying working class, manual identifying middle class, and won't commit	28.0%	40.0%	32.0%	2.04	(25)
Adult life in community: less than 75%					
white-collar identifying working class	36.4	36.4	27.3	1.91	(11)
manual identifying working class	30.0	60.0	10.0	1.80	(10)
Non-manual identifying middle class	55.2	27.6	17.2	1.62	(29)
Adult life in community: 75% or more					
White-collar identifying working class and non-manual identifying middle class	56.5	43.5	0	1.43	(23)
Manual identifying working class	71.0	22.6	6.5	1.35	(31)

[Cramers V, 0.29; Kendall's Tau-b, −0.30]

Table 6.5 Recruitment period, trade union activity, and tenure on Executive Committee: Alliance

	Favorable	Loosen	Abandon	Score	N
Recruited into Party 1935–44 and 1952–62					
Union actives and quasi-actives	25.0%	50.0%	25.0%	2.00	(24)
Union inactives and non-members	50.0	25.0	25.0	1.75	(28)
Recruited into Party during other periods					
Never on EC or served less than 5 years	53.5	34.9	11.6	1.58	(43)
Served on EC 5 years or more	64.7	32.4	2.9	1.38	(34)

[Cramers V, 0.23; Kendall's Tau-b, −0.24]

A fourth factor—age—also signalled its importance in the final regression run. Here again we found a curvilinear relationship, with both the oldest group and the youngest group registering the greatest opposition to the alliance. The scores for the various age categories were: 65 and older, 1.90; 55–64, 1.27; 45–54, 1.64; 35–44, 1.48; and under 35, 1.85.[34]

The major patterns drawn together in summary form are: (1) On a class breakdown, the activists whose subjective class mapping was the most incongruous with their objective status carried the brightest torch against the alliance. (2) Similarly and related, the people who had had secondary education and who held jobs as ordinary clerks or in the less established professions, i.e., those who had climbed up the ladder of success but had not made it all the way, were prone to take an extreme position. (3) The least resistance to the Anglo-American arrangement was exhibited by the activists who have had the most exposure to working-class norms through elementary education, stationary manual position on the social mobility table, and long residence in the community as an adult. (4) Activists who were recruited during the 'ideological' periods of the late 1930s and the 1950s conspicuously opposed the alliance, particularly those who were engaged in trade union work. But in general (and especially in the case of the people who entered the Party at other times) the more the activists were involved in party affairs, the more inclined they were to support the alliance.

TRADITIONAL DOCTRINE

We have already observed that some national Party leaders moved to a 'revisionist' position on socialist doctrine in the 1950s, setting the stage for explosive arguments over what the goals of the organization should really be. This disagreement over basic objectives still rages in the Party, as a glance at any British newspaper will show. In order to examine the socio-economic differences between the grass-roots workers who cling to the 'traditionalist' outlook and those who adhere to the 'revisionist' view, we asked the respondents whether they thought that the traditional socialist view of the class struggle was still applicable in the 1960s.

We hypothethized that the activists who had had the most sustained exposure to working-class norms would adhere most strongly to traditional socialist outlook on the class struggle. In other words, we expected the most support for traditional doctrine to come from those who had been born into the working class, had lived in working-class communities most of their adult lives, had left school after completing elementary education, were employed in manual jobs, and were active in their trade unions. We also anticipated a positive relationship between identification with the working class and support for traditional doctrinal precepts. (We predicted, however, that in objective/subjective social class the middle-class people who linked themselves with the working class would be more inclined to look to traditional doctrine than their colleagues who located themselves in the middle class. We also expected to find, as the literature points out, that individual mobility would tend to soften outlooks toward class conflict.)

The general tendency in the constituency breakdown offered few surprises. In terms of seeing the doctrine as currently relevant, the proportions were: Bermondsey, 61 per cent; Fulham, 69 per cent; and South Kensington, 39 per cent. The fact that Bermondsey's level of support was below expectations leads the author to suspect that some respondents in this group misread or misinterpreted the question.[35] Most of the simple calculations indicated that the class factor was noticeably operating, but the strength of the associations was less than we might have anticipated. The activists of working-class origin were more favorable to the traditionalist view than were those from the middle class (63 per cent to 40 per cent).[36] On occupation, the supporters of orthodox doctrine were: lesser-skilled manuals, 80 per cent; skilled manuals, 64 per cent; and non-manuals, 51 per cent.[37] The figures for education were in the same direction: elementary, 60 per cent; secondary, 62 per cent; and university, 39 per cent.[38] The trade union actives revealed their support for traditional doctrine (73 per cent), compared with an average of 51 per cent for the other categories of trade union activity. The only variable that failed to point clearly in the expected direction was proportion of adult life spent in the community.

We also suggested that the movement of individuals out of the working class would tend to soften their views on class conflict. About 69 per cent of the stationary manuals indicated preference for the traditional view, 56 per cent of the mobiles took this position, and 38 per cent of the stationary middle-class group did so. The degree of association, however, was not strong.[39] In fact, none of the relationships we have mentioned dazzles the reader with statistical significance.

The factor that does stand out, however, is class identification. When we look at objective/subjective social class, an interesting but not unexpected picture comes into view:

	Doctrine applies	N
Manuals identifying working class	72.3%	(47)
White-collar and prof./mgr. identifying working class	65.8	(38)
Manuals identifying middle class and won't commit	50.0	(18)
Non-manuals identifying middle class	34.3	(35)

[Cramers V, 0.31]

According to the pattern in this table, the more closely the activists were linked with the working class, the more likely they were to proclaim the relevance of the traditional class struggle. Those in non-manual occupations who identified with the middle class were more likely to be found in the revisionist camp.

The strongest predictor of doctrinal attitudes is a combined variable made up of class self-identification, period of entry into the Party, and social origin.[40] The data are presented in Table 6.6.

Table 6.6 Class self-identification, period of recruitment, and social origin: Traditional Doctrine

	Doctrine applies	N
Self-identification: working class		
Recruitment: 1952–62 and 1935–44	90.0%	(20)
other periods	63.1	(65)
Self-identification: middle class and won't commit		
Social origin: working class	48.4	(31)
middle class	27.3	(22)

[Cramers V, 0.37; Kendall's Tau-b, 0.34]

This table reveals differences in outlooks toward the traditional view of the class struggle between the working-class identifiers and those who adhered to the middle class or shied away from class analysis. Within the working-class category, the period of entry into the Party is particularly important. As is true with several other issues, the activists who were attracted to the organization during the 1950s and the period from 1935 to 1944 exhibited distinct ideological tendencies. The people recruited during the other periods were less inclined to support traditional doctrine, although the old-timers who came into the Party prior to 1925 were somewhat more orthodox in their attitudes than the others. In looking at the middle-class group, we can see that the activists who were from working-class homes were more inclined to cling to traditional doctrine than were their colleagues who were nurtured in a middle-class environment.

Although we had to be content with the regression computations from this new restructured variable, we need to report on two other factors which were ranked just below it. One of these was length of residence in the community, a variable in which there was theoretical interest on the assumption that long-term exposure to working-class attitudes was likely to have an effect upon outlooks toward traditional doctrine. If anything, the finding was in the other direction; in both South Kensington and Bermondsey, the relatively recent arrivals were more supportive of traditional doctrine than were those who had deeper roots in their communities. The two groups in Fulham were about evenly divided.

The other variable is a combination of constituency, office-holding, and Executive Committee membership, and we report the results in Table 6.7.

Table 6.7 Constituency, officers, and Executive Committee membership: traditional doctrine

	Doctrine applies	N
Bermondsey and Fulham		
Officers	76.9%	(26)
Non-officers		
Executive Committee: Members	69.2	(26)
Non-members	56.0	(50)
South Kensington		
Non-officers	50.0	(22)
Officers	21.4	(14)

[Cramers V, 0.32; Kendall's Tau-b, 0.26]

From the data we see that the people in Bermondsey and Fulham who bore responsibility in their parties tended to be more favorable toward traditional doctrine than were those who were not so involved in party affairs.[41] In South Kensington, however, the situation was reversed, with the officers being much less attached to doctrine. This is understandable when we recall that the young pragmatists in the South Kensington organization had taken control away from the more ideologically inclined group.

Obviously, the class factor exerts influence upon traditional/revisionist attitudes; it would be most surprising if this were not the case. But the possibility that some respondents misinterpreted the question raises doubts about the finer patterns of class relationships in this study.

REVISION OF CLAUSE IV

An important component of the Labour Party's traditional doctrine is the commitment to the 'common ownership' of basic industries, which is enshrined in Clause IV of the Constitution. Over the years this commitment has gradually evolved into a policy objective of nationalizing certain dominant industries. We have already seen that Hugh Gaitskell, after Labour's defeat in 1959, suggested that the Party should discard its 'cloth cap' image and whittle down the pledge for a sweeping program of nationalization. To many of the stalwarts in the organization, Gaitskell's idea was rank heresy, and in the ensuing confrontation some of the working-class members (including many trade unionists) who had usually supported their leader deserted him on this issue. The question of whether to expand the public sector through further nationalization still rocks the Labour Party today.

Since Clause IV is a meaningful symbol of the Party's long-established objective, we sought again to tap traditional socialist outlooks by asking the respondents whether they favored or opposed the revision of the Clause. The specificity of this issue sets it apart from the more general question we asked about the relevance of the traditional socialist approach to the class struggle. We knew that many unilateralists were opposed to tampering with the Clause, but we anticipated that many non-unilateralists would also take a dim view of any watering-down of public ownership commitment. Our expectations were simple and clearcut: (1) people most closely and intimately connected with the working class would be the most hostile to the revision of Clause IV; (2) those most active in their trade unions would tend to oppose revision, since many unions had been strong supporters of nationalization and had taken a stand against Gaitskell on the issue; and (3) the anti-revisionist posture would be especially characteristic of activists in the higher age-brackets who had been in the movement for a long time and who had always regarded public ownership as an untouchable marking on the blueprint for the new society. But we were alert to the possibility that a symbolic issue like nationalization would be attractive to some young people who had joined the Party during the ideological turbulence of the 1950s.

The responses in the three constituencies lived up to expectations. Bermondsey and Fulham were definitely against the revision of Clause IV (73 per cent and 72 per cent, respectively), while a majority of the GMC members in South Kensington (54 per cent) actually *favored revision*.[42] Preliminary analysis indicated the influence of a barrage of class factors: trade union affiliation, social origin, social mobility, class self-placement, objective/subjective class, education, and occupation. The initial tabulations showed that both the trade union actives and the non-members were heavy in their support of Clause IV. About 73 per cent of the activists from working-class backgrounds opposed the alteration of the Clause, compared with only 40 per cent of the people of middle-class origin. In terms of social mobility, the greatest opposition to modification came from activists who had moved from manual to routine clerical status, followed closely by the stationary manuals; the weakest opposition was registered by the stationary middle-class group and a small group of mobiles who had advanced to professional/ managerial status. A similar pattern emerged when we looked at class self-designation: 74 per cent of the activists who identified with the working class or refused to commit themselves on class breakdowns favored retention of the Clause, in contrast with only 45 per cent who identified with the middle class. When we refined the class categories to allow for the objective/subjective dimensions, the general pattern was sustained: white-collar workers associating themselves with the working class were the most antagonistic toward changing the Clause (79 per cent); next in line were the manual workers who placed themselves in their own class (73 per cent); the professional/managerial group that tied itself to the working class registered weaker opposition (63 per cent); and at the bottom of the list were the non-manual activists who saw themselves as middle class (42 per cent).[43]

These findings are buttressed when we turn to education and occupation. Opposition to the change in terms of education was: elementary, 75 per cent; secondary, 67 per cent; and university, 33 per cent. In the occupational breakdown, the activists in clerical jobs registered the most opposition (75 per cent), followed by the manual workers (70 per cent), and then by the professional/managerial group (44 per cent).[44]

In the regression results, the strongest factor is a new variable which combines social mobility, trade union affiliation, and class self-identification. The results are presented in Table 6.8.[45]

Table 6.8 Social mobility, trade union affiliation, and class self-identification: Clause IV

	Oppose Revision	N
Mobility: stationary manuals and mobiles to white-collar		
Non-members of trade unions	94.1%	(17)
Trade union actives	77.8	(36)
Trade union quasi-actives and inactives	65.7	(35)
Mobility: stationary middle and mobiles to prof./mgr.		
Working-class identifiers and won't commit	53.3	(15)
Middle-class identifiers	27.3	(22)

[Cramers V, 0.43; Kendall's Tau-b, -0.38]

The first group in the table – the non-mobile manual workers, together with the people who have moved a step beyond the manual category into white-collar jobs – obviously comprises the working-class core of the population and those who are not very far removed from that class, objectively and subjectively. It is within this group that trade union activity becomes influential. The GMC members who did not belong to a union (most of them women, with a median age of 56) exhibited the greatest opposition to revising Clause IV, followed by those who were the most involved in trade union work. The people in this group who were less involved or who were completely inactive in their unions were the least antagonistic toward revision, but, even so, nearly two-thirds of them were against tampering with the nationalization commitment.

The other major group in the table represents a middle-class element — those who were born into the middle class and remained there and those who moved from the working class into professional and managerial occupations. Here the factor of class self-placement makes a difference, with the small group of middle-class activists who identified with the working class or refused to accept class delineations registering much more objection to the revision of Clause IV than did their colleagues who maintained their affinity with the middle class.

The other two variables which appeared in the regression reveal a time factor at work: length of service on the Executive Committee and age. About 74 per cent of the people who had never been elected to the Executive Committee wanted to leave Clause IV untouched; the comparable figure for those who had served for less than five years was 66 per cent, and for those who had served for five years or more, 54 per cent.[46] In other words, there appears to have been a very slight tendency for the activists in positions of responsibility for relatively longer periods of time to be more flexible on the nationalization question than those with less or no official experience.[47]

When it comes to age, public ownership tended to appeal a bit more to the activists in the higher age-bracket: 78 per cent of the people 55 and over opposed the revision of Clause IV, compared with 58 per cent of those who were younger. This pattern held true when we controlled for social origin and class self-identification, and when we introduced the age factor into the analysis of trade union affiliation, the opposition to the revisionist position on the part of the older union actives and among the non-members increased.

Among the GMC delegates in the under-55 group, membership in the Labour youth organization had a slight influence. Thus, the age factor in the opposition to revising Clause IV reads: 55 and over, 78 per cent; members of the younger group who had had experience in the youth organization, 66 per cent ; and the young group without affiliation with the youth organization, 55 per cent.[48]

Quite apart from age differences, it would not be unreasonable to expect that activists who had been in the Party for a long time would be more inclined toward the preservation of Clause IV than their colleagues whose membership cards had been issued more recently. We did note that the people who joined the Party before 1925 recorded the highest vote against revision (82 per cent) – a reflection of attitudes nearly matched by the 1935–1944 group (80 per cent).[49] But the analysis of the length of Party membership and the length of GMC service yielded little more than jumbled tables.[50]

To sum up, the attitudes toward the public ownership of basic industries were largely a class phenomenon, as one would expect. The strongest support for nationalization came from activists with working-class backgrounds and sustained psychological links with their class. This support was reinforced both by trade union involvement and by non-membership (as opposed to intermittent activity or none at all). The support was also enhanced in the higher age categories. Approval for the revision of Clause IV, on the other hand, was to be found among the activists of middle-class origin and occupation who retained subjective links with their own kind.

COOPERATION WITH THE TORIES

In a further attempt to assess traditional outlooks, we asked the respondents whether they thought that cooperation with the Conservatives in political matters was possible. We requested them to mark one of three answers – on 'some issues', 'hardly at all', or 'not at all' – and to record their views in the space provided for open-ended comments.[51] We assumed that this question would tap an element of class feeling, since the Tories presumably represent the class 'enemy' whose political philosophy and social life-styles have always been the targets for Labour Party activists. While differences in philosophical orientation provided sufficient basis for confrontation, the fact that some Labour people had experienced personal conflicts with their Conservative opponents toughened their antagonism. Especially in Fulham, the activists' encounters with the Tories in the council chamber, in committee meetings, during election campaigns, and at official functions had sometimes been interpreted as 'Tory snubs'. To many Labour stalwarts, the Tories were a symbol of what the political struggle was all about.

We anticipated that the class factors would be especially prominent in the analysis of this issue – that the GMC delegates with the strongest linkages with the working class would be the most hostile to the idea of cooperating with the Tories, while the people with a middle-class orientation would have a more softened attitude toward them. In other words, anti-Tory sentiments would be most prevalent among those activists whose working-class origin was reinforced by limited educational attainment, lack of social mobility, long periods of residence in working-class districts, and continued subjective identification with the working class. Lengthy residence in working-class communities should be of particular importance, since it enables individuals to have prolonged exposure to the political milieu, as well as sustained contact with real-life Tory opponents. Finally, one can speculate that the longer a person has been a Labour Party member and the longer he has been involved in the management of the local party, the greater will be his reluctance to cooperate with the Tories.

For a start, the data from the three constituencies come close to the expected target. Hostility to the Conservatives was highest in Fulham, which had a weighted score of 2.22; Bermondsey was close behind with a rating of 2.14; South Kensington had a ranking of only 1.37.[52] Other class factors besides constituency were at the top of the list in the preliminary sorting: social origin, length of residence in the district, class self-identification, social mobility, and education. In this preliminary stage, length of service on the GMC was also a factor to be taken into account and period of entry into the Party was of some importance, but length of Party membership appeared to be of little consequence.[53] The analysis of such intercorrelated variables makes one realize again that the 'class factor' is an extremely complex phenomenon; a given class category may embrace sub-groupings which reflect the influence of 'refining' factors in the determination of political attitudes.

It will be instructive to begin by examining the variables that exhibited strength in the preliminary analysis. The most powerful factor appeared to be social origin. The Labour activists who came from working-class households continued to nurture more distrustful attitudes toward the Conservatives (2.12) than was true of the people of middle-class lineage (1.45).[54] In terms of community residence, those who had lived in their districts for 75 per cent or more of their adult lives expressed their apprehension about cooperating politically with the Tories by marking up a score of 2.33, while the more geographically mobile registered a lower score, 1.66.[55] The picture is the same when we look at education: elementary, 2.16; secondary, 2.04; secondary +, 1.72; and university, 1.44. Again, the same pattern obtains when we examine class self-identification: working class, 2.17; won't commit, 1.93; and middle class, 1.56.[56]

The pattern is reflected, though in a somewhat more refined way, when social mobility is put under the lens. The stationary manuals and those who had moved from manual status into routine clerical positions were at the top of the list (2.12 and 2.17); the people who were mobile into professional and managerial posts were next in line (1.92), and the stationary middle group was at the bottom (1.40).[57] In terms of objective/subjective class, the small group of professional/managerial people who identified with the working class registered the most skepticism about cooperating with the Tories (2.57); the manuals and clericals who placed themselves in the working class were also wary about such collaboration (2.11 and 2.17); the small 'won't commit' group was not as high in its distrust (1.93); and the contingent with the least concern was the non-manual category whose identification was with the middle class (1.49).[58]

In the regression, social origin becomes overshadowed by other factors because of intercorrelation. For this reason it merits separate treatment at this point. The relationship between social origin and constituency was as follows:

	Score	N
Bermondsey and Fulham		
Working-class origin	2.44	(90)
Middle-class origin	1.70	(10)
South Kensington		
Working-class origin	1.47	(15)
Middle-class origin	1.33	(20)

[Cramers V, 0.32]

The connections between social origin on the one side and education, residence, and class self-placement on the other are presented in Table 6.9.

Table 6.9 Social origin, education, length of residence, and class self-placement: Tories

	Score	N
Working-class origin		
Education: elementary and secondary	2.23	(86)
secondary + and university	1.63	(19)
Middle-class origin	1.45	(31)
Working-class origin		
Residence: 75% or more of adult life	2.28	(68)
Less than 75%	1.84	(37)
Middle-class origin*	1.45	(31)
Working-class origin		
Class self-placement: working	2.20	(75)
won't commit	2.20	(10)
middle	1.80	(20)
Middle-class origin†	1.45	(31)

* If we divide the middle-class groups, the breakdown is: 75% or more of adult life, 1.67 ($N=6$); less than 75%, 1.40 ($N=25$).

† If we divide the middle-class group, the breakdown is: working-class identifiers, 1.86 ($N=7$); middle-class identifiers and won't commit, 1.33 ($N=24$).

The data show that the antipathy toward the Conservatives on the part of Labour activists who grew up in working-class households was reinforced by constituency, long residence in the locality, limited attainment of formal education, and subjective identification with the proletariat.

This basic pattern retained its regularity when we analyzed education and social mobility in terms of constituency; education and class self-identification; and education and class self-identification with respect to length of residence. Introducing other sets of tables would serve no useful purpose, for these variables measure the same phenomenon we have already discussed.

One way to sum up this part of the analysis is to look at a confluence of variables in relatively 'pure' form. The Labour activists from working-class households who had gone no further than elementary school and who had lived in their communities for at least three-fourths of their adult lives (41 cases) rated an anti-Conservative score of 2.34, compared with a score of 1.39 for those of middle-class origin, more advanced education, and shorter periods of residence in their districts (23 cases). The score for the mixed 'in-between' group was 1.94. If we pull from the residue group the activists who were like the pure working-class group except that they had completed secondary school training (but not secondary [+] or university), the twenty cases had a score of 2.25, leaving the remainder (52 cases) with a score of 1.83.

In the regression analysis, two different combinations of variables turned out to be the strongest predictors; they masked some of the relationships we have already discussed. The first variable is a combination of social mobility, length of residence, and period of entry into

Table 6.10 Social mobility, length of residence, and period of recruitment into the Party: Tories

	Cooperate with Tories				
	Some	Hardly at all	Not at all	Score	N
Mobility: stationary manual and mobiles					
Residence: 75% or more adult life					
Recruitment: pre-1925, 1935–44 and 1952–62	15.2%	9.1	75.8	2.61	(33)
1925–34 and 1945–51	40.0	22.9	37.1	1.97	(35)
Residence: less than 75%	40.0	35.0	25.0	1.85	(40)
Mobility: stationary middle	67.9	25.0	7.1	1.39	(28)

[Cramers V, 0.37; Kendall's Tau-b, −0.40]

the party. The second variable is made up constituency and objective/subjective class.[59] The data on social mobility, length of residence, and period of recruitment are given in Table 6.10.

The first thing to notice in this table is the substantial difference between the stationary manuals and the socially mobile on the one hand and the stationary middle on the other. As we saw in the earlier analyses, the activists in the latter group were the most congenial to the idea of cooperating with their political opponents. A more complex set of associations is to be found within the first grouping – the manual workers who were following in the footsteps of their parents and the people who had moved into clerical or professional/managerial positions. Within this group a distinction has to be made between those who had spent most of their adult lives in their constituencies and were more distrustful of the Conservatives than the relatively new arrivals. Among the long-term residents, a further distinction has to be made on the basis of when they were recruited into the Party. The activists who had entered the ranks during the 'ideological' decades of 1952–62 and 1935–44 and during the difficult years prior to 1925 were the least hopeful of being able to cooperate with the Tories (and in the order listed). Somewhat less antagonistic were the activists who rallied to Labour in the mid-1920s and early 1930s and those who came into the organization in the immediate postwar years (again in the order listed).

The data supplied by the second variable, which links constituency with objective/subjective class, are recorded in Table 6.11.

Table 6.11 Constituency and objective/subjective class: Tories

	Cooperate with Tories				
	Some	Hardly at all	Not at all	Score	N
Bermondsey and Fulham					
Prof./mgr. identifying working class, manuals identifying middle class and won't commit	11.8%	29.4	58.8	2.47	(17)
White-collar identifying working class	28.6	17.9	53.6	2.25	(28)
Manual identifying working class	34.1	18.2	47.7	2.14	(44)
Non-manual identifying middle class	41.7	41.7	16.7	1.75	(12)
South Kensington	68.6	25.7	5.7	1.37	(35)

[Cramers V, 0.34; Kendall's Tau-b, -0.37]

We have already observed that the activists in Fulham and Bermondsey were much more reluctant to cooperate with the opposition party than were their colleagues from the middle-class areas of South Kensington. In this second variable we combined Fulham and

Bermondsey, and within this group objective/subjective class exerts some influence. At the top half of the group breakdown, subjective class identification is the most dominant, with the most incongruous elements – professional/managerial people who identified with the working class, the tiny band of manuals who claimed kinship with the middle class, and those who felt uncomfortable with class breakdowns – ranking highest in their opposition to the Tories. Next in line were the white-collar employees who designated their affinity with the workers. The objective part of class identification applies to manual workers who swore allegiance to their own class and who were somewhat less suspicious of the Tories, and to the non-manuals who placed themselves in the middle class and were noticeably more congenial with the idea of cooperating with their political opponents.

It would appear, then, that the outlooks of the Labour activists with respect to the Conservatives were influenced by a confluence of class factors: social origin and mobility, education, the type of area and the length of residence in it, the pattern of class identification, and to some extent the period of entrance into the Party. The findings definitely indicate that the tighter the middle-class context and the more sustained its influence, the greater the tendency of activists to be willing to cooperate with the Tories. By the same token, the activists who had closer associations with the working class and for lengthy time periods were much more reluctant to enter into any political liaison with the Tories. Within this working-class cluster, however, two groups of people tended to register slightly stronger objections to cooperation with the Tories than did the more solid proletarian core – a tiny fragment of professional people who had risen from working-class origins, and a larger group of routine clerical workers whose ties with the manual workers were still strong. All of these people had climbed a few rungs of the ladder, but they were still a good distance from the top.[60] For many, even the limited ascent had been difficult, and they still nursed wounds from the struggle.

Given the outline that has already been sketched, one might posit a linear relationship between the activists' length of Party membership and GMC service and their distrust of the Tories. The data, however, do not fit tidily into the several compartments. In terms of Party membership, those who had been in the organization for more than a quarter of a century did exhibit the greatest hostility (2.23), but the newcomers of five years' standing or less occupied second place (2.04), with the intermediate groups having scores of 1.67 and 1.87.[61] When we examine the length of GMC service, here again the oldest group – those who had served for more than sixteen years – ranked the highest (2.36), but there was little difference in the other categories, the scores ranging from 1.83 to 1.86.

When social class was controlled for length of Party membership and

GMC service, the older group always revealed a noticeable distaste for alliances with the Tories, but usually similar feelings were voiced by the younger, newer members, especially those associated with the working class. The same phenomenon was revealed through an analysis of age and social origin. Of the activists aged 55 and over, those of working-class origin were the most opposed to any Tory coupling (2.30), compared with those of middle-class origin (2.17). For the activists under 55, the comparable figures were: working-class origin, 2.00; middle-class origin, 1.28.[62] The respective scores for the younger activists in the under-35 bracket were 2.21 for those of working-class origin (24 cases) and 1.56 for those from the middle class (nine cases). Apparently the older activists with long records of Party involvement either entered the organization with anti-Tory outlooks or developed them while they were in harness. It seems likely, too, that some of the young newcomers into the Party, particularly those with working-class connections, became suspicious of the Tories relatively early in their political careers.

COMMON MARKET

The issue of the Common Market blurs the ordinary lines of schism between 'left' and 'right' in the Labour Party. To be sure, many enthusiasts lined up predictably in the opposition corner, but they were accompanied by many Labour people who usually took an orthodox line on other questions. Entry into the Common Market was a challenging issue which generated several types of cross-pressures: the need for an improved economic position for Britain vs. the threat to the Commonwealth nations; market opportunities vs. the prospect that foreign workers would be able to take employment in Britain; the idea of strengthening Labour's links with the working people and socialist parties on the continent vs. the psychological pull of the 'little England' posture.

The issue came to a head in its first phase while this study was under way. In July 1961, the Conservative Government gave notice of its intent to enter into negotiations for Britain's entry into the Market. The negotiations were carried on by Edward Heath during most of 1962, and the Market commanded attention in Britain until General DeGaulle announced his unwillingness to support Britain's application.

Our question on this issue was straightforward; we simply asked the respondents whether they favored Britain's entry, and we invited them to elaborate if they chose. Under ordinary circumstances, one would have expected that the Common Market would be a class issue, with the middle class generally supporting Britain's entry and the working class generally opposing it. But the fact that some elements of the left were beginning to shift from unilateralism to the Common Market as a focus for their enduring displeasure complicated the analysis. Basically, we expected to find that, as was the case with other issues, the ideological element of the middle class would cast its responses in opposition to the Market, and that the working-class delegates would be largely negative in their attitudes owing to the uncertainty about how it would affect their jobs. The least opposition, we predicted, would come from the non-ideological sector of the middle class which was presumed to be more internationalist in its outlook. We also speculated that age would be a factor, with the younger people tending to be more favorably disposed toward the Market.

In terms of disapproval of Britain's participation in the Common Market, the line-up of the three constituency parties was: Bermondsey, 66 per cent; Fulham, 83 per cent, and South Kensington, 35 per cent.[63] The startling thing about these figures was the low amount of opposition among the Bermondsey delegates. We have already indicated several reasons for this – the decline of traffic in the docks, the perception that France was benefiting from association with the Market, and the fact that the M.P., who was influential in matters of foreign policy, favored Britain's entry.

The preliminary analysis suggested the influence of these variables: objective/subjective class (and, of course, class self-placement), education, constituency, and social mobility. (These variables appear later, in our discussion of the regression.) Given our expectations, it appeared too that social origin might be worth looking at, since it would probably be suppressed owing to intercorrelation. Before we turn to this, however, we need to say a word about objective/subjective class. On all scores, it was the strongest single variable in its initial form.[64] As we shall note later, the activists who were subjectively deviant from their occupational groups were the most opposed to the Market, followed by the manual workers who identified with their class and then by the people who were uncomfortable with class designations and the middle class group whose objective and subjective assessments were congruent.[65]

The social origin table indicated that those from working-class homes were more opposed to Britain's joining than were the people of middle-class lineage (69 per cent to 44 per cent). It takes on more meaning, however, when it is modified to include class self-identification, as follows:

	Unfavorable to Market	N
Middle-class origin/working-class identifiers	88.9%	(9)
Working-class origin/working-class identifiers	74.7	(75)
Working-class origin/middle-class identifiers	54.8	(31)
Middle-class origin/middle-class identifiers	26.1	(23)

The strongest predictor for attitudes on the Common Market is a new variable composed of objective/subjective class and social mobility. The data are included in Table 6.12.

Table 6.12 Objective/subjective class and social mobility: Common Market

	Unfavorable to Market	N
Prof./mgr. and clerical identifying working class and manuals identifying middle class	85.7%	(42)
Manuals identifying working class	69.6	(46)
Non-manuals identifying middle class and won't commit		
Mobility: mobile to clerical and stationary manual	55.0	(20)
mobile to prof./mgr.	40.0	(10)
stationary middle	20.0	(20)

[Cramers V, 0.46; Kendall's Tau-b, -0.40]

The table is self-explanatory. The people whose subjective class status was incongruent with their objective position were the least favorable to Britain's entry into the Common Market. The solid working-class group was the next highest in opposition. The non-manuals who identified with the middle class and the group that refused to recognize social class were the most favorably disposed to Britain's participation. Within this latter category, however, social mobility made some difference: the mobiles were more in opposition to the Market than were the members of the stationary middle-class group.[66]

The other restructured variable is a combination of constituency and education.[67] This information is presented in Table 6.13.

Table 6.13 Constituency and education: Common Market

	Unfavorable to Market	N
Fulham		
Education: elementary	88.9%	(18)
post-elementary	78.6	(28)
Bermondsey		
Education: elementary	70.6	(34)
post-elementary	57.1	(21)
South Kensington		
Education: pre-university	43.5	(23)
university	21.4	(14)

[Cramers V, 0.41; Kendall's Tau-b, -0.35]

We have already noted the differences in constituency attitudes. When considered separately, the education data indicated that the higher the level of formal education attained, the more favorable the outlook toward the Common Market. This table shows that within each constituency increased education is associated with lessened antipathy toward Britain joining the continental partnership.

When we looked at the age factor, we noted a tendency for people under 45 to be more favorably disposed toward Britain's entry into the Market, but even though the result was statistically significant, the association was not strong. A more interesting revelation was uncovered when we divided the respondents into two groups — those who were born into working-class households and continued to identify with their class, and the remainder — and tested for length of Labor Party membership. For the working-class group, the outcome was contrary to expectations: of those who had been in the Party for more than fifteen years, 70 per cent opposed entry ($N=46$), while the figure for those with membership of shorter duration was 83 per cent ($N=29$). In the residue group, the situation was reversed. Among the respondents with more than fifteen years' tenure, 65 per cent opposed the Market ($N=26$), compared with 38 per cent for the people with less Party service ($N=37$).

The activists' opinions on Britain's entry into the Common Market appear to be largely related to social class attributes. Leading the opposition was a group of middle-class people who are eager to display working-class sympathies. Next in line were the people who can be identified as solidly working-class in terms of their origin, education, occupation, and class self-placement. Least hostile to the Market were the non-manuals who identified with the middle class, and within this category the stationary middle group assumed the most favorable attitude.

RESTRICTIONS ON IMMIGRATION

We move now to a different set of issues, those involving civil rights and moral and humanitarian concerns. At various times the GMC delegates discussed three questions which fit into this category: apart from medical checks (which had been in effect for some time), should further restrictions be imposed upon the immigration of people from the newer Commonwealth countries into Britain? Should capital punishment be abolished? Should more restrictions be placed upon the activities of the Communist Party?

In the immediate post-war years, immigrants from the newer parts of the Commonwealth began to move into England, and by the late 1950s the influx was perceived to be a 'problem'. The immigrants tended to settle in particular overcrowded sections of London, creating pressure on housing accommodations which were already inadequate for local needs. Many Labour Party activists, who could hardly be accused of supporting a color bar, were sincerely worried about the trend toward 'ghettoes', and some raised questions about the capacity of a small country to absorb the new arrivals from overseas.

The issue came to a head in the spring of 1962 when the Macmillan Government introduced a restrictive measure into the House of Commons. The Parliamentary Labour Party, under strong prodding from Gaitskell, took an official stand against the proposed regulations. Needless to say, the question of limiting immigration churned up many hours of discussion within local Labour parties. The author was privileged to attend a special meeting of the General Management Committee of the North Kensington party which had been convened for the purpose of airing the issue. He was impressed by the calm, rational approach taken by the delegates as they sought to improve race relations in their district.

Since the local parties involved in this study had discussed aspects of the immigration issue from time to time, we sought to probe the attitudes of the GMC members by asking them whether they favored additional restrictions upon the entry of people from these Commonwealth nations. Several studies of tolerance toward out-groups guided our expectations. The results of these studies became the bases for these hypotheses: (1) the higher the level of education, the greater the tolerance toward minority groups; (2) younger people are more liberal in racial matters than are older people; and (3) people who work in occupations that are high on the social prestige scale are inclined to be more tolerant than individuals in less prestigious jobs.[68] Obviously, these factors are interconnected; younger people are usually better educated, and the better educated people tend to hold the most prestigious jobs. In other words, we cannot get very far away from the class factor. People nurtured in a working-class milieu — in terms of social origin, elementary school training, manual work, and long exposure to the norms of a working-class community — are more likely than middle-class elements to resist the inroads of the immigrant; these are the people who feel the most threatened, in terms of jobs and housing.

The hypotheses took on a faint glow when we looked at the three constituencies. The figures against further restraints upon immigration were: South Kensington, 88 per cent; Fulham, 72 per cent; and Bermondsey, 30 per cent.[69] The Bermondsey folk, sensitive to problems that had arisen in nearby districts, found themselves bothered by the issue, and some were beset by cross-pressures. Further analysis revealed that eight of the twenty-two variables had simple correlations of more than 0.30, and five of them were above 0.40. Constituency ranked at the top, followed by objective/subjective class, social mobility, occupation, age, education, and class self-placement.[70] (It is interesting to note that constituency and certain class factors ranked ahead of age and education.)

Two of these variables, occupation and social mobility, need to be considered first because they were pushed aside in the regression. Opposition to further restrictions was expressed in the occupational groupings as follows: professional and managerial, 94 per cent; clerical, 58 per cent; and manual, 36 per cent.[71] The figures on social mobility point to the same pattern: mobiles to professional/managerial position, 94 per cent; stationary middle, 81 per cent; mobiles to clerical positions, 61 per cent; and stationary manual, 33 per cent.[72]

The other class factor, which ranked in second place behind constituency in all of the regressions, was objective/subjective social class. The results are listed below.

	Oppose Restrictions	N
Professional/managerial identifying working class and won't commit	90.5%	(21)
Non-manual and manual identifying middle class	78.4	(37)
White-collar identifying working class	50.0	(30)
Manual identifying working class	31.1	(45)

[Cramers V, 0 47]

In light of the importance of constituency and class factors, we looked at the age variable with special care. In general, the result adhered to the findings presented by other studies. The cut-off point was age 45, with the people below that age level expressing greater opposition to immigration controls (81 per cent) than the older group (41 per cent).[73] The age factor continued to hold influence when we controlled for constituency and occupation, as seen below.

	Oppose Restrictions	N
South Kensington		
Under 45	95.6%	(23)
45 and over	70.0	(10)
Fulham		
Under 45	94.7	(19)
45 and over	54.2	(24)
Bermondsey		
Under 45	40.0	(15)
45 and over	26.2	(44)
Professional and managerial		
Under 45	95.5%	(22)
45 and over	90.0	(10)

Clerical		
Under 45	81.8	(22)
45 and over	38.5	(26)
Manual		
Under 45	53.9	(13)
45 and over	30.0	(40)

When we analyzed age and education, we discovered that while age made a difference at the secondary level, it made no difference at all in the university ranks and very little at the elementary level. Moreover, among the older people there was virtually no difference between those who had completed elementary and secondary training. The older people in both educational categories opposed immigration controls at the low rates of 37 per cent and 36 per cent. When it comes to occupation, secondary education exerted some influence upon the people in non-manual occupations, but among manual workers there was little difference between those who had completed secondary education and those who went only to elementary schools.

Education, too, did not discriminate among the opinions of the Bermondsey activists, but it did in the case of the other two constituencies. In fact, a restructured variable composed of constituency and education turned out to be the strongest predictor.[74] The results are given in Table 6.14.

Table 6.14 Constituency and education: immigration

	Oppose Restrictions	N
South Kensington and Fulham		
Education: university	100%	(17)
secondary	85.0	(40)
elementary	47.4	(19)
Bermondsey	29.8	(57)

[Cramers V, 0.57; Kendall's Tau-b, -0.52]

Here the constituency differences are noticeable, and in the case of South Kensington and Fulham, the higher the educational level, the greater the opposition to restrictions upon immigration.

In this study, age and education were not the compelling factors we had thought they might be. While age was a significant discriminator among constituencies and within occupational categories, its influence upon education was restricted to the secondary level. Education as a variable had an effect in two constituencies and was discriminating among people in non-manual occupations, but it had little impact upon

Outlooks of the Activists

manual workers, especially those in the older age bracket. More important than age and education as single factors were constituency and objective/subjective class (which is really a combination of occupation and class self-identification). The data show that the activists at the working-class end of the spectrum were the most hostile to unrestricted immigration. Their disapproval was reinforced by age, but for the people solidly tied to the working class, education had only an attenuated influence at best.

CAPITAL PUNISHMENT

From time to time in the post-war years, the abolition of capital punishment has been a lively issue in British politics, and some Labour Members of Parliament have been involved in the movement. In December 1960, the National Campaign for the Abolition of Capital Punishment began a new effort, which was supported by some Labour people and by prominent religious groups.[75] This movement was countered by the Anti-Violence League, which urged greater use of capital punishment. The issue moved closer into the limelight while this study was in progress because a number of serious crimes attracted headlines.

Since the abolition of capital punishment is another moral/humanitarian question, we anticipated the same findings that we encountered when we studied immigration controls: sentiment for abolition would increase with more advanced education, it would vary inversely with age, and it would be higher among middle-class groups than among manual workers.

The returns seemed promising when we examined the support for abolition in the three constituencies: South Kensington, 89 per cent; Fulham, 82 per cent, and Bermondsey, 55 per cent.[76] Four variables had simple correlations of more than 0.40 – occupation, education, social mobility, and objective/subjective class. (Age was rather far down the list.)

Once again social mobility was subdued in the regression, as was objective/subjective class, and it will be instructive to examine these variables first. On social mobility, we found the same pattern that appeared in the opposition to restrictions on immigration. Support for the abolition of capital punishment was 100 per cent among the activists who were mobile to professional and managerial status, 92 per cent among the stationary middle group, 80 per cent among those who were mobile to clerical positions, and 47 per cent among the stationary manual people.[77] The pattern for objective/subjective class is also similar in basic contours to that involved in the immigration question, as seen below:

	Favors Abolition	N
Professional/managerial identifying working class and non-manual identifying middle class	97.7%	(42)
White-collar identifying working class, won't commit, and manual identifying middle class	74.0	(50)
Manual identifying working class	48.9	(47)

[Cramers V, 0.44]

Even though the age factor by itself did not appear to be as important as it was on the immigration issue, we nevertheless investigated it carefully. Here again the cut-off point was age 45, with the younger people being more favorable toward abolition than their elders. The effect of age upon constituency, occupation, and education can be seen in Table 6.15.

Table 6.15 The age factor and support for abolition

Constituency:	South Kensington		Fulham		Bermondsey	
Under 45	92.0%	(25)	95.0%	(20)	62.5%	(16)
45 and over	83.3	(12)	72.0	(25)	52.4	(42)

Occupation:	Professional/Managerial		Clerical		Manual	
Under 45	100%	(12)	87.5%	(24)	57.1%	(14)
45 and over	100	(23)	71.4	(28)	46.2	(39)

Education:	University		Secondary		Elementary	
Under 45	100%	(13)	94.7%	(38)	30.0%	(10)
45 and over	100	(6)	76.9	(26)	51.1	(47)

The data in this table suggest that the age factor was of little consequence in distinguishing among the GMC delegates in South Kensington and Bermondsey, but a little more so in the case of Fulham. By the same token, it was not very discriminating when controls were made for occupation and education. The most that can be said for it is that it had a slight effect upon the clerical workers and the people with limited education. The class factor – as represented by occupation, social mobility, and objective/subjective class – was more important than age. Education, however, was a matter of some consequence.

The strongest variable was a combination of occupation and education, the results of which are recorded in Table 6.16.[78]

Table 6.16 Education and occupation: Capital Punishment

	Favor Abolition	N
University	100%	(19)
Secondary		
Occupation: non-manual	92.0	(50)
manual	71.4	(14)
Elementary		
Occupation: non-manual	61.1	(18)
manual	41.0	(39)

[Cramers V, 0.52; Kendall's Tau-b, −0.46]

The message here is quite clear: the more advanced the education and the higher the occupation position, the more liberal the attitude toward the abolition of capital punishment.

COMMUNIST PARTY

During the course of the GMC meetings, a number of the delegates expressed concern about what they perceived to be the growing influence of the Communist Party in trade union affairs. In order to gauge attitudes on this question, we asked the respondents whether they thought that restrictions ought to be placed upon the Communist Party. This question resembled the immigration and capital punishment issues, we thought, in that it had a 'moral' flavor and involved civil rights. For this reason we expected to find the greatest opposition to restrictions among the more highly educated middle-class groups. We speculated that the least opposition was likely to come from working-class people, many of whom had had personal experience with the problem at their places of work. Within the working-class category, however, we anticipated that the trade union actives would offer some resistance to restrictions, since many trade unionists feel that Communist Party members do a good job of pressing the workers' demands. In other words, we expected that class factors, including education, would be strategic in the analysis. We recognized, however, that the small number of deviant cases (31) would not leave much scope for variance.

In terms of opposing restrictions upon the Communist Party, the three constituencies provided an interesting result. South Kensington and Fulham were tied at 86 per cent, while the figure for Bermondsey was 64 per cent. The preliminary screening provided a list of the significant factors: social mobility, education, occupation, constituency, objective/subjective class, and trade union affiliation.

Since some of these variables became veiled in the regression, it will pay to look at these patterns first. Here the class factor predominated, with the greatest opposition to restrictions coming from the higher socio-economic group, somewhat less coming from the middle social category, and the least being exhibited by the lower socio-economic cluster. Take education, for example. Opposition among the university people was 90 per cent; the secondary + group, 100 per cent; secondary, 76 per cent; and elementary, 67 per cent. In terms of occupation, the breakdown was: professional/managerial, 94 per cent; clerical, 74 per cent; and manual, 69 per cent.[79] When we look at objective/subjective class, the following result appears: professional/managerial activists who identified with the working class, 100 per cent; non-manual people who identified with the middle class, 86 per cent; clerical workers who identified with the working class and the tiny group of manual workers who attached themselves to the middle class, 82 per cent; and the manual workers who linked themselves with their own class and the group of people who refused to commit themselves on social class expressed the same degree of opposition, 67 per cent.

The best predictors are two reconstructed variables – one a combination of social mobility and trade union activities; the other a combination of constituency, borough council membership, and party officers. Although, as we have already pointed out, the number of deviant cases is small, resulting in small Ns in some groupings, social mobility and trade union activity appeared at the head of the list in nearly all of the regression runs. The data are presented in Table 6.17.

Table 6.17 Social mobility and trade union affiliation: Communist Party

	Oppose Restrictions	N
Mobiles to professional/managerial position	100%	(14)
Mobiles to clerical position and stationary prof./mgr.		
Trade union: actives	93.8	(16)
others	80.4	(46)
Stationary manual and stationary clerical		
Trade union: actives	75.0	(28)
quasi-active and inactive	63.2	(19)
non-members	46.2	(13)

[Cramers V, 0.35; Kendall's Tau-b, -0.30]

According to this breakdown, the people who were socially mobile to professional and managerial position were the strongest group in opposition to restrictions on the Communist Party. Next to them was a category of activists who were mobile to clerical status and the stationary professionals/managers. Within this category, however, the trade union actives were slightly more opposed than the rest. The least opposed to added regulation was a group composed of stationary manuals and of *lower-middle-class stationary clericals*. Again, within this grouping, the more the involvement in trade union work, the greater the tendency toward resisting restrictions upon the Communists.

The data on the second combined variable — constituency, borough council membership, and officers — are recorded in Table 6.18.

Table 6.18 Constituency, borough council membership, and party officers: Communist Party

	Oppose Restrictions	N
South Kensington and Fulham		
Borough council: members	96.2%	(26)
non-members	81.5	(54)
Bermondsey		
Non-officers	68.2	(44)
Officers	50.0	(12)

[Cramers V, 0.31; Kendall's Tau-b, −0.28]

The patterns here need little elaboration.[80] The reader will recall that South Kensington and Fulham were equal in their opposition to further controls over the Communist Party. Among the combined delegates, however, membership on the borough council made some difference, with the council members voicing slightly more opposition. Bermondsey, of course, was a case by itself, for it was in this party that the opposition to further restrictions was most muted. Within the Bermondsey group, the non-officers were more opposed to restrictions than were the officers.[81] [We could have used sex as a discriminating variable for Bermondsey: men, 70.3 per cent ($N=37$); women 52.6 per cent ($N=19$).]

On this issue, the higher the socio-economic status, the more the resistance to placing curbs upon the Communists. However, among several layers of the population, particularly in the stationary manual and stationary clerical groups, high involvement in trade union activity tended to influence opinions in opposition to controls. In other words, the lower the socio-economic status and the less involvement with the unions, the greater the tendency to support restrictions. In South Kensington and Fulham, involvement in the affairs of the borough was somewhat associated with opposition to controls. But in Bermondsey, the party officers and the women were the most inclined to regard restrictions as necessary.

REORGANIZATION OF LONDON GOVERNMENT

As we have already seen, the political institutions in the London area had been adapted to the problems of metropolitan growth in only piecemeal fashion. The outdated patterns of political organization were characteristic of other urban centers in Britain too, but the situation in London was the first to be tackled.[82] The Conservative Government set up a Royal Commission to study the problem, and it published a White Paper in late 1961. The Bill to reorganize London government was discussed in Parliament in the closing months of 1962 and was passed in the following year.

The proposed reform stimulated a great deal of opposition among the politically informed people in the counties of London and Middlesex, especially those connected with the Labour Party.[83] As mentioned earlier, some Labour people feared that the educational system developed by the old London County Council would be harmed, or that the welfare services and recreational services would be curtailed, or that the Labour majorities in existing borough councils would be swept away with the redrawing of boundary lines. Lord Morrison labelled the reform a 'contemptible plot' engineered by the Conservatives.[84] The London Labour Party sponsored protest conferences,[85] and the Parliamentary Labour Party opposed the reform when the Bill came before the House of Commons, with Michael Stewart of Fulham leading the attack and Robert Mellish of Bermondsey playing a very active role.[86]

We have noted, too, that the three constituency parties took different approaches to this problem. The South Kensington party exhibited little public interest in the matter. The Bermondsey people were vehemently opposed to the reform, and they decided not to submit evidence to the Royal Commission. The Fulham borough council, on the other hand, was sympathetic to the idea of widespread reform, and it offered testimony to the Commission. Fulham was one of two Labour-dominated councils in the entire London area to take this approach. The Fulham party, of course, officially backed the action of its council members, but, as we have seen, some of the activists were nervous about being out of step with the other boroughs and the London Labour Party. The Fulham organization, however, took no action to change its official position.

In the questionnaire we asked the respondents whether they favored the Government's plan to reorganize London government. But we were cognizant of the fact that some activists were opposed to the reform being suggested at that time but nevertheless recognized the long-term need to reorganize local government in London so that it would be more adequately equipped to handle the demands placed upon it. For this reason we asked the respondents a further question: whether they thought that it would be necessary to institute a sweeping reform five years from now. We expected, of course, that the Bermondsey delegates would be much more hostile than the other two parties to any tampering with London's governing structure. Beyond this, we anticipated that the opposition would be largely a class phenomenon: the more closely individuals came to meeting the criteria of the working class, the more likely they were to reject the notion of government reform. From our observations and interviews, we also speculated that the activists who were the most involved with the direction of party affairs and the management of the borough would be able to see the problem in broader perspective and would be more inclined to accept the need for basic reform. Finally, we hypothesized that the people who had lived in their communities for relatively long periods would have developed attachments to the existing structures and would be more reluctant than the newcomers to change them. We can now turn to an analysis of the responses to the two questions on London reorganization, handling them separately.

The 1962 Plan for Reorganizing London Government

We knew at the outset that the first question would be hard to handle because of the small number of deviant cases (23), but we nevertheless set about to make out of it what we could. In terms of resisting the proposed reform, the returns from the three constituencies lived up to expectations: Bermondsey, 95 per cent, and Fulham and South Kensington together at 76 per cent.[87] When we turned to the preliminary analysis, the key variables, in addition to constituency, appeared to be social mobility, trade union affiliation, education, objective/subjective class, party office-holding, and occupation. Following previous practice, we shall discuss first those factors that were later submerged in the regression.

In looking at these variables, we see evidence to support the proposition that the closer the linkages with the working class, the greater the opposition to the reform of London's local government. On education, we get the following pattern: elementary, 90 per cent; secondary, 86 per cent; and university, 58 per cent.[88] Similarly on occupation: lesser-skilled manual, 93 per cent; skilled manual, 89 per cent, clerical, 87 per cent; and professional/managerial, 69 per cent.[89] The pattern is essentially the same when we examine objective/subjective class: manual workers identifying with the working class and the tiny group of manuals who identified middle class, 92 per cent; clerical and professional/managerial people who claimed working-class affiliation and the 'won't commit' group, 85 per cent; and the non-manual activists who cast their lot with the middle class, 69 per cent.[90]

The best predictor is a combination of social mobility and trade union affiliation, the results of which are presented in Table 6.19.

Table 6.19 Social mobility and trade union affiliation: Reorganizing London Government

	Opposes	N
Trade union actives and quasi-actives	95.4%	(65)
Trade union inactives and non-members		
Mobility: Stationary manual and mobiles to white-collar positions	84.1	(44)
Stationary professional/managerial	76.9	(13)
Stationary white-collar and mobiles to professional/managerial positions	41.2	(17)

[Cramers V, 0.46; Kendall's Tau-b, −0.37]

The people who were the most involved in trade union work constituted the strongest opposition group to the reform of London government. Among the rest – the inactive trade unionists and the non-members – social mobility exerted some influence, with the opposition declining as social position improves. In this category, those who remained in the working class or had just barely moved out of it registered the greatest dissent; the stationary professional/managerial group expressed somewhat less opposition, but more than was expected, mostly because they feared that the existing welfare services would be endangered; and the stationary clerical group, along with the most mobile people, offered the least resistance to the proposed scheme.

Table 6.20 Constituency, borough council membership, and office-holding: Reorganizing London Government

	Opposes	N
Bermondsey		
Borough Council: non-members	100%	(21)
members	91.4	(35)
Fulham and South Kensington		
Borough Council: non-members		
non-officeholders in party	83.3	(42)
party officers	76.9	(13)
members	64.3	(28)

[Cramers V, 0.31; Kendall's Tau-b, −0.27]

The second reconstructed variable is one that combines constituency, borough council membership, and office-holding in the party.[91] The data are presented in Table 6.20. The information in this table shows the tendency for people who carried responsibility in their boroughs and their local parties to be more receptive to change than the people without such responsibility.[92]

We anticipated that period of residence in the community during the activists' adult lives would tend to develop attachments to the *status quo*. The figures show that those who had lived in their districts for 75 per cent or more of their adult lives were more opposed to the reorganization scheme than those who had lived there for a shorter time, but the difference is not statistically significant. More discriminating was the class factor and the responsibility held by the activists in their parties and in the borough council.

Reorganizing London Government in Five Years

The purpose of this analysis was to distinguish between those people who recognized the need for reform but were opposed for some reason to the suggested scheme and those who were resisting any reform. Since a majority of the respondents gave a positive answer to this question, we shall present the data in that fashion. The breakdown in the three constituencies was similar to that in the previous question: South Kensington, 89 per cent; Fulham, 87 per cent; and Bermondsey, 43 per cent.[93] Here again the important factors, in addition to constituency, were objective/subjective class, social mobility, occupation, education, membership on the Executive Committee, and party office-holding.

As was the case in the previous section, class factors were predominant, and we shall first examine those variables that were stifled in the regression. In terms of social mobility, we get this pattern: mobiles to professional/managerial position, 100 per cent; stationary middle, 85 per cent; mobiles to white-collar status, 78 per cent; and stationary manual, 44 per cent.[94] The pattern is repeated when we look at occupation: non-manual, 84 per cent; manual, 46 per cent.[95] On education, the results were: university, 84 per cent; secondary +, 90 per cent; secondary, 71 per cent; and elementary, 57 per cent.

On this more abstract question of governmental reform, however, social class appears to be less important than responsible involvement in party affairs and in the management of the borough. The most compelling variable is a combination of constituency, membership on the Executive Committee, and borough council membership, the results of which are recorded in Table 6.21. In South Kensington and Fulham, all of the members of the Executive Committees – who had discussed the matter often and were aware of the problems – favored governmental

Table 6.21 Constituency, Executive Committee membership, and borough council membership: reorganizing London government

	Favors	N
South Kensington and Fulham		
Executive Committee: current Members	100%	(41)
non-members	76.2	(42)
Bermondsey		
Borough Council: members	55.6	(36)
non-members	22.7	(22)

[Cramers V, 0.56; Kendall's Tau-b, 0.51]

reform in principle, while the activists with less responsibility were not quite so enthusiastic. Although the Bermondsey people had serious misgivings about any type of change, the borough councillors—the people who had had experience in this realm—were more receptive to the idea than their colleagues who played no such role.[96] We should also point out that in each constituency the party officers were more reform-minded than the non-officers.

The same class factor, however, was involved, and it was picked up by the second variable in the regression, objective/subjective class.[97] In terms of support for the eventual reform of London government, its components were: non-manuals identifying with the middle class, 91 per cent;[98] the professional/managerial people who identified with the working class and the group that refused to entertain class distinctions, 83 per cent; white-collar workers who retained their kinship with the working class, 74 per cent; and manual workers who identified with their own class, 39 per cent.[99] The idea of change came hardest for the working-class group and for those who were not far removed from that status.

SUMMARY OF ISSUES

In examining these twelve issues, we noted that a class factor was involved in all of them, and was heavily involved in most. In some cases, the best indicator was occupation, or education, or social mobility, etc. For this reason we thought it advisable to compile a scale of social class, which would combine the important factors, and then compare the responses for each issue at particular points on the scale.[100] The results of this exercise are given in Table 6.22.

Several observations need to be made about this table. (1) In the first grouping—unilateralism, leadership, and the Anglo-American alliance—the relationship is curvilinear, with Group II (the next to the highest middle-class element) receiving the largest 'ideological' score in *each* instance. Moreover, except for the leadership issue, on which the solid working-class people in Group IV felt strongly, the levels of association are very low—an indication that the class factor was not particularly discriminating on unilateralism and the alliance. (In fact, the Kendall's Tau-*b* scores for these two issues are the lowest in the table.)

(2) The Common Market issue begins the development of a different pattern. As we have already seen, many of the unilateralists turned their hostility toward the Market, but it also attracted opposition from the working-class activists in Groups III and IV. Indeed, Groups II, III, and IV are bunched together.

(3) The next issue grouping—traditional doctrine, Clause IV, and cooperation with the Tories—constitutes more of a 'traditional socialist' outlook. On these issues, the Group II people were much more 'ideological' than their middle-class colleagues in Group I. But, even more important, the working-class activists in Groups III and IV tended to take a stronger position than the Group II people, and they were certainly more 'ideological' in their attitudes than they were on defense and foreign policy (i.e., unilateralism and the alliance).

(4) When it comes to the next issue cluster—immigration, capital punishment, and the Communist Party—we get a strong class relationship, especially on the first two issues. In terms of a liberal position on immigration and capital punishment, the curve moves dramatically downward from the middle-class groups (I and II) to the working-class groups (III and IV). This, as we have seen, is congruent with the literature on this subject. With respect to the question of restricting the Communist Party, the curve definitely slopes downward from the middle-class to the working-class groups, but the differences are not so marked, partly because the number of deviant cases is not large and partly because the idea of restrictions attracted some of the middle-class people in Groups I and II.

(5) A general class pattern is noticeable in the issue grouping dealing with the reorganization of local government. In the case of the 1962 proposal, however, the pattern is lopsided, with the lion's share of support coming from Group I and the other three groups being clustered together. On the abstract question of reorganizing London government in the future, the drop-off is on the other side; the people in Groups I, II, and III are not far apart; but the solid working-class group (IV) exhibited vehement opposition.

The importance of social class in the analysis of the twelve issues was

Table 6.22 Summary analysis: issues and social class

Issue positions	I	II	III	IV	Cramers V	Kendall's Tau-b
For unilateralism	27%	58%	36%	36%	0.21	0.01
Against leadership	22	42	18	6	0.31	−0.22
Unfavorable to alliance	1.52	2.04	1.69	1.47	0.22	−0.10
Against Common Market	30	71	74	69	0.35	0.21
Traditional doctrine applies	35	58	56	71	0.26	−0.22
Against revising Clause IV	31	64	84	71	0.39	0.26
Against Tory Cooperation	1.35	2.00	2.21	2.11	0.30	0.23
Against immigration controls	92	79	56	31	0.48	−0.44
Against capital punishment	100	92	75	46	0.48	0.44
Against restricting communists	89	84	76	67	0.20	−0.18
For current London reform	41	12	10	11	0.32	0.21
For London reform in 5 years	85	92	80	41	0.46	0.38
	($N=27$)	($N=25$)	($N=40$)	($N=50$)		

underlined when we used the issues as independent variables and ran a regression with the class scale as the dependent variable. The rank-order of their importance was: capital punishment, traditional doctrine, immigration, reorganization of London government in the future, Party leadership, Clause IV, the 1962 plan for reorganizing London, and cooperation with the Conservatives. [Alliance, the Common Market, restrictions upon the Communist Party, and unilateralism (in that order) were of no consequence in the regression analysis.[101]]

On the basis of interviews and what we learned from the analysis of the twelve issues, we decided that the responses on five of them would constitute an index of 'ideological enthusiasm'. The issue responses are: support for unilateralism, antipathy toward the national Party leadership, suspicion of the Anglo-American alliance, resistance to the revision of Clause IV, and a positive answer to the relevance of traditional doctrine.[102] A glance at the matrix in note 14 shows that the correlations among the first three issues were higher than for the other two; Clause IV and traditional doctrine move into what we might call the 'traditional socialist' outlook. Using these five issues responses, we are in a position to ask ourselves: Who are the 'ideological enthusiasts'?

WHO ARE THE 'IDEOLOGICAL ENTHUSIASTS'?

For a long time the myth persisted that the activists in local parties were 'extremists', whose views were considerably to the left of their national leaders, the inactive Party members, and the Labour voters. In their writings, some scholars tended to assume that the activists were a solid, unified group pressing their militant views.[103] More recent research, however, has challenged this assumption.[104] In addressing the problem of 'ideological enthusiasm'. we formulated a simple scale on the five issue responses mentioned above, and divided the population into three groups on the basis of the scores: the 'ideological enthusiasts', a moderate or middle group, and a group of 'non-ideologicals'.[105]

The findings of this study line up with the more recent interpretation, namely, that the local parties at the time of this study were not hotbeds of ideological militancy. This is shown by the distribution among the categories of activists by constituency.

Constituency	Ideological Enthusiasts	Moderates	Non-Ideological
Fulham	33.3%	40.0%	26.7%
South Kensington	27.8	19.4	52.8
Bermondsey	11.1	44.4	44.4
Total	23.0	36.3	40.7

It is noteworthy that only about 23 per cent of the activists in all three constituency parties fell into the top ideological category. The relatively high number of 'moderates' in Fulham and Bermondsey represent 'traditional socialist' outlooks – people who claimed relevance for traditional doctrine and opposed the revision of Clause IV. That the parties were not overwhelmed by extremists can be seen when we look at the data from a different angle. Disregarding the ideological/moderate/non-ideological categories for a moment, we can average the scores for the five issue responses. Out of a possible score of 5.0, the constituency means were: Fulham, 2.56; South Kensington, 1.86; and Bermondsey 1.71. By all counts, the party that was rated the most ideological of the three was the one in the electorally marginal area, Fulham.

A fuller socio-economic profile of the ideological enthusiasts, moderates, and non-ideologicals can be seen when we compare one category with a grouping of the other two in terms of percentage differences.[106] These profiles are presented in Table 6.23. According to these profiles, the ideological enthusiasts tended to be people whose subjective class-placement was incongruent with their occupational position;[107] they were people with secondary education (and here the individuals who had gone slightly beyond secondary school were prominent) and from Group II on the social class scale. They were comparatively new to their communities. The activists from Fulham were conspicuous in the ideological category. In terms of exposure to politics, the ideologicals were a young group who had entered the Party in the 1950s and had served in the GMC and in party offices for relatively short periods of time.

The profile of the moderates is much different, following the contours of working-class existence. The moderates were people from working-class homes who had received elementary education, held manual jobs, identified with their own class, and had spent most of their adult lives in the area. As we would expect, they made Group IV on the class scale a significant point in the profile. It comes as no surprise that they had had considerable exposure to politics; they were an older group with long records of membership in the Party and on the GMC, and they tended to be active in their trade unions.

The non-ideologicals, of course, were an entirely different group from the other two. Their profile shows a middle-class complexion: university training, stable middle-class position, and identification with the upper social groups. In contrast with the ideological enthusiasts in Group II on the class scale, they were congregated in Group I. In terms of exposure to politics, the non-ideologicals were closer to middle age, and had had fairly lengthy tenure on the GMC and in party office. They were members of their unions but did not play active roles; their ambition was to get elected to the borough council.[108]

Table 6.23 Ideological profiles

Variables	Ideological Enthusiasts		Middle Group		Non-ideologicals	
			AREA			
Constituency	Fulham	+19.5				
Pct. Adult life in residence	Less than 75%	+27.3	75% or more	+22.0		
			SOCIAL CLASS			
Social origin	Secondary+	+19.4	Working-class	+20.0		
Education	Total secondary	+32.5	Elementary	+20.5	University	+16.1
Occupation			Manual	+21.9		
Social mobility			Stationary manual	+24.3	Stationary middle	+13.0
Class self-placement			Working-class	+23.2		
Objective/subjective class	Subjective deviants	+22.5	Manual identify working	+22.5	Non-manual identify middle	+19.4
Class scale	Group II	+31.3	Class IV	+20.2	Group I	+18.4
			EXPOSURE TO POLITICS			
Age	Under 35	+21.7	55 and over	+25.4	35–44	+14.8
Period of recruitment	1952–1962	+30.4				
Length of Party membership	5 years or less	+17.9	More than 15 years	+24.4		
Length of GMC membership	10 years or less	+38.7	More than 15 years	+18.4	More than 10 years	+20.7
Length of EC membership	Less than 5 years	+20.8				
Length of officer tenure	Less than 3 years	+15.9			3 years or more	+16.6
Trade union activity			Actives	+17.3	Inactives	+28.5
Political aspirations					Local council	+16.4

In looking at the profiles of the ideological enthusiasts and their opposite number, the non-ideologicals, we are faced with an interesting question: since both groups have certain middle-class attributes (the former, for example, represents Groups II and the latter Group I on the class scale), why is there a tendency for them to be on opposite sides of the ideological spectrum?[109] We knew that the people in these two groups had different educational levels and engaged in different types of professional activities, and we thought that the more extreme outlooks of the people in Group II might be related to their failure to advance farther up the educational ladder or to secure positions that their educational attainments might have entitled them to expect. In order to examine the educational and occupational patterns, we combined the middle-class groups (I and II on the class scale) so that the demarcation points on the scale would not be operative. Although we realized that the numbers would be small, we nevertheless established categories based upon both education and occupation and calculated the means scores on the five issue responses. The first group consists of university-trained people who held positions in law, medicine, and science. The second group is made up of respondents with university education and jobs in the newer professions: teachers, journalists, social workers, personnel officers, executive secretaries of voluntary organizations, etc. The third and fourth groups are distinguished on the basis of training beyond secondary education and the ordinary secondary school course, and they include people engaged in clerical work. The results are as follows:

Category	Mean Ideological Score	N
University: law, medicine, science	0.71	(7)
University: other professions	1.89	(14)
Secondary +: other professions and clerical work	2.83	(12)
Secondary: other professions and clerical work	2.11	(18)

It should be noted that, except for the top group, about half of the respondents came from working-class homes and might be expected to reflect this in their outlooks. When we calculated the scores on the basis of social origin, however, there was no real difference between the people of humble origin and those of more affluent upbringing, except in the case of the last group (people with regular secondary education), in which the respondents of working-class origin registered a higher score, 2.38 as compared with 1.90.[110]

In studying these results (which obviously can be nothing more than suggestive), one might conjecture that some of the respondents were suffering from career frustration which encouraged them to develop an 'against the system' syndrome. Conversations with some (by no means systematic) indicated unhappiness with their jobs and concern about unrealized aspirations. All of the school teachers and half of the journalists in the group were ideologically inclined.[111] Some scholars have suggested that people who are forced to pursue 'second choice' occupations tend to grow discontented and become vulnerable to unorthodox types of appeals.[112] Parkin hypothesizes that middle-class radicals enter certain types of 'creative' and value-oriented occupations through a process of self-selection.[113] But the data in this study do not permit us to make any judgments on this matter. We did not secure systematic information about occupational discontent; we do not know the incidence of second-choice positions or the degree of self-selection; and in any event the number of middle-class people in the activist population is far too small to be of much significance. It is sufficient to point out that in this study the most middle-class segment of the respondents were not ideological enthusiasts but that the people at the next middle-class level had a distinct tendency in this direction – a tendency that was observable in some of the individual issues we examined. The small size of the population we had to work with undoubtedly made it vulnerable in some respects to idiosyncracies in the three parties we were studying, but we suggest that this problem may be an interesting one for future research.

A body of social science literature indicates that the leaders of voluntary organizations are inclined to be more ideological than their followers. This finding usually applies to the national leaders and may not be applicable to the leaders of a local Labour party who have to contend with GMC delegates. The reader must remember, too, that the issues we are treating in this study comprise a particular ideological structure, although they are issues that are usually applied in 'left' and 'right' designations in British politics. In conducting the research, we concluded that the leaders' views on issues, while salient under certain conditions, were usually of only marginal importance; a more significant consideration was the ability of the potential officers to perform well in their roles and their willingness to work hard for the organization. It will be useful at this juncture, however, to examine the ideological tendencies of the activists who held major offices at the constituency level and those who served as chairmen and secretaries of their wards. In the three constituencies together, the mean scores of the officers as a group on the five issue responses were not as high as the scores for the non-officers (1.76, compared with 2.15). This pattern held true for each party treated separately. The ward officers, however, were more ideologically enthusiastic than were the constituency party officials (2.04, as opposed to 1.34). There was no difference between the two groups of officers in Bermondsey, but in Fulham and South Kensington the ideological scores of the ward officials were significantly higher. It is interesting to note that in Fulham, where the level of ideological zeal was the highest, the GMC delegates nevertheless elected constituency leaders who disagreed with them on controversial issues.

Another interesting question is this: compared with the moderates and the non-ideologicals, how involved were the ideological enthusiasts in the affairs of their local parties? The trade unions and the Co-operative societies? The work of the borough councils? One way of looking at these relationships was to calculate mean involvement scores for the three categories of activists, as given below.[114]

Type of Involvement	Ideological Enthusiasts	Moderate	Non-Ideologicals
Local party	3.69	4.05	4.55
Trade unions and Co-operatives	2.22	2.48	1.92
Borough council	0.71	0.73	1.15

Notice that the ideologically inclined were relatively less involved in the local party and the borough council, while the opposite was true of the non-ideolgicals.[115]

In his study of constituency parties, Janosik found that those in marginal areas and Labour strongholds followed a moderate policy line, while those in Conservative districts subscribed to more extreme views.[116] The findings from our study differ from this pattern in that the party in the most marginal constituency displayed the strongest commitment on ideological questions. As we have already noted, a measure of organized factionalism existed within the Fulham and South Kensington parties, with direct confrontations over defense and foreign policy sparking tensions. In Fulham, the political disagreements led to some personal antagonisms and resulted in alignments being carried over to unrelated issues. The non-ideological activists who controlled the South Kensington party were sensitive about the ideological split and sought to avoid head-on controversial discussions. By contrast, the intra-party disputes in Bermondsey lacked ideological underpinning, since most of the activists were inclined toward moderate, 'traditional socialist' outlooks and were influenced in defense and foreign policy matters by their Member of Parliament. Although not a problem, activists' discontents in Bermondsey were linked more to personal considerations than to severe clashes over doctrine.

Constituency differences with respect to these conflicts can be seen from the responses of the activists who perceived splits over doctrinaire socialism to be a problem: Fulham, 36 per cent; South Kensington, 29 per cent; and Bermondsey, 15 per cent. In the Fulham group, the majority of these activists — almost entirely from the non-ideological and moderate camps — stressed the need for unity, while slightly more than one-third of them — a mixture of enthusiasts and moderates — emphasized the importance of tolerance for minority viewpoints. No such distinction is possible in the South Kensington group; the people who recognized the problem of disunity either just mentioned the difficulty or pointed out why their ideological stance must prevail. The distribution of activists who spotted disunity on personal grounds was: Fulham, 23 per cent; South Kensington, 14 per cent; and Bermondsey, 8 per cent. In the former two constituencies, the ideological tensions had clearly been transformed into personality clashes so that issue differences and personal conflicts became noticeably interlaced. Apart from its impact upon the GMC meetings, however, the disunity appeared to have no effect upon the normal operations of the parties. When political campaigns got under way, the differences were submerged and people from both sides worked together in apparant harmony.

Now that we have completed our side-trip to survey the views of the activists on salient issues and have noted that certain categories of people tended to line up on opposite sides of these questions, we begin to get some notion of why political activity is important to many of them. We shall now return to our study of the three parties as organizations, looking at the patterns of involvement and the avowed reasons for such involvement and discussing the types of satisfactions that a party organization can bring to the people who are devoted to it.

7 Involvement, Motivations, and Inducements

During the course of this research undertaking, we observed a good many people working hard for their constituency party, sometimes at monetary cost to themselves and usually at the expense of their leisure interests and time spent with their families. Their effort was voluntary; they were free to withdraw from their association at any time. Though they were not vulnerable to the controls and sanctions that some other types of organizations are able to manipulate, they chose to remain in the party and to absorb themselves in its activities. This raises some interesting questions which will engage our attention in this chapter. What sorts of people were the most involved in the work of their parties? What motivated them to become caught up in local political work? What were their political aspirations? Given their interests and desires, what inducements did the local party have to offer, and how was it able to manipulate the inducements in an effort to achieve its own organizational purposes?

PARTY INVOLVEMENT

Although we assumed that the delegates to the General Management Committee were party activists (and the agents assured us that this assumption was largely justified), we noticed that some delegates were more involved with the organization than others. In looking for an explanation, one is immediately tempted to consider social class: much of the literature informs us that people in non-manual occupations are more heavily engaged in party effort than are manual workers. Indeed, some scholars have suggested a tendency for the middle-class element to displace the working class in the power structure of local parties. On the other hand, one might anticipate a strong relationship between party involvement and level of political aspirations; the more a party can assist the individual in achieving his political objectives, the more likely he is to work hard for the organization.

If social class is the compelling factor in the degree of party involvement, it will be useful to examine the reasons why the activists were interested in serving on the GMC. From what we already know about the class factor, we might expect the stated motivations of the working class to be largely party-oriented, while those of the middle class to be more issue-oriented and personal-oriented. If, on the other hand, the important variable in influencing party involvement is political aspirations, we would have good reason to conjecture that the people who wish to enter Parliament would express more issue- and personal-oriented motivations than the locally aspiring activists for whom party-oriented considerations would probably be more salient. These questions about political aspirations and motivations have important relevance for the sorts of inducements used by the local party to encourage people to work hard in its behalf.

The question of what types of people were the most involved in party work prompted us to sketch socio-economic profiles of organizational involvement, and we divided the activists from all of the parties into three categories – high party involvement, moderate involvement, and low involvement.[1] The profiles are displayed in Table 7.1, which is made up of percentage differences between the high and the low, between the moderate and the low, and between the low and a combination of the high and the moderate.[2]

Even a quick glance at the profiles reveals some interesting patterns. In terms of social class, the profile of the highly involved is similar to that of the moderately involved; both of them are dominated by clerical groups. The cluster includes the activists in routine clerical occupations, the clerical people who identified with the working class and who were mobile into the clerical stratum, and those who were heavily represented in Group III on the class scale. In terms of exposure to politics, the most active people were those who had been on the GMC for a relatively long period of time, were not involved in their trade unions, and had entered the Party through the youth organizations. Even more important, they had the *highest proportion of incumbent members of the borough councils, and this was their highest level of political aspiration.* The moderately involved people were distinguished by the fact that they found time to be active in their trade unions as well as in their parties.

The profile of the delegates who were the least involved in the work of their local parties is considerably different from the other two. They were a more solidly working-class group – in terms of occupation, class self-rating, and social mobility. These characteristics make Group IV on the class scale a visible point in the profile. The people in the low-involvement configuration had much less exposure to politics. They had never belonged to any Labour youth organization, they had never served on the borough council, they were not trade unionists, and they indicated no political aspirations.

As mentioned earlier, some scholars have detected a tendency for middle-class groups in some local parties to push aside the proletarian core. This study does not provide firm support for such a finding, despite

Table 7.1 Party involvement

Variable	High		Moderate		Low	
SOCIAL CLASS						
Occupation	Routine clerical	+34.6	Routine clerical	+32.9	Manual	+23.9
Objective/subjective class	Clerical identifying working-class	+27.1			Manual identifying working-class	+20.6
Social mobility			Mobiles to clerical jobs	+22.5	Stationary manual	+23.0
Class scale	Group III	+23.2			Group IV	+23.3
EXPOSURE TO POLITICS						
Length of GMC membership	More than 10 years	+22.9				
Youth organization membership	Members	+20.4			Non-members	+17.1
Borough council membership	Current members	+25.5			Never served	+23.4
Trade union activity	Inactives	+21.2	Actives	+18.6	Non-members	+16.8
Political aspirations	Local council	+28.8			None	+18.2

the working-class features of the low-involvement profile. The groups that were the most conspicuous in the high- and moderate-involvement categories were not the solidly middle-class element; they represented Group III on the class scale, not Groups I and II.[3] The reader will recall that these people who held routine clerical jobs still had close ties with the working class: more than three-fourths of them came from working-class homes, and nearly 60 per cent of them listed themselves as belonging to that class.

The profile would tempt us to expect that the class factor would have the strongest impact upon party involvement, except for the fact that borough council membership and local political aspirations also had distinctive points in the high-involvement contour. After having drawn the profiles, we ran a regression analysis with the party involvement scores as the dependent variable and the twenty-two factors used in the issue runs as the independent variables. (We were unable to include the data on motivations for serving on the GMC in the regression, since there was no way to order the categories.) The best predictor in the regression was not a class factor, but level of political aspirations, followed by recruitment through the youth organizations.[4] In other words, when such class factors as occupation were held constant, political aspirations still made the biggest impact upon party involvement. We must therefore examine these political aspirations in more detail.

POLITICAL ASPIRATIONS

When we asked the respondents which public office they would most like to have, we received the following result:

	Bermondsey	Fulham	South Kensington	Total
Member of Parliament	8.5%	34.8%	46.0%	26.8%
Advance on local council or become mayor	42.4	19.6	10.8	26.8
Get on local council	11.9	19.6	24.3	17.6
'None' and no answer	37.3	26.1	18.9	28.9
	($N = 59$)	($N = 46$)	($N = 37$)	($N = 142$)

Even though political aspirations turned out to have the strongest influence upon party involvement, a class factor was nevertheless at work. In fact, the data in this study show that political aspirations were strongly influenced by social class and by age when those who wrote 'None' or did not answer were dropped from the analysis. In other words, the people in the middle-class category and in the younger age bracket aspired to enter Parliament, while the people from the working class and in the higher age categories set their sights on local offices associated with the borough council. The relationships between social class and political aspirations are clearly visible in the following table, which is based upon occupation.[5]

	Professional managerial	Routine clerical	Manual
Member of Parliament	65.5%	32.4%	20.0%
Local public office	34.5	67.6	80.0
	(N = 29)	(N = 37)	(N = 35)

The age patterns are also quite distinct.

	Under 35	35–44	45 and Over
Member of Parliament	67.9%	55.0%	15.1%
Local public office	32.1	45.0	84.9
	(N = 28)	(N = 20)	(N = 53)

If we assume, tentatively, that the people who aspire to certain positions work hard in their parties in order to realize their goals, this should be reflected in their party involvement scores. We found this to be the case when we calculated the mean involvement scores for each level of aspiration: advance in council work, 5.30; Member of Parliament, 5.01; get on the council, 3.08; and no designated aspiration, 2.74.[6]

This brings us to the problem of avowed motivations. We asked the respondents the open-ended question of why they wanted to serve on the General Management Committee of their respective parties. One cannot, of course, be overwhelmingly confident about written responses to a question of this sort. We must confess, however, that we were surprised by the candor expressed in many of the questionnaires, and the results of the interviews we conducted gave us no reason to doubt the fidelity of the responses that the interviewees later made to this question on the written forms. In terms of social class, we expected that the working-class activists would be inclined to give party-oriented responses to the motivational inquiry, while those of the middle class would be more of an issue-oriented or personal-oriented nature. Since social class was so influential in determining political aspirations, the same phenomenon would be reflected in party-oriented motivations on the part of those who were interested in local offices and in issue- and personal-oriented responses by the parliamentary aspirants. For a start, we should look at the general motivational break-downs by constituency, which are presented in Table 7.2.[7]

Even though this table indicates a reasonable degree of congruence among the activists in three very different parties, we need to single out a few items for background purposes. The avowed motivations of the

Table 7.2 Motivations for service on GMC

	Bermondsey	Fulham	South Kensington	Total
Party-Oriented				
Serve Party, movement, community	29.0%	15.3%	17.6%	20.8%
Represent wards and affiliated units	11.8	19.4	6.8	13.2
Other*	5.4	8.2	9.5	7.6
Total Party-oriented	46.2	42.9	33.8	41.5
Personal-oriented				
Interest; desire to be involved	10.8	18.4	23.0	17.0
Social contacts	11.8	9.2	6.8	9.4
Keep informed	9.7	4.1	4.0	6.0
Total personal-oriented	32.3	31.6	33.8	32.5
Issue-oriented	21.5	25.5	32.4	26.0
	(N=93)	(N=98)	(N=74)	(N=265)

* Includes obligation to serve; inject new blood; see that party funds are spent wisely and that the Executie Committee does not get too much power; help in the selection of council candidates and see that they do their job.

Bermondsey and Fulham people were a bit more party-oriented than was the case in South Kensington. (Within the party-oriented category, the Bermondsey activists placed more emphasis upon serving the Party, the Labour movement, or the community, while the Fulham people were more concerned about their representative function.) Although the aggregate of personal-oriented motivations was evenly spread among the three parties, the Fulham and South Kensington activists were more concerned about 'getting involved' than were the Bermondsey folk, who placed more stress upon keeping informed about what was going on nationally and locally. Bermondsey and Fulham were a trifle more interested in the social benefits than South Kensington, but the social motivation was less prominent in all of the parties than might have been expected. Although the desire to participate in policymaking (issue-oriented motivation) was an important consideration in all three parties, it received fewer mentions in Bermondsey and Fulham than it did in South Kensington.

The speculation that the patterning of motivational responses would vary according to social class gets some support from the data in Table 7.3, which is based upon occupation.

Table 7.3 Occupation and motivations for GMC service

	Professional/ Managerial	Routine Clerical	Manual
Party-oriented			
Serve Party, movement or community	17.3%	13.6%	35.1%
Represent wards and affiliated units	9.9	11.8	18.9
Other	7.4	10.9	2.7
Total Party-oriented	34.6	36.4	56.7
Personal-oriented			
Interest, desire to be involved	16.1	20.9	12.2
Social contacts	13.6	9.1	5.4
Keep informed	4.9	5.5	8.1
Total personal-oriented	34.6	35.5	25.7
Issue-oriented	30.9	28.2	17.6
	(N=81)	(N=110)	(N=74)

The professional/managerial group and the routine clerical group differed hardly at all between themselves and over the three types of motivational responses. The deviating cluster was the manual workers who asserted their interest in the Party and the movement, exhibiting less concern about personal- and issue-oriented motivations.[8]

In light of this analysis of occupation, how do the stated motivations of the activists line up in terms of level of political aspirations? This information is given in Table 7.4. The messages in this table are fairly clear. The people who were already serving on the council and those who aspired to do so were more party-oriented and less issue-oriented in their motivations than were the parliamentary aspirants. On the party-oriented side, the incumbent councillors viewed themselves as serving the Party and the Labour movement, while those who wanted to become council members were concerned about their representative roles. In the personal-oriented group, the differences were surprisingly small, with the councillors being only slightly below the two aspiring groups in total proportions of mentions; the latter expressed an interest in politics and a desire to become involved. The people who wanted to go to the House of Commons seem to have been more motivated by the desire to wrestle with issues than were the people whose aspirations were entirely local.[9]

Now that we have examined the patterns of activists' involvement in the party, their political aspirations, and their stated reasons for wanting to serve on the General Management Committee, we need to move a step farther by asking several questions. Is a local party able to channel the interests and desires of its activists in directions that will help it to

Table 7.4 Political aspirations and motivation for GMC service

	M.P.	Get on Local Council	Advance on Local Council
Party-oriented			
Serve Party, movement, community	13.3%	16.7%	32.4%
Represent wards and affiliated units	8.4	21.4	13.5
Other	10.8	7.1	2.7
Total party-oriented	32.5	45.2	48.7
Personal-oriented			
Interest; desire to be involved	22.9	21.4	8.1
Social contacts	7.2	9.5	9.5
Keep informed	4.8	2.4	9.5
Total person-oriented	34.9	33.3	27.0
Issue-oriented	32.5	21.4	24.3
	(N=83)	(N=42)	(N=74)

achieve its own objectives? If so, how does the party do this? In other words, what 'satisfactions', 'rewards', or 'incentives' does it have available for its people so as to encourage them to labor industriously in the organization's behalf?

INDUCEMENTS FOR PARTY SERVICE

The author starts from the obvious premise that a person who works hard in a local Labour party does so because he wants to secure some gain/privilege for the organization or for himself, or for both reasons. If his *primary* interest extends beyond himself to the organization and its objectives, i.e., if he is largely concerned about its ideological position and its social program, we can say that he has a *normative* incentive to pour his energy into the party's effort. But if the individual's interests are mainly centered in personal benefits – to gain political experience, to make social contacts, to pursue a career in politics, etc., we can say that he is motivated by *personal* incentives.[10] In an abstract sense, a local Labour party has a 'supply' of these inducements which it can distribute. Obviously, it can provide normative incentives. (In fact, we shall argue later on that in many local communities it enjoys a near-monopoly of such rewards.) In terms of personal inducements, one would anticipate that a local party could offer to its activists: opportunities for social interaction, party offices, assistance in launching a parliamentary career, local council candidatures, and certain civic positions. As our discussion moves along, we shall see whether a party has all or just some of these incentives at its command.

As we have already intimated, some Labour activists appear to be stimulated primarily by normative concerns. It is also quite likely that some place more emphasis upon personal rewards. The discussion in the previous section, however, suggests that some people are motivated by a *variety of interests* – some normative and some personal – and that these tend to become interlaced and difficult to separate. It is probable, too, that some individuals are initially attracted to an organization by what it stands for and that subsequent involvement encourages them to develop interests of a more personal sort. By the same token, a person may join an organization in the hope of gaining personal benefits, but as he becomes engrossed in its affairs, he grows more committed to its values and goals. The organizational health of a party is improved when it is able to cater to both types of interests, the normative and the personal – when it is able to offer its members the 'rewards' that they seek.

Normative Incentives

As the research advanced, the author became impressed by the number of people who exhibited a devotion to the Labour cause and a fervent commitment to the organization's goals. He encountered many activists who were willing to invest huge amounts of time on the doorsteps and in the party quarters because they were convinced that their efforts would help a crusade in which they believed. In some instances the commitment seemed analogous to a religious experience with the accompanying flow of righteousness. For some veterans of humble origin, it was a matter of working-class solidarity. For some of the younger people it was the burst of idealism which produces dreams of a just social order. For many of the activists, their constituency organization was the local reflection of the national Party and should, wherever possible, be used as the vehicle for reform in the community. They perceived that with well-considered strategy and hard work they could exert pressure for local health centers, better libraries and schools, and improved employment exchanges. No less than 17 per cent of the middle-class people in South Kensington mentioned their 'obligation' to serve on the GMC, despite the dismal prospects. It would have been easy for the activists in South Kensington to sit back or to just 'go through the motions', but instead they opted for strategies designed to help the Party as a whole.

That the activists in this study were drawn from the ranks of the issue-oriented and the socially-motivated can be seen from a breakdown of the voluntary associations with which they were identified and the civic work in which they engaged.

Voluntary Associations	Bermondsey	Fulham	South Kensington
Labour Party only	55.9%	32.6%	21.6%
Other political organizations*	8.5	26.1	54.1
Civic committees and charities	23.7	23.9	8.1
Recreational groups and professional societies	11.9	17.4	16.2
	(N = 59)	(N = 46)	(N = 37)

* Includes Fabian Society, Campaign for Nuclear Disarmament, Movement for Colonial Freedom, Co-operative Party, etc. The Fabian Society received the most mentions.

Note that for a good many people, especially in Bermondsey, the Labour party was the *only* outlet for their spare-time activities. If all of the political organizations are combined (most of the 'mentions' were affiliated with the Labour Party anyway), the proportions of identification with purely political organizations were: Bermondsey, 64 per cent; Fulham, 59 per cent; and South Kensington, 76 per cent. The activists' involvement on school and hospital boards, in old folks' welfare, and in various charitable organizations is especially noticeable in Bermondsey and Fulham where the Labour party dominated the councils. Of course, the South Kensington activists had less opportunity for formal civic work because they had no influence on the borough council, but the sponsorship of the annual old folks' party was a recognition of social responsibilities which had to be discharged informally. These lists of organizational identifications give some indication of what activities the respondents placed value upon – and the overwhelming response was political involvement and community service.

For this involvement in political and civic work, the activists relied heavily upon their local Labour parties. Most of them either had no other organizational ties or linked themselves only with Party-affiliated units, such as the Fabian Society. In other words, a local Labour party was able to offer them something that was congenial with their interests. Unlike the intermittent 'crusades' and 'movements' which suddenly sprang into being and then gradually withered away, a Labour party was an ongoing organization with a staff (and usually a headquarters) and visible activities. Its regular meetings could be used as a forum for the discussion of a wide range of contemporary and philosophical problems. Moreover, its policy stands were tied to programs of political action for social benefit; for someone really interested in engaging in social service and welfare activities in the local community, involvement in the Labour party was a sure route. It is important to recognize that these kinds of normative incentives could be distributed only in a group context.

Apart from the fact that a local party, compared with alternative voluntary associations, offered advantages to the politically conscious and the socially aware, was the organization able to make use of its advantageous position to influence the behavior of the activists? We should at least take note of the fact that the party has the authority to impose negative sanctions on individual members (and groups as well). The Fulham Young Socialists, in consultation with the party's governing bodies, would not admit a person from the radical 'Keep Left' group because he would be an unsettling force within the organization. And in South Kensington the members of one of the wards came close to passing a resolution of censure against a comrade for allegedly having participated in CND 'disruptive tactics' at the Party's May Day rally in Hyde Park. While proscriptions, votes of censure, and threats of expulsion may be a form of group or peer pressure, they are probably not very effective, and, in any event, are not used very often.

We wondered what the party involvement record of the people who seemed to be primarily interested in normative concerns would look like compared with the record of those who stressed personal motivations.[11] This, of course, is difficult to get at because many people listed both types. In an admittedly crude attempt to investigate the problem, we divided the respondents from each constituency into two types – those who had listed party-oriented and/or issue-oriented motivations but made no mention of personal strivings,[12] and those whose mentions included personal-oriented considerations. Then we calculated the mean party-involvement scores for each group:

Stated Motivations	Bermondsey	Fulham	South Kensington
Party- and issue-oriented	(31) 4.35	(20) 3.83	(15) 2.83
Personal-oriented	(23) 2.93	(23) 5.00	(21) 5.57

Only in the case of Bermondsey were the normative objectives and the degree of party involvement positively related; while commitment to the party's purposes were important in Fulham and South Kensington and prompted many people to sacrifice in their organization's behalf, the fact remains that the people who listed motivations of a more personal sort tended to be more deeply involved in party work. Although we recognized that commitment to the party could not be equated with ideological enthusiasm (indeed, we have seen that on some issues, e.g., unilateralism, the two were in conflict), we could probe the relationship between strong ideological views and effort put forth in party work by separating the respondents from each constituency into three groups on the basis of high party involvement, moderate, and low, and then calculating the mean ideological scores for each group. In Bermondsey and South Kensington, the relationship was inverse – the lower the level of involvement, the higher the ideological scores. In Fulham, however, the ideological scores were relatively high at all levels of involvement, but highest in the moderately involved and then the highly involved groups.[13]

Thus it would appear that only part of the picture comes into view when we focus upon the normative aspects of the inducement system. As we have been careful to point out, a good many people in the three constituencies worked very hard because of their avowed loyalty to the party and their devotion to its program. But the data collected in this study indicate that many activists, in addition to being concerned about the party and its ideological flavor, had interests that were oriented toward themselves as individuals. From the viewpoint of the organizations, plurality of motivations was probably a steadying force in some respects; an organization that is forced to rely primarily upon normative incentives and is not restrictive in its recruitment policy tends to attract different shades of ideological belief which precipitate schism in the ranks.

Personal Incentives

While signifying devotion to the Labour Party and its basic creed, many respondents indicated certain desires which may be classified as rewards beneficial to them as individuals. Some, for example, expressed a desire to be on the GMC because they had a general interest in politics and they wanted to be where the action was, or because they enjoyed the social fellowship. As we have seen, many of them indicated political aspirations – to get on the borough council, to advance in the hierarchy of the council, to become mayor, or to pursue a career in parliament.[14] Organizational theory informs us that if a local party is able to 'distribute' these 'individual rewards' to those people who work the hardest for the collective effort while denying them to the less diligent, it is in a position to improve the quality of its operation. It has an opportunity, in other words, to take advantage of the consistency between individual wants and group goals. A local Labour party, of course, has fewer inducements at its command then do the American parties; it has, for example, virtually no 'material' incentives to fall back upon. In examining this question of inducements, we shall consider a number of possible 'rewards' which constituency parties may have at their disposal: (1) social interaction; (2) party offices; (3) assistance in launching parliamentary careers; (4) local council candidacies; and (5) civic positions.

Social Interaction. As we have already seen, the women's and youth organizations ran a schedule of social events in order to maintain the interest of their members, and the constituency party itself arranged social gatherings for its activists from time to time. But all of these events were usually open to the members without regard to work contribution. More relevant for our purposes would be the distribution of passes to the election 'count' on the basis of campaign effort, and the after-the-count gathering in the party headquarters, with invitations often going to people who had done their stint on the doorstep. This type of social activity, however, hardly qualifies for 'inducement' classification. Some of the hardest-working activists did not take advantage of it; and, besides, one does not expect people to spend their valuable time in a political contest only because they want to be invited to observe the count or to attend a party afterward.

A few respondents mentioned that they enjoyed being on the GMC in part because they liked to chat with their Member of Parliament. It is likely that some activists, especially those from the working class, take pride in their first-name relationship with the M.P., and they get a feeling of being 'in the know' when he tells them what is really going on in the House of Commons – the happenings that never appear in the newspaper. For people whose lives evolve in a narrow setting, such personal association widens their horizons, and they may be stimulated to work hard in order to insure that their M.P. retains his seat.

In this study, however, we are forced to conclude that 'social interaction' was not of much significance as an inducement for political effort. Only about 16 per cent of the GMC delegates – equally distributed among the three constituencies – mentioned reasons that could be fitted into the social rubric.[15] Social life *per se* could be found in other organizations; even in a relatively isolated community like Bermondsey, the party had to compete with a variety of social clubs and recreational associations.[16]

Party Offices. At the ward level the group decided who would represent them on the General Management Committee and who the ward officers would be. The GMC as a group elected the party officers and the members of the Executive Committee. At election time, the agent, sometimes in consultation with the main party officers, selected the staff of campaign leaders.

From the evidence we have, we can say that nearly everyone was interested in being elected to the GMC where the political 'excitement' was, but some people who wanted to serve on the GMC were not interested in any party offices. The average length of time that an individual puts in as a local party member before taking a seat on the GMC should provide a rough measure of upward mobility within a party organization.[17] For purposes of this analysis, we drew from each GMC list the delegates who had been elected to that body within the previous five years. The average number of years spent in local party membership before being selected for GMC service was: Bermondsey, 9.6 years; Fulham, 3.2 years; and South Kensington, 1.6 years. In South Kensington, the high rate of removals and the existence of vacant seats from time to time meant that a young person who was interested in politics could rise much more rapidly than was the case in many other constituency parties. In fact, some people become GMC members within a month or two after they had moved into the constituency. We noted earlier that the South Kensington party received special dispensation from the National Executive Committee to have more representation on the GMC than would ordinarily be permitted; it wanted to have a relatively large governing body as an inducement for its activists. Preferment could also be fairly rapid in Fulham; a sizeable group of younger people saw GMC service within six months or a year after they had taken out their Party membership cards. In Bermondsey, several individuals fitted into this pattern of rapid selection for the GMC, but the intake and elevation of young people was not so marked, and a number of the new recruits to the GMC during 1961–62 were people who had been members of the party for relatively long periods of time and who had been persuaded by the agent to become active.

One can safely say that a person who did not carry his share of the party load endangered his chances of being selected for the GMC by his ward comrades; a few cases of rejection emerged during this study. But the reward/sanction structure did not operate very effectively at this level. The people who were selected for GMC seats varied considerably in the amount of time they devoted to party work. The negative sanction of non-election was applied only to the most serious cases of negligence, and it was usually rendered ineffectual because the people involved could get on the GMC by other routes, e.g., their trade unions or their connections with the Co-operative movement.

Some of the major constituency offices were sought after. The party chairmanship in all three constituencies, for example, was considered to be a prestigious post and was in most instances filled competitively. Similarly, in some of the wards the office of chairman carried certain status. Some people liked the position of ward secretary because it enabled them to be on the GMC automatically or because they wanted to expand their knowledge about politics and Labour Party organization. Often, however, activists avoided the secretarial post, and the people who took the job did so out of a sense of obligation to the party. In the case of the party offices that people were interested in holding (for whatever reason), the important criterion for election by their peers was whether or not a given individual had worked hard in behalf of the organization. Ideological outlooks might be taken into account if the competition was between two hard-working individuals with differing political views, but the doctrinal posture of the competitors was often disregarded if the question of effort in behalf of the party arose. We encountered cases in which unilateralists were supported for party office by their non-unilateralist peers because they had done a commendable job of organizing their wards. Conversely, moderate GMC members voted against the re-election of their moderate colleagues because, in their view, they had not performed conscientiously.

In the most competitive constituency party, Fulham, three groups seemed to emerge: (1) the activists who were 'pragmatists' in outlook and followed the national leadership on most controversial issues; (2) the people who inclined 'leftward' on nearly all of the controversial issues; and (3) those who were in the 'center' — interested in the goals of the party and its organizational health but not committed to any integrated doctrinal stance. In this constituency, neither the 'pragmatists' nor the 'leftists' had sufficient strength to win control over key posts in the wards and thereby command a sustained majority on the GMC. As a result of a near-equilibrium of ideological forces, the people in the 'center', whose primary concern was less with inflaming passions over issues than with building an effective organization designed to achieve concrete objectives, were often in a position to tilt the balance for or against particular candidates for party offices. When placed in this position, the 'centrists' tended to support those activists — regardless of their 'pragmatic' or 'leftist' orientations — who had demonstrated their loyalty to the organization by their work on the doorstep.

Quite often we came across people who worked hard in their wards and for the constituency party because they were interested in politics and wanted to gain political experience. Occasionally, too, we met people who had initially joined the Party as a result of ideological inclination, but once they had become involved in party work, the satisfaction they derived from administrative responsibility operated independently of their doctrinal commitment. Some of these people were victims of the British 'class system'. Though intelligent individuals, they had been forced to terminate their formal education at an early age in order to take jobs that provided little scope for their real talents. Bored by the monotony of the assembly line or the dulling noise of the typewriter, these people were eager for new challenges when they left their places of work and could turn to the administrative tasks provided by the party.[18] It is from the group of people who desire political experience or who want an outlet for their unused talents that the agent and his colleagues select their campaign staffs at election time. In other words, the party is able to channel the personal interests of its members toward the realization of its own objectives. As one local leader expressed it, 'The people who work the hardest are the ones who rise to positions of influence in our party.'

To what extent were young people able to rise to party office in the three constituencies? We have a rough gauge of this in the following statistics.

Party Offices	Mean Ages		
	Bermondsey	Fulham	South Kensington
Membership on General Management Committee	55.6	47.0	40.3
Major constituency offices	60.0	49.0	42.4
Ward offices	55.8	45.1	43.9
Membership on Executive Committee (excluding officers)	50.7	47.9	31.5
Holding no posts	54.0	47.8	41.8

The office-holding patterns were naturally influenced by the age structure of the parties. In each constituency, the major offices were held by people who were above the average age level of the GMC as a whole; this was especially true in Bermondsey. South Kensington drew its ward officers from a slightly older group (in order to maintain stability in a highly mobile area), while Bermondsey recruited its ward leaders at the average age level and Fulham reached down into a younger age bracket. Both Bermondsey and South Kensington offered some mobility to their younger non-officers through membership on the Executive Committee, but Fulham kept some of the older members on in this capacity.[19] It is interesting to observe that of the Bermondsey and Fulham people who were below the age of 45 and who had been on the GMC for three years or more, only 9 per cent held no positions at the constituency and ward levels or on the Executive Committee; the comparable figure for South Kensington was 11 per cent. In other words, opportunity for young people to hold some form of office existed in all of the three parties.

Assistance in launching a parliamentary career. At the time of this study, no fewer than thirty-eight activists (27 per cent of the respondents) were either seeking parliamentary candidatures or aspired to do so. A total of seven eventually appeared before selection conferences, four of them became candidates, and two of them managed to enter the House of Commons. As we have already pointed out, aspirations for parliamentary careers were a class phenomenon. The overwhelming majority of the aspirants were from the middle class, including the seven individuals just mentioned; of the handful of working-class people with such aspirations, all but one were active trade unionists.

The question arises, then, as to whether the local constituency organization is in a position to help these people achieve their political objective in return for industrious effort on their part. We have already noted the various steps in the candidate-selection process: (1) entry of name on candidates' lists through either (*a*) the trade union; or (*b*) nomination by the ward, recommendation by the GMC, and approval by the National Executive Committee; and (2) acceptance by a constituency party's selection conference. Where in this process is an individual's work record in the party likely to be taken into account, and with what result?

A local trade unionist who wishes to launch a parliamentary career will probably try to get on the A List of his trade union, and here his record of trade union activity will be much more important than his performance record in the local party. If he is unsuccessful in his attempt, however, he will then have to take steps to get his name placed upon the B List, which means that he must go through the local party machinery.

The initial stage in the B List procedure involves a nomination of the individual by one of the wards, usually his own. During this study, two people sought nomination from their wards. Neither of them had been among the most active members of their ward units, and the question of their work in the party was not raised at the ward meetings. Both nominations were sent forward to the General Management Committee. The rejection rate at the ward level for inadequate handling of party responsibilities is probably very low.

When the question of nomination for the B List appears on the GMC's agenda, the delegates may give the aspirants a rough passage by asking pointed questions. This happened in the two cases observed during the course of this study. The questions, however, dealt entirely with policy matters; no one asked about his or her work in the party. It is likely that a comrade may occasionally seek to embarrass a potential nominee by asking why he has ignored work on the doorstep. We know of one individual who was reluctant to submit himself to interrogation by his GMC colleagues because he had neglected the activities in his ward, but he eventually decided to go through the process anyway and he won endorsement. In the two cases we observed, the GMC delegates, after considerable grilling, voted to send the names on to Transport House. Probably in the overwhelming number of cases the GMC delegates give their approval to such nominations regardless of the work records of the aspirants.

Nor is the candidates' screening procedure of the National Executive Committee likely to be an impediment to individuals who wish to have their names inscribed on the B List but whose record of activity in the party is deficient. The NEC is primarily interested blocking people with extremist political views, although its rejection rate on this score is apparently very low. If the NEC officials decide to call a potential candidate in for an interview, they may exhibit some displeasure at his lack of effort in behalf of his party, but it is extremely unlikely that they would keep him off the B List for this reason.

Once his name appears on an official candidates' list, the individual begins his search for a constituency which is willing to accept him. At this juncture, a good record of party service may help him, but in most instances probably not. The South Kensington party made it a practice to select a local person in order to give him campaign experience. Since the party had a number of parliamentary aspirants, competition for the candidature sometimes emerged. In such a situation, the GMC members were unlikely to support an individual who made it a habit to avoid work. The person selected, however, need not have been among the most hard-working; sometimes his views on policy issues were more important. It is probably a safe generalization, though, that a local party will not select as its candidate a person who had done little or no work at all for the organization.

Sedulous effort in support of his local party may enable a parliamentary aspirant to become visible to a neighboring party which is beginning the search for a candidate. If his work record has won the respect of his comrades, he may be chosen to represent them at wider party meetings and conferences, and here he may have an opportunity to go to the rostrum to enunciate his views. His work in the street-corner meetings in South Kensington brought the name of Ivor Richard, who had been the local Labour candidate in the 1959 election, to the attention of one of the wards in the Barons Court constituency. The ward nominated him, and he survived the selection conference to become the candidate.

It is possible that an outstanding party record may excite the attention of the regional organizer, and he may be prompted to suggest the name of the individual to local party leaders who are looking for qualified candidates. When this is done, it has to be done judiciously, however, because constituency parties tend to be suspicious of Transport House direction in the choosing of candidates. Hence, cases of commendable party records being brought to the attention of other constituency parties through the medium of the regional offices are rare.

An aspirant's performance in his local organization could make a difference when the members of the Executive Committee prepare their short list. They may be suspicious of a person who has not held party offices in his local bailiwick or whose selection form reveals other evidence of lack of devotion to his own constituency party. We know that this happens, but we have no notion about its frequency.

Once an aspirant makes the short list, the chances are remote that he will be denied the candidature because his work in the party has been less than steadfast. Occasionally an individual may have to field a question or two about it at the selection conference, but if it were a serious consideration it would probably have been picked up at the time of the short-listing. Most of the interrogation involves policy issues. If a few members of the selection conference who were not on the Executive Committee begin to entertain doubts about an aspirant's party record, they have no opportunity to convey misgivings to their colleagues, since the conference moves to an exhaustive ballot without any discussion.

Thus, we are forced, on balance, to make a tentative negative judgment about the ability of a local Labour party to make use of the parliamentary nominating machinery in order to elicit hard work from the aspirants. We do this largely because most of the people who dreamed of going to Westminster did not themselves *perceive* that lack of arduous effort on their own turf would be held against them.[20] But we do say this: if work in the party is ever a factor in helping to launch a parliamentary career, it is important for an aspirant to do it in his own territory, moving into other districts only when his party's campaign plan calls for it. In contrast with the Conservative Party, the decisions affecting his candidacy are made by his home organization. If anyone is likely to judge his party record in ways that may be helpful or harmful, it will be his peers.[21]

Thus far we have avoided the real benefits that a parliamentary aspirant sees as flowing from untiring work in his local organization. The people we conversed with were very interested in gaining political experience. They wanted to understand politics and to get used to talking about politics. Quite apart from the cause they believed in, they 'took the stump' on Saturday mornings in order to develop their speaking ability. They accepted an invitation to supervise a portion of the campaign effort so as to sharpen their administrative skills. Some of them felt that work in their wards helped them to become better known in their party, and that visible identification with their party made them more widely known in the area. And most of them worked very hard. We have already seen that their party involvement scores were among the highest. Their aspiration and their willingness to work in pursuit of their objective made them an important resource upon which the local party could draw.

Local council candidacies. One of the striking things about this study is the number of people who were interested in continuing to serve on or in getting elected to the local councils. If we lump together the people who were already serving, those who were elected for the first time in May 1962, and those who expressed a desire to become councillors, we get this result: Bermondsey, 76 per cent; Fulham, 70 per cent; and South Kensington, 46 per cent. We have already noted that local political aspirations were a working-class phenomenon. This proved to be the case when we made the breakdown for each constituency.

That so many of the activists were interested in getting elected to local councils or, if they were incumbents, in continuing to serve is both praiseworthy and understandable. No small number of them viewed such a role as a means by which they might help to improve the quality of life in their communities. As we have already seen, the most frequently mentioned reason given by the sitting councillors for wanting seats on the GMC was to serve the Labour Party, the Labour movement, or the community. If their stated motivations have any validity, 35 per cent of them enunciated this objective without listing any other reason that could be classified as 'personal'. (In Bermondsey, the proportion was 46 per cent.)

Council service, of course, brings other satisfactions, which some respondents mentioned in their conversations with the author. An individual who bears the title 'Councillor' gets some visibility on the local scene and commands a degree of prestige in the community. For people who feel crushed by the monotony of their regular jobs, it is a welcome relief to enter the door of the Town Hall where they immediately get recognition. When a person has had a 'set-to' with his boss at the workshop, he may derive psychic gratification from having a 'bash at the Tories' in the council chamber. As the freshmen councillors begin to exhibit skill in their legislative roles, they will be given opportunities to move up the ladder in their committee assignments. Eventually they may move on to the chairmanship of the Housing Committee or the Finance Committee, or even to the top post as Leader of the Council, a position that is graced with both power and status. To hold a formal office in their local community can be important to Labour party members, especially those from the working class. They have a lot to lose when electoral opinion shifts against them; they not only forfeit the right to carry out policies to which they are devoted, but they have to give up their cherished committee assignments and they lose the standing they have come to appreciate. As one ex-councillor remarked, 'There will be an emptiness in my life for a time.'

We come now to the question we have asked before: Is a local Labour party able to 'reward' its hardest-working activists by helping them to get on the council or by assisting them to receive the committee assignments they desire? A good way to begin is to list the types of positions the allocation of which are within the party's control, i.e., they are assigned on the basis of a vote by party people in certain organs of the party. These include: (1) approval of the panel of council candidates by the GMC; (2) selection of particular candidates by the ward members, in collaboration with the members of the Executive Committee: (3) selection of councillors by the Labour Group to serve on the various committees; and (4) selection of people by the council to serve as aldermen (when the Labour party dominates the council, the effective decision is made by the Labour Group). We recognize that the people who are chosen to fill these roles are expected to have a number of qualifications; but, according to analysis attempted here, the minimal essential quality is demonstrated service to the organization – in other words, an individual's party colleagues will probably not support him if he has not carried his share of the work-load.

As one goes canvassing with party activists or observes an Executive Committee meeting on candidate-selection policy, one soon realizes the importance placed upon diligence. 'We hardly ever see Councillor X at our ward meetings', or 'He hasn't been at the GMC for the last four meetings', or 'He always wants help when he is standing for a seat, but he doesn't spend much time on the doorstep for anyone else' are the most common complaints one hears. As a local activist suggested, a councillor can usually get away with *only* one term of neglect. When incumbent council members are not re-selected, local party members are in effect applying negative sanctions against them. 'Mr Brown's speech at the selection meeting was lousy, compared with Mr Smith's, but Brown is much more conscientious about his party and council work – so we selected him.' This norm is clearly enunciated in local political circles; only the most imperceptive aspirants would be unaware of its existence.

When the question of approving the panel of borough council candidates appears on the GMC agenda, the matter is usually a formality. Any problems will probably have been worked out in advance by the Executive Committee. On the question of whether the hard-working activists are the people who secure the council candidatures, the best evidence we can muster is to compare the mean party involvement scores of the council candidates with those of the non-candidates. (In the case of South Kensington, we have included only the serious council candidates, i.e., those who were contesting seats in North Kensington. This means that the genuine candidatures available to the South Kensington activists were within the gift of the North Kensington party. An aspirant from the South, of course, would probably have to do some work in his home territory in order to become visible to his comrades in the North.) The mean party involvement scores for the two groups are as follows:

	Bermondsey	Fulham	South Kensington
Council candidates	5.13	5.85	7.25
Non-candidates	1.58	3.02	4.02

The people who survived the candidate screening were clearly more 'involved' (i.e., 'hard-working') than were those who did not apply or were eliminated in the early stages.[22] When we controlled for age, the result did not damage the initial formulation; only in Bermondsey were the involvement scores of the younger candidates slightly lower than those of the older group.

Once the candidate list has been compiled, is the organization able to offer preferment to its more diligent activists in terms of the wards they will be permitted to represent? For a person who desires a political career in local government, it obviously makes a difference whether he is accepted to fight for a seat in a safe Labour ward, for a winnable seat in a marginal ward, or for an unwinnable seat in a Tory ward. The ward members decide whom they wish to interview, but they are required to interview any incumbents who desire to stand again. In addition, the Executive Committee may send along potential candidates to be considered, and it can make recommendations to each ward. Thus, opportunities exist for the party to sponsor the candidacies of deserving stalwarts and, conversely, to shift its preference from those whose performance may not be up to acceptable standards. It is not difficult to cite instances of incumbent candidates having to shift their base of operations to a marginal ward or even a less hopeful site because they had been denied readoption by their party colleagues in a safe ward on the ground that they had 'neglected' their organizational responsibilities. But reliable data that go beyond the mere citation of anecdotes are hard to come by. We cannot derive any information from South Kensington for this purpose, since the party there had no real ward candidacies of its own to distribute. Nor can we use the information from Bermondsey because for all practical purposes all of the wards were safe, and, besides, the candidates were given the option of selecting the wards they would like to stand for.

This leaves us with Fulham, and though it is only a single case, it is one in which the selection of council candidates was highly competitive. Although factional disputes over ideology sometimes entered the picture, there can be no doubt that energetic performance in party work was an important consideration. Indeed, negative sanctions for neglect of duty were applied in a few instances during the course of this study. We at least address the issue when we compare the mean party involvement scores of candidates who stood in Fulham's safest wards (Walham, Sands End, and Munster) with those of candidates who went to the doorsteps in the more marginal areas (Town Ward and Hurlingham Ward). The involvement scores were: candidates in safe wards, 6.50; in marginal wards, 4.50. We should also note that while more than two-thirds of the Labour councillors from Fulham represented the wards they lived in, some of them left their home districts to win acceptance in safer areas, and their mean party involvement score was 7.33. We should note, too, that the newcomer candidates in Fulham (average age 32) had already turned in good records of party service; their mean involvement score was 6.25.

The effect of the competitive environment in Fulham on career advancement can be seen in another way: the length of time a person served on the GMC before taking a seat on the council. The Fulham activists who joined the Labour Party after the war had to serve only 2.8 years on the GMC before they entered the council chamber. The comparable figure for Bermondsey was 4.3 years and for South Kensington, 5.3 years.

Once the election has resulted in a Labour council, the Labour Group is faced with the task of allocating the committee assignments and the council offices. It should be recorded that, under a recent rule change, the GMC has the right to submit names for consideration for the mayoralty and aldermanic posts and for other council offices, although the decision lies with the Labour Group.[23] We are faced with the question, then, of whether the councillors take assiduous party and council work into account when they make the appointments that are within their jurisdiction. In order to examine the hypothesis in this context, we divided the respondents from each constituency into three categories on the basis of their party involvement scores – high, moderate, and low. We then calculated the mean council involvement scores (based on council positions held in 1961–62)[24] for each category. The scores are:

Mean Council-Involvement Scores

Party Involvement	Bermondsey	Fulham	South Kensington
High	2.09	2.08	0.43
Moderate	1.32	0.86	0.12
Low	0.85	0.23	0.23

This table has some interesting findings. Turn first to Fulham, where preferment was the most competitive. Obviously, a close relationship exists between high party involvement and responsibilities held in the council.[25] When we look at Bermondsey, the situation is slightly different. To be sure, there is still the same relationship between high party involvement and high council involvement. But, compared with Fulham, council involvement is a bit higher than we might expect for the people who have only moderate or low party involvement. This can be explained on two grounds. First, some of the Bermondsey folk who were elected to the council gave some of their effort to the trade unions – a form of activity that was very much respected in that constituency. Second, it was sometimes a job to get a full roster of council candidates, and the relative lack of competition meant that they occasionally had to fall back on people who had little experience, or whose party work recorded was a bit thin. The figures for South Kensington appear to be somewhat ragged, but actually they lend some support to the thesis. As we know, the South Kensington party did not have any influence on borough council candidacies or council assignments; those matters were decided by the sister organization in North Kensington. It is important to note, though, that the South Kensington people who held seats on the borough council had high involvement scores for work in their own party. Without some work in the South Kensington organization, they could hardly expect to become known to the activists in North Kensington who made the decisions on the inducements they were interested in.

Another reward for loyal party effort which a constituency party has at its disposal is appointment to the aldermanic bench. Traditionally, appointments as aldermen were a civic honor bestowed upon people who had valued experience in local affairs and had performed distinguished service on the borough council and in the community; the six-year term was established to provide continuity of expertise. As political parties developed in the boroughs, it became customary in many places for the aldermanic posts to be divided proportionally among the competing groups. In recent decades, however, the Labour party – like the Conservatives – has often manipulated the aldermanic appointments so as to increase its majority in the chamber. Not faced with the problem of Tory competition in the council, Bermondsey tended to appoint its aldermen from the ranks of senior councillors who had rendered faithful service to the Labour movement in their borough. Fulham, too, sometimes honored its party veterans by aldermanic appointment, but usually it took a more practical approach to the bench. At times the party people felt a need to increase their voting strength in the council, and in 1962 they reserved one of the posts for a younger member who had barely missed victory when he stood for a council seat in the strongest Tory ward. When Labour controls the borough council, the party people who have been elected to the council in effect determine the allocation of the aldermanic positions. Under ordinary circumstances they are unlikely to bestow such rewards upon individuals whose work record is below the level of expectation.

Civic Positions. We have already noted that a large number of the activists, especially in Bermondsey and Fulham, were busily engaged in the work of school governors and managers, hospital boards, and other civic bodies. Most people sincerely viewed these endeavors as contributing to the betterment of conditions in their communities. Such work, of course, often brings satisfactions of a different sort, including visibility and respect for the individual in the locale. The people who are interested in such civic appointments are usually able to receive them only through association with the party.

One of the more important civic positions which involves both service and prestige is that of justice of the peace. This post, which reaches far back into England's rural past when the justices were people of social standing in their counties, carries with it judicial and some administrative responsibilities. Sometimes facetiously referred to as a 'poor man's baronetcy', it requires service several times each week, and ordinary workers often experience difficulty in fitting its demands into their job schedules. For this reason an appointment as justice of the peace may be more attractive to Labour people in the professions or in business who are in a better position to adjust their regular work to the responsibilities of the office. In any event, the justices of the peace are in effect selected by advisory committees, to which the local parties and other voluntary associations submit names.[26] In other words, a local Labour party is in a position to make nominations, and its nominees are usually chosen from the ranks of its diligent activists.[27]

The most sought-after civic position, however, is that of mayor of the borough, a post that is filled through election by the councillors and aldermen. The recipient of this 'prize' has the privilege of wearing the chain of office for a one-year term. While serving as the ceremonial 'monarch' of the borough, the mayor cuts his formal ties with his party so that he can preside in neutral fashion over the local 'parliament' and the civic affairs of the community. Most of the Labour people who are selected for this role accept it at a financial sacrifice, for they have to take leave from their regular jobs and the expense allowance is usually inadequate to cover the cost of official entertainment. Nevertheless, the 'Dick Whittington spirit' is very much alive in Labour-controlled councils, and a good number of activists look forward to the day when they can take their turn in the mayor's office. In a Labour-controlled area, the people who select the mayor are the Labour members of the council. That they are unlikely to choose a person who has failed to do his share of doorstep work can be seen in an examination of the party-involvement scores in the three constituencies. The mean involvement score for all of the respondents in the population was 4.10, but the score for those who had either served as mayors since 1950, or became mayors shortly after this study was completed, or indicated a desire to become mayor was 6.48.

The Constituency Party and Its Supply of Inducements

From our discussion of inducements for party service, we can recognize a convergence, in important respects, between the 'desires' and 'wants' of the individual activists and the interests and objectives of the local party organization. Although the 'incentives' were limited in all three parties and more were available in one party than in another, each was in a position to allocate some 'rewards' to individuals who had worked resolutely for the cause.

As mentioned earlier, it is extremely difficult to disentangle the effects of *normative* and *personal* incentives, partly because many Labour people seem to be stimulated by both types. The researcher can easily be swayed by the personal rewards because the evidence, though usually circumstantial, is easier to collect. But in this study a sizeable number of activists showed signs of being motivated to a large extent by normative concerns; their avowed interests were to serve the organization and to help it achieve its socialist goals. For the people who desired sustained involvement directed toward social reform at the local level, the Labour party probably had more to offer than alternative voluntary associations. The organizations in Bermondsey and Fulham were endowed with local prestige, and the political power they commanded could be turned toward social ends. This meant that the parties in these two districts had something to offer those activists who were devoted to the socialist mission and had no other vehicle available to them. Needless to say, the parties in Bermondsey and Fulham welcomed the services of these dedicated people and put their talents to good use. The Labour party in South Kensington enjoyed little prestige in the community, but it nevertheless attracted a group of keen activists who were willing to work hard under its auspices. They had to be strongly motivated to pursue their activities in such barren terrain where visible results in the foreseeable future obviously could not be achieved. Despite the poor prospects, they designed an agenda of political work aimed at helping the Labour cause beyond the boundaries of their own constituency. To be sure, a good number of the South Kensington people labored industriously because they had political ambitions. But a significant number of them who apparently nurtured no such aspirations also gave a large amount of their time to the party. The reader will recall that some of these people felt compelled to take seats on the GMC because they 'had an obligation to serve'.

An aspect of the normative inducement is the desire to discuss issues and to hammer out policy, since this type of activity is related to the 'socialist' end. On this score the opportunities offered by the three parties differed. Probably Bermondsey provided the greatest scope for such endeavor. As we have seen, the Bermondsey GMC devoted more of its discussion time to contemporary issues; apart from the discussion in the Labour Group on the council, the GMC was the only place in which differing opinions on vital questions could be aired. The Fulham party, more taken up with organizational matters pressed upon it by its competitive environment, spent comparatively less of its meeting time on divisive issue questions. In South Kensington, the moderates in control of the organization sought to avoid disruptive arguments over issues in their GMC meetings. The monthly forums in South Kensington were designed to take care of such deliberation; but these were hardly a 'reward' for those who worked hard for the party, since anyone could attend and derive the benefits without having to share the burdens on the doorstep.

In considering personal inducements, we can make two statements to start with. Social interaction was not a significant incentive to encourage hard work on the part of the activists. Nor was the prospect of being elected to a seat on the General Management Committee a noteworthy inducement. If, in places like Bermondsey and Fulham, people were rejected for GMC posts on grounds of inadequate performance, it was a relatively simple matter for them to go to their trade unions or other affiliated organizations and win seats through that route. The lack of trade unions and Co-operative organizations in South Kensington rendered such a procedure almost impossible, but the mobility of the population resulted in frequent GMC vacancies so that those who wanted to serve could do so with little difficulty, regardless of their work records. The most important rewards for the energetic appear to have been some party offices, assistance in launching parliamentary careers, and especially the allocation of positions in local government.

Personal inducements in a safe labour constituency. In a constituency that lacks a competitor, dedication must replace the lure of political excitement. Usually the local party gets caught in the chains of its secure environment: apathy creates a recruitment problem – the organization tends to age – low turnover and slow growth diminish promotion opportunities – the dim prospect of preferment exacerbates the recruitment problem. All of this means that, although the party has many positions to fill, it often encounters difficulty in filling them. The lack of competition for posts thus renders the organization incapable of maximizing the inducements it would ordinarily have at its disposal.

Except for the party chairmanship and an occasional ward office, the activists do not compete for posts in the organization; indeed, people have to be encouraged or persuaded to take on these responsibilities. Under such circumstances, most of the party offices cannot be regarded as awards for resolute service. In addition, the party cannot make much use of the 'launching a parliamentary career' incentive; not many people in a working-class community entertain such aspirations, and the few who do are dependent more upon their trade unions than they are upon the local party.

The biggest inducements available to a party in a safe Labour area come in the form of local government positions. But here again their use is circumscribed. The wards, to be sure, can occasionally apply negative sanctions against incumbent councillors whose performance does not meet accepted standards. But the need to fill such a large number of council seats from a limited pool of aspirants means that the party does not have much control over the panel of candidates. Moreover, it is estopped from rewarding its best workers with safe-ward candidatures because all of the wards are usually secure.

Important rewards are available and can be used, however, when it comes to selecting people for positions that are within the domain of the borough council – the chairmanship of important committees, assignment to desirable committees, and, of course, the office of mayor. The party – through the borough council or by itself – can also be influential in appointments to such posts as school managers, membership on health boards, justices of the peace, and the like. It is in this domain that the party members in a safe Labour area can judge their peers and vote in support of those who have rendered conspicuous service to their organization.

Personal inducements in a marginal Labour constituency. The political challenge confronting the Labour party in a marginal constituency makes recruitment less of a problem. A larger reservoir of workers for not quite so many posts generates more competition within the organization, thereby making the operation of the incentive system potentially more effective.

Compared with a party in safe Labour territory, the party in a marginal constituency is likely to have more activists who are interested in holding party offices if for no other reason than they are younger and want to gain political experience. Not only is the party chairmanship sought after, but also the ward seats on the Executive Committee and occasionally the post of secretary or chairman in the wards.

In addition to the rewards of party office, the Labour organization is in a better position to elicit the services of people who aspire to become M.P.s. Since it draws upon the middle class for some of its members, more of its activists see entry into parliament as a political goal, and they are dependent upon the party to help them get on the B List of candidates. *If* a good record of work in their local party is helpful at all, the activists have opportunities to compile one in this type of environment. Such a record may give them the visibility that will help them in other constituencies and will enable them to have respectable résumés so that an Executive Committee searching for a candidate will not be tempted to keep them off the short list because they have not been steadfast in handling their responsibilities on the home ground. At the very minimum, the local party is able to give them experience in public speaking and in political organization which is essential for those who wish to move beyond the local scene.

In terms of positions in local government, the party is also in a position to give more recognition to its hard-working activists. Since the number of aspirants for council seats invariably exceeds the number of candidatures, the wards can afford to reject those with deficient records. Moreover, since some wards are safer than others, the party can move its most devoted people into the safe-ward candidacies so that they do not have to spend so much time working a marginal area with the risk of defeat.

When it comes to assignments to council posts and civic positions, the party has access to nearly all of the awards that are available in a solidly Labour district, including committee chairmanships, aldermanic posts, justices of the peace, and the mayoralty. Given the higher degree of competition which characterizes its operations, the party is in a much more favorable position to make distinctions between those who deserve recognition for their diligence and those who do not quite measure up.

Personal inducements in a hopeless constituency. A Labour party tilling infertile soil is beset by all of the problems that afflict a party in a Labour stronghold and at the same time has few of the rewards that are at the disposal of a party in a marginal district. As we have already noted, the hopelessness of the cause generates long-term apathy, making recruitment a serious problem and thwarting the development of competition among the activists for political advancement.

A party in this type of environment has very few attractive posts under its command. While the party chairmanship may be in contention most of the time, sometimes it is not, and the party is often reduced to calling for volunteers to fill the other major constituency offices and all of the ward posts. Borough council candidacies and other civic positions are not within its discretion but are distributed – if they are available at all – by the neighboring party at the other end of the borough. While the person who wants to become a councillor may be inspired to work for his own party so that he can attract the attention of the activists in the party next door which may have candidatures to distribute, he naturally turns his attention to the other organization which becomes a strong competitor for his time.

This leaves us, then, with one other personal incentive to consider, assistance in launching parliamentary careers. The party can help its parliamentary aspirants to get on the B List and, more important, it can give them some political experience. It even has parliamentary candidature which can serve this purpose and which can be awarded to one of its own people. As we have already seen, many South Kensington activists had parliamentary aspirations and were seriously interested in getting some experience in practical political work. To be attractive to individuals who entertained no desire to enter the House of Commons, however, the party had to rely upon normative incentives or to attempt to harness their energies because they liked politics. (For the convenience of the reader, the author has drawn up a summary list of incentives by constituency characteristics in Table 7.5. Within the normative and personal incentive groups, the various inducements are rank-ordered according to their importance, but the rank-ordering is merely impressionistic.)

In concluding this section on inducements for party service, we must remember this important point: any rewards at the disposal of the party – whether it operates in a safe, marginal, or hopeless area – are dispensed by the local activists themselves. The 'reward system' is not even under the control of the agent. It is administered in a group context, and an individual's work record is taken into account in many instances. In other words, the most actively involved workers who are in a position to assess the situation pass judgment upon the effectiveness of the contributions made by their peers. This becomes an important source of strength for the local party because it is often able to give desired recognition to the people who exert substantial effort in the organization's behalf.

Table 7.5 Inducements available to the local party

Safe Area		Marginal Area		Hostile Area	
Normative		Normative		Normative	
Help the cause		Help the cause		Help the cause	
Discuss issues affecting locality		Discuss broad issues and issues affecting locality		Discuss broad issues	
Personal		*Personal*		*Personal*	
Council positions		Council positions		Help in launching parliamentary career	
Committee chairmanships		Committee chairmanships		Political experience	
Committee assignments		Committee assignments		Parliamentary candidature	
				Initiate proceedings for B List	
Civic posts		Civic posts			
Mayor		Mayor			
Justices of the peace		Justices of the peace			
School managers, etc.		School managers, etc.			
		Borough council candidatures			
		Safe			
		Marginal			
		Less desirable			
Party posts		Party posts			
Party chairmanship		Main party offices			
		Membership on Executive Committee			
		Ward secretary or chairman			
		Help in launching parliamentary career			
		Political experience			
		Initiate proceedings for B List			

8 Summary and Conclusions

To summarize the study of three very different local Labour parties along the various dimensions is not an easy assignment. If it is too detailed, it grows tiringly redundant; but if it is too brief, it is of little more use than a street map of New Underwood, South Dakota. In this concluding chapter, we shall bring the main threads together under the following topics: the impact of environment upon the structures and operation of the three parties; the three constituency parties as organizations; class patterns in the analysis of salient issues; constituency marginality and ideological moderation; and the inducement system.

THE IMPACT OF ENVIRONMENT

The organization literature offers little concerning the impact of the socio-economic environment upon the structure and operation of voluntary associations, especially political parties. This study shows that the environmental repercussions on a local Labour organization can be profound, and while some of these influences are self-evident, we can derive some benefit from specifying them in at least summary fashion. Obviously, the socio-economic character of a parliamentary district stamps its print upon the social structure and establishes a spectrum of social and political issues to be decided. The social structure, in turn, is an important determinant of political values, political attitudes, and political preferences. The socio-economic composition of the population will determine whether the Labour party is challenged by a viable opposition, whose presence or absence will affect the goals of the organization. The social structure of a community also influences the size of the pool of potential recruits from which the Labour activists will be drawn. In addition, a stable or an unstable population is likely to have an effect upon the stability of the local party, and this will influence both the recruitment of new members and the operation of the 'reward' system.

Assuming that the local party wins its battle for survival in a politically secure environment, we can safely say that the more solid the Labour area, the more stable the party structure. Working-class people are not usually geographically mobile, and the activists who are attracted to the organization tend to remain associated with it for long periods of time. As veterans in a party that is never threatened by the opposition, they develop routinized ways of dealing with problems which have an element of 'sameness' about them, and the patterns of response gain sanctity with age. Since the political monopoly is beyond challenge, the party's main goals remain unchanged. Even the idea of helping out in the marginals may encounter some resistance, and when the obligation is accepted, it is often ranked in second place behind the work in the home garden. Furthermore, long residence in a working-class community, where the life experiences are similar, fosters the growth of common values and perspectives which are reinforced by tightly-knit social bonds. The attitudes of the older people who have grown up with the organization are often colored by their memories of personal deprivations, and these tend to be picked up by the younger folk who respond to their elders with understanding and respect. The ideological milieu can hardly be classified as 'extremist'; it is more the 'traditional socialist' outlook, with widespread support for nationalization and the social services rather than unilateralism and other intermittent crusades. The disagreements that arise are rooted not so much in ideology as in differing approaches to the resolution of the workaday problems that fall within the jurisdiction of the town hall. Here the clash of opinions may be aggravated by the existence of two centers of power – the General Management Committee and the borough council chamber. The lack of real contest with the Tories, of course, inevitably results in apathy, and this, combined with the low turnover of activists, gives rise to recruitment problems. The limited intake of new members, especially young people – whether stemming from declining interest or the perception that advancement opportunities are meager – means that the organization denies itself the fresh ideas and the enthusiasm they might bring to it. Equally important, the stability of the party, lagging recruitment, and the low degree of competition for posts that must be filled tend to obstruct the working of the incentive system, even though the organization has a good supply of inducement resources at its command.

A Labour party in a marginal constituency operates, by definition, in an insecure environment. Even though it has to contend for power against a lively opposition, it often has to work through a party structure which is less stable than that found in a safe district. In the first place, the higher rate of population movement into and out of the constituency makes for some turnover of personnel within the organization. This can result in an influx of new ideas which challenge the 'traditional' way of doing things. Then, too, the more heterogeneous social structure is reflected in a greater variety of social groups that are attracted to the organization, resulting in a mixture of values, ideas, and attitudes, which often adds an ideological dimension to personal differences. Discord may also arise when a growing threat from the opposition dictates changes in party strategy which may be regarded by some activists as 'goal displacement'. Higher activist turnover, of course, opens up opportunities for preferment, and this, together with the expectation of political excitement in a contested arena, makes the recruitment problem a bit easier. The infusion of new blood and the resulting competition in the filling of posts obviously have an effect upon party stability, but they also render the incentive system more workable.

The Labour party in a hopeless constituency is the least stable of the three. The potential clientele of the organization is usually disproportionately represented among the large numbers of people who are forced to move out of the high-rent districts – and this, combined with the futility of the cause, creates a serious recruitment problem. The newcomers who move into the party as replacements have less opportunity to be socialized in the mores of the group by 'old-timers', and the lack of an effective 'organization memory' renders them less knowledgeable about previous routinized procedures and frees them from the constraints of precedent. Moreover, since the party operates on the fringe of a middle-class-dominated culture, it draws from the non-manual stratum a group of activists who are at odds with their own social class. Hence, the party can hardly escape intellectual jousting and the sharp clash of ideas, with the likelihood that ideological splits will be interwoven with personal rivalries. Disagreements may emerge over the question of what the party's role should be – whether it should function as a 'sect' or as a 'missionary' organization. The turnover of personnel can lead to abrupt changes in goals and tactics, as when a 'moderate' group is depleted by removals and ideological enthusiasts move in to take their place. The instability of a party in hopeless territory naturally results in rapid promotion of a limited sort (such as being elected to the GMC shortly after arrival in the community), but the party usually has few tangible rewards to bestow upon its hard-working activists. It has to depend largely upon their desire for practical experience in politics and upon their sense of dedication to the larger movement.

In more specific terms, we have noted the impact of environment upon the voting patterns in the three constituencies – a situation that was hardly surprising. It was to be expected, too, that the Bermondsey party would draw heavily upon the manual workers for its GMC delegates, that Fulham would recruit a sizeable proportion of its delegates from the ranks of clerical people, and that the South Kensington organization would have a disproportionately large representation from the professional/managerial class.[1] More interesting was the environmental influence upon the social composition of the borough council candidates.[2] In their social characteristics, the opposition candidates in Bermondsey bore a fairly close resemblance to the Labour people, and this was even more the case in Fulham. In South Kensington, however, the Conservatives and Liberals recruited the bulk of their candidates from the professional/managerial category, while Labour drew its candidates in roughly similar proportions from both the professional/managerial group and the routine clerical people. With respect to trade union and co-operative affiliations, we noted that these organizations were significant in Bermondsey and somewhat less so in Fulham, but that they are virtually non-existent in South Kensington. The availability of these affiliations affected the operation of the local parties in two ways: (1) they were an important source of monetary resources; and (2) they provided alternative routes to the GMC when people were rejected by their wards, thereby influencing to some extent the functioning of the reward system.

THE THREE CONSTITUENCY PARTIES AS ORGANIZATIONS

In this section we need to make summary appraisals of the three parties, and we shall try to do this in terms of the constituency party profiles and the party functions which were set forth in Chapter 1.

Bermondsey. Operating in a working-class area where the crisis threats of an opposition were but memories, the Bermondsey party was so stable that its veterans were able to routinize their procedures and virtually convert them into traditions. The long-established power of the wards/areas, reinforced by independent financial resources and the inadequacy of the headquarters for all-party functions, resulted in a decentralized pattern of organization in which older people – dedicated and experienced – occupied key roles. The diffused authority relationships and the stabilized behavioral patterns made 'task' leadership difficult and 'maintenance' leadership even more necessary. Under conditions of stability and decentralization, the role of the agent as coordinator/manager became crucial, the encouragement and guidance offered by the M.P. was significant, and the flow of information from the units to the GMC and back again was a requirement.

The interests of the Bermondsey delegates were focused in strong measure upon the local scene and its two centers of power, the GMC and the borough council. Tension between these two groups was bound to surface from time to time, but the strong linkages between them, the regularized procedures for resolving controversial issues (like council housing rents), and the activists' long-term commitment to a social program enabled them to carry out their responsibilities with relative calm. Even the opposition could register few complaints about the way in which Labour managed the borough. Most of the political aspirations of the activists were locally centered, and efforts were made to feed talent into the council. The councillors were expected to do their work conscientiously, and negative sanctions were occasionally applied. The political leaders sought to interest new people in council work, and they sponsored a training program to prepare the candidates for their responsibilities.

When we consider liaison between public officials and ordinary citizens, the Bermondsey party has to be given good marks. The Member of Parliament, a native of an adjacent constituency, had come up through the ranks and thoroughly understood the problems and concerns of the Bermondsians. Unlike most M.P.s from impregnable districts, he had become a prominent national figure, assuming major responsibility in the Parliamentary Labour Party and in the Labour Governments. But these added responsibilities did not prevent him from taking care of the home front; he kept his eye on local problems and gave personal attention to the difficulties of his constituents. The Bermondsey party not only established liaison with the citizenry through formal mechanisms (the surgery and the advice bureaus), but it also picked up complaints informally through the wards and the GMC and transmitted them to the borough council.

Every Labour party in a secure political environment has to wrestle with the problem of apathy, which is reflected in poor voter turnout and lagging membership recruitment. The Bermondsey activists were concerned about doing well in their subdued electoral contests, and during the period of this study they compiled a good record. In the general election of 1964, Bermondsey suffered a smaller decline in voter turnout than most of the comparable districts in the London area, and the party scored the biggest majority of any organization in the group. Voter turnout was also improved in the 1962 borough council election, and the size of the Labour vote was increased over the previous campaign; indeed, the workers managed to convert Saints Ward from marginal to safe territory. In all elections, the activists sought to keep their majority formidable enough to maintain their prestige, but they still did not overlook the need to send some of their most experienced people to marginal districts, although this type of effort was not given as much emphasis as the agent wanted.

One might have expected the Bermondsey party to have an overwhelming recruitment problem. It could hardly offer its potential members exciting political contests, and, given the nature of the community, many local citizens could become involved in social interaction without having to rely upon the party. Then, too, the organization was not so dependent upon membership subscriptions as was the case with parties that had no trade union support. The Bermondsey people, however, paid attention to the recruitment of new members and they achieved better results than nearly all of the other parties in the 'safe' category. In fact, the number of names on the membership roster constituted a respectable percentage of the Labour electorate. The party seemed to experience more difficulty in persuading

Summary and Conclusions 317

new people to become actively involved in its affairs. The GMC delegates were conscious of the need to infuse the activist corps with young blood, and the agent and the M.P. made special attempts to encourage people to take more interest in party work. But, despite the fact that Bermondsey had a relatively young population, the GMC drew a disproportionately large number of its representatives from the higher age brackets, and it showed signs of aging. The shortage of active personnel meant that relatively few party posts attracted competitors and there was declining competition for council seat candidatures. As a consequence, the dedicated workers were over-burdened with responsibilities.

The Bermondsey party took its policymaking function seriously. It devoted a conspicuous amount of GMC time to the discussion of issues, and the area units submitted a number of resolutions during the course of the year, quite apart from the one that was to be sent to Conference. The activists as a group did not hold extreme ideological views, but a strong current of 'traditional socialist' feeling ran through the organization. In general, they fixed their attention upon local issues and upon those national questions that were likely to have an impact on their community (such as immigration and the Common Market). Compared with other organizations in safe districts, the party sent forward an average number of Conference resolutions, and these adhered to the expected pattern, being concerned with local issues and avoiding questions of foreign policy.

In terms of motivation for party service, it would appear that many Bermondsey people were influenced by normative incentives. They expressed a desire to engage in community welfare and service activities, and their work records indicated that they were quite heavily involved. Under their leadership, the area organizations carried out specific welfare projects, especially for the old people. The operation of the personal incentive system was thwarted by the relatively small number of activists and the large number of positions to be filled. Personal incentives worked more effectively in the distribution of council posts and in appointments to civic positions.

As one studied the Bermondsey party, one soon became impressed by that fact that its leaders were very much aware of the problems that beset an organization in a non-competitive political environment and were interested in doing something about them. In the absence of an effective opposition, they established an Action Committee which served as a mechanism for self-assessment. It drew representation from the various party units and from the borough council so that it was in a good position to detect problems and to solicit ideas that stood a reasonable chance of gaining acceptance. While the Action Committee was unable to win approval for all of its suggested reforms, it was the source of some important changes. The Bermondsey party was concerned about adapting to its environment, and it certainly did not fit the stereotype of a Labour organization in an impregnable constituency undergoing a process of decay.

Fulham. The activists in the Fulham party, who had to carry out their work in marginal territory, listed the winning of elections as their first priority. In pushing toward this objective, the party was able to be flexible in its overall approach largely because it could (if it wished) follow a centralized pattern of organization. Several factors combined to make such flexibility in organizational patterns possible: (1) the wards, which had access to only meager financial resources of their own, were oriented toward the central headquarters and the GMC, and they operated as units within an integrated party; (2) the location and size of the party premises facilitated the central direction of election campaigns and other activities; (3) when young people were moved into positions of responsibility, they were quickly socialized into the appropriate organizational modes by the experienced veterans and by the agent; and (4) the agent was respected for his organizational skills, and the people in the party's governing bodies were receptive to his innovative ideas. The role of the task leader is difficult in a marginal constituency because the party's heterogeneous composition tends to produce divergent outlooks. But in Fulham the recognized need to win elections dampened the fires of controversy at campaign time, and the activists' willingness to defer to the agent's organizational expertise enabled him to fill the task role effectively.

Although many of the GMC delegates were concerned about the broad national questions, their interests were for the most part deflected to the local scene. Under prompting by the agent, they perceived that if the party developed a good reputation in handling local problems, they would have an easier time electing their Member of Parliament. Their electoral success in council races, together with the favorable appraisal given reluctantly by the opposition, would lead one to conclude that the party rated good points for its management of the borough. The problem of the relationship between the GMC and the council is especially difficult in a divided borough, but the Fulham people were able to establish workable linkages between their organization, the Barons Court party, and the Labour Group. Although some GMC members aspired to enter Parliament, a larger number of them were interested in council service. The party claimed the allegiance of so many activists that competition emerged for the candidatures, thus making an incentive system operative. A well-planned training course for the aspiring council members prepared them for their new roles.

In terms of liaison between the public officials and ordinary citizens, the Fulham party would have to be ranked high on any listing. It not only sought to keep in touch through the advice bureaus and the M.P.'s surgery, but it also ferreted out citizen's complaints through informal contacts and brought them to the attention of the local authorities. In these contacts with the local community, the Member of Parliament played a strategic role. People respected him for his integrity and diligence, and they sought him out when they ran into personal difficulty. Moreover, a local resident could not fail to be impressed when a person of such national stature appeared on the doorstep in behalf of Labour's council candidates. Because he was such a 'good constituency man', the Fulham activists who disagreed with him on defense and foreign policy were unwilling to cross swords with him personally on these issues.

Apathy was not as formidable an opponent in this marginal district because the uncertainty of the electoral outcome generated some political enthusiasm. The competitive nature of Fulham politics meant that more tasks had to be carried out, and the party usually set up training courses so that the activists would be equipped to handle their responsibilities. A sizeable corps of people were involved in the parliamentary election of 1964, and the agent's thorough communications system insured proper coordination. In terms of voter turnout, Fulham was tied for first place in its category of constituencies. This was not reflected in a proportionately large shift of voters to the Labour column, however, because that shift had occurred, comparatively speaking, in the 1959 election. In the 1962 contest for the borough council, the size of the poll was also increased, and the Labour vote was augmented in three of the five wards, including the two marginal areas which were the most crucial and where much of the work had been concentrated.

Although apathy was more noticeable in the recruitment of new members, the Fulham party did quite well in resisting the general downward trend which was evident in the national organization. It ranked well above the average for the parties in its category, and the size of its membership roll as a proportion of the Labour vote was also above expectation. The Fulham organization stressed the importance of recruiting younger people, including young married women, and its age distribution was the most balanced of the three. The party was unusal in having an active branch of Young Socialists who were constructively involved in its work, and the GMC delegates were generally interested in entrusting the young people with responsibility.

The Fulham people devoted a good part of their discussion time to housekeeping matters and planning for the borough council campaign. But they were also concerned about policy issues, especially those involving local affairs. In addition to the Conference resolution, the GMC dealt with five statements submitted by the party's units, nearly all of them on local matters. In comparison with the constituency organizations in its group, Fulham was below the average in the submission of Conference resolutions, and it was distinctive in that the resolutions it did send forward avoided the defense/foreign policy syndrome.

Fulham, like Bermondsey, had a good number of activists who appeared to be motivated by normative concerns. They were caught up in welfare work and civic service, and they were dedicated to the improvement of life in their district. For those who held such interests, the Labour party was an attractive route for pursuing them. A sizeable proportion of the activists also indicated that they had political aspirations, and here the personal incentive system had a wider scope in which to operate than was the case in the other two constituencies. The ratio of aspirants to official positions made the competition relatively brisk so that the party could occasionally impose negative sanctions upon those whose work schedules had been too light and, even more important, could reward the people whose service had been meritorious.

The Labour party in Fulham adapted flexibly to its competitive environment. Each election was looked upon as a new challenge requiring changed strategy. The agent's systematic records were used to pinpoint weaknesses and to target particular social sectors and geographic areas for recruitment and other types of party effort. The activists recognized that young people would have to be enlisted if the organization was to be kept vital, and they sought to give them preferment. Despite sharp divisions over some issues, the Fulham party was a healthy, well-integrated organization; its objectives were clear-cut and widely supported, and it was able to achieve most of them.

South Kensington. Being called upon to operate in a hostile environment with rapid changes in population, the South Kensington party naturally suffered from instability. But this was not as serious an organizational problem as one might have anticipated. The party did not develop the types of procedures that sometimes become constraints, and the newcomers often brought in fresh ideas which the activists were willing to try. Moreover, people were reluctant to take on responsibilities as officials until they thought that their residence in the constituency would last for more than just a few months; hence the party's leadership corps was more stable than the GMC membership or the membership of the rank and file.

In view of the paucity of Labour supporters and the absence of a central headquarters with a full-time agent, the South Kensington party was reasonably well integrated. The wards, which were impecunious and lacking in long-established loyalties, did not develop parochial outlooks but were oriented towards the GMC, which served as an important center for the exchange of information. The party was held together by an enthusiastic group of party and ward officers who, under the leadership of the dedicated secretary/agent working without salary, sought to give the organization vitality and a sense of purpose.

Since it was generally recognized that the party was latently fissiparous as a result of ideological cleavage and the possibility of individual interests being diverted to adjacent constituencies, the leaders were determined to keep the organization intact by engaging its members in a variety of 'practical' activities. Thus the party opted to become a missionary organization rather than a sect, putting forward a set of realistic goals. Its objective during election campaigns was to tie down the opposition with token contests, while transferring most of its resources to marginal constituencies; its goal during the period between elections was to develop programs of political education for the general public with a view toward the initial recruitment of individuals regardless of what local Labour party they might join.

The problem of task and maintenance leadership is especially difficult in a constituency party of this type. A task leader is needed at election time to coordinate the division of effort between the home district and the marginals. A maintenance leader is necessary because middle-class people are inclined to resist edicts and because ideological splits have to be papered over. Since there is no Member of Parliament to assume the maintenance role, both the task and maintenance functions have to be handled by the voluntary secretary/agent or shared with someone else. For one person to take over both roles creates difficulties because the two are basically incompatible. Probably the best solution is to have the secretary/agent serve as the coordinator of the party's activities in the interim between elections and as maintenance leader during political campaigns – and to have some other individual become the agent/task leader at election time. In this way the 'hurts' inflicted by task directives issued under campaign pressure are of relatively short duration and are not tied to the person who is charged with holding the party together on a long-term basis; indeed, his position as coordinator will have been strengthened as a result of his maintenance role during the political contest.

The problem of apathy on the part of the Labour voters in South Kensington could not be attacked with immediate results. The activists worked very hard in the early stages of the 1964 parliamentary campaign and then pulled out at the strategic moment for work in other constituencies where the harvest was more promising. For them to have remained at home to turn out a slightly larger Labour vote would have been poor strategy, given their ojectivies. The same can be said of their activities in the 1962 council election; indeed, one could even question the advisability of using scarce resources for the preparation of an imaginative election address when a standard format would have been less expensive and would probably have served the purpose just as well.

The problem of apathy as reflected in membership recruitment was a bit more serious. While this study was under way, the South Kensington party did not carry out a systematic recruitment campaign; yet an increase in membership subscriptions would have improved the financial picture somewhat. As it was, the organization depended upon individuals taking the initiative themselves to become members, or upon existing members recruiting people with certain political orientations in order to bolster support for their respective factions. Given the lack of recruitment effort and the high turnover of rank-and-file membership, the party did well to keep its roll of members from being reduced in size. It should be pointed out, however, that the people who did come into the organization were enthusiastic and willing to work; the proportion of members who were actively involved in a party that faced hopeless odds was amazingly high.

The GMC members of the South Kensington party were very much interested in policy matters. The wards sent to the governing body about twice as many resolutions as the component units of the other two parties. Although a few of these resolutions dealt with local questions, the fact that Labour had little influence on the Kensington council stimulated the activists to address broader issues; besides, these were the issues that were congenial with their intellectual interests. Their interest in policy concerns, however, was not reflected in the GMC meetings as much as one would have expected. This was due in part to the desire of some of the officers to avoid ideological confrontation which might disrupt the organization and render it less effective in carrying out its practical tasks. Discussion of issues was also hampered by the need to spend time on housekeeping affairs and the relaying of information, since the organization did not have full-time staff and regular premises. Like most of the parties in its group, the South Kensington organization always sent a resolution forward to the Annual Conference; but the subject-matter of the resolutions did not conform to the pattern established by local parties in hopeless districts in that they did not deal with defense or foreign policy.

Normative concerns were noticeably evident among the South Kensington activists. Some of these people were issue-oriented, determined to keep the party on its 'socialist' course. Some who were more flexible about the party's program claimed no political aspirations but took an active role in the organization because they felt an obligation to do so. A good number of the South Kensington people, however, were avowedly interested in personal incentives because they had a love for politics and desired to pursue political careers. As we have seen, the party had relatively few personal rewards to offer its diligent workers. But the few it had were of some importance to individuals who wanted to gain political experience so that they might be better equipped to appear before a parliamentary selection conference. The activists who aspired to become members of the borough council had to turn their attention to the party in North Kensington, and this tended to make them somewhat ambivalent about the work at their home base.

When the author, in conversing with friends in other parts of London, mentioned that South Kensington was one of the parties he was studying, the usual response was one of implicit derision: 'What on earth does that group of "intellectuals" find to do there?' And when he outlined the party's goals and listed the activities designed to reach them, he would encounter reactions of surprise. As pointed out several times before, the South Kensington people could have retreated into a closed circle of ideological discussion and rabbit-chasing disputation, or it could — as it did — map out a set of objectives aimed at helping the Labour cause in a wider arena. Given the hopelessness of its environment and the severity of the problems it faced, one feels compelled to award the party a verbal medal for the way in which it adapted to adversity.

CLASS PATTERNS IN THE ANALYSIS OF SALIENT ISSUES

Although it was only a side excursion from the main journey through the three constituencies, we were able to examine the outlooks of the activists on a variety of important issues. The small size of the responding population diminishes confidence in the results in a number of places, but we can nevertheless draw conclusions about the class patterns in some of the issue responses and in some of the others we can suggest potential relationships which invite further examination.

The way in which the respondents located themselves on the social map varied according to type of community. The non-manual people in Bermondsey and Fulham strongly identified with the working class, while in South Kensington the tendency was in the opposite direction. Apart from the area of residence, education exerted the next greatest influence upon self-rating, with the elementary school people overwhelmingly listing the working class, those with secondary education identifying less strongly with that class, and the activists with university training claiming virtually no proletarian kinship. The evidence suggests that in the Labour Party the social gulf between the manual workers and the people engaged in routine clerical jobs was very small.

On 'humanitarian' and civil rights types of issues, the patterns we encountered were clear-cut and were congruent with the findings in the literature. The Labour party activists who had had the greatest exposure to working-class norms (in terms of social origin, education, occupation, and length of residence in working-class areas) favored restrictions upon immigration, the retention of capital punishment, and the regulation of the Communist Party. The middle-class respondents were clustered in the opposite corner on these issues, except that on the Communist Party question an element of the lower middle class engaged in routine clerical jobs united with the workers in support of restrictions. In this issue group we found that the class patterns were noticeably affected by age on the immigration question and by education in the case of capital punishment.

The same class pattern emerged when we analyzed the respondents' attitudes toward the reorganization of local government in London. The working-class group expressed stubborn opposition, while the middle-class people were much more responsive to the need for reform.

The working-class component of the population was distinctive in its support for the national Party leadership and traditional doctrine and in its opposition to the revision of Clause IV and to the idea of cooperating with the Conservatives. It was also opposed to Britain's entry into the Common Market, but its posture was not as strong as it was on these other issues. Again, the bulk of the middle-class respondents lined up on the other side of the fence on all of these questions.

The class patterns were not so clearly marked on the issues involving foreign policy and defense. The working-class activists were the least hostile to the Anglo-American Alliance, but sectors of the middle-class group were more divided on the issue. The middle-class element was also split on the unilateralist question, and although the number of unilateralists among the working-class activists was surprisingly high, they were not the most prominent group of disarmers. As we noted when we examined the Alliance and unilateralist issues, other factors appeared to be more important than social class.

Throughout much of the analysis of these salient issues, we observed deviant behavior on the part of two small groups: a core of professional/managerial people who subjectively identified with the working class, and an aggregation of people who objected to class designations and refused to commit themselves. In sharp contrast with the bulk of the people in middle-class occupations, the professional/managerial dissidents were the most supportive of traditional doctrine, the most skeptical of cooperation with the Tories, and the least sympathetic toward the Common Market. These dissentients, together with the 'won't commit' group, were the most favorably disposed toward unilateralism and the most hostile toward the Anglo-American Alliance. In addition, they were conspicuously suspicious of the national Party leadership and noticeably antagonistic toward the revision of Clause IV.

These groups were for the most part made up of people with a mixture of middle-class and working-class backgrounds who had completed secondary or training-school education and who held clerical jobs or positions in the non-traditional professions. On a good number of these issues they were joined by people who had similar characteristics except that their subjective class identification was more congruent with their occupational status. The reader will recall that we sometimes found significant differences in attitudes between the people in Groups I and II on the class scale. The people in Group II, which includes most members of the two deviant elements we have just discussed, represent a 'marginal' middle-class category, which is always difficult to analyze in the class terms because it is an 'in-between' group. It fits into an ambiguous category because its members are in a somewhat ambiguous social position. They meet the criteria of clear-cut classification in some respects but fall short of the criteria in other respects: they are beyond the level of elementary schooling, but they did not attend a university; they completed a distinctive level of education, but they have to be content with ordinary clerical jobs or professional positions that do not quite match those of more prestigious social standing. In other words, they have climbed up some rungs of the educational and occupational ladder, but other rungs are still ahead of them. Our study suggests that the outlooks and attitudes of these people differ significantly from the outlooks and attitudes of the people who fit the conventional standards for unquestioned middle-class ranking. Further investigation is needed to determine whether in fact the attitudes of the 'marginal' middle-class group differ significantly from those of the solidly middle-class category, and if they are important, we need some rigorously designed studies to provide an explanation of the differences.

Our research also suggests that in certain types of issues (such as defense) the period of recruitment will have an impact upon activists' attitudes. The small number of respondents made rigorous cohort analysis impossible, but we did notice certain attitudinal patterns among those who entered the Party during the peace struggle of the late 1930s and during the period of ideological upheaval in 1951–62. This was especially noticeable on the questions of unilateralism and the Anglo-American Alliance. We observed, too, that the veterans who had come into the organization before 1925 were strongly opposed to cooperation with the Tories and the revision of Clause IV. The possibility of employing cohort analysis on issues of this type is worth examining.

This study also suggests that when a single-issue 'crusade' (such as unilateralism) sweeps across the Labour Party, threatening to weaken its effectiveness, opposition will develop among those people who have been the most attached to and involved in the organization. Definitive statements about this relationship must await further study, but in this rather limited project it turned out to be quite strong.

CONSTITUENCY MARGINALITY AND IDEOLOGICAL MODERATION

During the last two decades Anthony Downs and other scholars have opened up an inviting terrace of research challenges on the relationship between the marginality of a district and the ideology of the political competitors.[3] The model that is relevant to this study hypothesizes that in a marginal district the competing candidates (and, of course, their parties) tend to move toward middle-point positions on salient issues in order to maximize their voting strength. Simply stated, the proposition is that constituency marginality (i.e., increased competition between two parties) attracts ideological moderation.

Some research findings presumably support the formulation and others call it into question. One reason why we are confronted with conflicting research results is that many of the studies did not subject the hypothesis to a direct test – that is, they examined the voting records of successful candidates from categories of districts after the election instead of analyzing electoral attitudes and party positions *within* contrasting types of constituencies during the campaign.[4] Moreover, to the author's knowledge, no study has involved an ideological party which is able to compete for power.

Although this analysis of three local Labour parties has only a trickle of evidence which can be channeled into a discussion of this problem, it is nevertheless worth looking at because it is based upon constituency data and not upon that deriving from parliamentary behavior, and because it deals with an ideological party which successfully competes for power.

According to the postulation, we would expect the Fulham party, which was forced to play the game of politics on marginal turf, to have been the most moderate of the three constituency organizations. Yet in all of the analyses we have made it turned out to be the most ideologically oriented. This means that on significant issues it was moving *away* from the Tories and away from what the experts would consider to be the middle-point positions of the electorate. Moreover, not once during all of the discussions held in the party during 1961–62 did any of the activists raise a question about whether an ideologically enthusiastic posture might antagonize strategic sectors of the voting public.

We would be inclined to pass this off as possibly idiosyncratic except that we recalled the results of the pilot study we made of Conference resolutions. In that study the constituency Labour parties in the most marginal districts – those in which the voters had switched from one party to the other – tended to be among the highest in submitting resolutions that were antithetical to the position of the national leaders, i.e., much less moderate.[5] If it persists in further in-depth studies, this phenomenon is not beyond comprehension. An ideological party in a highly marginal district draws its activists from a variegated social spectrum. Compared with safe Labour areas or those that are less safe but still have a substantial working-class base, a Labour party operating in a district that alternates between the two parties is likely to have a strong component of marginal middle-class people who have loaded their ideological guns against other members of their social class and are determined to push forward to the new Jerusalem, whatever the immediate cost.

It could be argued, of course, that the Party manifesto is written by moderate national leaders and that the attitudes of the local GMC make no difference in a campaign, and besides both the moderates and the ideologicals agree to an uneasy truce during the election period. This argument overlooks the fact that the national Party manifesto is often given a local interpretation and that in any event the policy struggles and issue stands of the local activists between campaigns get reported in the Tory press and help to create a general 'image' of the local party in the minds of the local voters. The author remembers that the unilateralists in the marginal constituency proudly displayed their CND buttons when the leader of the Party, Hugh Gaitskell, came to officially open the borough council campaign in the district. One thing is clear: the proposition that marginality promotes moderation needs further investigation at the constituency level; and the sample of cases will be enriched and the results more firmly grounded if an ideological organization from a different culture (such as the British Labour Party) is included in the study.

THE INDUCEMENT SYSTEM

The political motivations of people who are actively involved in an ideological party are complex and difficult to study. The author anticipated that some of the incentive/sanctions literature would be helpful in his study of Labour activists, but he did not find it very useful – and for several reasons: (1) Much of the literature, which is heavily influenced by the American experience, assumes that ideological parties are always out of power – that they put up candidates merely for the purpose of 'educating' the general public. The classification system does not provide for a category of ideological parties which actually compete for power because they have a chance of winning. The typology thus excludes a good number of viable political organizations in Western Europe and Japan. (2) Much of the literature also fails to take account of the *mixed* motivations of activists who attach themselves to ideological parties. Often the conceptual framework sets up particular motivations as 'ideal types', and the usual assumption is that people in ideological organizations are motivated only by 'purposive' incentives. No provision is made conceptualy for mixed or hybrid types, although reference may be made to their existence in concrete cases. But the researcher who braves the winds of the real world encounters many instances of mixed motivations and has to find some way to deal with them.

The problem of tracing the mixed motivations of activists in left-wing ideological movements is not easy to handle. Researchers will converse with people who claim to be motivated by devotion to the cause but who also express interest in certain objectives which can readily be classified as 'solidary' or personal. When pressed to make a choice as to which is the more compelling motivation, the activists in the ideological party will be strongly prompted to list the normative as having priority because the mores emphasize selfless dedication and are scornful of 'careerists'. Thus, sooner or later we are brought into the domain of psychology and are confronted with the question that scholars have met in other research areas: what really takes place in people's heads – is their *real* motivation for political activity different from what they say it is?

This study can do little more than point up the problem. The limited evidence we have unearthed suggests that some people were influenced primarily by normative incentives – that they were committed to the organization *per se* or were concerned about its ideological pronouncements – and were willing to spend time on the doorstep or to incur the wrath of their associates in defending the fine points of socialist principle. These people were incurring personal costs with no hope of direct benefit to themselves, at least in the calculable future.

In discussing the question of normative inducements, we must avoid underestimating the power that such incentives give to a local Labour party. The activists who are concerned about broad programs of social reform or who defend ideological positions in the hope that one day the socialist principle will be brought into full bloom have no realistic alternative to an association with Labour. As a rule, their interests cannot be well served through affiliation with intermittent associations. The Labour party is the one *enduring* organization which can fit their needs and desires. When we looked at the activists' voluntary affiliations, we saw how dependent they were upon the party machinery. In Bermondsey and Fulham, it was largely through the Labour organization that they became absorbed in civic and welfare endeavors. If the local Labour party were suddenly to disappear, a good many of the satisfactions that come to the people who are normatively involved would also vanish. Many local Labour leaders are probably unaware of the party's organizational power in this realm and do not make sufficient demands upon the people who are influenced by normative incentives and have no other appropriate political organizations available to them.

The study also indicated that a sizeable number of activists had 'mixed' motivations, apparently being oriented toward personal as well as normative concerns. We are not in a position to state that the personal-oriented motivations were more important than the normative, but the data suggest that personal incentives, even in an ideological party, carry some significance. Of special importance is the fact that the rewards under this system are distributed by the group – the people who are knowledgeable about the individual contributions to the party effort. The listing of inducements in Table 7.5 may be useful for a systematic investigation of the relative weights of the various incentives. At this stage we are inclined to make two tentative generalizations. First, a local Labour party in a safe district – which has relatively abundant resources – is constrained by personnel shortages from making optimal use of the personal incentive system. Second, a party in a marginal district – with comparatively fewer resources in terms of money, safe candidatures, etc. – is better situated than its counterpart in safe territory to make effective use of the system of personal inducements.

Professor Etzioni indicates that congruent relationships between type of organization and type of incentive/compliance structure are found more frequently because an organization that is characterized by this congruency is more effective.[6] This formulation does not seem to be applicable to ideological parties that seek to compete for power. Such an organization probably starts out by being congruent in that the primary emphasis is upon what we have called normative incentives. But as it becomes more successful in appealing for votes, in winning elections, and in implementing its platform (i.e., as it becomes more 'effective'), it gets command of a greater variety of incentives – both normative and personal – and this enables it to grow more attractive to different social groups, which in turn makes it even more successful. Under these circumstances, the pressure may be for an accommodation to a hybrid compliance structure rather than pressure toward congruency.

Of course, accommodation toward a mixture of incentives is sometimes difficult; our study has indicated the tension between the 'traditionalists' and the 'revisionists', which is often related to differences in activists' motivations. For a local Labour party to rely too heavily upon personal rewards is likely to create disappointments and some dissension, especially when its ideology proclaims the importance of the cause and the collectivity. Similarly, an over-reliance upon normative satisfactions can be unsettling because the doctrinal script is often unclear and its reinterpretation for electoral purposes can generate charges of goal dislocation by ideological enthusiasts. In other words, each incentive system nurtures its own set of problems for an ideological party. It is likely that both sets of problems come into play when a party develops a 'mix' of these rewards and satisfactions. But somehow or other, the desire to win at the polls in order to carry out programs of social reconstruction permits an accommodation to be worked out.

The three parties we have just studied managed to utilize both normative and personal incentives and to adapt to their local conditions. That these organizations were able to perform as admirably as they did is testimony to the effectiveness of their leaders and the dedication of their activists.

Notes

PREFACE

1. Bary Hindess, *The Decline of Working-Class Politics*, (London: MacGibbon & Kee, 1971) p. 17.
2. A. H. Birch, *Representative and Responsible Government* (London: Allen & Unwin, 1964) p. 240.
3. Reg Race, 'Attitudes to Political Activity', in Inigo Bing (ed.), *The Labour Party: An Organisational Study* (London: Fabian Society, Fabin Tract No. 407, June 1971) p. 7.

CHAPTER 1

1. Labour Party Constitution, Clause IV, 4.
2. Quoted in *A Pictorial History of the Labour Party, 1900–1975* (London: The Labour Party, Sep 1975) p. 64. See also *Report of the Sixty-First Annual Conference of the Labour Party*, 1962, p. 89. (Hereafter the latter source will be cited as *Annual Conference Report*.)
3. James Q. Wilson, *Political Organizations* (New York: Basic Books, 1973) Chapters 3 and 6 and especially pp. 46–9. Wilson's typology is based upon incentives/motivations and is greatly influenced by the American context. In his classification, an 'ideological' party is a subtype of a 'purposive' party, and the distinction appears to be the degree to which an organization pushes toward its image of a 'desirable state of affairs'. Some will argue that, in view of the diluting of the Labour Party's program in recent years, the Party will more appropriately fit the general 'purposive' or 'programmatic' categories. The criteria are a trifle ambiguous, but, in the view of this writer, the Labour Party – in recognizing the class basis of politics and in questioning the fundamental underpinnings of the *status quo* – rests more congenially in the ideological category. Its factional splits over socialist doctrine, which the writer has observed for several years both in the national Party and in local Labour parties, would support such a classification. Since Wilson lists the Non-Partisan League in the United States as an ideological organization, surely the British Labour Party should be similarly labeled. The treatment of the conflict over 'socialist principles' which appears at various places in this book presents additional evidence.
4. For a discussion of the reorganization of local government, see below, pp. 268–73.
5. See Richard L. Leonard, 'Grass Roots Electioneering', *Plebs*, Sep 1965, pp. 486–7.
6. See below, pp. 21–2.
7. *Annual Conference Report*, 1974, *passim*. The Conference made its decisions

on the reogranization of the Party on the basis of a two-year study made by the 'Simpson Committee'. The Committee submitted two reports: *Labour Party Interim Report of the Committee of Enquiry into Party Organisation* (London: The Labour Party, 1967) and *Labour Party Report of the Committee of Enquiry into Party Organisation* (London: The Labour Party, 1968). A similar study had been made in 1955 by the 'Wilson Committee': *Interim Report of the Sub-Committee on Party Organisation* (London: The Labour Party, 1955).

8. See the Model Rules for Constituency Labour Parties, *Annual Conference Report*, 1974, Appendix 3, pp. 345–52.
9. *Annual Conference Report*, 1974, p. 161.
10. *Report of the Committee of Enquiry into Party Organisation* (1968) p. 8.
11. See especially Inigo Bing (ed.), *The Labour Party: An Organisational Study*, (Fabian Tract No. 407, June 1971). This is a collection of thoughtful essays.
12. The reader's attention is called to the fine essay by Ben Pimlott, 'Are CLPs Necessary?', ibid., pp. 11–19. Negative findings on organizational impact have been reported by the authors of the various Nuffield Election Studies and by Dennis A. Kavanagh, *Constituency Electioneering in Britain* (London: Longmans, Green & Co., 1970) especially Chapter 4.
13. See Ben Pimlott, 'Are CLPs Necessary?', pp. 12–15.
14. One enterprising constituency party once undertook a study of council tenants' complaints, using survey research methods. The investigation resulted from a ward resolution calling the attention of the GMC to the problems of the tenants. (Barons Court Constituency Labour Party, *The Report of the Special Subcommittee inquiring into Council Tenants' Complaints*, 20 Jan 1967, mimeographed.)
15. A ward party with fewer than ten members can have only one delegate – the secretary or some other person.
16. When meeting to choose a parliamentary candidate, the GMC is technically called a 'selection conference'.
17. Allen Kornberg and Robert C. Frasure, 'Constituency Agents and Conflict in Labour Parties', *Political Quarterly*, Vol. 45, No. 4, (Oct – Dec 1974) p. 490.
18. For a treatment of the agent's responsibilities during an election campaign, see Rober T. Holt and John E. Turner, *Political Parties in Action: The Battle of Barons Court* (New York: The Free Press, 1968) pp. 41–5.
19. See A. L. Williams, 'Lessons of the 1950 General Election', *Labour Organiser*, Vol. 30, No. 349 (Apr 1951) p. 64; *Annual Conference Report*, 1976, p. 6. See also *Interim Report of the Sub-Committee on Party Organisation*, 1955, p. 17. In the 1974 October election, only 88 constituencies had full-time agents in their employ, while an additional 28 had the services of full-time agents who were handling two constituencies. The remaining 507 constituencies had to recruit voluntary workers as election agents, many of whom had served in that capacity during the previous campaign in February. The shortage of agents on a regular basis is especially serious in the rural areas. (*Annual Conference Report*, 1974, pp. 25, 232.)
20. See Richard L. Leonard, 'Labour's Agents', *Plebs*, Vol. 57, No. 10, Oct 1965. p. 15.
21. *Annual Conference Report*, 1974, p. 33.
22. Richard L. Leonard, 'Labour's Agents', p. 17.
23. Harold Croft, *Party Organisation* (London: The Labour Party, 1957). A

later edition suggested that 10 per cent of the vote in a general election is a modest target – or 20 per cent of the vote in a local election. (*Party Organisation*, 1966, p. 31.)

24. See *Annual Conference Report*, 1976, p. 61. Only 12 out of 623 local parties reported a membership in excess of 2000. (Ibid., p. 7.) See also *The Mechanics of Victory* (London: The Fabian Society, Feb 1962) p. 17. The number of people affiliating with the Labour Party through their unions peaked in 1957 and has declined only slightly since that time. Because the local parties are encouraged by the system of reporting to record a minimum enrollment, the official membership figures may be regarded as maximum calculations. In many constituencies – especially in the non-competitive areas – the actual number of individual members is less than the figure reported.

25. *Interim Report of the Sub-Committee on Party Organisation* (1955) p. 6.

26. See Robert T. Holt and John E. Turner, 'Change in British Politics: Labour in Parliament and Government', in William G. Andrews (ed.), *European Politics II: The Dynamics of Change* (New York: Van Nostrand Reinhold Co., 1969) pp. 56–64.

27. In reporting on Stafford Cripps' poor performance before the Party Conference that expelled him, Richard Crossman wrote: 'The Party likes to have a Left wing to challenge those in authority, and the Left has always received as much affection as anger from the rank and file . . . A Left may be fanatical and Utopian but it must never be dull.' *New Statesman and Nation*, June 3, 1939, p. 850.

28. Interview, *The Listener*, Oct 20, 1964, p. 656.

29. For the diagnosis presented by Hugh Gaitskell, see *Annual Conference Report*, 1959, pp. 105–14. See also Anthony Crosland, *Can Labour Win?* (Fabian Society Tract No. 324, May 1960); 'The Transition from Capitalism', in R. H. S. Crossman (ed.), *New Fabian Essays* (London: Turnstile Press, 1953) pp. 33–68. This outlook was later given support by a survey of popular attitudes conducted by Mark Abrams and his colleagues, *Must Labour Lose?* (Harmondsworth: Penguin Books, 1960). Subsequent research has raised some doubts about the validity of the general thesis. (See, for example, John H. Goldthorpe *et al.*, *The Affluent Worker: Political Attitudes and Behaviour* (London: Cambridge University Press, 1968); John C. Goyder, 'A Note on the Declining Relation between Subjective and Objective Class Measures', *British Journal of Sociology*, Vol. 26, No. 1 (Mar 1975) pp. 102–9.)

30. Richard H. S. Crossman, *Labour in the Affluent Society* (Fabian Tract No. 325, June 1960) p. 6.

31. *Glasgow Herald*, June 18, 1951.

32. For a discussion of the 'left' in local Labour parties, see T. E. M. McKitterick, 'Membership of the Party', *Political Quarterly*, Vol. 31, No. 3 (July – Sep 1960) especially pp. 315–18.

33. These caricatures have been drawn from such works as Sir Ivor Jennings, *Political Parties*, Vol. I (Cambridge: Cambridge University Press, 1960) pp. 278–85; from a variety of journalistic reports of election campaigns in daily newspapers and weekly magazines; and from conversations with Labour Party agents and officials in Transport House.

34. E. E. Schattschneider, *Party Government* (New York: Farrar & Rinehart, 1942) pp. 95–6.

35. That the problem has existed for some time is suggested by J. W. Raisin, 'London and Middlesex', *Labour Organiser*, Vol. 30, No. 349 (Apr 1951) p. 77.
36. *The Mechanics of Victory*, p. 17.
37. *An Economic Theory of Democracy* (New York: Harper & Row, 1957) pp. 117–18.
38. Mark Abrams, 'Politics and the British Middle Class', *Socialist Commentary*, Sept 1962, p. 9.

CHAPTER 2

1. See *Interim Report of the Sub-Committee on Party Organisation* (1955) pp. 22–23.
2. When two organizations wish to form an all-purpose party – and such a plan is 'practical' – the amalgamation is to be considered on its merits. An all-purpose party, however, is not allowed to embrace more than two constituencies, since it would grow 'unwieldy'. (See *Annual Conference Report*, 1974, p. 270.)
3. See 'Model Rules for District Labour Parties', *Annual Party Conference*, 1974, Appendix 6, pp. 359–61.
4. See the 'Rules for County Labour Parties', *Annual Conference Report*, 1974, Appendix 5, pp. 356–8.
5. For a treatment of the relationship between the Party Conference and the Parliamentary Labour Party, see below, pp. 52, 63–7.
6. See Sara Barker, *How the Labour Party Works* (London: The Labour Party, revised edition) p. 8.
7. For reports of regional council meetings and party work in the regions, see London Labour Party, *Annual Report*, 1961; *Report and Resolutions, The Labour Party, Scottish Council*, Mar 1966; *Agenda and Executive Committee Report, 27th Annual Meeting of the East Midlands Regional Council of the Labour Party*, June 21, 1969.
8. The author attended the Conference. The resolutions are recorded in London Labour Party, *Final Agenda, Forty-Eighth Annual Conference*, Mar 1962.
9. See David J. Wilson, 'Constituency Party Autonomy and Central Controls', *Political Studies*, Vol. 21, No. 2 (June 1973) pp. 169–70.
10. The best treatment of the National Executive Committee is found in Robert T. McKenzie's classic work, *British Political Parties: The Distribution of Power within the Conservative and Labour Parties* (New York: Frederick A. Praeger, 1964) pp. 516–31, 599–601.
11. *Constitution and Standing Orders of the Labour Party*, Clause VIII, 2(c).
12. For Conference rulings on some of the more serious cases of disciplinary action by the NEC, see *Annual Conference Report*, 1949, pp. 18, 112, 119–27; ibid., 1959, pp. 21–2; ibid., 1961, pp. 13, 246–7; ibid., 1974, pp. 36–7.
13. While no thorough-going study has been made of Transport House, one can gain a view of the responsibilities of the various divisions by studying the annual reports submitted to the Party Conference. Also to be considered are *Our Penny-Farthing Machine* (London: Socialist Commentary Publications, 1965), one of the authors of which was a former official in the national headquarters;

and Gerald Kaufman, 'Transport House: The Truth', *New Statesman*, May 7, 1965, pp. 706–7. *Our Penny-Farthing Machine* originally appeared as a supplement to *Socialist Commentary*, Oct 1965.

14. Sara Barker, *How the Labour Party Works* (London: The Labour Party, revised edition,) p. 4.

15. For a fuller treatment of the conflicts between the Party Conference and the Parliamentary Labour Party, see below, pp. 63–7.

16. Ian Aitken, 'The Structure of the Labour Party', in Gerald Kaufman (ed.), *The Left* (London: Anthony Blond, 1966) p. 30.

17. See, for example, *Annual Conference Report*, 1974, pp. 57–8, 71.

18. An illustration of such a policy statement is *Labour's Programme 1973* (London: The Labour Party, 1973). This resulted from the reports of a network of study groups, as well as rank-and-file discussion in the local parties.

19. See *Labour and the Common Market: Report of a Special Conference of the Labour Party*, July 17, 1971. Another special conference on the Common Market was held in Apr 1975.

20. Ibid., p. 42.

21. See *Annual Conference Report*, 1974, Appendix I, p. 325.

22. *Participation '69* (London: The Labour Party, 1969); *Participation '72*, (London: The Labour Party, 1972). See also L. J. Sharpe, 'How the Labour Party evolves Policies', *New Society*, Vol. 21, No. 511 (July 13, 1972) pp. 66–9. The Party has developed other policy discussion papers since the *Participation* series.

23. For a short discussion of how the resolutions are drawn up, see Richard Rose, *The Problem of Party Government* (New York: The Free Press, 1974) p. 201. For a description of how a constituency party formulated its resolution for the 1968 Conference, see Paul Foot's article in the *Sunday Times*, Sep 29, 1968.

24. The information on these resolutions is taken from George W. Jones, 'Who Opposes the Party Leadership?', *Socialist Commentary*, Oct 1962, pp. 12–14.

25. Saul Rose, 'Policy Decision in Opposition', *Political Studies*, Vol. 4, No. 2 (June 1956) pp. 131–2.

26. See *Annual Conference Report*, 1965, pp. 203–4.

27. The bases of representation are given in the *Party Constitution and Standing Orders*, Clause VI.

28. According to the Simpson Report, the 1966 Conference had on its agenda 556 motions covering 83 subjects, as well as two NEC policy statements, the report of the Parliamentary Labour Party, and several other reports. Decisions were made on only 25 of the 83 subjects. (*Labour Party Report of the Committee of Enquiry into Party Organisation*, 1968, p. 4.)

29. See *Annual Conference Report*, 1975, p. 335. See also ibid., 1974, p. 321; 1973, p. 341.

30. See *Annual Conference Report*, 1974, p. 145.

31. For an excellent treatment of political policymaking in the trade unions and their role in the Party Conference, see Martin Harrison, *Trade Unions and the Labour Party since 1945* (Detroit: Wayne State University Press, 1960) pp. 129–261.

32. See Keith Hindell and Philip Williams, 'Scarborough and Blackpool: An Analysis of some Votes at the Labour Party Conferences of 1960 and 1961', *Political Quarterly*, Vol. 33, No. 3 (July–Sep 1962) pp. 306–21.

33. Sir Tom Williamson, *Annual Conference Report*, 1960, p. 186. See also Hugh Gaitskell's statement, ibid., p. 201
34. Some mandated party delegates, of course, see fit to use their own judgment and are willing to risk censure by their home organizations. For the statement of a delegate who was prepared to violate the directive of her local party, see *Annual Conference Report*, 1958, p. 215.
35. See, for example, the statement of Charles Geddes, *Annual Conference Report*, 1955, pp. 165–6.
36. This analysis has been drawn from all of the Party Conference Reports since 1945. A catalogue of the issues on which the Conference delegates have rejected the advice of their leaders is as follows: defense policy, the Vietnam war, the military regime in Greece, Rhodesia, and the Common Market; education housing, the distribution of consumer goods, unemployment, prices and incomes policy, the development of coal resources, prescription changes, the economic policy of the Trades Union Congress, business mergers, motor vehicle insurance, public ownership, the legal status of Conference decisions, limiting imports on leather and textiles, the National Health Service, pensions, and care for chronically sick and disabled persons. The 1951 Conference was devoted almost entirely to the Party Manifesto, and the 1959 Conference was a postmortem on the general election of that year.
37. Since 1955, the Leader of the Labour Party in opposition has assumed authority to appoint Labour M.P.s who are not technically members of the parliamentary committee to certain 'shadow posts', where they handle special assignments during parliamentary debates.
38. For an account of a conflict between one of the PLP committees and an NEC study group, see Aitken, 'The Structure of the Labour Party', in Kaufman (ed.), *The Left*, p. 21.
39. For statements of this position, see the speech of Christopher Mayhew (*Annual Conference Report*, 1960, pp. 162–3) and Gaitskell's speech, previously cited (ibid., p. 201). A good treatment of the problem is presented in A. H. Birch, *Representative and Responsible Government* (London: Allen & Unwin, 1964) pp. 122–30.
40. See *Annual Conference Report*, 1970, pp. 181–2. See also *Let Labour Lead* (London: Victory for Socialism Pamphlet, 1961).
41. On the solidarity of the big trade unions during this era, see Stephen Haseler, *The Gaitskellites: Revisionism in the British Labour Party, 1951–61*, (London: Macmillan, 1969) pp. 23–42.
42. For an account of the struggle between Gaitskell and Bevan, see Hugh Dalton, *High Tide and After: Memoirs 1945–1960* (London: Frederick Muller, 1962) pp. 358–63, 408–10, 425–35.
43. See McKenzie, *British Political Parties*, pp. 597–631.
44. For detailed discussions of the question, see the issues of *New Statesman* from June 30, 1961 through July 28, 1961; Leon D. Epstein, 'Who Makes British Party Policy: British Labour, 1960–1961', *Midwest Journal of Politics*, Vol. 6, No. 2 (May 1962) pp. 165–82; Saul Rose, 'Policy Decision in Opposition', *Political Studies*, Vol. 4, No. 2 (June 1956) pp. 128–38; Robert T. McKenzie, 'Policy Decisions in Opposition: A Rejoinder', *Political Studies*, Vol. 5, No. 2, (June 1957) pp. 176–82. An excellent analysis of the problem in light of events in the 1950s and 1960s is found in McKenzie, *British Political Parties*, pp. 596–631.

See also Harold Wilson's statement at the 1970 Conference (*Annual Conference Report*, 1970, p. 184).

45. *Annual Conference Report*, 1948, p. 214. See also the statement by A. Len Williams, ibid., 1960, pp. 165–7; Morgan Phillips, *Constitution of the Labour Party* (London: The Labour Party, 1960) pp. 3–4.

46. According to some reports, Harold Wilson and the head of the Research Department in Transport House were involved in the writing of the 1964 Manifesto, and the NEC hardly had time to study it. (See, for example, Aitken, 'The Structure of the Labour Party', in Kaufman (ed.), *The Left*, p. 22.)

47. See *The Guardian*, Nov 28, 1968; Dec 19, 1968; *The Times*, Dec 2, 1968. See also Aitken, 'The Structure of the Labour Party', in Kaufman, *The Left*, pp. 21–4.

48. See David Butler and Michael Pinto-Duschinsky, *The British General Election of 1970* (London: Macmillan, 1971, pp. 59–61); Rose, *The Problem of Party Government*, p. 342.

49. See Peter Paterson, *The Selectorate: The Case for Primary Elections in Britain* (London: MacGibbon & Kee, 1967) pp. 58–63.

50. Austin Ranney, *Pathways to Parliament: Candidate Selection in Britain* (Madison: University of Wisconsin Press, 1965) p. 210. See also Michael Rush, *The Selection of Parliamentary Candidates* (London: Thomas Nelson & Sons, 1969) Chapter 8.

51. McKenzie, *British Political Parties*, p. 556.

52. Ranney, *Pathways to Parliament*, pp. 185–8.

53. A. D. R. Dickson, 'M.P.s' Readoption Conflicts: Their Causes and Consequences', *Political Studies*, Vol. 23, No. 1 (Mar 1975) p. 65.

54. *Daily Telegraph*, Apr 1–3, 1947; *The Times*, Aug 14, 1947. Blackburn followed a course of increased dissidence and eventually left the Labour Party.

55. For Walden, see *The Times*, July 1, 1968; Robertson: *The Times*, Dec 19, 1975; Colquhoun: *The Times*, Feb 2 and 21, 1977.

56. *The Times*, Sep 18–19, 1969; Oct 8, 14, 20 and 22, 1969; Jan 15, 1970; Feb 26, 1970; May 6, 1970.

57. This compilation has been made from an analysis of the *Resolutions for the 59th Annual Conference of the Labour Party* and the known views of the M.P.s on the defense question. Eighteen of the unilateralist resolutions sent forward by constituency parties were from those with unilateralist Members of Parliament.

58. Peter G. Richards, *Honourable Members: A Study of the British Backbencher* (London: Faber & Faber, 1964) p. 164. For an excellent analysis of the problem, see Leon D. Epstein, *British Politics in the Suez Crisis*, (London: Pall Mall Press, 1964) pp. 136–8, 205–10.

59. See *The Times*, Oct 22 and Nov 16, 1964; May 18 and 20, and Nov 27, 1965.

60. See Ranney, *Pathways to Parliament*, pp. 183–4; *The Times*, Apr 19 and 28, 1948; May 13 and 17, 1948.

61. For the details of this case, see Epstein, *British Politics in the Suez Crisis*, pp. 128–32.

62. Evans jumped the whip on the American Loan issue and the Bretton Woods Agreement in December 1945.

63. *Daily Herald*, Mar 26, 1953; *Observer*, Mar 29, 1953.

64. *Tottenham Herald*, Mar 14, 1961; *Daily Telegraph*, Mar 23, 1961.

65. In the period from 1945 to 1970 (when the rules on readoption were

relaxed), there were other cases of resignation by Labour members who objected to the leftward movement of the Party on certain issues. But the role of the local organizations in precipitating the resignations is not as clear as in the cases we have recorded.

66. *The Times*, Mar 8–10 and 28, 1968; Apr 8–10, 1968; *The Guardian*, May 8, 1968.
67. *News Chronicle*, Apr 30, 1951.
68. See, for example, *Northern Echo*, Apr 4, 1955.
69. *The Times*, Mar 27, 1961.
70. See *Yorkshire Observer*, Feb 12, 1951; June 30, 1952; *The Times*, Dec 14, 1954. For the censure of a left-wing M.P. by an affiliated trade union branch, see *Paddington Mercury*, Nov 17, 1961.
71. See *Annual Conference Report*, 1948, p. 17.
72. For the reaction of the local parties in Finsbury, Dulwich, and Nelson and Colne, see *The Times*, Apr 29–30, 1948; May 3–4, 1948; *News Chronicle*, May 2, 1948.
73. See *The Times*, Apr 30, 1948; May 11, 31, 1948; *Manchester Guardian*, May 3–4, 1948.
74. See Ranney, *Pathways to Parliament*, pp. 155–9; *Annual Conference Report*, 1949, pp. 18, 119–27.
75. Richards, *Honourable Members*, pp. 22–3. Transport House had to come to the rescue of several other Labour members on the German rearmament issue, including Herbert W. Butler, Hackney Central.
76. Ranney, *Pathways to Parliament*, pp. 188–90; *Daily Telegraph*, Apr 29, 1954; *Manchester Guardian*, July 26, 1954; Jack and Bessie Braddock, *The Braddocks*, (London: Macdonald, 1963) pp. 90–2.
77. Ranney, *Pathways to Parliament*, pp.190–1; *The Times*, Mar 17, 1955; *Daily Herald*, Mar 18, 1955.
78. In the period before 1970, the NEC did not always intervene to protect a sitting member who happened to be in difficulty with his local party because his views on a particular policy were unpopular, though congenial with those of the national leaders. In 1963, the General Management Committee of the party at Wolverhampton North-East voted 38 to 21 to request the M.P., John Baird, to retire at the next general election. According to Baird, the dissatisfaction arose because of his vigorous position against racial discrimination. He was associated with the left wing of the Party and had engaged in several floor rebellions. When he appealed his case to Transport House, the officials ruled that the local party had followed the proper procedures in trying to replace him. (*The Times*, Feb 6, 8 and 28, 1963.)
79. See 'Model Rules for Constituency Labour Parties', Clause XIV (7), *Annual Conference Report*, 1974, Appendix 3, pp. 348–9.
80. An American party does not provide this kind of protection for its incumbents. When a Congressman from a safe district runs into trouble, the organizational fight usually takes place in a primary election, and the national party rarely intervenes in a significant way, regardless of how loyal he has been to the party's leadership in the Congress. He will probably be given a small amount of funds from one of the Congressional campaign committees, but this is usually the extent of the assistance. Forced to mobilize local resources on his own, he has to appeal in the primary to an electorate that is likely to be less

moderate than the national leadership. If he loses – and this happens in a relatively few cases – he will be finished politically; at least he can entertain little hope of getting another constituency. But if he wins renomination in this safe district, he recognizes that he and his local supporters saved his political life. He then returns to Washington owing very little to the 'national team', and under the seniority principle he reassumes his powerful post as committee chairman in a diffused power structure. By the same token, even the legislators from marginal districts in a general election have to rely heavily upon the financial and human resources they can mobilize themselves. For an interesting bit of evidence on this point, see Frank E. Smith, *Congressman from Mississippi* (New York: Capricorn, 1967).

81. See *Annual Conference Report*, 1973, p. 11. *The Times* reported that at a meeting of the National Executive Committee James Callaghan expressed concern about extremist elements moving into some constituency parties, especially those that had eliminated their proscribed lists. (See the issue of Mar 25, 1976.) In late 1975, the National Agent submitted a report to the NEC of increasing attempts by people with Trotskyist allegiances to infiltrate local Labour parties. (*The Times*, Dec 12, 1975; Dec 2, 1976.)

82. *Annual Conference Report*, 1970, p. 158.

83. See *Annual Conference Report*, 1974, pp. 170–3. On attempts to get this idea endorsed by the National Executive Committee, see *The Times*, Jan 27 and 29, 1976; Feb 10, 1976; Mar 25, 1976.

84. *Annual Conference Report*, 1974, p. 173.

85. *The Times*, Feb 11, 1974. The party's case against Milne was issued as a fact-sheet advertisement during the campaign. The author visited the constituency during the election battle.

86. See *The Times*, July 20, 1974; Sep 12, 16 and 18, 1974. The issue for Sep 16 presents the local party's reasons for wanting dismissal and the M.P.'s reply.

87. *The Times*, Nov 17, 1971; Dec 7, 1971; June 20, 1972; Aug 4, 1972; Oct 4 and 17, 1972. Taverne's statement is printed in the Aug 4 issue.

88. *Daily Telegraph*, Nov 5, 1971; *The Times*, Dec 6, 1971; Mar 16, 1972. One of the pro-Marketeers who had to face the critics in his local party was Douglas Houghton, chairman of the Parliamentary Labour Party. After a three-hour discussion, the GMC delegates, by a vote of 18 to 3, approved Houghton's explanation of why he voted with the Conservatives for Britain's entry. E. L. Mallalieu was also called upon by his party at Brigg to explain his pro-Market vote. (*The Times*, Nov 16, 1971.)

89. For early accounts of the Prentice case, see the July 1975 issues of *The Economist*. *The Times* covered the case for more than two years. The most important citations are: 1975 – Mar 2–5, 20; July 4, 10, 17, 19, 21–2, 24; Nov 10–12, 27; 1976 – Jan 7, 30; Feb 26–7; Mar 10, 25; Apr 13; May 3–4, 11; Sep 20; Dec 9; 1977 – Feb 8, 24–6; Apr 9.

90. For the press reports, see *The Times*, Oct 28, 1974; July 25, 1975; Aug 11 and 23, 1975; Sep 15, 1975; Oct 16, 1975; Mar 1, 1976; May 27 and 29, 1976; Nov 19, 1976; June 26, 1976; July 3, 1976; Mar 12, 1977; *Sunday Times*, Feb 20, 1977.

91. *The Times*, Sep 22 and 25, 1975; Oct 25, 1976; Nov 25 and 27, 1976; Jan 17 and 24, 1977.

92. *The Times*, Nov 29–30, 1976; Dec 9, 1976; Feb 21, 1977.

93. *The Times*, Sep 11, 1971; Nov 9, 1971; July 2–3, 1976; Mar 12 and 21, 1977.

94. *The Times*, Oct 28, 1974; Aug 30, 1975; Oct 31, 1975; Feb 13 and 27, 1976; July 13 and 29, 1976.
95. *The Times*, Mar 15–16, 1977; Apr 5, 1977.
96. *The Times*, July 28, 1976; Aug 6 and 10, 1976.
97. *The Times*, June 26 and 30, 1975; July 21, 1975; Oct 23, 1975. The political committee of the London Co-operative Society indicated agreement with the restrictions imposed by the Yorkshire area council. According to the committee, their M.P.s could not be dictated to, but no one could make the Society pay funds to M.P.s or candidates who were out of sympathy with the political views of the organization. (*The Times*, July 2, 1975.)
98. The proportion of dissident M.P.s during the other intake periods was: pre-1964: 5 per cent; 1964–6: 13 per cent; 1966–70: 27 per cent; 1970–4: 21 per cent. The figure for ex-M.P.s who returned to parliament in 1974 was 21 per cent. The divisions used in this analysis are Prevention of Terrorism, Nov 28, 1974; Defense, Dec 16, 1974; Civil List, Feb 26, 1975; Defense, May 7, 1975; Counter-Inflation, July 22, 1975; Employment, Jan 29, 1976; and Public Expenditures, Mar 10, 1976.
99. For a discussion of the M.P.'s constituency business, see Richards, *Honourable Members*, pp. 169–78. See also the work by Raymond E. Wolfinger and his colleagues, 'Popular Support for the British Party System', which presents some interesting information on the expectations of Labour supporters with respect to their M.P.s. The authors are careful to present the methodological weaknesses of their study. (Paper presented to the American Political Science Association, 1970, pp. 11–14.)
100. See Robert E. Dowse, 'The M.P. and His Surgery', *Political Studies*, Vol. 9, No. 3 (Oct 1963) pp. 333–41; Rosemary Dinnage, 'Parliamentary Advice Bureau', *New Society*, Vol. 19, No. 491 (Feb 24, 1972) pp. 392–3; Lionel H. Cohen, 'Local Government Complaints: The M.P.s' Viewpoint', *Public Administration*, Vol. 51 (summer 1973) pp. 175–84.

CHAPTER 3

1. The three districts were greatly affected by the reorganization of the London boroughs in 1965. The borough of Bermondsey became part of the new borough of Southwark, the borough of Fulham was joined with Hammersmith to form the borough of Hammersmith, and the borough of Kensington was linked with Chelsea to become the borough of Chelsea and Kensington. The parliamentary constituencies, however, remained the same until the redistribution which went into effect in 1974 and which brought major changes to all three of them.
2. For the high points of Bermondsey's past, see E. J. Beck, *History of Rotherhithe* (London: Cambridge University Press, 1907); *Bermondsey Official Guide* (London: Pyramid Press, 1963); *The Official Guide to the Borough of Bermondsey* (London: Pyramid Press, 1960); Edward T. Clark, *Bermondsey: Its Historic Memories and Associations* (London: Elliot Stock, 1901); V. Leff and C. H. Blunden, *Riverside Story: The Story of Bermondsey and Its People* (London: Civic Publicity Services, Publicity House, 1965).
3. Since the completion of the research for this project, a new development program has greatly diminished the importance of the Bermondsey docks.

4. Leff and Blunden, *Riverside Story*, p. 9.
5. See ibid., pp. 7–16; Pearl Jephcott, *Married Women Working* (London: Allen & Unwin, 1962) pp. 40–52. Fenner Brockway gives an interesting account of life in Bermondsey during the pre-war period in his *Bermondsey Story: The Life of Alfred Salter* (London: Allen & Unwin, 1949).
6. See Jephcott, *Married Women Working*, p. 48; *Bermondsey Official Guide*, pp. 53–55; Leff and Blunden, *Riverside Story*, pp. 17–51. For an account of the changes made under the Labour council, see Brockway, *Bermondsey Story*, pp. 85–112, 163–74.
7. A man of pacifist convictions, Dr Salter served as the Labour Member of Parliament for Bermondsey West from 1922 to 1923 and from 1924 until his death in 1945.
8. Jephcott, *Married Women Working*, p. 51.
9. Leff and Blunden, *Riverside Story*, p. 45.
10. For the wartime devastation, see Leff and Blunden, *Riverside Story*, pp. 59–60.
11. Unless otherwise indicated, the statistics dealing with the socio-economic features of the three constituencies are drawn from census data. The Bureau of the Census made special runs for each constituency on a ward basis.
12. The affiliated branches included: Transport and General Workers Union, 28; National Union of Public Employees, 6; Amalgamated Engineering Union, 2; National Union of Railwaymen, 2; Electrical Trades Union; 2 Amalgamated Society of Woodworkers, 1; National Society of Operative Printers and Assistants, 1; Amalgamated Union of Building Trade Workers, 1; Transport Salaried Staffs Association, 1; National Society of Painters, 1; and Fire Brigades Union, 1.
13. This discussion of Fulham's history is basd on T. Faulkner, *An Historical and Topographical Account of Fulham, including the Hamlet of Hammersmith* (London: J. Tilling, Chelsea, 1813); *Fulham: The Official Guide* (London: Edward J. Burrow & Company, 1950); C. M. L. Wickham and F. E. Hansford, *The Story of Bishop Creighton House*, Fulham History Society Publications, No. 5, 1965, mimeographed.
14. Interestingly enough, the two areas were amalgamated again in the reorganization of London government in 1965.
15. These figures include Fulham workers who held jobs outside the district.
16. The affiliated branches were: Transport and General Workers Union, 4; National Union of General and Municipal Workers, 3; National Union of Railwaymen, 3; Electrical Trades Union, 2; Amalgamated Engineering Union, 2; Union of Shop, Distributive, and Allied Workers, 2; Amalgamated Society of Woodworkers, 1; Fire Brigades Union, 1; National Society of Pottery Workers, 1; National Association of Operative Plasterers, 1; Amalgamated Union of Building Trade Workers, 1; National Amalgamated Union of Life Assurance Workers, 1; and Vehicle Builders, 1.
17. For the history of the Kensington area, see William Gaunt, *Kensington* (London: Batsford, 1958); W. J. Loftie, *Kensington: Picturesque and Historical*, (London: Field & Tuer, 1888); *The Royal Borough of Kensington* (London: Edward J. Burrow & Company); Eric Whelpton and Barbara Whelpton, *The Intimate Charm of Kensington* (London: Nicolson & Watson, 1948).

18. For a discussion of the use of the concept 'social class', see Milton M. Brown, *Social Class in American Sociology* (New York: McGraw-Hill Book Company, 1963), especially Chapter 1.
19. The census divides the 'lesser skilled' into two groups: 'semi-skilled' and 'unskilled'. In this study, the two groups have been treated as a single category. Similarly, the professional and employer/manager groups have at various times been combined. Retired persons have been listed in the occupational grouping they were situated in prior to retirement; hence, the term 'gainfully employed males' includes them. The census breakdown takes into account both economic and social status.
20. In the census returns, about 19 per cent of the Bermondsey respondents did not disclose the extent of their formal education; the comparable figures for Fulham and South Kensington are 6 per cent and 9 per cent. The lack of response in Bermondsey was highest in three of the most heavily working-class wards – more than one-fourth of the sample.
21. Jephcott, *Married Women Working*, pp. 44–5.
22. This study does not record the full amount of housing constructed by the Fulham council, since it has allocated a good slice of its housing resources to that part of the borough which was included in the Barons Court constituency.
23. In the 1966 and 1970 elections, Bermondsey was in second place, behind Poplar, in terms of the size of the Labour vote in the London region.
24. The eight wards are: Abbey, Dockyard, Leathermarket, Neckinger, Park, South, Southwest, and Willow Walk. Interviews with party organizers also identified the five contested wards as the areas of greatest opposition strength in relative terms.
25. In reporting on education, the census uses age at termination of education. For the purposes of this table, we have converted the age categories to an approximation of educational level so that they would roughly correspond to the data for GMC membership. The percentages for the population do not add up to 100 per cent owing to the fact that the category 'current students' has been omitted.
26. The correlation between occupation and education is 0.69.
27. Many of the people who served on the General Management Committees of the three constituencies in 1961–62 were victims of the British educational system. Confronted by economic pressures at home, they were forced to terminate their formal education at an early age and had to develop their talents on their own, either by private study or through adult education programs. Two people in Bermondsey, for example, enrolled as 'external students' for university work and eventually won their diplomas through extension study. Several of the people in the other constituencies managed to complete their advanced training by winning scholarships to a university.
28. An 'active' trade unionist is defined as one who attended 'all' or 'nearly all' of the branch meetings. Some unions, of course, do not hold regular meetings, and when in some instances the union meetings conflict with GMC meetings, the most loyal party people opt to attend the GMC sessions. These figures apply only to the questionnaire respondents.
29. These figures cover all GMC delegates, including those who did not return their questionnaires.

CHAPTER 4

1. Although the Conservatives contested four of the thirteen Bermondsey wards in the 1962 borough council elections, they put up a full slate of candidates in only two of them.
2. After the reorganization of London, the six areas were converted into five wards.
3. The author's set of questions on the area organizations was returned by only two of the secretaries. Hence, the informtion presented here is drawn from interviews and from four annual reports. The reports were complete for the other two constituencies and cover the period from January 1961 through June 1962.
4. This figure includes representation from whatever sources – regular area delegates, representatives from the special sections and the affiliated organizations, and *ex officio* members.
5. The largest number of Transport and General Workers Union delegates sent to the Bermondsey GMC was forty-eight in 1948–49, when political excitement in the country and in the constituency ran much higher.
6. Four of the delegates had moved away during the year and some of the trade union appointees had not been active at all.
7. The median age is the better measure in the case of party officers. Three out of four of the major officers in Bermondsey had lived in the district for 75 per cent or more of their adult lives.
8. The questionnaire was sent to thirty-eight GMC members, even though the regular membership was about thirty. The discrepency stems from instability in the membership roster. The author sent questionnaires to all who had ever served during the period of the study.
9. The GMC officers included an honorary president and an honorary vice-president. These posts were reserved for veteran party members and the leader of the Labour Group on the Kensington borough council.
10. The South Kensington party, of course, did not have an M.P.
11. For a treatment of the incentive system, see below, pp. 289–311.
12. John W. Thibaut and Harold H. Kelley, *The Social Psychology of Groups* (New York: John Wiley & Sons, 1959) pp. 278–86. This statement about the Thibaut-Kelley analysis is borrowed from the treatment in Holt and Turner, *Political Parties in Action*, pp. 291–2.
13. Mr Mellish became Minister of Housing and Local Government three weeks before the 1970 election, in which the Labour Party was defeated.
14. See Holt and Turner, *Political Parties in Action*, p. 294.

CHAPTER 5

1. For comparisons with Bermondsey, we shall use the fourteen other parties in the Greater London area which compiled the largest Labour vote in the 1959 and 1964 elections, the two parliamentary contests that were the closest to the time period of this study. With Bermondsey in the rank-order, the constituency parties were: West Ham South, Bermondsey, Poplar, Stepney, Bethnal Green, Dagenham, West Ham North, Battersea North, Southwark, Shoreditch and

Finsbury, Banking, Islington South-West, Woolwich East, Camberwell, Peckham, and Walthamstow West.

In the case of Fulham, we shall make the comparison with fourteen other parties that were operating in the most marginal areas and had a sitting M.P. as a result of both elections. These parties, including Fulham, were: Kensington North, Southall, Edmonton, Romford, Wood Green, Paddington North, Feltham, Fulham, Lambeth, Brixton, Leyton, Lewisham South, Enfield East, Hayes and Harlington, East Ham North, and Islington North.

For the comparison with South Kensington, we shall use the fourteen parties that amassed the largest Conservative majorities in the 1959 and 1964 elections. With South Kensington in the rank-order, these parties were: South Kensington, Chelsea, Wanstead and Woodford, Southgate, Harrow West, Bromley, Beckenham, Cities of London and Westminster, St. Marylebone, Enfield West, Sutton and Cheam, Kingston-upon-Thames, Wimbledon, Surbiton, and Wandsworth, Streatham.

2. Occasionally, one encounters the observation that some local Labour parties are not interested in expansion and growth, since an influx of new members would threaten the existing oligarchy and make decision-making more difficult. Not a trace of this sentiment was to be found in the three parties with which this study is concerned. We should point out that the membership records in Bermondsey and Fulham were probably more accurate than the figures in many constituency parties.

3. The 1955 figures are taken from *Annual Conference Report*, 1956, pp. 242–3. We have also made comparable calculations from *The Labour Party: List of Affiliated Organisations, Membership, Affiliation Fees and by-Election Premiums paid for 1968, with Secretaries and with Delegates appointed to attend the Brighton Conference, 1969, and Ex-Officio Members of the Conference.* (London: The Labour Party, 1969) pp. 15–16. The 1955 figures are the best for comparative purposes, since they represent actual memberships. Later reports have a minimum membership (usually 1000) on which each party paid the affiliation fees even though the number of actual members was less. Even when the later, inaccurate figures are used, the rank-order of the top parties is not changed.

4. Cramers V, 0.32. The same pattern emerges when we examine education.

5. The manual workers group includes four workers who identified with the middle class. Since the number was too small to be of any use, we placed them in the manual workers category because they had kinship with this group and usually resembled it in their attitudes. The Cramers V is 0.34.

6. Phi, 0.30.

7. About 80 per cent of the executive officers of the parties expressed concern about recruitment, compared with 58 per cent of the ward officials and 56 per cent of the people who did not hold major office. Two-thirds of the current members and ex-members of the Executive Committee listed the recruitment problem, while the figure for those who had never served was 43 per cent. Neither of these breakdowns, however, met the cut-off standard for the Cramers V significance test.

8. The distribution was: low involvement, 50 per cent; moderate involvement, 81 per cent; high involvement, 86 per cent. (Cramers V, 0.38)

9. Cramers V, 0.37. In 1959, the Bermondsey party submitted to the Annual

Conference a resolution urging more effective use of modern methods of publicity.

10. The author attended all of the GMC meetings in the three constituencies during the period December 1961 through June 1962, taking copious notes and keeping a stop-watch record of the amount of time spent on each item or issue. The November meeting in South Kensington was used as a pilot session so that the author could become familiar with the proceedings. The 'information flow' referred to here largely includes information about special meetings, conferences, training schools, etc., and reports to the GMC on these affairs. It does not include decisions on matters of policy which, of course, would also be reported to the subordinate units.

11. Cramers V, 0.39.

12. Robert Michels, *Political Parties: A Sociological Study of Oligarchical Tendencies of Modern Democracy* (Glencoe, Illinois: The Free Press, 1949).

13. See, for example, Reg Race, 'Attitudes to Political Activity', in Inigo Bing (ed.), *The Labour Party: An Organizational Study*, Fabian Tract No. 407, June 1971, pp. 7–10.

14. Cramers V, 0.45.

15. In discussing the Michels thesis at the constituency party level, we must recognize immediately that all of the officials except the agent were voluntary workers involved with the party only on a part-time basis.

16. Most of the attention that scholars give to the resolutions of constituency Labour parties is focused upon the statements prepared for the Annual Conference. Each party, of course, sends forward only one issue resolution each year, if it sends any at all. But in many cases the Conference resolution represents only a small proportion of the resolutions submitted by the units and approved by the General Management Committee. As already indicated, the other resolutions may be sent during the course of the year to the National Executive Committee, the Parliamentary Labour Party, some other Party agency, or to a ministry. A full assessment of the sentiments of the local party activists would have to include more than just the resolutions submitted to the Party's Annual Conference.

17. A visitor at the meetings in Bermondsey and Fulham, the older and more stable of the three organizations, would be struck by the warm feelings of sympathy and respect expressed by the members when party veterans became ill or died. In Fulham, these sentiments were expressed at the annual meeting when the delegates stood in silent tribute to their comrades who were no longer with them. The activists in Bermondsey were especially sensitive to the adversities suffered by their colleagues. They always authorized the secretary to send bouquets of flowers and notes of greeting to veterans who were ill, and when these individuals returned to service, the GMC delegates made a special effort to welcome them back. The Bermondsey people did not wait until the annual meeting to pay homage to the deceased as a group, but stood to honor each individual silently at the next GMC meeting. This type of recognition was rarely extended in the South Kensington organization, partly because there was less illness among the youthful delegates and partly because the mobility of the population in the district thwarted the development of 'comradely ties'.

The visitor would also note that the minutes of the GMC meetings in Bermondsey and Fulham were very detailed and usually took about five or ten minutes of the agenda time. This is traditional in the two parties, where a history of disputed points stimulates the minute secretaries to record every item of deliberation in intricate detail. The same caution is noticeable in the elections for party offices in the two constituencies. At the annual meetings great care was exercised to check the delegates' credentials and to see that the ballots were distributed properly and tabulated by the scrutineers. The delegates from South Kensington, who had had much less experience with controversy over parliamentary procedure, did not exhibit much concern over these matters.

Obviously, copious note-taking and the use of a stop-watch are a crude way to analyze the content of party meetings. In this research context, however, the author had no alternatives. The findings are not meant to be *precise* differences, but rather general tendencies. They are also designed to provide a general indication of what issues the constituency activists were most concerned about.

18. Note that Bermondsey did not submit a resolution in 1960, the year when the unilateralist controversy shook the Conference.
19. The Fulham party was more concerned about resolutions in the 1955–56 era, when the GMC approved a total of nineteen. All but two of the statements dealt with the social services, housing, local transport, and the like. The other two resolutions were concerned with the abolition of capital punishment and the evils of advertising. The activists in the party have tended to stress issues that appealed to the local electorate; in their view, a party that handles local problems effectively wins popular approoal which carries over into parliamentary contests.
20. During 1960–61, the South Kensington people had three clashes on the unilateralist question. The unilateralists carried the day on two occasions, and the multilateralists once. The delegate to the 1960 Conference, a unilateralist, was mandated by a small majority to vote for the multilateralist position and in support of the missile bases and the training of German troops.
21. Several resolutions dealt with the same subject, especially the Common Market.
22. For the resolution and the debate, see *Annual Conference Report*, 1962, pp. 126–30.
23. See *Annual Conference Report*, 1963, pp. 153–63. Controversy erupted over the issue of private, fee-paying schools.
24. *Labour Party Manifesto*, 1964, pp. 13–14.
25. The criteria of classification were as follows. Group I (impregnable Labour) consists of those constituencies that had an average Labour majority of more than 25 per cent in the 1955, 1959 and 1964 elections. Group II (moderate to marginal Labour) includes the constituencies that had an average majority of less than 25 per cent but returned a Labour M.P. in all three elections. Group III (alternating in party control) is made up of two elements: (*a*) the constituencies that shifted allegiance during the three elections, and (*b*) marginal Tory constituencies where the majority declined during this period and Labour took over in 1966. Group IV (moderate to marginal Conservative) embraces constituencies in which the average Tory majority was less than 25 per cent, but the Tories held on to the seats, even in 1966. Group V (impregnable Conservative) is composed of constituencies where the average Tory majority was more than 25 per cent in the three parliamentary contests.
26. The result is not an artifact stemming from certain constituencies in a given category submitting resolutions that were nearly all challenges to the leadership.

We get roughly the same result when we calculate the *proportion of constituencies* that submitted incongruent resolutions: Group I, 26.3%; Group II, 52.3%; Group III, 78.3%; Group IV, 76.5%; and Group V, 75%.

27. See, for example, Ben Pimlott, 'Does Local Party Organization Matter?' *British Journal of Political Science*, Vol. 2, Part 3 (July 1972) pp. 381–3; 'Local Party Organization, Turnout, and Marginality', ibid., Vol. 3, Part 2 (Apr 1973) pp. 252–5; and J. M. Bochel and D. T. Denver, 'Canvassing, Turnout, and Party Support: An Experiment', ibid., Vol. 1, Part 3 (July 1971) pp. 257–69; 'The Impact of the Campaign on the Results of Local Government Elections,' ibid., Vol. 2, Part 2 (Apr 1972) pp. 239–44 . See also John C. Brown, 'Local Party Efficiency as a Factor in the Outcome of British Elections', *Political Studies*, Vol. 6, No. 2 (June 1958) pp. 174–8.

28. The author observed the elections in each constituency in 1962 and 1964. He also had interviews with the agents and/or key party officials in each constituency during the 1966 parliamentary election. He was privileged, too, to be an inside observer of the parliamentary elections in Fulham in 1970 and February 1974.

29. The author has attended three parliamentary selection conferences and has interviewed the agents of four other constituencies concerning their selection conferences.

30. Useful information abour parliamentary candidate selection can be found in Michael Rush, *The Selection of Parliamentary Candidates* (London: Nelson, 1969); Peter Paterson, *The Selectorate: The Case for Primary Elections in Britain* (London: MacGibbon & Kee, 1967).

31. Some of the union branches did not get their delegates appointed at least one month before the meeting, and for this reason they were not permitted to attend the proceedings.

32. In 1953, the Bermondsey party had 70 aspirants for the 45 candidatures, and six incumbents who were members of the housing committee were not selected. Their formal complaint to Transport House produced no change in their situation. (*News Chronicle*, Apr 11, 1953.)

33. The 'code' consisted of the following items: (1) Sitting members have a right to be considered in the wards they represent. (2) If the record of a sitting member is good, if there is not valid reason why the member should not be readopted, and if he is willing to stand again, then that person should be supported by the Executive Committee. (3) Other things being equal, a candidate should reside in the ward that he may be called upon to represent. (4) In marginal wards, the type of person the nominee is and the appeal he is likely to make should weigh heavily in the choice. (5) In considering all candidates, the Executive Committee realizes that, from the viewpoint of the party's interests, special considerations will make some people better candidates in some areas than in others, and that these should be taken into account even when they conflict with the feelings in a given ward. (6) Normally it is unwise to have a husband and wife contesting seats in the same ward. (7) In cases of disagreement between the Executive Committee and a ward, the GMC adjudicates. (8) All Executive Committee members are required to attend all selection conferences and to support the Committee's recommendations. (9) If a member of the Executive Committee is informed that the Committee is recommending that he be adopted in a certain ward, he is to decline to be on the

short-list for another ward.

34. Compared with the 1959 election, the number of voters on the register declined by 8 per cent, but the Labour vote decreased by 15 per cent and the Labour majority was reduced by 10 per cent. The Tory vote was diminished by 26 per cent.

35. One of the public meetings was held on the 'eve of the poll'; it was largely a pep rally for the campaign workers so that they would be inspired for the next day's effort.

36. The Bermondsey Conservatives suffered from a paucity of workers. They were assisted, however, by about twenty-five people from the outside. These people were friends of the candidate and were not brought in through any organized effort. The campaign was carried out from a central location. Canvassing was sporadic, but the candidate visited about 3000 homes. One of the ways in which the Conservatives attracted attention was by writing letters to the local press – 34 over a two-year period.

37. One evening toward the end of the campaign, the author counted 69 people working in the central headquarters or being sent from the headquarters to work elsewhere in the constituency. Other volunteers, of course, were working out of the committee rooms.

38. The borough council candidates who were unilateralists ostentatiously displayed their buttons during the proceedings.

39. Eight people attended the first of the small indoor meetings, but the second was a non-starter, with only one auditor appearing. The South Kensington people followed the practice of inviting the Barons Court candidate to speak at their large public meetings in the hope that his appearance would help him to attract workers for his campaign.

40. The Conservatives in South Kensington divided their party resources so that workers from two wards went to Fulham and the people from the other two wards went to North Kensington. They also sent out forty letters requesting people to offer their services in Barons Court.

41. A study of this type would require a systematic analysis of canvassing returns, the proportion of Labour 'promises' redeemed at the polls, participant observation of campaign decision-making, etc.

42. This means that we shall be comparing Bermondsey with seven other safe Labour constituencies in which there was a 'straight fight' in the 1959 and 1964 elections. Similarly, we shall contrast the voting result in Fulham for these two elections with the outcome in seven other Labour marginal districts that did not have Liberal interventions. In the case of South Kensington, we shall have to match the increase in the Labour vote with that of the ten other impregnable Tory areas. This format for comparison works something of a hardship on the Fulham party, since it puts the organization into competition with areas where the Labour vote was heavier; the Liberals tended to enter races in the more marginal areas which could ordinarily be compared with Fulham, except for the fact that the Liberal intervention makes the comparison impossible.

43. Of the 'permanent Labour majority boroughs' in London, Bermondsey ranked second in terms of voter turnout in the local elections between 1945 and 1956. (See L. J. Sharpe, 'The Politics of Local Government in Greater London', *Public Administration*, Vol. 38, No. 2 (Summer 1960) p. 171.)

44. Three of the four wards were contested in both the 1959 and the 1962

elections. Saints Ward had not been contested in 1959, but the majority was heavier in 1962 than it had been in any of the other post-war elections.

45. On London's borough councils in which the majority party held 70 per cent of the seats but less than 100 per cent of them, Fulham ranked highest in voter turnout in the local elections conducted in the period 1945–1956. (See L. J. Sharpe, 'The Politics of Local Government in Greater London', op. cit.)

46. The Conservative vote decreased by 18.6 per cent, and the Liberal vote increased by 5.4 per cent.

47. The representative function of the Bermondsey councillors was facilitated by the fact that two-thirds of them represented the wards they resided in; if we consider areas rather than wards, the figure rises to 89 per cent.

48. The GMC delegates were aware of the problems, too. A section of the questionnaire inquired about the difficulties that are likely to arise when a borough council is completely controlled by the Labour Party. About 70 per cent of the Bermondsey activists indicated types of problems that tend to emerge in such a situation: lack of alternative views being presented, difficulty in maintaining public interest and in keeping citizens informed, general apathy, decline in the quality of councillors, etc.

49. The proposals from the party's Action Committee were sent to the Executive Committee, then to the General Management Committee, and finally to the Labour Group in the council.

50. See *Constitution and Standing Orders of the Labour Group of the Fulham Borough Council*, 1960, mimeographed.

51. For discussion of the M.P.'s work with ordinary citizens, see, in addition to the works cited in note 100 on page 339, Anthony Barker and Michael Rush, *The British Member of Parliament and His Information* (Toronto: University of Toronto Press, 1970) pp. 173–215.

52. See *The Times*, Oct 13, 1964.

53. The sale of land is an idiosyncratic entry for the Bermondsey party and its elimination would reduce the amount of income considerably. Most of the items in the three income distributions are net figures, but not all of them.

The income and expense listings have been converted into American denominations at the rate of $2.40 to the pound.

CHAPTER 6

1. On most runs we used twenty-two independent variables: constituency, sex, age, proportion of adult life in local residence, occupation, education, social origin, social mobility, class self-identification, objective/subjective social class, office-holders, length of officers' service, Executive Committee membership, length of tenure on the Executive Committee, tenure on the General Management Committee, period of entry into the Labour Party, length of Party membership, trade union activity, Co-operative society activity, borough council membership, recruitment through the youth organization, and political aspirations.

2. Norman H. Nie, *et al.*, *Statistical Package for the Social Sciences* (New York: McGraw-Hill Book Company, 1970).

3. See, for example, Richard P. Boyle, 'Path Analysis and Ordinal Data', *American Journal of Sociology*, Vol. 75, No. 4, Part I (Jan 1970) pp. 461–80;

Sanford Tabovitz, 'The Assignment of Numbers to Rank Order Categories', *American Sociological Review*, Vol. 35, No. 3 (June 1970) pp. 515–24. The author is indebted to Stanley Feldman for discussing these matters with him.

4. This, of course, was a difficult undertaking, but the work was made a bit easier by the fact that the author had interviewed many of the respondents, had had contact with all of them, and was familiar with the data. The preliminary testing on possible combinations could be done from the data compiled on McBee Selector cards. The final testing required a good many computer runs.

5. Robert R. Alford, *Party and Society: The Anglo-American Democracies* (Chicago: Rand McNally & Company, 1963) pp. 101–7. See also David Butler and Donald Stokes, *Political Change in Britain: Forces Shaping Electoral Choice* (New York: St. Martin's Press, 1969) Chapter 4.

6. The Greenwich study found that the subjective assessment of the respondents appeared to be more closely associated with party choice than was the objective categorization according to their occupations. (Mark Benney, A. P. Gray, and R. H. Pear, *How People Vote: A Study of Electoral Behaviour in Greenwich* (New York: Grove Press, 1956) p. 115.)

7. Mark Abrams, 'Some Measurements of Social Stratification in Britain', in J. A. Jackson (ed.), *Social Stratification* (Cambridge: Cambridge University Press, 1968) p. 138. See also Butler and Stokes, *Political Change in Britain*, p. 70.

8. A total of fifteen people refused to commit themselves on the social class question. Twelve of these people were in the middle class by objective standards, and their responses betrayed a certain sensitivity to their social position. One GMC delgate did not answer the question at all. All sixteen of these people have been dropped from this analysis of class self-designation.

9. The results of the regression analysis were:

Variable	R	R^2	Cumulative R^2	F Score	B	Beta
Constituency	0.66	0.43	0.43	92.78 (0)	0.26	0.45
Education	0.63	0.11	0.54	29.97 (000)	0.26	0.40

[F Score 72.31]

Occupation was one of the twenty-one independent variables used in this regression, but it did not rank very high. This means that, with occupation being held constant, both constituency and education still had an impact.

10. Peter Willmott, *The Evolution of a Community: A Study of Dagenham after Forty Years* (London: Routledge & Kegan Paul, 1963) p. 102. See also W. G. Runciman, 'Embourgeoisment and Self-Rated Class and Party Preferences', *Sociological Review*, Vol. 12, No. 2 (July 1964, new series) pp. 137–54. The same tendency was reported by Frank Bealey, J. Blondel, and W. P. McCann, *Constituency Politics: A Study of Newcastle-under-Lyme* (New York: The Free Press, 1965) pp. 183–4. Peter Willmott and Michael Young put the generalization this way: '. . . the more the middle class predominates in a district, the more working-class people identify themselves with it . . .' [*Family and Class in a London Suburb* (London: Routledge & Kegan Paul, 1960) p. 115.]

11. Michael Young and Peter Willmott, 'Social Grading by Manual Workers', *British Journal of Sociology*, Vol. 7, No. 4 (Dec 1956) pp. 337–45.

12. The tiny number of middle-class identifiers made it impossible to make a separate run for Bermondsey.

The regression results were:

Variable	R	R^2	F Score	B	Beta
Education	0.63	0.40	81.65 (0)	0.41	0.63

It is important to note that the education variable was not affected by age.

Recognizing that some studies have indicated that party leaders were more likely than the rank and file to list themselves as working class, we made a special calculation. We discovered that nearly half of the constituency party officials either identified with the middle class or were unwilling to recognize social class, while more than three-fourths of the ward officials designated themselves as working class. (When we refer to ward officials in this study, we mean the chairman and the secretary.)

13. For an excellent discussion of how revisionism, unilateralism, and the internal power struggle became intertwined, see Frank Parkin, *Middle Class Radicalism: The Social Bases of the British Campaign for Nuclear Disarmament*, (Manchester: Manchester University Press, 1968) pp. 113–24.

14. The correlations among the issues are:

	Alliance	Leadership	Clause IV	Doctrine	Market	Tories	Immigration	Capital Punishment	Communist Party	London Reorganization Later	Current London Reorganization
Unilateralism	−0.50	−0.42	−0.39	0.24	−0.27	−0.21	−0.09	−0.01	−0.09	0.07	−0.07
Alliance		0.52	0.40	−0.24	0.38	0.21	0.03	−0.03	0.12	−0.23	−0.13
Leadership			0.23	−0.15	0.15	0.12	0.08	−0.15	0.17	−0.11	0.08
Clause IV				−0.38	0.33	0.27	−0.13	0.17	0.02	0.04	0.17
Doctrine					−0.24	−0.39	0.15	0.02	−0.09	−0.12	−0.05
Market						0.34	−0.06	0.16	0.10	0.09	0.06
Tories							−0.15	0.12	0.01	0.18	0.12
Immigration								−0.38	0.28	−0.29	−0.21
Capital Punishment									−0.22	0.34	0.12
Communist Party										−0.05	−0.05
London Reorganization Later											0.30

A factor analysis gave us the groupings we were entitled to expect on the basis of what we already knew. The groupings were: (1) Leadership, Unilateralism, and Alliance; (2) Cooperation with the Tories, Traditional Doctrine, Clause IV, and the Common Market; (3) Capital Punishment, Immigration, and Restrictions on the Communist Party; and (4) the two questions on the Reorganization of London Government.

15. *Political Change in Britain*, pp. 198-9.

16. In December 1961, the Gallup Poll reported that 33 per cent of the voters who had supported Labour in 1959 approved of having their country give up her H-bombs even if the other nations did not. About 54 per cent of them opposed such a policy. (*Gallup Political Index*, Report No. 24, p. 14.)

17. In this study we speculated that outlooks toward certain issues might be influenced by the period in which individuals were recruited into the Labour Party. The dividing lines are, of course, somewhat arbitrary. The delineations we used are:

1. *1924 and earlier.* These were the years when the Labour Party was divided over its goals and it was struggling to become a significant political force. (Average age of GMC members who were recruited during this period, 69.8.)

2. *1925-34.* This was the period of the general strike, depression, unemployment, and disillusionment over Ramsey MacDonald's leadership. (Average age, 58.5.)

3. *1935-44.* This was an era of pacifist appeals with spirited debates over rearmament, and eventually the entrance into World War II. (Average age, 52.6.)

4. *1945-51.* These were the immediate post-war years when the Labour Party achieved majority control of the House of Commons for the first time. The experience of these people was largely pre-war Britain; had it not been for the war, many of these people would have entered the Party earlier. (Average age, 45.3.)

5. *1952-62.* This was the period of Suez, increasing material affluence, and basic disagreements within the Party over defense and foreign policy. The people who were recruited during this period did not experience pre-war Britain as adults. (Average age, 31.1.)

18. The cumulative R^2 was 0.20. GMC tenure was highly correlated with period of entry. This variable, however, gave some support to the involvement hypothesis. The mean years of GMC service for the unilateralists was 7.4 and for the non-unilateralists it was 12.5. This pattern was the same for the constituencies individually. The mean years of Labour Party membership yielded the same result: unilateralists, 15.9; non-unilateralists, 20.9.

19. Of the sixteen people in this group, ten had joined the Party during the middle and late 1930s and nine of them were unilateralists. The remaining six, who had entered the organization after the onset of the war, were equally divided between unilateralists and non-unilateralists.

20. The breakdown of trade union activity was: active – those who attended all or nearly all of the branch meetings; quasi-active – those who attended about one-half or one-fourth of the time; inactive – those who attended very infrequently or not at all.

The regression results are:

R	R^2	F Score	B	Beta
0.53	0.28	50.06 (000)	0.21	0.53

21. We calculated a set of party involvement scores as follows: major

constituency office, 4 points; minor constituency office, 2; Executive Committee membership, 2; ward chairman or secretary, 3; minor ward office, 1; attendance at all ward meetings, 2; attendance at nearly all of the ward meetings, 1.5; attendance at half of the ward meetings, 0.5. For purposes of presenting the data in tables, we set up three categories on a scale: scores 0–2, low party involvement; scores 2.5–6.5, moderate involvement; scores 7–13, high involvement. On this scale, 51 per cent of those with low party involvement favored unilateralism; moderate involvement, 34.5 per cent; high involvement, 25.9 per cent. (Cramers V, 0.20) Put another way, the mean party involvement score for the unilateralists was 3.31, compared with a score of 4.48 for the non-unilateralists.

22. The number and types of complaints were as follows:

Complaint	Bermondsey	Fulham	South Kensington	Total
Defense	7	13	10	30
Public ownership	3	11	3	17
Weak attacks on Tories	5	8	4	17
Drift from socialist principles	2	6	5	13
Common Market	1	–	8	9
Ignoring Conference decisions	2	4	3	9
Intolerance of dissent	–	1	5	6
Foreign affairs	1	3	1	5
Too 'middle-class'	2	–	1	3
Education	–	2	1	3
Immigration	2	–	–	2
Reorganization of London government	–	2	–	2
Miscellaneous	–	1	6	7

23. The few people who wrote 'uncertain' have been combined with those who listed themselves as negative.

24. The figures on education are particularly interesting in terms of support for the national leadership: elementary, 93 per cent; secondary, 74 per cent; secondary+ (training college and other work beyond the regular secondary level), 53 per cent; and university, 90 per cent (Cramers V, 0.31).

25. Cramers V, 0.29. In June 1962, 67 per cent of the Labour voters in the 1959 election thought that Gaitskell was a good leader, while 20 per cent took the opposite view. (*Gallup Political Index*, Report No. 30, p. 100.)

26. Cramers V, 0.30.

27. Phi, 0.29. The respective mean proportions of adult residence were: in support of the leadership, 74.3 per cent; against the leadership, 45.2 per cent.

28. While this category covers only 55 per cent of the respondents, it includes 78 per cent of the manual workers and the people with elementary education, 77 per cent of those who had served on the GMC for more than sixteen years, 72 per cent of the activists who had been in the Party for more than a quarter of a century, 70 per cent of those who identified with the working class, and 62 per cent of the people 45 years of age and over. In terms of constituency, it embraced 76 per cent of the Bermondsey respondents, 63 per cent of the Fulham activists,

but only 11 per cent of the South Kensington people.
There was a tendency for those who had been in the Party and on the GMC for longer periods to be the most favorably disposed toward the leadership.

29. The regression results:

Variable	R	R^2	Cumulative R^2	F Score	B	Beta
Residence, Objective/ Subjective Class	0.35	0.12	0.12	9.13 (0.003)	0.10	0.27
Constituency	0.29	0.02	0.14	3.27 (0.073)	0.08	0.16

[F Score 11.08 (0.000)]

30. Since only a few of the respondents in Fulham and South Kensington thought that the alliance should be strengthened, this category was combined with the 'remain as is' group. Because of the trichotomized percentages, the results in some of the tables have been converted to scores for ease of reading: strengthen or remain as is (henceforth listed as 'Favorable'), 1; 'Loosen', 2; 'Abandon', 3.

31. In November 1961, 53 per cent of the Labour Party voters indicated a preference to have their country remain neutral rather than have it be on good terms with either the United States or the USSR at the expense of good terms with the other (*Gallup Political Index*, Report No. 23, p. 48). In November 1962, 60 per cent of the respondents in a sample of the entire British population felt that Britain was not being treated as an equal partner with the United States. (Ibid., Report No. 35, p. 207.)

32. The mean scores for party involvement were: those favorable to the alliance, 4.31; those who wanted a looser arrangement, 4.34; and those who wanted to abandon it, 2.87.

33. First, education was broken into three dummy variables:

Educational Level	E 1	E 2	E 3
Elementary	0	0	0
Secondary	1	0	0
Secondary+	1	1	0
University	1	1	1

In this way E 1 measures the difference between secondary and elementary, E 2 measures the difference between secondary + and secondary, and E 3 measures the difference between university and secondary +. Since each dummy variable is one unit long $(0-1)$, the unstandardized regression coefficient (*b*-weight) gives the mean difference in the dependent variable owing to that step in the education variable. Through the use of these weights, the education variable was reconstructed, with elementary education being given the arbitrary value of 0 and the other levels of education being assigned values in the same ratios as the regression weights. The recoded variable is equivalent to the three dummy variables, whose weights were empirically determined as optimal for that regression equation. [See Morgan Lyons, 'Techniques for Using Ordinal Measures in Regression and Path Analysis', in Herbert L. Costner (ed.),

Sociological Methodology, 1971 (San Francisco: Jossey-Bass, 1971) pp. 147–71.]

34. Cramers V, 0.25. The results of the regression were:

Variable	R	R^2	Cumulative R^2	F Score	B	Beta
Objective/Subjective class and Residence	−0.35	0.13	0.13	10.01 (0.002)	−0.11	−0.27
Recruitment period, trade union, and Exec. Cttee tenure	−0.29	0.05	0.17	12.56 (0.001)	−0.22	−0.33
Education	0.28	0.03	0.21	6.28 (0.013)	0.90	0.21
Age	−0.04	0.03	0.24	5.19 (0.024)	0.01	0.21

[F Score: 9.72 (0.000)]

35. A band of older clerical workers in Bermondsey who identified with the working class were, unlike their counterparts in Fulham, weak in their support for traditional doctrine.

36. Phi, 0.19.

37. When the non-manuals were categorized on the basis of social origin, the figures were: working-class origin, 57 per cent; middle-class origin, 39 per cent.

38. The slightly higher figure for secondary education is a result of the responses from manual workers of working-class origin who had completed schooling at the secondary level; all but two of this group of twelve supported the traditional outlook.

39. Cramers V, 0.23.

40. The regression results were:

Variable	R	R^2	F Score	B	Beta
Class Self-Placement, Period of Entry, & Social Origin	0.38	0.14	22.29 (0.000)	0.16	0.38

41. The same pattern held when we examined each constituency separately.

42. In March 1962, 54 per cent of the Labour voters favored the extension of nationalization, while 29 per cent were opposed. (*Gallup Political Index*, Report No. 26–27, p. 49.)

43. A tiny band of manual workers who identified with the middle class and the small group that refused to make a class designation were both strongly opposed to revision.

44. These findings on the relationship between working-class factors and support for the preservation of Clause IV and the opposite relationship with respect to the middle class are at variance with the study of active ward members and a small group of inactive members, which was reported in Manchester in 1952. In that study it was the middle class that supported nationalization most strongly. No specific data were presented. [See Wilfred Fienburgh and the Manchester Fabian Society, 'Put Policy on the Agenda', *Fabian Journal*, No. 6 (Feb 1952) p. 29.]

45. Taking into account two other variables which we shall discuss next, the regression results are as follows:

Variable	R	R^2	Cumulative R^2	F Score	B	Beta
Mobility, trade union, and class self-identification	−0.43	0.18	0.18	20.26 (0.000)	−0.14	−0.37
Executive Committee tenure	0.17	0.02	0.20	5.16 (0.025)	0.12	0.19
Age & Youth orgn membership	−0.21	0.03	0.23	4.16 (0.044)	−0.10	−0.18

[F Score 12.04 (0)]

46. Cramers V, 0.17.
47. A similar pattern can be detected when we look at the length of tenure of party officers: whereas between 69 and 71 per cent of the people who had held office for less than three years or who had never been elected to an officer's post were against revision, the figure for officers who had served for three years or more was 44 per cent. [Cramers V, 0.21]
48. Cramers V, 0.21 (low).
49. The proportions for the other periods of entry were: 1952–62, 68 per cent; 1925–34, 60 per cent; and 1945–51, 51 per cent.
50. None of the differences proved to be significant. One reason why the patterns were not clear was because Fulham was the deviant case. There the young people, most of them newcomers to the party, supported Clause IV to a greater extent than did the older veterans.
51. Rather than present so many percentages in the descriptive parts of this section, we shall make it a bit easier for the reader by presenting weighted scores. Those who thought that cooperation with the Tories was possible on 'some issues' were given a rating of 1; 'hardly at all', 2; and 'not at all', 3. The higher the score, the greater hostility toward the Conservatives.
52. Cramers V, 0.32.
53. Occupation does not give us quite the picture that we expected. The small group of lesser skilled workers was the most hostile to the Tories (2.31); the skilled workers and the clerical group were virtually identical in their responses (2.03 and 2.04); and the professional/managerial people were the most receptive to cooperation (1.67).
54. Cramers V, 0.33.
55. Cramers V, 0.36.
56. Cramers V, 0.27.
57. Cramers V, 0.27.
58. Cramers V, 0.33. The four manual workers who listed themselves as middle class had a score of 2.25.
59. The regression result from the use of the two variables was:

Variable	R	R^2	Cumulative R^2	F Score	B	Beta
Mobility, Residence and Period of Entry	−0.46	0.21	0.21	16.14 (0.000)	−0.27	−0.33
Constituency, Subjective/Objective Class	−0.44	0.07	0.28	12.53 (0.001)	−0.19	−0.29

[F Score: 25.48 (0.000)]

The Beta for the social mobility, residence, and period of recruitment variable was reduced by the advent of the second variable, constituency and objective/subjective class, and, as we would expect, by the entry of social origin into the regression. While the first variable was picked up first by the stepwise procedure because of its own direct impact and probably because it was reflecting indirect variance from the second variable, its final Beta was below that of the second variable. The constituency and objective/subjective variable immediately picked off variance of its own which had initially been represented by the first variable, and it remained stable throughout the regression.

60. Only one of the professional people had had the equivalent of a university education, and only two were employed in the 'established' professions. The highest level of formal education for the clerical people was secondary school, and nearly all of them held routine clerical jobs.

61. This curvilinear relationship is mostly generated by the GMC members in Bermondsey, where the comparatively recent affiliates displayed greater antipathy toward the Tories than did the old-timers (2.37, compared to 2.03).

62. There are only six cases in the older group of middle-class origin. The point would still obtain if the two elements in the higher age category were combined. (Cramers V, 0.32)

63. Cramers V, 0.38. For purposes of this analysis, the respondents who wrote 'uncertain' were listed in the negative category. (There were sixteen of these, nine of them from Bermondsey, five from Fulham, and two from South Kensington.)

In April-May 1962, 38 per cent of the Labour voters in the previous election supported Britain's joining the Market, while 33 per cent were opposed. (*Gallup Political Index*, Report No. 28–29, p. 68.)

64. Cramers V, 0.41. In the original regression, the R^2 was 0.17.

Occupation presented an unusual pattern. The skilled manual workers registered their opposition at 74 per cent, but the figure for the lesser skilled was only 57 per cent. (The latter category was comprised almost entirely of dockers.) In the non-manual category, the routine clericals listed their opposition at 66 per cent; the teachers, journalists, research workers, clerical supervisors, etc., of the professional/managerial category at 58 per cent; and the people from the more established professions (solicitors, barristers, medical people) at 22 per cent. The categories permitted us to introduce social origin into only the routine clerical group and the lower echelon of the professional/managerial group. When we did this, the people of working-class origin were always more opposed to the Market than were their colleagues of middle-class origin.

65. The 'won't commit' people have been included with the middle-class identifiers, since their responses were very similar.

66. The stationary manual group consisted of only two people who were in the 'won't commit' category. The mobiles to professional/managerial status were a small group which could have been combined with the other mobiles except that its outlooks were different. Had it been included the other mobiles, the figure would have been 50.0 per cent ($N = 30$).

67. The results of the regression were:
   (*See Table on page 357*)

68. See, for example, Samuel A Stouffer, *Communism, Conformity, and Civil Liberties: A Cross-section of The Nation Speaks Its Mind* (Garden City, N. Y.: Doubleday, 1955) pp. 89–90; Christopher Bagley, *Social Structure and Pre-*

Variable	R	R^2	Cumulative R^2	F Score	B	Beta
Objective/Subjective class and social mobility	−0.46	0.21	0.21	14.58 (0.000)	−0.12	−0.34
Constituency and education	−0.41	0.04	0.25	6.63 (0.011)	−0.07	−0.23

(F Score 22.00 (0.000))

judice in Five English Boroughs (London: Institute of Race Relations, 1970); Christopher Bagley, 'Racial Prejudice and the 'Conservative Personality: A British Sample', *Political Studies*, Vol. 18, No. 1 (Mar 1970) pp. 134–41. There seems to be some doubt as to which group – manual workers or routine clericals with low educational attainment – rates lowest on the tolerance scale.

69. Cramers V, 0.51. In late 1961, 56 per cent of the Labour voters approved of the government's measures for controlling immigration, while 30 per cent were opposed. About 73 per cent of the Conservative voters gave their approval. (*Gallup Political Index*, Report No. 24, Dec 1961, p. 10.)

70. In the initial regression, constituency, objective/subjective class, and age appeared in that order: R^2, 0.32.

71. This finding corresponds with the research results obtained by Mark Abrams. ('The Lost Labour Voter', *Socialist Commentary*, Feb 1969, pp. 28–9.)

72. Cramers V, 0.45. As one would expect, 74 per cent of those who were relatively new to their districts opposed controls, while only 45 per cent of those who had lived in their communities most of their adult lives were in this category. (Phi, 0.29.)

73. Phi, 0.40.

74. In the regression South Kensington and Fulham were combined so as to increase the numbers in the cells. When examined separately, the results were almost identical. The final regression included this variable, objective/subjective class, and age. The results of the regression are:

Variable	R	R^2	Cumulative R^2	F Score	B	Beta
Constituency and education	−0.57	0.32	0.32	21.15 (0.000)	−0.19	−0.42
Objective/subjective class	0.46	0.02	0.35	3.60 (0.060)	0.07	0.17
Age	−0.35	0.01	0.36	2.57 (0.112)	−0.01	−0.13

(F Score, 23.99)

75. See Peter G. Richards, *Parliament and Conscience* (London: Allen & Unwin, 1970) p. 49.

76. Cramers V, 0.34. In early 1962, Lord Pakenham made this statement: 'Capital punishment is opposed by the overwhelming majority of Labour M.P.s, and by almost every Labour Peer. I should imagine that the same is true of Party workers as a whole.' ('The Labour Party and Penal Reform', *Socialist Commentary*, Feb 1962, p. 7.)

In July 1961, only 21 per cent of the Labour voters in 1959 favored the abolition of capital punishment, while 66 per cent of them opposed such a move. The Conservative voters were stronger in their opposition. (*Gallup Political Index*, July 1961, p. 10.)

77. Cramers V, 0.46.
78. The regression results are as follows:

Variable	R	R^2	F Score		B	Beta
Occupation and Education	0.51	0.26	49.61	(0.000)	0.16	0.51

In the final regression, the Beta weight for length of Party membership remained high, even though the stepwise procedure did not pick the variable as a leading contender. Of the people who had been in the Party for fifteen years or less, 80 per cent of them favored the abolition of capital punishment. For those who had been in the organization for longer periods, the comparable figure was 66 per cent.

79. There was a difference here within the manual group: skilled manual, 72 per cent; lesser-skilled, 60 per cent.
80. The regression run produced the following results:

Variable	R	R^2	Cumulative R^2	F Score		B	Beta
Social mobility, Trade Union	−0.34	0.12	0.12	10.93	(0.000)	−0.08	−0.27
Constituency, Borough Council, Officers	−0.31	0.05	0.16	7.63	(0.007)	−0.11	−0.23

(F Score 12.99 (0.000))

81. The trade union analysis, which has already been used in connection with social mobility, gets some confirmation in Bermondsey: trade union actives and quasi-actives; 75 per cent ($N=32$); inactives and non-members, 50 per cent ($N=24$).
82. For good treatments of the reorganization of London government, see Frank Smallwood, *Greater London: The Politics of Metropolitan Reform* (New York: Bobbs-Merril Co., 1965) Gerald Rhodes (ed.), *The New Government of London: The First Five Years* (London: Weidenfeld and Nicolson, 1972).
83. The Gallup Poll's analysis was based upon a sample drawn from the general population, not divided into Labour and Conservative voters. About 11 per cent of the respondents approved of the Government Bill, and 10 per cent were opposed. A total of 63 per cent, however, had not heard about the reform. (*Gallup Political Index*, Report No. 40, May 1963, p. 93.)
84. *Daily Herald*, March 15, 1962.
85. For the attitude of Peter Robshaw, secretary of the London Labour Party, see *Annual Conference Report*, 1962, pp. 194–5.
86. See, for example, the debate on the second reading of the London Government Bill and accompanying Money Bill. (*House of Commons*, Debates, Dec 10, 1962, Col. 37–164, 223–344; Dec 11, 1962, Col. 345–60.)
87. Cramers V, 0.25.

88. Cramers V, 0.28.
89. Cramers V, 0.25.
90. Cramers V, 0.25. The various groups were combined when the percentages were nearly alike; in the original form, the Cramers V was 0.26.
91. The results of the regression were:

Variable	R	R^2	Cumulative R^2	F Score	B	Beta
Mobility and Trade Union activity	−0.44	0.19	0.19	23.59 (0.000)	−0.14	−0.38
Constituency, Borough Council, Officers	−0.31	0.04	0.23	6.94 (0.009)	−0.06	−0.21

(F Score, 20.40)

92. The number of Bermondsey people who supported reform is too small for analysis on a constituency basis. But in Fulham and South Kensington, taken separately, the party officers were more disposed toward reform than were the non-officers. Similarly, those who were serving or had served on the Executive Committee were more favorable to the change than those who had never served on this body. Moreover, the people who had been officers or Executive Committee members for relatively long periods gave more support to reorganization than their colleagues whose tenure had been shorter.
93. Cramers V, 0.48. The analysis of this issue is made easier by the fact that the number of deviant cases is 43.
94. Cramers V, 0.45.
95. All of the people in the staid professions supported reform, but only 77 per cent of the activists in the newer professions and in managerial posts gave it their favor. The difference between the non-manual and manual groups was nevertheless significant.
96. The same patterns prevail in each constituency.

	South Kensington		Fulham		Bermondsey	
Executive Committee members	100.0%	(16)	100.0%	(25)	59.1%	(22)
Non-members	81.0	(21)	71.4	(21)	33.3	(36)
Borough council members	100.0%	(8)	100.0%	(20)	55.6%	(36)
Non-members	86.2	(29)	76.9	(26)	22.7	(22)

We preferred to use the borough council figures for Bermondsey, since the council was such an important body there when it came to issues of this sort. In Bermondsey, the experience factor was reflected in the period of recruitment: 57% of those who had entered the Party prior to 1945 supported the idea of reform, compared with 30% for those who had joined the Party after the war.

97. The results of the regression were:

	R	R^2	Cumulative R^2	F Score	B	Beta
Constituency, EC Membership, BC Membership	0.56	0.32	0.32	28.96 (.000)	0.20	0.45
Objective/Subjective Class	−0.46	0.03	0.35	6.41 (.012)	−0.08	−0.21

[F score, 36.42]

98. The four manual workers who identified with the middle class all supported the idea of reform.
99. Cramers V, 0.48.
100. The categories were scaled on the basis of social origin, education, occupation, and class self-rating. Occupation, education, and class self-rating were highly correlated; the *weakest* correlations were between social origin and class self-identification (−0.35) and between social origin and education (−0.37). The small group of activists who refused to place themselves in a social class were graded according to the other criteria. Below is a categorization of the four groups, with an indication of the types of people who fell into each group.

Group IV ($N = 50$), the most solidly working class. The general criteria were: working-class origin, elementary education, manual jobs, and subjective identification with the working class. All but ten of the people in this group met all of the criteria. The ten had secondary education, but they were all from working-class homes, held manual jobs, and identified with the workers.

Group III ($N = 40$). The general criteria were: working-class origin, routine clerical jobs, elementary or secondary education, and identification with the working class. The exceptions were: four people of lower middle-class origin who had elementary education, held clerical positions, and identified with the working class; and three manual workers who met the other criteria but who identified with the middle class.

Group II ($N = 25$). All of the respondents in this group had either secondary+ or secondary education. They fall into two sub-categories: (1) Working-class origin (14). Nine held routine clerical posts, three were teachers, and two were small-scale supervisers. Nine of them identified with the middle class, three with the working class, and two refused to designate class. (2) Middle-class origin (11). Two were manual workers, five were clerks, and three were in teaching, journalism, or supervisory work. Five of them identified with the workers, one identified with the middle class, and five would not commit themselves. One person in this middle-class origin group was a non-university trained professional who claimed subjective kinship with the working class.

Group I ($N = 27$), the most solidly middle class. All of the people in this category held professional/managerial positions and two-thirds of them had a university education. The activists in this group also divide into two sub-categories. (1) Middle-class origin (18). Eleven people had university training and seven had secondary+ or secondary education. Five were employed in the established professions, and thirteen were engaged in the newer professions (journalism, social work, etc.) or in some form of supervisory work. Sixteen

identified with the middle class, one person from the established professions identified with the workers, and one would not accept class analysis.
(2) Working-class origin (9). Seven in this group were university trained and two had secondary + or secondary education. Three were from the established professions and six were employed in the newer professions. All of the people in this sub-group identified with the middle class.
101. The regression results were:

Variable	R	R^2	Cumulative R^2	F Score	B	Beta
Capital punishment	0.52	0.27	0.27	16.03	0.86	0.31
Traditional doctrine	−0.35	0.14	0.40	7.66	−0.49	−0.21
Immigration	−0.48	0.07	0.47	6.84	−0.47	−0.20
Future London reorganization	0.45	0.04	0.51	4.07	0.39	0.16
Party leadership	−0.27	0.02	0.53	8.63	−0.59	−0.21
Clause IV	0.32	0.04	0.57	4.85	0.42	0.18
Current London reorganization	0.28	0.02	0.58	3.18	0.39	0.13
Cooperation with Tories	0.36	0.01	0.59	2.33	0.14	0.11

(F Score 16.49)

102. A Guttman scaling of the five issues yielded 92 per cent reproducibility.
103. See, for example, Ralph Miliband, *Parliamentary Socialism: A Study in the Politics of Labour* (London: Allen & Unwin, 1961) pp. 107, 300, 307, 319; Norman Birnbaum, 'The Year Zero of British Socialism', *Antioch Review*, Summer 1960, p. 137; David E. Butler, 'The Paradox of Party Difference', *American Behavioral Scientist*, Vol. 4, No. 3 (Nov 1960) p. 5; T. E. M. McKitterick, 'The Membership of the Labour Party', *Political Quarterly*, Vol. 31, No. 3 (July – Sep 1960) p. 315. Maurice Duverger is often cited in support of the notion that local party activists are militants. But in his analysis the activists are militants by definition. (See *Political Parties: Their Organization and Activity in the Modern State* (New York: John Wiley & Sons, 1951) pp. 90–1, 110–16.)
104. See, for example, Richard Rose, 'The Political Ideas of English Party Activists', *American Political Science Review*, Vol. 56, No. 2 (June 1962, pp. 364, 366, 368–9; Frank Bealey, J. Blondel, and W. P. McCann, *Constituency Politics: A Study of Newcastle-under-Lyme* (New York: The Free Press, 1965) p. 295; Edward G. Janosik, *Constituency Labour Parties in Britain* (New York: Frederick A. Praeger, 1968) pp. 28–58.
105. One point was allocated for each of the following responses: support for unilateralism and for traditional doctrine, and opposition to the national leadership, to the revision of Clause IV, and to the Anglo-American Alliance. (When the response on the Alliance was 'Loosen', the score was 0.5.)

The category 'ideological enthusiasts' ($N=31$) includes the respondents who followed this pattern on at least four issues, receiving scores of 3.5 and above. All opposed the revision of Clause IV and all but two were unilateralists. The variance within this group was over the questions of leadership and doctrine. More than half of the respondents in this category received a score of at least 4.5.

The category 'moderates' ($N=49$) is composed of people whose scores ranged from 2.0 to 3.0. Their pattern of responses on the two or three issues varied: 37 of them supported traditional doctrine; 36 opposed the revision of Clause IV, 21 were unilateralists, 18 favored loosening the Alliance and two wanted to abandon it, and four opposed the leadership.

The category 'non-ideological' ($N=55$) embraces the respondents with scores ranging from 1 to 1.5, and it contains no unilateralists and no opponents of the leadership. A total of 25 received a score of 0; four had 0.5; 17 had scores of 1.0 (nine opposed Clause IV and eight supported traditional doctrine); and nine had scores of 1.5 (all of them favoring a loosening of the Alliance, five voting to retain Clause IV, and four supporting traditional doctrine).

Seven GMC delegates – five from Bermondsey and one each from Fulham and South Kensington – were dropped from this analysis owing to an inadequate number of responses.

It is important to note that, unlike some of the literature on this subject, our definition of 'ideological enthusiast' or 'militant' is based upon expressed attitudes toward certain issues – not on the number of meetings attended or the amount of work done.

106. In other words, using the constituency variable as an illustration, we found that the ideological enthusiasts in Fulham made up 48.4 per cent of the total in that category, but only 28.9 per cent of the respondents in the rest of the population. Hence the percentage difference for Fulham was $+19.5$ per cent. All of the percentage differences were significant at the 0.05 level or better.

107. On the ideological preferences of middle-class socialists, see Mark Abrams, 'Politics and the British Middle Class', *Socialist Commentary*, Oct 1962, p. 9. See also N. J. Demerath III and Victor Thiesson, 'On Spitting against the Wind: Organizational Precariousness and American Irreligion', *American Journal of Sociology*, Vol. 71, No. 6 (May 1966) p. 682.

108. In order to examine the tendencies of people with certain socio-economic characteristics to become ideological enthusiasts, moderates, or non-ideologicals, we made the calculations in a different direction. For example, what proportion of all the people in a certain age bracket fell into each category? Below is a listing of the socio-economic attributes for which the percentage differences were high.

Socio-Economic Feature	Ideological Enthusiasts	Moderates	Non-Ideologicals	N
Education				
Secondary+	47.4%	26.3%	26.3%	(19)
University	15.8	15.8	68.4	(19)
Officers' tenure				
3 years or more	3.9	34.6	61.5	(26)
Less than 3 years	50.0	28.6	21.4	(14)
Trade union inactives	19.5	17.1	63.4	(41)
Class scale				
Group I	14.8	22.2	63.0	(27)
Group II	54.2	16.7	29.2	(24)

109. The reader will recall that they were not in opposite corners on humanitarian issues. (See Table 6.22.)

110. We should note that in each constituency party the people who refused to recognize the validity of social class analysis were overwhelmingly those with secondary school education.

111. The teachers in Britain have grown increasingly militant since the early 1960s. See R. D. Coates, *Teachers' Unions and Interest Group Politics: A Study in the Behaviour of Organized Teachers in England and Wales* (Cambridge: Cambridge University Press, 1972) Chapter 6.
112. See Seymour M. Lipset and Juan J. Linz, *The Social Bases of Political Diversity* (Stanford: Center for Advanced Study in the Behavioral Sciences, 1956) p. 9, mimeographed.
113. Frank Parkin, *Middle Class Radicalism*, pp. 184–92.
114. We have already indicated how the party involvement scores were figured. The score for trade union involvement were: active, 3; quasi-active, 2; membership, 1. The cooperative scores were: active, 3; quasi-active, 1; member, 0.5. The basis for the borough council involvement scores was: committee chairman, 3; other offices, 2; member, 1.
115. When we examined each constituency separately, the patterns held up except in the case of Fulham. There the ideological enthusiasts were more active in the party and in the borough council than were the moderates, and all the people in all three categories were about equally involved in the trade union and co-operative affairs.
116. Janosik, *Constituency Labour Parties in Britain*, especially p. 59. For the treatment of factionalism in this work, see pp. 97–108.

CHAPTER 7

1. The basis for the involvement scores has already been given in note 21 on pp. 351–2. The high involvement group ($N = 30$) includes activists with scores of 7 or more; the moderate group ($N = 60$) has scores ranging from 2.5 through 6.5; and the low-involvement people ($N = 52$) have scores of less than 2.5. The cut-off lines were drawn at points where group differences appeared in the distribution table.
2. This profile table is similar to the one we compiled for ideological outlooks. Take, for example, occupation. The routine clerical group accounted for 50 per cent of the high involvement group but only 15.4 per cent of the low involvement group. The percentage difference is thus +34.6 per cent. All percentage differences listed in the table are statistically significant at least at the 0.05 level.
3. The mean party involvement scores of the occupational groups were: professional/managerial, 3.99; routine clerical, 5.24; and manual, 3.08.
4. The results of the regression were:

Variable	R	R^2	Cumulative R^2	F Score	B	Beta
Political aspirations	−0.37	0.14	0.14	23.16 (0.000)	−0.93	−0.37
Youth organization	−0.22	0.04	0.18	7.40 (0.007)	−1.53	−0.21

[F Score 15.50 (0.000)]

5. The same pattern emerged when we used education and the class scale as the bases for analysis and when we examined each constituency separately. Those who wrote 'None' or did not answer were dropped from this analysis. These non-aspirers were included in the original regression, and the correlation between occupation and political aspirations was low.
6. The Cramers V is 0.29. The patterns of party involvement and aspiration levels were the same for each constituency.

7. This table and the other two tables on motivations (7.3 and 7.4) are based upon the number of responses. Most individuals offered more than a single response.

8. When the asserted motivations were further analyzed in terms of social mobility, the stationary middle and the stationary manual groups were strongest in the party-oriented category, while the socially mobile group emphasized personal-oriented considerations. In the issue-oriented responses, the stationary manual group stood by itself, offering the smallest number of mentions.

9. Of the people with local aspirations, those who located themselves in the middle class or who refused to commit themselves on social class were the least issue-oriented of all; only 6 per cent of their responses fell into this category.

10. In this analysis, 'normative' incentives come close to fitting what James Q. Wilson defines as 'purposive', and our 'personal' incentives are akin to his 'solidary' inducements. (See *Political Organizations*, pp. 33–5.)

11. The relationship between the organizational and ideological commitment to a local party and the amount of work done in its behalf is difficult to tap in this study for two reasons: (1) We have no information on personal costs, which vary greatly and which have to be held constant; (2) The question on reasons for serving on the GMC was open-ended, and most respondents listed several which fell under the party, personal, or issue categories. We have no way of weighting the responses to determine which are of greater importance.

12. The result was not changed by combining the people with party-oriented and issue-oriented responses. The two were separate in the initial analysis.

13. The mean ideological scores were: Bermondsey – highly involved, 1.36; moderate, 1.61; low, 1.92. South Kensington – highly involved, 0.93; moderate, 1.63; low, 2.65. Fulham – highly involved, 2.58; moderate, 2.64; low, 2.38.

14. A good many people on the councils regarded their work as service to the community, although they admitted that they derived personal satisfaction from it.

15. Social rewards appear to be of much more importance in a local Conservative party. (See Robert T. Holt and John E. Turner, *Political Parties in Action*, pp. 280–2.)

16. There was a number of husband-and-wife teams on each GMC. Bermondsey had nine, Fulham had six, and South Kensington had five.

17. The average length of Party membership for the questionnaire respondents was: Bermondsey, 23.3 years; Fulham, 18.8 years; and South Kensington, 12.1 years.

18. Individuals of this type might, of course, find an outlet for their latent abilities by joining other voluntary organizations than political parties. In other words, the personal satisfaction that a person feels from taking on responsibility in a local party does not explain why he is working there when he might receive similar gratification in a different type of organization. The author is inclined to speculate, however, that the working-class people we are referring to tend to gravitate toward organizations that are socially reformist in goals and have a relatively permanent existence. Moreover, they are not likely to feel comfortable working in other types of voluntary associations, many of which are dominated by middle-class people.

19. It should be noted that Fulham had a balanced age representation at all levels.

20. We did encounter two people who did some work in adjacent parties on the assumption that they might earn 'brownie points' if parliamentary seats were suddenly to become vacant. But these efforts were made to offset the 'carpetbagger' image, since both parties were partial toward local candidates.

We should also point out that the trade unionists who were very active in their unions and would have been eligible to further their parliamentary ambitions by getting on the A List of candidates had a mean party involvement score of 4.50. The comparable figure for aspirants who lacked such trade union connections and would be forced to secure local approval as the initial step to getting on the B List was 5.15.

21. On the difference in the reward system between the Conservative and Labour parties with respect to work done outside the home constituency, see Holt and Turner, *Political Parties in Action*, pp. 254–56.

22. We have party involvement information on about two-thirds of the people on Bermondsey's candidate list and three-fourths of the people on Fulham's list. Some of the Bermondsey people did not return their questionnaires. In the case of Fulham, the lack of information stems from the fact that some of the candidates were outsiders from Barons Court, and a few others were not on the GMC. The Fulham agent was on the candidates' list (he had been a council member for some years), but he was not included in this analysis. The South Kensington candidates represented in the table were *bona fide*, appearing on the North Kensington list. The incentive hypothesis is hardly torn apart by South Kensington; the members of the London County Council who lived in South Kensington and were on the GMC but who secured their candidatures in *other districts* had a mean party involvement score in South Kensington of only 1.75!

Presumably, the active members are more likely to submit themselves for candidacy than are the less active people. In this study, however, we were not in a position to test for this.

23. See *Annual Conference Report*, 1975, p. 217.
24. See above, note 114, p. 362.
25. Of the twenty-three Fulham people who served on the local council in 1961–62, eighteen (78 per cent) were engaged in the party's 'donkey-work' in their wards, women's organizations, and the Young Socialists. Two more were active in their trade unions, and another had valuable expertise in local government and local government law.
26. Political and Economic Planning, 'Government by Appointment', in Richard Rose (ed.), *Policy-Making in Britain* (New York: The Free Press, 1969) pp. 55–6, 62.
27. The mayor is a justice of the peace during his term of office and for one year thereafter.

CHAPTER 8

1. See Table 3.8, p. 114.
2. See Table 3.7, p. 112.
3. See Anthony Downs, *An Economic Theory of Democracy* (New York: Harper & Row, 1957); Peter C. Odeshook, 'Extensions to a Model of the Electoral Process and Implications for the Theory of Responsible Parties', *Midwest*

Journal of Political Science, Vol. 14, No. 1 (Feb 1970) pp. 43–70.
4. For a good critique of the literature on this problem, see Morris P. Fiorina, 'Electoral Margins, Constituency Influence, and Policy Moderation: A Critical Assessment', *American Politics Quarterly*, Vol. 1, No. 4 (Oct 1973) pp. 479–98.
5. See above, pp. 195–7.
6. See Amitai Etzioni, *A Comparative Analysis of Complex Organizations: On Power, Involvement, and Their Correlates* (New York: The Free Press, 1975) pp. 12–14.

Bibliography

GENERAL WORKS ON BRITISH PARTIES AND POLITICS

Sydney D. Bailey (ed.), *Political Parties and the Party System in Britain: A Symposium*, (New York, Frederick A. Praeger, 1952).
Allen Beattie (ed.), *English Party Politics, 1660–1970* (London: Weidenfeld and Nicolson, 1970, two volumes).
Samuel H. Beer, *British Politics in the Collectivist Age* (New York: Alfred A. Knopf, 1965).
A. H. Birch, *Representative and Responsible Government* (London: Allen & Unwin, 1964).
Jean Blondel, *Voters, Parties, and Leaders: The Social Fabric of British Politics* (Harmondsworth, Middlesex: Penguin, 1963).
Ivor Bulmer-Thomas, *The Party System in Great Britain*, (London: Phoenix House, 1953).
Ivor Bulmer-Thomas, *The Growth of the British Party System*, (London: John Baker, 1967, two volumes).
George O. Comfort, *Professional Politicians: A Study of British Party Agents*, Washington, D. C.: Public Affairs Press, 1958.
Leon D. Epstein, *Political Parties in Western Democracies*, (New York: Frederick A. Praeger, 1967).
Leon D. Epstein, 'British Mass Parties in Comparison with American Parties', *Political Science Quarterly*, Vol. 71, No. 1, (Mar. 1956), pp. 97–125.
Martin Harrison, 'Britain', in 'Comparative Studies in Political Finance', *Journal of Politics*, Vol. 25, No. 4 (Nov 1963) pp. 664–85.
Sir Ivor Jennings, *Party Politics: Appeal to the People* (Cambridge: Cambridge University Press, 1960) Vol. I.
James G. Kellas, *The Scottish Political System* (Cambridge: Cambridge University Press, 1973).
John D. Lees and Richard Kimber, *Political Parties in Modern Britain: An Organizational and Functional Guide* (London: Routledge & Kegan Paul, 1972).
Robert T. McKenzie, *British Political Parties: The Distribution of Power within the Conservative and Labour parties* (New York: Frederick A. Praeger, 1964).
Ian McLean, 'The Rise and Fall of the Scottish National Party', *Political Studies*, Vol. 18, No. 3 (Sep 1970), pp. 357–72.

Allen M. Potter, 'British Party Organization, 1950', *Political Science Quarterly*, Vol. 66, No. 1, (Mar 1951), pp. 65–86.
R. M. Punnett, *British Government and Politics* (New York: W. W. Norton & Company, 1968).
Geoffrey K. Roberts, *Political Parties and Pressure Groups in Britain* (London: Weidenfeld & Nicolson, 1970).
Richard Rose (ed.), *Policy-Making in Britain* (New York, Free Press, 1969).
Richard Rose, *Politics in England: An Interpretation* (Boston: Little, Brown & Company, 1964).
Richard Rose, *The Problem of Party Government* (New York: Free Press, 1974).
Richard Rose (ed.), *Studies in British Politics : A Reader in Political Sociology*, (New York: St. Martin's Press, 1966).
Richard Rose, 'Parties, Factions, and Tendencies in Britain', *Political Studies*, Vol. 12, No. 1 (Feb 1964), pp. 33–46.
Richard Rose, 'The Professionals of Politics', *New Society*, Aug 8, 1963, pp. 10–12.

SOCIOLOGICAL STUDIES

Mark Abrams and Richard Rose, *Must Labour Lose?* (Harmondsworth, Middlesex: Penguin, 1960).
Mark Abrams, 'Disturbing Thoughts for the Next Election', *Socialist Commentary*, Oct 1957, pp. 16–19.
Mark Abrams, 'The Lost Labour Voter', *Socialist Commentary*, Feb 1969, pp. 17–34.
Mark Abrams, 'Politics and the British Middle Class', *Socialist Commentary*, Oct 1962, pp. 5–9.
Mark Abrams, 'Social Class and British Politics', *Public Opinion Quarterly*, Vol. 25, No. 3 (Fall 1961) pp. 342–51.
Philip Abrams and Alan Little, 'The Young Activist in British Politics', *British Journal of Sociology*, Vol. 16, No. 4 (Dec 1965) pp. 315–33.
Paul R. Abramson and John W. Books, 'Social Mobility and Political Attitudes: A Study of Intergenerational Mobility among Young British Men', *Comparative Politics*, Vol. 3, No. 3 (Apr 1971) pp. 403–28.
Christopher Bagley, *Social Structure and Prejudice in Five English Boroughs* (London: Institute of Race Relations, 1970).
Christopher Bagley, 'Racial Prejudice and the "Conservative Personality": A British Sample', *Political Studies*, Vol. 18, No. 1, (Mar 1970) pp. 134–41.
Frank Bechhofer and Brian Elliott, 'An Approach to the Study of Small Shopkeepers and the Class Structure', *European Journal of Sociology*,

Vol. 9, No. 2 (1968) pp. 180—202.
Colin Bell, *Middle Class Families: Social and Geographical Mobility*, (London: Routledge & Kegan Paul, 1969).
David Berry, *The Sociology of Grass Roots Politics* (London: Macmillan, 1970).
Alan P. Brier and Robert E. Dowse, 'The Politics of the A-Political', *Political Studies*, Vol. 17, No. 3 (Sep 1969) pp. 334—9.
Samuel Brittan, *Left or Right: The Bogus Dilemma* (London: Secker & Warburg, 1968).
Peter B. Clark and James Q. Wilson, 'Incentive Systems: A Theory of Organization', *Administrative Science Quarterly*, Vol. 6, No. 2 (Sep 1961) pp. 129—66.
Ivor Crewe, 'The Politics of "Affluent" and "Traditional" Workers in Britain: An Aggregate Data Analysis', *British Journal of Political Science*, Vol. 3, Part 1 (Jan 1973) pp. 29—52.
Arthur Cyr, 'Class in Britain through Liberal Eyes', *Comparative Politics*, Vol. 5, No. 1 (Oct 1972) pp. 63—82.
Christopher Driver, *The Disarmers; A Study in Protest* (London: Hodder & Stoughton, 1964).
Leon D. Epstein, 'British Class Consciousness and the Labour Party', *Journal of British Studies*, Vol. 1, No. 2 (May 1962) pp. 136—50.
Amitai Etzioni, *A Comparative Analysis of Complex Organizations: On Power, Involvement, and Their Correlates* (New York: Free Press, 1975).
H. J. Eysenck, 'Primary Social Attitudes as Related to Social Class and Political Party', *'British Journal of Sociology*, Vol. 2, No. 3 (Sep 1951) pp. 198—209.
John H. Goldthorpe, David Lockwood, Frank Bechhofer, and Jennifer Platt, *The Affluent Worker: Political Attitudes and Behaviour* (Cambridge: Cambridge University Press, 1968).
John H. Goldthorpe, David Lockwood, Frank Bechhofer, and Jennifer Platt, 'The Affluent Worker and the Thesis of *Embourgeoisement*: Some Preliminary Research Findings', *Sociology*, Vol. 1, No. 1 (Jan 1967) pp. 11—31.
John H. Goldthorpe and David Lockwood, 'Affluence and the British Class Structure', *Sociological Review*, Vol. 11, No. 2 (new series) (July 1963) pp. 133—63.
John C. Goyder, 'A Note on the Declining Relation between Subjective and Objective Class Measures', *British Journal of Sociology*, Vol. 26, No. 1 (Mar 1975) pp. 102—9.
W. L. Guttsman, *The British Political Elite* (London: MacGibbon & Kee, 1963).
John Hall and D. Caradog Jones, 'Social Grading of Occupations', *British Journal of Sociology*, Vol. 1, No. 1 (Mar 1950) pp. 31—55.
Murray Hausknecht, *The Joiners: A Sociological Description of Volun-*

tary Association Membership in the USA, New York: Bedminster Press, 1962).

J. A. Jackson (ed.), *Social Stratification* (Cambridge: Cambridge University Press, 1968).

Edward A. Johns, *The Social Structure of Modern Britain* (New York: Pergamon Press, 1972)

R. W. Johnson, 'The British Political Elite, 1955–72,' *European Journal of Sociology*, Vol. 14, No. 1, (1973) pp. 35–77.

Michael Kahan, David Butler, and Donald Stokes, 'On the Analytical Division of Social Class', *British Journal of Sociology*, Vol. 17, No. 2 (June 1966) pp. 122–32.

Dennis Kavanagh, 'The Deferential English: A Comparative Critique', *Government and Opposition*, Vol. 6, No. 3 (Summer 1971) pp. 333–60.

David Lockwood, *The Blackcoated Worker: A Study in Class Consciousness* (London: Allen & Unwin, 1958).

David Lockwood, 'The "New Working Class"' *Archives Européenes de Sociologie*, Vol. 1, No. 2 (1960) pp. 248–59.

David Lockwood, 'Sources of Variation in Working Class Images of Society', *Sociological Review*, Vol. 14, No. 3 (new series) (Nov 1966) pp. 249–67.

Richard Mabey (ed.), *Class*, (London: Anthony Blond, 1966).

Robert McKenzie and Allan Silver, *Angels in Marble: The Working Class Conservatives in Urban England* (London: Heinemann, 1968).

Eric Nordlinger, *The Working-Class Tories: Authority, Deference, and Stable Democracy* (London: MacGibbon & Kee, 1967),

Frank Parkin, *Middle Class Radicalism: The Social Bases of the British Campaign for Nuclear Disarmament*, (Manchester: Manchester University Press, 1968).

Frank Parkin, 'Working-Class Conservatives: A Theory of Political Deviance', *British Journal of Sociology*, Vol. 18, No. 3 (Sep 1967) pp. 278–90.

Anthony Piepe, Robin Prior, and Arthur Box, 'The Location of the Proletarian and Deferential Worker', *Sociology*, Vol. 3, No. 2 (May 1969) pp. 239–44.

D. E. G. Plowman, W. E. Minchton, and Margaret Stacey, 'Local Social Status in England and Wales', *Sociological Review*, Vol. 10, No. 2 (new series) (July 1962) pp. 161–202.

John Raynor, *The Middle Class* (London: Longmans, Green, 1969).

John P. Roche and Stephen Sachs, 'The Bureaucrat and the Enthusiast: An Exploration of the Leadership of Social Movements', *Western Political Quarterly*, Vol. 8, No. 2 (June 1955) pp. 248–61.

Richard Rose, 'Class and Party Divisions: Britain as a Test Case', *Sociology*, Vol. 2, No. 2 (May 1968) pp. 129–62.

W. G. Runciman, ' "Embourgeoisment", Self-Rated Class, and Party Preference', *Sociological Review*, Vol. 12, No. 2 (new series) (July

1964) pp. 137–54.

W. G. Runciman and C. Bagley, 'Status Consistency, Relative Deprivation, and Attitudes to Immigrants', *Sociology*, Vol. 3, No. 3 (Sep 1969) pp. 359–75.

Joseph A. Schlesinger, 'Political Party Organization', in James G. March (ed.), *Handbook of Organizations* (Chicago: Rand McNally & Company, 1965) pp. 764–801.

Philip Stanworth and Anthony Gibbens, *Elites and Power in British Society* (Cambridge: Cambridge University Press, 1974).

Rodney Stark, 'Class, Radicalism, and Religious Involvement in Great Britain', *American Sociological Review*, Vol. 29, No. 5, (Oct 1964) pp. 698–706.

Samuel A. Stouffer, *Communism, Conformity, and Civil Liberties: A Cross-section of the Nation Speaks Its Mind* (Garden City, New York: Doubleday, 1955).

D. F. Swift, 'Social Class, Mobility-Ideology and 11 + Success', *British Journal of Sociology*, Vol. 18, No. 2 (June 1967) pp. 165–86.

A. J. M. Sykes, 'Some Differences in the Attitudes of Clerical and of Manual Workers', *Sociological Review*, Vol. 13, No. 3 (Nov 1965) pp. 297–310.

James D. Thompson, *Organizations in Action: Social Science Bases of Administrative Theory* (New York: McGraw-Hill Book Company, 1967).

Peter Townsend, 'The Family Life of Old People: An Investigation of Old People', *Sociological Review*, Vol. 3, No. 2 (new series) (Dec 1955) pp. 175–95.

William Watson, 'Social Mobility and Social Class in Industrial Communities', in Max Gluckman (ed.), *Closed Systems and Open Minds: The Limits of Naïvety in Social Anthropology*, (Chicago: Aldine Publishing Company, 1964) pp. 129–57.

James Q. Wilson, *Political Organizations* (New York: Basic Books, 1973).

Michael Young and Peter Willmott, 'Social Grading by Manual Workers', *British Journal of Sociology*, Vol. 7, No. 4 (Dec 1956) pp. 337–45.

Mayer N. Zald and Roberta Ash, 'Social Movement Organizations: Growth, Decay, Change', *Social Forces*, Vol. 44, No. 3 (Mar 1966) pp. 327–41.

Elia T. Zureik, 'Party Images and Partisanship among Young Englishmen', *British Journal of Sociology*, Vol. 25, No. 2 (June 1974) pp. 179–200.

VOTING STUDIES

Mark Abrams, 'Social Trends and Electoral Behaviour', *British Journal of Sociology*, Vol. 13, No. 3 (Sep 1962) pp. 228–42.

Philip Abrams and Alan Little, 'The Young Voter in British Politics', *British Journal of Sociology*, Vol. 16, No. 2 (June 1965) pp. 95–110.

Robert R. Alford, *Party and Society: The Anglo-American Democracies* (Chicago: Rand McNally & Company, 1963).

A. J. Allen, *The English Voter* (London: English Universities Press, 1964).

A. J. Allen, 'Voting Recollections and Intentions in Reading: An Opinion Poll Experiment', *Parliamentary Affairs*, Vol. 20, No. 2, (Spring 1967) pp. 170–7.

William G. Andrews, 'Social Change and Electoral Politics in Britain: A Case Study of Basingstoke, 1964 and 1974', *Political Studies*, Vol. 22, No. 3 (Sep 1974) pp. 324–36.

Malcolm J. Barnett, 'Aggregate Models of British Voting Behavior', *Political Studies*, Vol. 21, No. 2 (June 1975) pp. 121–34.

F. Bealey and D. J. Bartholomew, 'The Local Elections in Newcastle-under-Lyme, May 1958', *British Journal of Sociology*, Vol. 13, No. 3 (Sep 1962) pp. 273–85; No. 4 (Dec 1962) pp. 350–68.

R. J. Benewick, A. H. Birch, J. C. Blumler, and Alison Ewbank, 'The Floating Voter and the Liberal View of Representation', *Political Studies*, Vol. 17, No. 2 (June 1969) pp. 177–95.

Mark Benney, A. P. Gray, and R. H. Pear, *How People Vote: A Study of Electoral Behaviour in Greenwich* (London: Routledge & Kegan Paul, 1956).

Mark Benney and Phyllis Geiss, 'Social Class and Politics in Greenwich', *British Journal of Sociology*, Vol. 1, No. 4 (Dec 1950) pp. 310–27.

Hugh Berrington, 'The Election Drama: Act One', *Aspect, No. 12* (Jan 1964) pp. 12–18.

Hugh Berrington, 'Local Election Results: Their Relevance to a General Election', *Aspect*, (May 1963) pp. 48–54.

Hugh Berrington, 'Prisoners of Convention', *Insight* (Jan 1965) pp. 2–7.

A. H. Birch, 'Citizen Participation in England and Wales', *International Social Science Journal*, Vol. 12, No. 1 (1960), pp. 15–26.

A. H. Birch 'The Habit of Voting', *Manchester School of Economic and Social Studies*, Vol. 18, No. 1 (Jan 1950) pp. 75–82.

A. H. Birch and Peter Campbell, 'Voting Behaviour in a Lancashire Constituency', *British Journal of Sociology*, Vol. 1, No. 3 (Sep 1950) pp. 197–208.

J. M. Bochel and D. T. Denver, 'Canvassing, Turnout and Party Support: An Experiment', *British Journal of Political Science*, Vol. 1, Part 3 (July 1971) pp. 257–69.

J. M. Bochel and D. T. Denver, 'The Impact of the Campaign on the Results of Local Government Elections', *British Journal of Political*

Science, Vol. 2, Part 2, (Apr 1972) pp. 239–44.
J. M. Bochel and D. T. Denver, 'Religion and Voting: A Critical Review and a New Analysis', *Political Studies*, Vol. 18, No. 2 (June 1970) pp. 205–19.
John Bonham, *The Middle Class Vote* (London: Faber & Faber, 1954).
Ian Budge and Derek W. Urwin, *Scottish Political Behaviour: A Case Study in British Homogeneity* (London: Longmans, Green, 1966).
David E. Butler, *The British General Election of 1951* (London: Macmillan, 1952).
David E. Butler, *The British General Election of 1955*, (London: Macmillan, 1955).
David E. Butler and Richard Rose, *The British General Election of 1959*, (London: Macmillan, 1960).
David E. Butler and Anthony King, *The British General Election of 1964*, (London: Macmillan, 1965).
David E. Butler and Anthony King, *The British General Election of 1966* (London: Macmillan, 1966).
David E. Butler and Michael Pinto-Duschinsky, *The British General Election of 1970*, (New York: St. Martin's Press, 1971).
David E. Butler and Dennis A. Kavanagh, *The British General Election of February 1974* (London: Macmillan, 1974).
David E. Butler and Dennis A. Kavanagh, *The British General Election of October 1974* (New York: St. Martin's Press, 1974).
David E. Butler, *The Electoral System in Britain, 1918–1951* (Oxford: Clarendon Press, 1953).
David Butler and Donald Stokes, *Political Change in Britain: Forces Shaping Electoral Choice* (New York: St. Martin's Press, 1969).
Peter Campbell, David Donnison, and Allen Potter, 'Voting Behavior in Droylsden in October, 1951', *Manchester School of Economic and Social Studies*, Vol. 20, No. 1 (Jan 1952) pp. 57–65.
Chris Chamberlain, 'The Growth of Support for the Labour Party in Britain', *British Journal of Sociology*, Vol. 24, No. 4 (Dec 1973) pp. 474–89.
S. B. Chrimes (ed.), *The General Election in Glasgow, February 1950*, (Glasgow: Jackson, Son and Company, 1950).
E. J. Cleary and H. Pollins, 'Liberal Voting at the General Election of 1951', *Sociological Review*, Vol. 1, No. 2 (Dec 1953) pp. 27–41.
J. P. Cornford and J. A. Brand, 'Scottish Voting Behavior', in J. N. Wolfe (ed.), *Government and Nationalism in Scotland* (Edinburgh: Edinburgh University Press, 1969, pp. 17-40).
H. Daudt, *Floating Voters and the Floating Vote: A Critical Analysis of American and English Election Studies* (Leyden: H. E. Stenfert Kroese, 1961).
Nicholas Deakin (ed.), *Colour and the British Electorate, 1964: Six Case Studies*, (London: Pall Mall Press, 1965).

Nicholas Deakin and Jenny Bourne, 'Powell, the Minorities, and the 1970 Election', *Political Quarterly*, Vol. 41, No. 4 (Oct – Dec 1970) pp. 399–415.

Robert E. Dowse and Jeffrey Stanyer, 'The General Election in Exeter', *The Listener*, Nov 5, 1964, pp. 715–17.

Leon D. Epstein, 'The Nuclear Deterrent and the British Election of 1964', *Journal of British Studies,* Vol. 5, No. 2 (May 1966) pp. 139–63.

Peter Fletcher, 'An Explanation of Variations in "Turnout" in Local Elections', *Political Studies*, Vol. 17, No. 4 (Dec 1969) pp. 495–502.

Wilma George, 'Social Conditions and the Labour Vote in the County Boroughs of England and Wales', *British Journal of Sociology*, Vol. 2, No. 3 (Sep 1951) pp. 255–9.

C. A. E. Goodhart and R. J. Bhansali, 'Political Economy', *Political Studies*, Vol. 18, No. 1 (Mar 1970) pp. 43–106.

W. P. Grant, 'Size of Place and Local Labour Strength', *British Journal of Political Science*, Vol. 2, Part 2 (Apr 1972) pp. 259–60.

N. Greenwald, 'Labour's Reading Victory: A Technical Examination', *Southwestern Social Science Quarterly*, Vol. 37, No. 2 (Sep 1956) pp. 111–21.

Roy Gregory, 'Local Elections and the "Rule of Anticipated Reactions" ', *Political Studies*, Vol. 17, No. 1 (Mar 1969) pp. 31–47.

J. Grundy, 'Non-Voting in an Urban District', *Manchester School of Economic and Social Studies*, Vol. 18, No. 1 (Jan 1950) pp. 83–99.

William Hampton, 'The Electoral Response to a Multi-Vote Ballot', *Political Studies*, Vol. 16, No. 2 (June 1968) pp. 266–72.

L. H. Harrison and F. E. Crossland, 'The British Labour Party in the General Elections, 1906–1945', *Journal of Politics*, Vol. 12, No. 2 (May 1950) pp. 383–404.

Barry Hindess, 'Local Elections and the Labour Vote in Liverpool', *Sociology,* Vol. 1, No. 2 (May 1967) pp. 187–95.

Dean H. Jaensch, 'The Scottish Vote 1974: A Re-Aligning Party System?', *Political Studies*, Vol. 24, No. 3 (Sep 1976) pp. 306–19.

C. O. Jones, 'Inter-Party Competition in Britain – 1950–1959'. *Parliamentary Affairs*, Vol. 17, No. 1 (Winter 1963–64) pp. 50–6.

Marion R. Just, 'Causal Models of Voter Rationality, Great Britain 1959 and 1963', *Political Studies*, Vol. 21, No. 1 (Mar 1973) pp. 45–56.

Richard L. Leonard, *Elections in Britain* (Princeton, N. J.: D. Van Nostrand, 1968).

Richard L. Leonard, *Guide to the General Election* (London: Pan Books, 1964).

Warren L. Mason, 'Cognitive Patterns among British Labour Party "Regulars" ', *Comparative Politics*, Vol. 6, No. 1 (Oct 1973) pp. 147–55.

R. B. McCallum and Alison Readman, *The British General Election of*

1945 (London: Oxford University Press, 1947).
F. M. Martin, 'Social Status and Electoral Choice in Two Constituencies', *British Journal of Sociology*, Vol. 3, No. 3 (Sep 1952) pp. 231–41.
Michael Meecher and Molly Meecher, 'Maverick Voters', *Plebs*, May 1967, p. 19–21.
G. Mercer, 'Political Contagion and Party Affiliation: A Case Study of Adults and Adolescents in Scotland', *Political Studies*, Vol. 22, No. 2 (June 1974) pp. 210–14.
R. S. Milne and H. C. Mackenzie, *Straight Fight: A Study of Voting Behaviour in the Constituency of Bristol North-East at the General Election of 1951* (London: Hansard Society, 1954).
R. S. Milne and H. C. Mackenzie, *Marginal Seat 1955: A Study of Voting Behaviour in the Constituency of Bristol North-East at the General Election of 1955* (London: Hansard Society, 1958).
R. S. Milne, 'The Study of Parliamentary Elections', *Cambridge Journal*, Vol. 5, No. 11 (Aug 1952) pp. 688–98.
D. S. Morris and K. Newton, 'Marginal Wards and Social Class', *British Journal of Political Science*, Vol. 1, Part 4 (Oct 1971) pp. 503–7.
K. Newton, 'Turnout and Marginality in Local Elections', *British Journal of Political Science*, Vol. 2, Part 2, (Apr 1972) pp. 251–5. For criticism and rejoinder, see No. 4 (Oct 1972) pp. 513–16.
H. G. Nicholas, *The British General Election of 1950* (London: Macmillan, 1951).
'Active Democracy – A Local Election', *Planning*, Vol. 13, No. 261 (Jan 24, 1947) pp. 1–20.
'Local Elections: How Many Vote?', *Planning*, Vol. 15, No. 291 (Nov 29, 1948) pp. 163–78.
'Voting for Local Councils', *Planning*, Vol. 21, No. 379 (May 9, 1955) pp. 49–64.
D. E. G. Plowman, 'Allegiance to Political Parties: A Study of Three Parties in One Area', *Political Studies*, Vol. 3, No. 3 (Oct 1955) pp. 222–34.
Harry Pollins, 'The Significance of the Campaign in General Elections', *Political Studies*, Vol. 1, No. 3 (Oct 1953) pp. 207–15.
Peter C. J. Pulzer, *Political Representation and Elections: Parties and Voting in Great Britain* (New York: Frederick A. Praeger, 1967).
Colin S. Rallings, 'Two Types of Middle-Class Labour Voter?' *British Journal of Political Science*, Vol. 5, Part 1 (Jan 1975) pp. 107–12.
James C. Robertson, 'The British General Election of 1935', *Journal of Contemporary History*, Vol. 9, No. 1 (Jan 1974) pp. 149–64.
Richard Rose and Harve Mossawir, 'Voting and Elections: A Functional Analysis', *Political Studies*, Vol. 15, No. 2 (June 1967) pp. 173–201.
Ralph Samuel, 'The Deferent Voter', *New Left Review*, No. 1, (Jan –

Feb 1960) pp. 9–13.
G. N. Sanderson, 'The "Swing of the Pendulum" in British General Elections, 1832–1966', *Political Studies*, Vol. 14, No. 3, (Oct 1966) pp. 349–60.
L. J. Sharpe, *A Metropolis Votes: The London County Council Election of 1961*, Greater London Papers No. 8 (London: London School of Economics and Political Science, 1962).
L. J. Sharpe (ed.), *Voting in Cities: The 1964 Borough Elections*, (London: Macmillan, 1967).
M. Spiers and M. J. Le Lohé, 'Pakistanis in the Bradford Municipal Election of 1963', *Political Studies,* Vol. 12, No. 1 (Feb 1964) pp. 85–92.
Leslie Stone, 'What Happened in Smethwick?' *Socialist Commentary* (Dec 1964) pp. 5–8.
G. J. G. Upton and D. Brook, 'The Importance of Positional Voting Bias in British Elections', *Political Studies*, Vol. 22, No. 2 (June 1974) pp. 178–90.
J. R. Vincent, 'The Electoral Sociology of Rochdale', *Economic History Review*, Vol. 16, No. 1 (second series) (Aug 1963) pp. 76–90.
Philip M. Williams, 'Two Notes on the British Electoral System', *Parliamentary Affairs*, Vol. 20, No. 1 (Winter 1966–67) pp. 13–30.

COMMUNITY STUDIES

A. H. Birch, *Small-Town Politics: A Study of Political Life in Glossop* (Oxford: Oxford University Press, 1959).
Elizabeth Bott, *Family and Social Network: Roles, Norms, and External Relationships in Ordinary Urban Families* (London: Tavistock Publications, 1957).
Ian Budge, J. A. Brand, Michael Margolis, and A. L. M. Smith, *Political Stratification and Democracy* (London: Macmillan, 1972).
Peter Collison and John N. Mogey, 'Residence and Social Class in Oxford', *American Journal of Sociology*, Vol. 64, No. 6 (May 1959) pp. 599–605.
Council of Citizens of East London, *Our East London: A Study in Diversity* (Southend-on-Sea, Essex: Unicorn Press, no date).
Ruth M. Crichton, *Commuters' Village: A Study of Community and Commuters in the Berkshire Village of Stratfield Mortimer* (London: David & Charles, Dawlish Macdonald, 1964).
Elwyn Davies and Alwyn D. Rees (eds.), *Welsh Rural Communities* (Cardiff: University of Wales Press, 1960).
Norman Dennis, Fernando Henriques, and Clifford Slaughter, *Coal is Our Life: An Analysis of a Yorkshire Mining Community* (London: Eyre & Spottiswoode, 1956).

Bibliography

Ruth Durant, *Watling: A Survey of Social Life on a New Housing Estate* (London: P. S. King & Son, 1939).

N. Elias and J. L. Scotson, *The Established and the Outsiders: A Sociological Enquiry into Community Problems* (London: Frank Cass & Co., 1965).

Isabel Emmett, *A North Wales Village: A Social Anthropological Study* (London: Routledge & Kegan Paul, 1964).

Raymond Firth (ed.) *Two Studies of Kinship in London*, Monographs on Social Anthropology, No. 15, London School of Economics (London: Anthlone Press, 1956).

Ronald Frankenberg, *Communities in Britain: Social Life in Town and Country* (Harmondsworth, Middlesex: Penguin, 1966).

William Hampton, *Democracy and Community: A Study of Politics in Sheffield* (Oxford: Oxford University Press, 1970).

Barry Hindess, *The Decline of Working-Class Politics* (London: MacGibbon & Kee, 1971).

Brian Jackson, *Working Class Community: Some General Notions Raised by a Series of Studies in Northern England* (London: Routledge & Kegan Paul, 1968).

Hilda Jennings, *Societies in the Making: A Study of Development and Redevelopment within a County Borough* (London: Routledge & Kegan Paul, 1962).

Madeline Kerr, *The People of Ship Street* (New York: Humanities Press, 1958).

James Littlejohn, *Westrigg: The Sociology of a Cheviot Parish*, (London: Routledge & Kegan Paul, 1963).

University of Liverpool, Department of Social Science, *The Dock Worker: An Analysis of Conditions of Employment in the Port of Manchester* (Liverpool: University Press, 1954).

Peter J. Madgwick, *The Politics of Rural Wales: A Study of Cardiganshire* (London: Hutchinson, 1973).

E. W. Martin, *The Shearers and the Shorn: A Study of Life in a Devon Community* (London: Routledge & Kegan Paul, 1965).

J. M. Mogey, *Family and Neighbourhood: Two Studies in Oxford* (Oxford: Oxford University Press, 1956).

Harold Orlans, *Stevenage: A Sociological Study of a New Town* (London: Routledge & Kegan Paul, 1952).

R. E. Pahl, 'Class and Community in English Commuter Villages', *Sociologia Ruralis*, Vol. 5, No. 1 (1965) pp. 5–22.

T. S. Simey (ed.), *Neighbourhood and Community: An Enquiry into Social Relationships on Housing Estates in Liverpool and Sheffield* (Liverpool: University Press, 1954).

Margaret Stacey, *Tradition and Change: A Study of Banbury* (Oxford: Oxford University Press, 1960).

W. M. Williams, *The Sociology of an English Village: Gosforth* (London:

Routledge & Kegan Paul, 1956).
W. Morgan Williams, *A West Country Village: Ashworthy — Family, Kinship, and Land* (London: Routledge & Kegan Paul, 1963).
Peter Willmott, *The Evolution of a Community: A Study of Dagenham after Forty Years* (London: Routledge & Kegan Paul, 1963).
Peter Willmott and Michael Young, *Family and Class in a London Suburb,* (London: Routledge & Kegan Paul, 1960).
Michael Young and Peter Willmott, *Family and Kinship in East London,* (Harmondsworth, Middlesex: Penguin, 1962).

THE LABOUR PARTY

John Ardagh, 'The Future of Britain's Labour Party', *Realities*, No. 274 (Sep 1973) pp. 66–7, 80.
Inigo Bing (ed.), *The Labour Party: An Organisational Study*, Fabian Tract No. 407, June 1971 (London: Fabian Society).
Norman Birnbaum, 'Great Britain: The Reactive Revolt', in Morton A. Kaplan (ed.), *The Revolution in World Politics* (New York: John Wiley & Sons, 1962) pp. 31–68.
Norman Birnbaum, 'The Year Zero in British Socialism', *Antioch Review* (Summer 1960) pp. 133–52.
James M. Burns, 'The Parliamentary Labour Party in Great Britain', *American Political Science Review*, Vol. 44, No. 4 (Dec 1950) pp. 855–71.
Anthony Crosland, *Can Labour Win?* Fabian Tract No. 324, May 1960, (London: Fabian Society).
Anthony Crosland, 'Socialism in a Dangerous World', *Socialist Commentary*, (Nov 1968) supplement.
Richard H. S. Crossman, *Labour in the Affluent Society*, Fabian Tract No. 325, June 1960 (London: Fabian Society).
Hugh Dalton, *High Tide and After: Memoirs, 1945–1960* (London: Frederick Muller, 1962).
Leon D. Epstein, 'Who Makes British Party Policy: British Labour, 1960–1961', *Midwest Journal of Politics*, Vol. 6, No. 2 (May 1962) pp. 165–82.
Martin Harrison, *Trade Unions and the Labour Party since 1945* (Detroit: Wayne State University Press, 1960).
Stephen Haseler, *The Gaitskellites: Revisionism in the British Labour Party, 1951–1964* (London: Macmillan, 1969).
Bernard Hennessy, 'Trade Unions and the British Labour Party', *American Political Science Review*, Vol. 49, No. 4 (Dec 1955) pp. 1050–66.
Keith Hindell and Philip Williams, 'Scarborough and Blackpool: An Analysis of Some Votes at the Labour Party Conferences of 1960 and

1961', *Political Quarterly*, Vol. 33, No. 3 (July-Sep 1962) pp. 306–21.
George W. Jones, 'Who Opposes the Party Leadership?', *Socialist Commentary* (Oct 1962) pp. 12–14.
Gerald Kaufman (ed.), *The Left* (London: Anthony Blond, 1966).
Gerald Kaufman, 'Transport House: The Truth', *New Statesman*, May 7, 1965, pp. 706–7.
Let Labour Lead, London: Victory for Socialism Pamphlet, 1961.
Gerhard Loewenberg, 'The British Constitution and the Organization of the Labour Party', *American Political Science Review*, Vol. 52, No. 3 (Sep 1958) pp. 771–90.
Dean E. McHenry, *The Labour Party in Transition, 1931–1938* (London: George Routledge & Sons, 1938).
Robert T. McKenzie, 'Labour Party Organization', *Fabian Journal* (July 1955) pp. 11–13.
Robert T. McKenzie, 'Policy Decisions in Opposition: A Rejoinder', *Political Studies*, Vol. 5, No. 2 (June 1957) pp. 176–82.
T. E. M. McKitterick, 'The Membership of the Labour Party', *Political Quarterly*, Vol. 31, No. 3 (July-Sep 1960) pp. 312–23.
Ralph Miliband, *Parliamentary Socialism: A Study in the Politics of Labour* (London: Allen & Unwin, 1961).
Our Penny-Farthing Machine, special supplement, *Socialist Commentary*, (Oct 1965).
'The Labour Party', *Political Quarterly*, Vol. 31, No. 3, (July-Sep 1960).
Ben C. Roberts, 'Trade Unions and Party Politics', *Cambridge Journal*, Vol. 6, No. 7 (Apr 1953) pp. 387–402.
Saul Rose, 'Policy Decision in Opposition', *Political Studies*, Vol. 4, No. 2 (June 1956) pp. 128–38.
Saul Rose, 'Thoughts on the Constitution', *Socialist Commentary* (Sep 1960) pp. 9–11.
L. J. Sharpe, 'How the Labour Party Evolves Policies', *New Society*, Vol. 21, No. 511 (July 13, 1972) pp. 66–9.
Patrick Gordon Walker, 'A New Party Structure', *Socialist Commentary* (Jan 1956) pp. 18–20.
David J. Wilson, 'Party Bureaucracy in Britain: Regional and Area Organization', *British Journal of Political Science*, Vol. 2, Part 3 (July 1972) pp. 373–81.
Ivan Yates, 'Power in the Labour Party', *Political Quarterly*, Vol. 31, No. 3 (July-Sep 1960) pp. 300–11.

MEMBERS OF PARLIAMENT

Anthony Barker and Michael Rush, *The British Member of Parliament and His Information* (Toronto: University of Toronto Press, 1970).
Philip W. Buck, *Amateurs and Professionals in British Politics, 1918–*

1959 (Chicago: University of Chicago Press, 1963).

Philip W. Buck, 'Election Experience of Candidates for the House of Commons, 1918–1955', *Western Political Quarterly*, Vol. 12, No. 2 (June 1959) pp. 485–91.

Lionel H. Cohen, 'Local Government Complaints: the M.P.'s Viewpoint', *Public Administration*, Vol. 51 (Summer 1973) pp. 175–84.

A. D. R. Dickson, 'M.P.s' Readoption Conflicts: Their Causes and Consequences', *Political Studies*, Vol. 23, No. 1 (Mar 1975) pp. 62–70.

Rosemary Dinnage, 'Parliamentary Advice Bureau', *New Society*, Vol. 19, No. 491 (Feb 24, 1972) pp. 392–3.

Robert E. Dowse, 'The M.P. and His Surgery', *Political Studies*, Vol. 9, No. 3 (Oct 1963) pp. 333–41.

Leon D. Epstein, *British Politics in the Suez Crisis* (London: Pall Mall Press, 1964).

Leon D. Epstein, 'Cohesion of British Parliamentary Parties', *American Political Science Review*, Vol. 50, No. 2 (June 1956) pp. 360–77.

Leon D. Epstein, 'New M.P.s and the Politics of the PLP', *Political Studies*, Vol. 10, No. 2 (June 1962) pp. 121–9.

Lyndelle D. Fairlie, 'Candidate Selection Role Perceptions of Conservative and Labour Party Secretary/Agents', *Political Studies*, Vol. 24, No. 3 (Sep 1976) pp. 281–95.

Roger Fulford, *The Member and His Constituency* (Ramsay Muir Educational Trust, 1957).

Robert T. Holt and John E. Turner, 'Change in British Politics: Labour in Parliament and Government', in William G. Andrews (ed.), *European Politics II: The Dynamics of Change* (New York: D. Van Nostrand, 1969, pp. 23–116).

Dennis A. Kavanagh, 'The Orientations of Community Leaders to Parliamentary Candidates', *Political Studies*, Vol. 15, No. 3 (Oct 1967) pp. 351–6.

Richard L. Leonard and Valentine Herman (eds.), *The Backbencher and Parliament* (London: Macmillan, 1972).

T. E. M. McKitterick, 'The Selection of Parliamentary Candidates: The Labour Party', *Political Quarterly*, Vol. 30, No. 3 (July-Sep 1959) pp. 219–23.

John D. May, 'Opinion Structure of Political Parties: The Special Law of Curvilinear Disparity', *Political Studies*, Vol. 21, No. 2 (June 1973) pp. 135–51.

Nigel Nicolson, *People and Parliament* (London: Weidenfeld & Nicolson, 1958).

Peter Paterson, *The Selectorate: The Case for Primary Elections in Britain* (London: MacGibbon & Kee, 1967).

Austin Ranney, *Pathways to Parliament: Candidate Selection in Britain* (Madison: University of Wisconsin Press, 1965).

Jorgen S. Rasmussen, 'The Implication of Safe Seats for British Democracy', *Western Political Quarterly*, Vol. 19, No. 3 (Sep 1966) pp. 516–29.
Peter G. Richards, *Parliament and Conscience* (London: Allen & Unwin, 1970).
Peter G. Richards, *Honourable Members: A Study of the British Backbencher* (London: Faber & Faber, 1964).
Richard Rose, *Influencing Voters: A Study of Campaign Rationality* (London: Faber & Faber, 1967).
Michael Rush, *The Selection of Parliamentary Candidates*, (London: Nelson, 1969).

LOCAL GOVERNMENT

Hervey Benhem, *Two Cheers for the Town Hall* (London: Hutchinson, 1964).
J. Blondel and R. Hall, 'Conflict, Decision-Making and the Perceptions of Local Councillors', *Political Studies*, Vol. 15, No. 3 (Oct 1967) pp. 322–50.
Noel Boaden, *Urban Policy Making: Influences on County Boroughs in England and Wales* (Cambridge: Cambridge University Press, 1971).
J. M. Bochel, 'The Recruitment of Local Councillors: A Case-Study', *Political Studies*, Vol. 14, No. 3 (Oct 1966) pp. 360–4.
Ian Budge, 'Elections' Attitudes towards Local Government: A Survey of a Glasgow Constituency', *Political Studies*, Vol. 13, No. 3 (Oct 1965) pp. 386–92.
J. G. Bulpitt, *Party Politics in English Local Government*, (London: Longmans, Green, 1967).
J. G. Bulpitt, 'Party Systems in Local Government', *Political Studies*, Vol. II, No. 1 (Feb 1963) pp. 11–35.
Ruth Butterworth, 'Islington Borough Council: Some Characteristics of Single Party Rule', *Politics*, Vol. 1, No. 1 (May 1966) pp. 21–31.
Centre for Urban Studies, *London: Aspects of Change* (London: MacGibbon & Kee, 1964).
Roger V. Clements, *Local Notables and the City Council* (London: Macmillan, 1969).
John Dearlove, 'Councillors and Interest Groups in Kensington and Chelsea', *British Journal of Political Science*, Vol. 1, Part 2 (Apr 1971) pp. 129–53.
Hugh H. Heclo, 'The Councillor's Job', *Public Administration*, Vol. 47, No. 2 (Summer 1969) pp.185–202.
George W. Jones, *Borough Politics: A Study of the Wolverhampton Town Council, 1888–1964* (London: Macmillan, 1964).
John M. Lee, *Social Leaders and Public Persons: A Study of County*

Government in Cheshire since 1888 (Oxford: Clarendon Press, 1963).
James E. MacColl, 'The Party System in English Local Government', Public Administration, Vol. 27 (Summer 1949) pp. 69–75.
Bruce Miller, 'Citadels of Local Power', Twentieth Century, Vol. 162, No. 968 (Oct 1957) pp. 325–30.
Austin Mitchell, 'Clay Cross', Political Quarterly, Vol. 45, No. 2 (Apr – June 1974) pp. 165–78.
F. Musgrove, 'The Educational and Geographical Background of some Local Leaders', British Journal of Sociology, Vol. 12, No. 4 (Dec 1961) pp. 363–74.
Paul E. Peterson and Paul Kantor, 'Political Parties and Citizen Participation in English City Politics', Comparative Politics, Vol. 9, No. 2 (Jan 1977) pp. 197–217.
Ioan B. Rees, Government by Community (London: Charles Knight, 1971).
The Report of the Royal Commission on Local Government in Greater London (Herbert Report), Comnd. 1164 (HMSO, October 1960).
Gerald Rhodes, The Government of London: The Struggle for Reform (London: Weidenfeld & Nicolson, 1970).
Gerald Rhodes (ed.), The New Government of London: The First Five Years (London: Weidenfeld & Nicolson, 1972).
L. J. Sharpe, 'Elected Representatives in Local Government', British Journal of Sociology, Vol. 13, No. 3 (Sep 1962) pp. 189–209.
L. J. Sharpe, 'The Politics of Local Government in Greater London', Public Administration, Vol. 38, No. 2 (Summer 1960) pp. 157–72.
Frank Smallwood, Greater London: The Politics of Metropolitan Reform (New York: Bobbs – Merrill Company, 1965).
W. Thornhill, 'Agreements between Local Political Parties in Local Government Matters', Political Studies, Vol. 5, No. 1 (Feb 1957) pp. 83–8.
H. V. Wiseman, 'The Working of Local Government in Leeds. Part I. Party Control of Council and Committees', Public Administration, Vol. 41, No. 1 (Spring 1963) pp. 51–69; 'Part 2. More Party Conventions and Practices', ibid., No. 2 (Summer 1963) pp. 137–55.

LOCAL LABOUR PARTIES

Frank Bealey, J. Blondel, and W. P. McCann, Constituency Politics: A Study of Newcastle – under – Lyme (New York: Free Press, 1965).
Jean Blondel, 'The Conservative Association and the Labour Party in Reading', Political Studies, Vol. 6, No. 2 (June 1958) pp. 101–19.
John C. Brown, 'Local Party Efficiency as a Factor in the Outcome of British Elections', Political Studies, Vol 6, No. 2 (June 1958) pp. 174–78.

Angus Buchanan, 'East End Politics', *Socialist Commentary* (Mar 1961) pp. 13–15.
Ian Budge and Dennis Farlie, 'Political Recruitment and Dropout: Predictive Success of Background Characteristics over Five British Localities', *British Journal of Political Science*, Vol. 5, Part 1 (Jan 1975) pp. 33–68.
P. W. Campbell and A. H. Birch, 'Politics in the North-West', *Manchester School of Economic and Social Studies*, Vol. 18, No. 3 (Sep 1950) pp. 217–43.
Jim Daly, 'A Tale of Four Cities', *Socialist Commentary*, (Oct 1970) pp. 10–14; 'Action in Four Cities', ibid. (Sep 1971) pp. 6–11.
D. V. Donnison and D. E. G. Plowman, 'The Functions of Local Labour Parties: Experiments in Research Methods', *Political Studies*, Vol. 2, No. 2 (June 1954) pp. 154–67.
Robert E. Dowse and Jeffrey Stanyer, 'The Party Activists', *New Society*, (Oct 15, 1964).
Leon D. Epstein, 'British M.P.s and Their Local Parties: The Suez Case', *American Political Science Review*, Vol. 65, No. 2 (June 1960) pp. 374–90.
Wilfred Fienburgh and the Manchester Fabian Society, 'Put Policy on the Agenda', *Fabian Journal*, No. 6 (Feb 1952) pp. 25–33.
Paul Foot, 'In the Grass Roots of Politics: The State of the Labour Party', *Sunday Times* (Sep 29, 1968) pp. 13–14.
Tom Forester, 'Anatomy of a Local Labour Party', *New Statesman* (Sep 28, 1973) pp. 414–16; (Oct 5, 1973) pp. 464–7.
Robert C. Frasure, 'Constituency Racial Composition and the Attitudes of British M.P.s', *Comparative Politics*, Vol. 3, No. 2, (Jan 1971) pp. 201–10.
Julius Gould, ' "Riverside": A Labour Constituency', *Fabian Journal*, No. 14 (Nov 1954) pp. 12–18.
W. P. Grant, ' "Local" Parties in British Local Politics: A Framework for Empirical Analysis', *Political Studies*, Vol. 19, No. 2 (June 1971) pp. 201–12.
H. J. Hanham, 'The Local Organization of the Labour Party', *Western Political Quarterly*, Vol. 9, No. 2 (June 1956) pp. 376–88.
Richard Heller, 'East Fulham Revisited', *Journal of Contemporary History*, Vol. 6, No. 3 (1971) pp. 172–96.
Robert T. Holt and John E. Turner, *Political Parties in Action: The Battle of Barons Court* (New York: Free Press, 1968).
Edward G. Janosik, *Constituency Labour Parties in Britain*, (New York: Frederick A. Praeger, 1968).
Hugh Jenkins, 'Enfield to Mitcham to Putney: Fifteen Years in Pursuit of a Constituency', *Insight* (Nov 1965) pp. 16–22.
Dennis A. Kavanagh, *Constituency Electioneering in Britain*, (London: Longmans, Green, 1970).

Allen Kornberg and Robert C. Frasure, 'Constituency Agents and Conflict in Labour Parties', *Political Quarterly*, Vol. 45, No. 4 (Oct – Dec 1974) pp. 489–92.

Richard L. Leonard, 'Grass Roots Electioneering', *Plebs* (Sep 1965) pp. 486–7.

Richard L. Leonard, 'Labour's Agents', *Plebs*, Vol. 57, No. 10 (Oct 1965) pp. 14–17.

W. J. M. Mackenzie and Cynthia Arditti, 'Co-operative Politics in a Lancashire Constituency', *Political Studies*, Vol. 2, No. 2 (June 1954) pp. 112–27.

David Marquand, 'At the Hustings', *Encounter*, Vol. 25, No. 2 (Aug 1965) pp. 84–7.

Arthur Norris, 'Our Ward: Keeping Account' *Socialist Commentary*, (Oct 1956) p. 27.

Ben Pimlott, 'Does Local Party Organization Matter?' *British Journal of Political Science*, Vol. 2, Part 3 (July 1972) pp. 381–3.

Ben Pimlott, 'Local Party Organization, Turnout and Marginality', *British Journal of Political Science*, Vol. 3, Part 2 (Apr 1973) pp. 252–5.

Jorgen S. Rasmussen, 'The Impact of Constituency Structural Characteristics upon Policy Preferences in Britain', *Comparative Politics*, Vol. 6, No. 1 (Oct 1973) pp. 123–45.

Richard Rose, 'The Political Ideas of English Party Activists', *American Political Science Review*, Vol. 56, No. 2 (June 1962) pp. 360–71.

Michael Steed, 'Case Study: My Own By-Election', *Government and Opposition*, Vol. 9, No. 3 (Summer 1974) pp. 345–58.

Henry J. Steck 'Grassroots Militants and Ideology: the Bevanite Revolt', *Polity*, Vol. 2, No. 4 (Summer 1970) pp. 426–42.

Nigel Todd, 'Labour Women: A Study of Women in the Bexley Branch of the British Labour Party (1945–1950)' *Journal of Contemporary History*, Vol. 8, No. 2 (Apr 1973) pp. 159–73.

William Wallace, 'The British General Election of 1970 – Impressions of an Academic Candidate', *Government and Opposition*, Vol. 6, No. 1 (Winter 1971) pp. 36–57.

Philip Whitehead, 'Views', *The Listener*, (Oct 18, 1973) p. 506.

David J. Wilson, 'Constituency Party Autonomy and Central Control', *Political Studies*, Vol. 21, No. 2 (June 1973) pp. 167–74.

Robert Worcester, 'The Hidden Activists', *New Society*, Vol. 20, No. 506 (June 8, 1972) pp. 512–13.

BERMONDSEY, FULHAM, AND SOUTH KENSINGTON

E. J. Beck, *History of Rotherhithe* (Cambridge: Cambridge University Press, 1907).

Bermondsey Official Guide (London: Pyramid Press, 1963).
Edward T. Clarke, *Bermondsey: Its Historic Memories and Associations* (London: Elliot Stock, 1901).
Pearl Jephcott, *Married Women Working* (London: Allen & Unwin, 1962).
V. Leff and C. H. Blunden, *Riverside Story: The Story of Bermondsey and Its People* (London: Civic Publicity Services, Publicity House, 1965).
The Official Guide to the Borough of Bermondsey (London: Pyramid Press, 1960).
Fenner Brockway, *Bermondsey Story: The Life of Alfred Salter* (London: Allen & Unwin, 1949).
T. Falkner, *An Historical and Topographical Account of Fulham, including the Hamlet of Hammersmith* (London: J. Tilling, Chelsea, 1813).
Fulham: The Official Guide (London: Edward J. Burrow and Co., 1950).
C. M. L. Wickham and F. E. Hansford, *The Story of Bishop Creighton House*, Fulham History Society Publications, No. 5, 1965, mimeographed.
William Gaunt, *Kensington* (London: Batsford, 1958).
W. J. Loftie, *Kensington: Picturesque and Historical* (London: Field & Tuer, 1888).
The Royal Borough of Kensington (London: Edward T. Burrow & Co.).
Eric Whelpton and Barbara Whelpton, *The Intimate Charm of Kensington* (London: Nicolson & Watson, 1948).

LABOUR PARTY DOCUMENTS

Sara Barker, *How the Labour Party Works* (London: Labour Party, revised edition).
Harold Croft, *Party Organization* (London: Labour Party, 1957).
Fabian Society, *The Mechanics of Victory*, Young Fabian Pamphlet No. 3 (Feb 1962).
Mary A. Hamilton, *The Labour Party Today: What It Is and How It Works* (London: Labour Book Service).
Handbook: Facts and Figures for Socialists (London: Labour Party, 1951).
Interim Report of the Sub-Committee on Party Organization, (London: Labour Party, 1955).
Labour Party Interim Report of the Committee of Enquiry into Party Organisation (London: Labour Party, 1967).
Labour Party Report of the Committee of Enquiry into Party Organisation (London: Labour Party, 1968).
Labour's Programme 1973 (London: Labour Party, 1973).

Labour and the Common Market: Report of a Special Conference of the Labour Party (London: Labour Party, July 17, 1971).
Participation '69 (London: Labour Party, 1969).
Participation '72, (London: Labour Party, 1972).
Morgan Phillips, *This is the Labour Party* (London: Labour Party, no date).
Morgan Phillips, *Labour in the Sixties*, (London: Labour Party, 1960).
Reorganization of Party Structure (London: Labour Party 1973).
Reports of the Annual Conference of the Labour Party (London: Labour Party, 1945–75).

Index

Abbey Ward (Bermondsey), 105, 108, 341n.24
Abrams, Mark, quoted, 38; cited, 229
Action Committee (Bermondsey), 134–5, 139–40, 146, 176, 179, 215, 317, 348n.49
Activists, 162; characteristics of, 1–3; as council candidates, 201, 202, 214; interests of, 169–70, 176, 178, 185; number of, 15, 159, 160, 204, 206–7, 210, 316–17, 322, 347n.37
Age: of candidates and officers, 126, 129, 131, 134, 297, 302, 303; discords, 77, 145, 150; distribution in CLPs, 102, 116, 149, 161–2; influence on issue attitudes, 247, 249, 250, 256, 257, 259, 260–4 *passim*, 323–4; influences political aspirations, 285–6, 296–7; *see also* Factional rivalries; listing for three parties
Agents, 6, 8, 20, 54–5, 73, 76, 90, 282; in Bermondsey, 125, 126, 144–6, 147, 158, 171, 203, 204, 224, 315, 317; in Fulham, 148–52, 154, 159, 163–4, 166, 167, 172, 173, 184, 185, 202, 205–9, 218, 225, 318, 319, 320, 365n.22; links with other units, 21, 43–4, 46, 47, 170, 217, 218; and National Agency Service, 47; number of, 23, 42, 331n.19; role and tasks of, 21–2, 25, 54–5, 115, 143–4, 165, 168, 176, 199, 203, 221, 294, 296, 310, 321; in South Kensington, 132, 154–6, 160, 164, 167, 169, 173, 174, 202–3, 209, 210, 219, 225, 320
Aldermen, 172, 216, 301, 304–9 *passim*.
Alford, Robert R., cited, 229
Anglo-American Alliance, 226; tie-up with other issues, 231–2, 350n.14; views on, 239–43, 273–5, 324, 325
Annual Conference, 6, 8, 41, 49, 67; agenda of, 57–8, 334n.28; composition of, 11, 57; conflict with PLP, 44, 52, 57, 63–7, 75, 76–7, 213; debates in, 58–63 *passim*.; policymaking role of, 52, 53, 55–6, 66, 335n.36; and resolutions, 33, 55, 70, 177, 182, 184, 185, 188, 193–7, 317, 319–20, 322, 326; and sanctions, 10, 49–50, 78; and Transport House, 49–50; voting in, 48, 59–62, 64, 335n.34
Annual Conferences, 335n.36; *1960*: 60, 65, 187, 231; *1961*: 60, 65; *1962*: 194–5; *1963*: 194–5; *1970*: 64, 74; *1974*: 10, 58, 59, 63, 75
Anti-Violence League, 263
Apathy, 2, 9, 177, 308, 309; in hopeless Labour areas, 39, 321; in marginal areas, 36, 130, 319; in safe Labour areas, 33–4, 121, 145, 180, 313, 316
Aspirations, political, 283–4, 285–9, 293, 297, 300, 364n.9; in hopeless Labour areas, 40, 285, 310, 322; and ideological views, 276; in marginal areas, 37, 40, 318, 320; and motivations, 288–9; and party involvement, 282, 285, 286; in safe Labour areas, 34–5, 40, 315; *see also* Incentives; Motivations
Association of Engineering and Shipbuilding Draughtsmen, 96
Attlee, Clement, 64, 73
Attlee Government, 26, 61, 70, 71, 72

Baird, John, 337n.78
Barber, Maurice, 154–6, 209; *see also* Agents
Barking CLP, 158, 343n.1
Barons Court CLP, 171, 172, 173–4, 200, 208, 210, 216, 217, 218, 299, 347n.39
Barons Court parliamentary district, 90, 128, 150, 199, 201, 347n.40
Battersea North CLP, 171, 342n.1
Beckenham CLP. 343n.1
Bermondsey, 83; history, 84–8; location, 84; as parliamentary district, 84; postwar economy of, 88–9; socioeconomic features of, 85–6, 96–7, 100–7, 112–13, 294; voting patterns in, 108–12
Bermondsey CLP: Action Committee in, 134–5, 140; appraisal of, 315–18; candidate selection in, 199, 303, 346n.32;

388   Index

electoral performance of, 211, 316; Executive Committee structure in, 134; external contacts of, 121, 146, 170–1, 204, 205, 316; finance of, 223–5; General Management Committee structure in, 132–4; goals of, 120–2; incentives in, 291, 294, 295, 303, 306–7, 328, 364n.17; liaison with borough council, 214–17 *passim.*; membership recruitment in, 157–9; officers of, 127, 133, 297; policymaking in, 147–8, 163, 195, 197, 215–16, 317; social composition of, 114–16, 314, 317, 323; stability of, 96, 117–18, 315; training programs in, 163; views on issues in, 234, 237, 239, 244, 247, 251, 254–5, 257, 260, 262, 265, 267–9, 270–2, 276–7, 279, 317, 323, 359n.96; ward organization in, 124–7, 163; Women's Section in, 139–40; Young Socialists in, 140; *see also* Agents; Borough Council; Borough Councillors; Campaigns, election; Factional rivalries; Finance; GMC, Bermondsey; Incentives; Local Affairs Management; Membership, Labour Party; Trade Unions; Wards/Branches

Bermondsey West CLP, 139, 166
Bermondsey West parliamentary district, 84, 125, 199, 340n.7
Bethnal Green CLP, 342n.1
Bevan, Aneurin, 64, 72, 73; quoted, 27, 65
'Bevanism', 25, 27, 28, 60, 64, 72, 73
Birch, A. H., quoted, ix
Blackburn, Raymond, 70, 336n.54
Blyth CLP, 75–6
Borough council, 32, 82, 147; in Bermondsey, 86–7, 121, 134–5, 147, 214–15, 301, 315–17; in Fulham, 91–2, 122, 130, 177, 183, 184, 216–19, 268, 318, 322; functions and organization of, 9, 47, 212, 213, 301, 305, 313; incentives in, 308; in Kensington, 95, 98–9, 154, 174, 187, 219; *see also* Borough councillors; Labour Group; Local Affairs Management
Borough councillors, 9, 51, 77, 213, 301–2; in Bermondsey, 127, 133, 180, 214; and CLPs, 15, 33, 216–19, 308; contact with citizens, 81, 86–7, 220, 221; duties of, 11, 213–14, 306; in Fulham, 129, 151, 164, 216–19, 302, 365n.25; in Kensington, 154–5; and motivations, 288–9, 300–1, 364n.14; and political aspirations, 283–4, 285; social composition of, 34, 214, 302, 303, 314–15; views on issues, 266, 267, 270–2; *see also* Borough councillors; Labour Group; Local Affairs Management

Borough Labour party, 5, 41–2, 44, 70, 73; *see also* District Labour party
Borough local government committee, 43
Braddock, Elizabeth, 73
Bradford South CLP, 72
Bradford West CLP, 78
Brentford and Chiswick parliamentary district, 171
Brigg CLP, 338n.88
Bromley CLP, 343n.1
Brown, Alan, 71
Burton, Elaine, 73–4
Butler, David, cited, 233
Butler, Herbert W., 337n.75
By-elections, 4, 46, 49, 71, 76, 122, 171, 173, 199

Callaghan, James, 338n.81
Camberwell, Peckham CLP, 343n.1
Campaign for Nuclear Disarmament, 184, 233, 234, 291, 292
Campaigns, election, 7–9, 12–14, 17, 165, 175; agent's role in, 22; in Bermondsey, 32, 170–1, 178, 203–5; conduct of, 17, 42, 46, 50, 197–211; finance of, 50, 224–5; in Fulham, 35, 149–53 *passim.*, 167, 178, 184–5, 318, 319, 320; problems in, 24–5; in South Kensington, 37, 154, 178, 187, 321; training for, 163–4; voting results in, 211–12, 316, 319
Candidates, local, 8, 9, 11, 311; conflict over, 36, 174–5; occupations of, 112–13; recruitment and training of, 145–6, 163–4, 215, 318; selection of, 12, 33, 42–3, 44, 128, 129, 170, 172, 173, 200–3, 216–17, 301–3, 308, 309, 310, 317
Candidates, parliamentary, 11, 22, 57; selection of, 8–9, 12, 20, 32, 35, 37, 47, 49, 67–8, 74, 173–4, 197–200, 297–300, 310
Capital punishment, 226, 259; linked with other issues, 232–3, 265, 350n.14; views on, 79, 263–5, 273–5, 323, 345n.19
Central Ward (Bermondsey), 108, 111, 125, 127
Chelsea CLP, 56–7, 160, 173, 343n.1
Chief Whip, 66, 67, 147
Cities of London and Westminster CLP, 343n.1

Index

Citizens, contact with, 9, 11, 14, 17, 81–2, 214, 219–21; in Bermondsey, 135, 147, 180, 214, 215, 221, 316; in Fulham, 153, 218, 221, 318–19; in South Kensington, 219, 222; *see also* Mellish, Robert J.
Clause IV, 226; activists' views on, 55–6, 246–50, 273–6 *passim.*, 324, 325; linked with other issues, 231–3, 350n.14
Clerical and Administrative Workers Union, 95
Colquhoun, Maureen, 70
Common Market, 27, 55, 148, 178, 226; activists' attitudes on, 163, 179, 180, 184, 186–7, 273–4; discussed at Conferences, 53–4, 334n.19, 335n.36; linked with other issues, 231–3, 350n.14; M.P.s' views on, 65, 75–9, 80, 338n.88; South Kensington resolution on, 189–93, 317, 324, 345n.21
Communication, 214, 216, 217; *see also* Coordination; Diffusion of information
Communist Party, 108, 226, 259; attitudes towards, 265–8, 273–5, 323; tied to other issues, 232–3, 350n.14
Conservative Government, 76–7, 172, 180, 182, 183, 184, 190, 209, 256, 268
Conservative Party, 16, 25, 26, 27, 59, 71, 77, 108, 222, 300, 305, 347n.40; in Bermondsey, 111, 120–1, 145, 204–5, 215, 216, 313, 315, 342n.1, 347nn.34, 36; in Fulham, 122, 130, 141, 150, 206, 216, 219, 318; local candidates of, 112–13; in South Kensington, 109, 122, 123, 202, 314–15, 347n.40, 348n.46
Conservatives, co-operation with, 226; attitudes towards, 250–6, 273–5, 324, 325; linked with other issues, 232–3, 350n.14
Constituency Labour Party (CLP), activities and organization of, 5, 16–22, 41–2, 293–4; criticism of, 16–17; functions of, 6–10; and M.P.s, 67–82; and National Executive Committee, 48–50, 64–5; and Party Conference, 8, 57–63; problems of, 22–9; profiles of, 29–40; and Transport House, 44–5, 46–7, 50–1; *see also* Bermondsey CLP; Fulham CLP; South Kensington CLP
Constitution, Labour Party, 5, 52, 55, 64, 74, 76, 246
Co-operative Party, 47, 54, 93, 136, 291

Co-operatives, 4, 17; in Bermondsey, 89, 118, 127, 132–3, 134, 315; in Fulham, 93, 118, 136, 137, 315; represented in Labour Party, 48, 170, 295; in South Kensington, 118, 307, 315
Coordination, 17, 173, 174; in CLPs, 44, 125, 128, 149, 154, 166, 172, 217, 319; importance of, 165; in national Party, 43–4, 47, 50, 66; *see also* Diffusion of information
County Labour party, 6, 43–6, 64
Coventry South CLP, 73–4
Craddock, George, 72
Cripps, Sir Stafford, 332n.27
Crossman, Richard H. S., quoted, 27, 332n.27

Dagenham, 230
Defense policy, 55, 56, 65, 72, 281, 319, 320, 322, 325; *see also* Unilateral disarmament
DeGaulle, General Charles, 256
Deputy Leader, Labour Party, 48, 67
Dickson, A. D. R., cited, 69, 336n.53
Diffusion of information, 18, 19, 21; in Bermondsey, 168, 169, 178, 315; in Fulham, 158–9, 178; importance of, 8, 168, 169, 214; in South Kensington, 167, 168, 169, 178, 186, 320, 322; *see also* Coordination
Discipline: of local parties and individuals, 49–51, 73; in Parliamentary Labour Party, 63, 69, 70–3; *see also* Incentives; Members of Parliament
District Labour party, 5–6, 42–6 *passim*.
Dockyard Ward (Bermondsey), 100, 104, 105, 108, 341n.24
Doctrine, 226; activists' views on, 243–6, 273–5, 276, 277–8, 324; basis for factionalism, 25–9, 65; and candidate selection, 67–8; in hopeless Labour areas, 38, 173; linked with other issues, 231–3, 350n.14; in marginal areas, 35–6, 325–7; and M.P. – CLP relations, 81; *see also* Factional rivalries; Ideological 'enthusiasts'
Donnelly, Desmond, 71–2
Downs, Anthony, cited, 36, 325–6
Dulwich CLP, 171

Earls Court Ward (South Kensington), 98, 104, 107, 109–11, 131, 138, 160, 187–9, 190, 192, 200, 209
East Ham North CLP, 343n.1
Ebbw Vale CLP, 72

Edmonton CLP, 343n.1
Education: as indicator of class, 99, 101–2; of party members, 7, 17, 25, 114–15, 162–4, 173, 321; and views on issues, 230–1, 237, 239, 240, 243, 244, 247, 248, 251–5 *passim.*, 258–9, 260, 262–5, 266, 269, 271, 276–9, 323–4, 349n.9, 352n.24, 353–4n.33, 354n.38, 362n.108; and voting patterns, 111
Education policy, 178, 186–7, 188, 190–5, 335n.36
Edwards, Alfred, 71
Elections: for borough council, 42–3, 108, 109, 112, 122, 123, 172, 197; CLP performance in, 211–12; impact on parties, 3–4, 197; for London County Council, 109; for Parliament, 109
Ellis, Harry, 209
Enfield East CLP, 343n.1
Enfield West CLP, 343n.1
Environment, 96; impact on parties, 6, 30–2, 83, 118, 120, 312–15; and voting patterns, 108–12
Epstein, Leon, cited, 71
Eton and Slough CLP, 172
Etzioni, Amitai, 329
Evans, Stanley, 71, 336n.62
Executive Committee, 175, 176; in Bermondsey, 134; and candidate selection, 12, 198, 201–3, 299, 301, 302, 303, 309, 346–7n.33; in Fulham, 137, 159, 176; make-up and powers, 20–1, 176, 294, 309; in South Kensington, 138–9; views on issues in, 161, 240, 242, 246, 249, 271–2, 277, 343n.7, 359n.92; *see also* Constituency Labour Party; General Management Committee; listing for three parties

Fabian Society, 4, 136, 138, 200, 291
Factional rivalries, 6, 27–9, 68, 293, 344–5n.17; in Bermondsey, 146, 148, 214, 234, 281; in Fulham, 129, 137, 142, 150–4 *passim.*, 176, 184–5, 234, 281, 296, 303, 318, 319, 320, 347n.38; generational basis of, 24, 34; in hopeless Labour areas, 38–40, 314; ideological basis of, 5, 25–9, 240, 246–7, 273, 280–1; in marginal areas, 35–6, 40, 313–14, 326–7; in national Party, 58–9, 62–7 *passim.*, 80, 231, 243, 256, 329; over readoption of M.P.s, 75; role of agent in, 21–2; in safe Labour areas, 32–3, 40, 77, 313; in South Kensington, 130–2, 138–9, 155, 160, 186–93 *passim.*, 238, 281, 320–1, 322, 345n.20; *see also* Doctrine; Ideological 'enthusiasts'
Feltham CLP, 343n.1
Fernyhough, Ernest, 72
Finance, 6, 7, 11–12, 17, 22, 23–4, 157, 165, 176; in Bermondsey, 125–6, 166, 178, 223–5, 315, 316; in Fulham, 137, 149, 166, 167, 171–2, 178, 223–5, 318; of CLPs, 9, 16, 42, 56, 165, 222, 315; of national Party, 50, 222; in South Kensington, 130, 178, 223–5, 321–2
Foot, Michael, 72
Foreign policy, 79, 187, 239, 281, 317, 319, 322
Fulham, 83; history, 90–2; location, 90; as parliamentary district, 90, 128, 347n.40; postwar economy of, 92–3; socio-economic features of, 97–8, 100–7, 113, 149; voting patterns in, 108–12 *passim.*
Fulham CLP, appraisal of, 318–20; candidate selection in, 199–202, 346–7n.33; electoral performance of, 205–9, 211–12, 319; Executive Committee structure in, 137; external contacts of, 128, 171–3, 201, 208, 216–18, 318; finance of, 157, 223–5 *passim.*; General Management Committee structure in, 135–7; goals of, 122, 318, 320; incentives in, 130, 158, 291, 294, 295, 306–7, 328, 364n.17; membership recruitment in, 157, 158, 159–60; officers in, 128–30, 297, 303, 364n.19; policymaking in, 195, 197, 218, 319–20; social composition of, 114–16, 176, 314; stability of, 98, 117–18; training programs in, 318, 319; views on issues in, 234, 237, 239, 244, 247, 250, 251, 254–5, 257, 260, 262, 263, 264, 265, 267, 268, 269, 270–2, 276–8, 280, 323, 326, 359n.96, 363n.115; ward organization in, 127–30; Women's Section in, 140–1; Young Socialists in, 141–2; *see also* Agents; Borough council; Borough councillors; Campaigns, election; Factional rivalries; Finance; GMC, Fulham; Incentives; Local Affairs Management; Membership, Labour Party; Trade Unions; Wards/Branches
Fulham East CLP, 159
Fulham East parliamentary district, 90, 127–8, 152, 199
Fulham West CLP, 159, 166

Fulham West parliamentary district, 90, 127–8, 148, 199

Gaitskell, Mrs. Dora, 141
Gaitskell, Hugh, 60, 64, 171, 238; and Clause IV, 231, 246–7, 370; criticism of, 56, 352n.22; and Fulham campaign, 209, 327; and immigration, 260; and Party Conference, 65; and unilateralism, 187, 231, 236; *see also* Leaders, national Party
General Management Committee (GMC): and candidate selection, 198, 200–1, 298–302 *passim.*; incentives in, 143, 176, 294–5, 303–4, 364n.17; in intermediate organizations, 42–3; and Labour Group, 33, 35, 213–14, 219, 313; make-up of, 8, 11, 17–18, 176, 294; in policymaking, 10–11, 54–8 *passim.*, 63, 82, 177–8, 344n.16; and readoption of M.P.s, 74–5; views on issue stands in, 235, 255–6; *see also* listing for three parties
General Management Committee, Bermondsey: content of meetings, 147, 163, 168, 178, 179–82, 307, 344–5n.17; social composition of, 113–16, 314, 317; stability of, 116–18; structure of, 132–4; *see also* Bermondsey CLP
General Management Committee, Fulham: content of meetings, 153, 168, 178, 182–5, 187, 307, 319, 344–5n.17; social composition of, 113–16, 176, 314; stability of, 116–18; structure of, 135–7; *see also* Fulham CLP
General Management Committee, South Kensington, 138, 167; content of meetings, 167, 168, 169, 178, 185–7, 307, 322, 344–5n.17; social composition of, 13–16, 173; stability of, 116–18; structure of, 138, 295; *see also* South Kensington CLP
General Secretary, Labour Party, 50, 57, 66, 67
German rearmament, 27, 60, 73, 148
Goals, Party, 6, 143, 157, 290, 293, 306, 312; of CLP in hopeless Labour areas, 37, 40, 122–4, 314, 321, 323; of CLP in marginal areas, 35, 40, 122, 151–2, 313–14, 318, 320; of CLP in safe Labour areas, 32, 40, 120–2, 145, 313; in national organization, 5, 67, 231, 246–7
Green Paper, 51, 54–5

Griffiths, Edward, 76

Hackney Central CLP, 337n.75
Hammersmith borough, 90
Hammersmith North CLP, 79, 171
Hampstead parliamentary district, 124
Harrison, Martin, cited, 60
Harrow West CLP, 343n.1
Hayes and Harlington CLP, 73, 211, 343n.1
Hayward, Ronald, quoted 14
Heath, Edward, 256
Henderson, Arthur, 4
Hilliard, Leslie, 148–52, 172; *see also* Agents
Hillingdon, Hayes and Harlington CLP, 78
Hindess, Barry, quoted, ix
Holland Ward (South Kensington), 102, 104, 107, 109–11, 132, 138, 190, 200
Home Policy Committee (NEC), 53
'Hopeless' Labour district, 2; characteristics of, 29, 31–2; CLP organization in, 23, 28, 37–40, 55–6, 67, 156, 177, 195–6, 281, 314; incentives in, 309–11
Houghton, Douglas, 338n.88
House of Commons, 6, 9, 32, 52, 65, 68, 71, 79, 80, 81, 184, 220–1, 260, 268, 288, 294, 310
House of Lords, 6
Housing, 30, 31, 32, 112, 178, 220, 259–60; in Bermondsey, 88, 105–6, 179–80, 181, 214, 221; in Fulham, 91, 106–7, 172, 185, 206, 209, 341n.22, 345n.19; in South Kensington, 93, 95, 107, 186–7, 189
Hurlingham Ward (Fulham), 101, 102, 104, 106, 107, 109–11, 128, 129, 137, 209, 216, 303
Hutchinson, H. Lester, 73

Ideological 'enthusiasts', 28–9, 35–6, 38, 138, 295, 313, 317; number and characteristics of, 276–81, 362n.108; *see also* Doctrine
Ideology, *see* Doctrine
Immigration, 53, 70, 178, 226, 337n.78; activists' attitudes on, 180–3, 195, 259–63, 273–4, 317, 323; as election issue, 203–4, 206; linked with other issues, 232–3, 265, 350n.14; PLP policy on, 182
Incentives, 9, 11, 21, 22, 32, 82, 115–16, 118, 143–4, 165–6, 213, 214, 281, 283, 288–311, 327–9; in hopeless Labour areas, 37, 39, 40, 124, 154, 178, 314,

322; in marginal areas, 36, 37, 122, 130, 150, 153, 154, 158, 178, 314, 315, 318, 320; in safe Labour areas, 34–5, 121–2, 140, 148, 166, 178, 215, 313, 315, 317; *see also* Aspirations, political; Discipline; Motivation
International Committee (NEC), 53
International Department (Transport House), 53
Involvement, party, 282–5; and attitudes towards issues, 235–6, 240, 243, 351–2n.21, 352n.32, 353n.32; and borough councillors, 302, 303, 304, 306, 365n.25; and GMC motivation, 292; and parliamentary candidates, 300; and perceptions of problems, 161, 223, 269, 280, 281, 343n.8; in the three CLPs, 291, 292–3, 364n.13
Irvine, Sir Arthur, 78–9
Islington North CLP, 78, 343n.1
Islington South-West CLP, 343n.1

Jarrow CLP, 72
Justices of the peace, 305–6, 308, 309, 311

Kelley, Harold H., cited, 144
Kensington and Chelsea CLP, 79–80
Kensington North CLP, 173, 174–5, 210, 260, 302, 304, 310–11, 322, 343n.1
Kensington North parliamentary district, 93, 124, 202, 212, 219
Kettering CLP, 78
Kingston-upon-Thames CLP, 343n.1

Labour Agents Union, 148
Labour Group, 8, 19, 37, 42–4, 301; and council assignments, 303–4; liaison with CLPs, 32–5, 43, 134–5, 213–19, 307, 318; *see also* Borough council; Borough councillors
Labour Party, national organization: early organization of, 4, 52; finance of, 187, 222; as ideological organization, 5, 189, 330n.3; manifesto of, 66, 188, 195, 336n.46 membership of, 4, 158; *see also* listings under specific organs and the three parties
Lambeth, Brixton CLP, 343n.1
Lambeth, Vauxhall CLP, 78, 79
Leader, Labour Party, 48, 50, 58, 63, 64–5, 67, 213, 335n.37; *see also* Gaitskell, Hugh; Wilson, Harold
Leaders, national Party 226; activists' attitudes towards, 236–8, 273–5, 324; criticism of, 55–6, 60, 352n.22; issue linkages with, 231–2, 350n.14; and Party Conference, 60–3 *passim.*, 65, 80; and readoption of M.P.s, 73–81
Leathermarket Ward (Bermondsey), 104, 341n.24
Lewisham South CLP, 160, 343n.1
Leyton CLP, 343n.1
Liberal Party, 25, 71, 108, 109, 111–13, 185, 212, 314–15, 348n.46
Lincoln CLP, 76
Liverpool, Edge Hill CLP, 78–9
Liverpool, Exchange CLP, 73
Liverpool, Toxteth CLP, 78
Local Affairs Management, 9, 17, 212–14; in Bermondsey, 121, 145, 178, 214–16; in Fulham, 122, 149, 151–2, 178, 216–19, 318; in hopeless Labour areas, 37, 38, 40; in marginal areas, 35, 40; in safe Labour areas, 32–3, 40; in South Kensington, 178, 219; *see also* Borough councils; Borough councillors; Labour Group
Local government reform, Britain, 6, 10, 41, 42, 43
Local government reform, London, 171, 178, 202, 226, 339n.1; attitudes towards, 268–75 *passim.*, 324; in Bermondsey, 179–80, 181–2, 205; in Fulham, 168–9, 171, 183–4, 209, 340n.14; linked with other issues, 232–3, 350n.14; in South Kensington, 187
London Co-operative Society, 339n.97
London County Council (LCC), 108, 144, 164, 225, 268
London Labour Party, 45, 121, 123, 135, 147, 170–1, 173, 179, 181, 183, 186, 209, 210, 268
Lyons, Edward, 78

McKay, Margaret, 70
Macmillan Government, 260
Mallalieu, E. L., 338n.88
Manchester, Blackley CLP, 78
Marginal district, 2; characteristics of, 29–31, 150; CLP organization in, 23, 28, 35–7, 46, 50, 51, 80, 177, 280–1, 313–14, 325–7; incentives in, 308–9, 311, 329; *see also* Fulham CLP
Mayor, 3, 34, 133, 285, 293, 304, 306, 308, 309, 311
Mellish, Robert J., 121, 146–8, 158, 170, 199, 204, 205, 221, 268, 342n.13; selected as candidate, 199, 346n.31; role in policymaking, 163, 179, 181, 281
Members of Parliament (M.P.s), 34, 164,

285; contact with citizens, 9, 220, 316, 318–19; under discipline, 63, 65, 68–73 *passim.*, 75–7, 80, 338n.98; on NEC, 48, 66; and Party Conference, 52, 57, 76–7; readoption of, 69–70, 73–81; relations with CLPs, 19, 32, 51, 55, 67–82, 146–8, 152–4, 158, 163, 177, 182–3, 294, 315, 317; role of, 64, 143–4
Membership, Labour Party, 9, 10, 17, 47, 83, 176, 177, 293, 308, 312, 313; decline of, 24, 332n.24; effects of population instability on, 15–16, historical development of, 4–5; importance of, 6–7, 24–5, 157–8, 161–2; qualifications for and types of, 10–11; period of entry into and issue stands, 234, 235, 236, 240, 242, 243, 245, 253–6, 259, 277–8, 325; recruitment in Bermondsey, 116, 145–6, 147, 158–9, 161–2, 316, 317; recruitment in Fulham, 116, 117, 140–1, 149, 157–60, 161, 162, 319, 320; recruitment in hopeless Labour areas, 38, 39, 309, 314; recruitment in marginal areas, 36–7, 308–9, 314; recruitment in safe Labour areas, 33–4; recruitment in South Kensington, 116, 123, 160, 162, 209, 321–2; *see also* Bermondsey CLP; Fulham CLP; South Kensington CLP
Methodology, xi–xiii, 226–9, 348n.1, 350n.17, 351–2n.21, 360–1n.100, 361n.105, 363n.114
Metropolitan counties, 43
Michels, Robert, 175–7, 344n.15
Middlesbrough East CLP, 71
Milne, Edward J., 75–6, 338n.85
Mineworkers, Yorkshire, 80
'Missionary' organization model, 39, 122–3, 177, 314, 321
Morrison, Lord, quoted, 268
Motivations, 186, 283, 286–9, 292, 293, 306, 307, 317, 320, 322, 327, 329, 364n.8; *see also* Aspirations, political; Incentives
Movement for Colonial Freedom, 291
Munster Ward (Fulham), 106, 109–11, 128, 129, 130, 135–7, 212, 303

National Agency Service, 23, 47, 50
National Agent, 45, 50, 75, 338n.81
National Campaign for the Abolition of Capital Punishment, 263
National Executive Committee (NEC), 8, 45, 46; composition of, 48–50, 64, 66, 67; and discipline of M.P.s, 63, 71–3; and the Parliamentary Labour Party, 64–7; and Party Conference, 56–8, 61, 62, 66–7, 177, 182, 193, 194, 344n.16; powers and functions of, 6, 10, 11, 18, 43, 47–50, 74, 173, 218, 295; role in candidate selection, 198, 298; role in policymaking, 53–7, 60, 62, 66; and readoption of M.P.s, 70, 73–9, 337n.78
National Union of General and Municipal Workers, 93
National Union of Journalists, 95
National Union of Public Employees, 132, 181
National Union of Railwaymen, 96
National Union of Teachers, 95
National Union of Vehicle Builders, 93
Nationalization, *see* Clause IV; Public ownership
Neckinger Ward (Bermondsey), 105, 108, 125, 127, 341n.24
Nenni telegram, 72
Newham North-East CLP, 77–8
Non-ideologicals, 27–9, 138, 276–81, 362n.108; *see also* Doctrine
Normanton CLP, 78
Northampton North CLP, 78
Nottingham East CLP, 78.

Occupation: of borough council candidates, 112–13, 214; and class identification, 229; distribution in three districts, 99–101; of GMC members, 113–14; impact on issue stands, 235–8, 243–4, 247–8, 255, 257, 259–66 *passim.*, 269, 271, 277–9, 348n.9, 355n.53, 356n.64, 358n.79, 359n.95; as indicator of class, 99–101; and motivation, 287–8; and party involvement, 176, 282–5, 363n.2; and voting patterns, 109–11; *see also* Education; Social Class
Officers, CLP, 18, 20, 36, 176–7, 344–5n.17; age and tenure of, 234, 235, 297; in Bermondsey, 127, 133, 176, 178, 297; in Fulham, 130, 137, 140–1, 142, 178, 182, 185, 202, 219; policymaking role of, 175–6; in South Kensington, 131, 138–9, 176, 178, 187; views on issues, 161, 176, 184, 187, 240, 246, 266–72 *passim.*, 277–8, 280, 343n.7, 350nn.12, 47, 359n.92, 362n.108
Officers, ward, 14, 295; activities of, 161,

214, 219–20, 343n.7; in Fulham, 128–9, 135, 184, 202, 218; ideological outlooks of, 280, 350n.12, in safe Labour areas, 34, 126; in South Kensington, 131, 132, 138, 160, 167, 188–9, 209; *see also* Wards/Branches
Organization Committee (NEC), 79
Organization Department (Transport House), 50

Paddington North CLP, 343n.1
Paddington South CLP, 173
Paddington South parliamentary district, 124
Pakenham, Lord, quoted, 357n.76
Park Ward (Bermondsey), 341n.24
Parkin, Frank, cited, 234, 279
Parliamentary Committee ('Shadow Cabinet'), 63, 66–7, 335n.37
Parliamentary Labour Party (PLP), 6, 19, 45, 54, 68–9, 152, 153, 172, 316, 344n.16; composition of, 63, 67, 68; discipline in, 74; and immigration, 182, 260; linkage with National Executive Committee, 66–7; and London reorganization, 268; relations with Party Conference, 44, 52, 57, 62, 63–7, 75, 213; *see also* Discipline
Party Conference, *see* Annual Conference
Party headquarters, *see* Premises
Pembrokeshire CLP, 71–2
Policymaking: in Bermondsey, 134–5, 147–8, 163, 178, 179–82, 215–16, 317; in CLPs, 8, 11, 17, 19, 21, 63; in Fulham, 137, 168–9, 178, 182–5, 218; at intermediate levels, 43–5; in local government, 43, 47; in national Party, 51–67; nature of, 175–8, 344n.16; in South Kensington, 139, 169, 178, 185–95; *see also* Resolutions; listing for three parties
'Political sect' organization model, 39, 122, 177, 314, 321
Poplar CLP, 342n.1
Population changes: in Bermondsey, 84, 88, 124–5; effect on CLPs, 15–16, 29, 39, 96, 98, 117, 307–8, 312, 313
Powell, Enoch, 70
Premises, 8, 23, 50; in Bermondsey, 139, 140, 165, 315; in Fulham, 128, 165–6, 206, 318; importance of, 165–6; in South Kensington, 166, 186, 320, 322
Prentice, Reginald, 77–8
Press and Publicity Department (Transport House), 51

Proscribed organizations, 10, 49, 74, 292, 338n.81
public ownership, 26–7, 33, 185, 187, 246–7, 313, 335n.36; *see also* Clause IV
Putney CLP, 171, 258

Queens Gate Ward (South Kensington), 107, 109–11, 132, 138, 190–3

Race, Reg, quoted, ix
Ranney, Austin, cited, 68, 69
Raymouth Ward (Bermondsey), 103–4, 105, 108, 111
Redcliffe Ward (South Kensington), 101, 102, 104, 107, 109–11, 131–2, 138–9, 155, 160, 189–90, 200, 209
Redistribution, 29–30, 90, 148, 152, 159, 199, 200
Regional councils, 44–5
Regional organization, 6, 8, 32, 44–7, 49
Regional organizers, 54; and candidate selection, 170, 198 199, 299; relations with CLPs, 123, 140, 165, 168, 170–1, 172, 173, 177, 183, 222; role of, 45–7; sponsors training programs, 163–4
Research Department (Transport House), 51, 53, 54, 66, 336n.46
Residence, length: impact on issue outlooks, 161, 237, 238, 239, 240–1, 243, 244–6, 250–1, 252, 253, 254, 255, 269, 271, 276–8, 323, 352–3nn.27, 28
Resolutions, 8, 11, 19, 49, 52, 177, 344n.16; in Bermondsey, 134–5, 181–2, 317, 343–4n.9, 345n.18; comparative analysis of, 33, 38, 195–7, 345n.25, 345–6n.26; in Fulham, 129, 137, 182–3, 185, 218, 319–20, 345n.19; at Party Conference, 53, 55–62 *passim.*, 70, 334n.28; in regional councils, 45; in South Kensington, 187–95, 322; *see also* Bermondsey CLP; Fulham CLP; Policymaking; South Kensington CLP
Revisionism, 26–7; *see also* Doctrine
Richard, Ivor S., 200, 299
Richards, Peter G., quoted, 71
Robertson, John, 70
Robshaw, Peter, x
Romford CLP, 343n.1
Rotherhithe CLP, 133, 166
Rotherhithe parliamentary district, 84, 85, 125, 146, 199
Russell, Bertrand, 187

St. Marylebone CLP, 343n.1

Safe Labour district, 2; characteristics of, 29–30; elections in, 17; incentives in, 308, 311, 329; M.P. selection in, 67; nature of CLP in, 18, 23, 28, 32–5, 55–6, 177, 195, 312–13; *see also* Bermondsey CLP; Newham North-East CLP
Saints Ward (Bermondsey), 100, 104, 108, 111, 121, 125, 127, 205, 316, 347–8n.44
Salter, Dr. Alfred, 166, 340n.7
Sandelson, Neville, 78
Sands End Ward (Fulham), 90, 91, 92, 101, 104, 106, 109–11, 128, 129–30, 137, 212, 303
Schattschneider, E. E., quoted, 32
Sex distribution: on Communist Party issue, 267–8; in constituencies, 102–3
'Shadow Cabinet', *see* Parliamentary Committee
Sheffield, Attercliffe CLP, 78
Sheffield, Brightside CLP, 76
Shoreditch and Finsbury CLP, 342–3n.1
Simpson Report, 54, 334n.28; quoted, 15
Skeffington, Arthur, 73
Social class, 296; comparative distribution of, 97–102 *passim.*, 114–16, 314–15; definition and analysis of, 98, 229; in hopeless Labour areas, 31–2, 37–8, 314; in marginal areas, 31, 313; and motivation, 286–8, 290, 294, 364n.8; and outlooks on issues, 161, 162, 235–8 *passim.*, 260–4, 265–7, 269–72, 273–5, 276–9, 323–5, 326–7, 354n.44, 362n.108; and party involvement, 282–5; and political aspirations, 285–6, 297, 300, 364n.9; in safe Labour areas, 30, 313–14; self-mapping of, 229–31; and voting patterns, 109–12; *see also* Education; Occupation
Socialist Medical Association, 4, 136
Socialist societies, 4, 16, 17, 48, 137; *see also* Fabian Society
Solley, Lester J., 73
South Kensington, 83; history, 94–5; location, 93–4; as parliamentary district, 93; post-war economy, 95–6; socio-economic features of, 98–9, 100–7, 113; voting patterns, 108–12 *passim.*
South Kensington CLP: appraisal of, 320–3; candidate selection in, 200, 202–3, 299; election campaigns in, 209–12; Executive Committee structure in, 138–9; external contacts of, 124, 154, 173–5, 210, 222, 321, 323, 347n.39;

finance of, 157, 223–5; General Management Committee structure in, 138, 295; goals of, 122–4, 321, 323; incentives in, 131, 290, 291, 292, 294–5, 303, 307, 364n.17; membership recruitment in, 157, 158, 160; officers of, 131, 297; policymaking in, 169, 195, 197, 322; social composition of, 114–16, 126, 314; stability of, 98, 117–18, 132, 307–8, 320; training programs in, 123, 321; views on issues in, 234, 237, 238, 239, 244, 247, 251, 254–5, 257, 260, 262, 263, 264, 265, 267, 268, 269, 270–2, 276–7, 280, 359n.96; ward organization in, 130–2; Young Socialists in, 142; *see also* Agents; Borough council; Borough councillors; Campaigns, election; Factional rivalries; Finance; GMC, South Kensington; Incentives; Local Affairs Management; Membership, Labour Party; Trade Unions; Wards/Branches
South Ward, 341n.24
Southall CLP, 343n.1
Southgate CLP, 343n.1
Southwark CLP, 342n.1
South-west Ward (Bermondsey), 104, 341n.24
Stead, Barrie, 200, 209
Stepney CLP, 342n.1
Stewart, Michael, 152–4, 221; in election campaigns, 206, 208; role in policymaking, 183, 268; selected as candidate, 199–200
Stokes, Donald, cited 233
Summerskill, Dr. Edith, 199
Surbiton CLP, 343n.1
Sutton and Cheam CLP, 343n.1

Taverne, Richard, 76
Thibaut, John W., cited, 144
Thomas, John R., 144–6, 148, 158; *see also* Agents
Thorborn Ward (Bermondsey), 105, 108, 111
Tomney, Frank, 79
Town Ward (Fulham), 101, 102, 104, 107, 109–11, 128, 129, 137, 209, 303
Tottenham CLP, 71
Trade unions/trade unionists, 4, 47, 52, 54, 77, 116, 130, 265, 295; and attitudes on issues, 235, 236, 240, 242, 243, 244, 247–9, 250, 265–7, 269–70, 276–8, 341n.28, 351n.20, 358n.81, 362n.108; in Bermondsey, 30, 34, 86, 89, 118,

127, 132–6 *passim.*, 157, 170, 177, 181, 223–5, 307, 315, 316, 342n.5, 346n.31; in Fulham, 31, 93, 130, 135–7, 142, 158, 217, 225, 307, 315; and intermediate-level organizations, 41, 44; and Labour Party membership, 4–5, 10, 11; and parliamentary candidates, 32, 35, 68, 76, 80, 146, 147, 149, 198, 200, 297, 298, 365n.20; and Party Conference, 48, 57, 59–61, 64, 65; and Party finance, 23, 42, 222; and party involvement, 283–4, 304; reform of, 55–6; and representation in CLPs, 5, 16, 17, 18, 20–1, 118; in South Kensington, 31, 37, 95–6, 118, 131, 138, 225, 307, 315
Trades Union Congress, 4, 48, 52, 53, 335n.36
Transport and General Workers Union, 59, 96, 132, 146, 166, 199, 342n.5
Transport House, 8, 18, 44, 49, 50, 74, 145; and candidate selection, 69, 73–81, 298, 299, 340n.32; and CLPs, 23, 55, 56, 158, 159, 160, 165, 168, 170, 172, 210, 222, 225; and Party organization, 21, 46–53 *passim.*
Treasurer, Labour Party, 48
Tunnel Ward (Bermondsey), 104, 105, 108, 111

Unilateral disarmament, 25, 27, 28, 45, 178, 226, 325; activists' views on, 56, 70, 129, 137, 142, 151, 176, 181, 184–5, 187–9, 191, 233–6, 273–5, 292, 295, 313, 324, 327, 345n.20; as campaign issue, 206; endorsed at Party Conference, 60, 65, 335n.36; linked with other issues, 186, 231–3, 239, 247, 256–7, 350n.14; M.P.s' attitudes on, 71, 336n.57
Union of Agricultural Workers, 91

Victory for Socialism, 28
Voluntary associations, 291, 292, 305, 306, 364n.18
Voter identification, 12–13, 207, 209
Voting patterns, 29–30, 104–5, 108–12, 314–15

Walden, Brian, 70
Walham Ward (Fulham), 91, 92, 106, 109–11, 128, 129–30, 202, 303
Walthamstow West CLP, 343n.1

Wandsworth, Clapham CLP, 70
Wandsworth, Streatham CLP, 343n.1
Wanstead and Woodford CLP, 343n.1
Wards/Branches: activities and organization of, 5, 10–20, 42, 56, 58, 143, 163, 177, 219, 294, 308, 344n.16; in Bermondsey, 124–7, 163, 179, 181, 203, 214, 315, 316, 317; and candidate selection, 74, 198, 201, 297, 298, 302–3, 309; in Fulham, 127–30, 137, 185, 218, 318; in South Kensington, 130–2, 138, 164, 167, 186–9, 320, 322; *see also* listing for three parties
Warley East CLP, 78
Webb, Sidney, 4
Wednesbury CLP, 71
West Ham North CLP, 342n.1
West Ham South CLP, 342n.1
White Paper, 55, 183, 268
Williamson, Sir Tom, quoted, 60
Willmott, Peter, cited 230; quoted, 349n.10
Willow Walk Ward (Bermondsey), 341n.24
Wilson Government, 62, 66, 80, 147, 152
Wilson, Harold, 56, 62, 63, 77–8, 171, 208, 336n.46; quoted, 5, 26; *see also* Leaders, national Party
Wilson, James Q., cited 5, 364n.9
Wilson Report, 42; quoted 24
Wimbledon CLP, 343n.1
Wolverhampon North-East CLP, 337n.78
Women: in national Party, 48, 57; in three constituencies, 98, 102–3
Women's Sections, 5, 17–19, 47, 170, 293; in Bermondsey, 125, 134, 139–40, 179; in Fulham, 128, 136, 137, 140–1, 159
Wood Green CLP, 343n.1
Woodford parliamentary district, 230
Woolwich East CLP, 158, 211, 343n.1
Wyatt, Woodrow, 71

Young, Michael, cited, 230; quoted, 349n.10
Young Socialists, 5, 18, 19, 24, 47, 170, 283–4, 293; in Bermondsey, 33, 140; in Fulham, 136, 137, 141–2, 159, 292, 319; in national organization, 48, 57; and party involvement, 285; in South Kensington, 138, 142, 174, 187, 193; views on Clause IV, 249
Youth organization *see* Young Socialists

Zilliacus, Konni, 73

LIBRARY OF DAVIDSON COLLEGE